Handbook of Banking Regulation and Supervision in the United Kingdom

Handbook of Banking Regulation and Supervision in the United Kingdom

Third Edition

Maximilian J.B. Hall

Senior Lecturer, Department of Economics,
Loughborough University, UK

Edward Elgar

Cheltenham, UK • Northampton, MA, USA

Published by
Edward Elgar Publishing Limited
Glensanda House
Montpellier Parade
Cheltenham
Glos GL50 1UA
UK

Edward Elgar Publishing, Inc.
136 West Street
Suite 202
Northampton
Massachusetts 01060
USA

A catalogue record for this book is available from the British Library

Library of Congress Cataloguing in Publication Data

Hall, Maximilian.
    Handbook of banking regulation and supervision in the United Kingdom/
Maximilian J.B. Hall. — 3rd ed.
    Rev. ed. of: Handbook of banking regulation and supervision. 2nd
ed. c1993.
        Includes index.
        1. Banking law—Great Britain. 2. Banking law—United States.
    3. Banks and banking—State supervision. I. Hall, Maximilian.
    Handbook of banking regulation and supervision. II. Title.
    K1066.H35   1999
    346.41'082—DC21   98–55210
                                                                        CIP

ISBN 1 85898 818 7

Printed and bound in Great Britain by MPG Books Ltd, Bodmin, Cornwall

Contents

Exhibits

Foreword
Howard Davies, *Chief Executive,*
Financial Services Authority

In the case of most industries the primary purpose of regulation is to prevent the growth and abuse of monopoly power. The financial services industry is different. It is not a monopoly – indeed it is usually highly competitive – but it is regulated in almost every country of the world. The purpose of financial regulation reflects the special position of the industry for all of us – namely that we entrust financial institutions with our savings and want to know that they are being looked after properly.

With banks, there is an additional dimension. They provide the mechanism for money transfer around the economy, ranging from small retail payments to multi-million pound transactions between large companies. This is a service that is so much part of our everyday lives, and in the main invisible to us, that we can easily forget how essential it is to the performance of the modern economy.

The banking regulator must tread a fine line. He or she needs to look to the interests of depositors and the financial system as a whole without being over-intrusive into the affairs of private companies, which also have a legitimate duty to their shareholders for whom the regulator has no brief. The regulator must ensure that the standards set do not impose an undue burden on the regulated. It would be easy to stifle innovation and competition by inhibiting risk-taking by banks, but regulators understand that risk is fundamental to banking. Their job is to ensure that risks are understood, controlled and contained within manageable limits.

The UK has a very dynamic and innovative banking industry and the City of London's success as an international financial centre is a great national asset. Proper and well-balanced regulation is an important part of that success. The markets would not be here if their participants were not satisfied that the regulators were working to keep out the crooked and the reckless, but if our regulation became over-intrusive it could drive them away in a very short time.

Regulators must also be very sensitive to the costs that they impose on the banks. Providing the information that regulators need and making management time available to them can be expensive. On top of this the banks must also pay the regulator's own costs. Many consumers think of regulation as a free good, so it is not surprising that they sometimes demand more of it. But of course banks have to recover regulatory costs like any others if they are to make a profit for their shareholders so the consumer pays in the end. The FSA makes extensive use of cost–benefit analysis to ensure that it does not impose unreasonable costs on the industry and no new policy, rule or requirement is allowed to go forward unless it passes the cost–benefit test. To help us pass that test we have recently formalized a system of risk-based supervision. This sharpens the supervisor's focus as never before and ensures that the process concentrates on the things that matter most.

Meeting regulatory standards for systems and controls and for the various financial buffers such as liquidity and capital also carries a price. Of course, left to their own devices, banks would undoubtedly put in place standards of their own, which theoretically might be tighter or looser. It is entirely legitimate to ask what the regulators can add to this process in a good bank, whose management brings its expertise to bear on creating safeguards that will protect the institution from harm. It is the regulators' job to work with the grain of such management and to allow it to find its own solutions. There is almost always more than one way to get to where we want to go and regulators recognize that they do not have a monopoly of wisdom. But, sadly, history shows that there have been many banks which have not made prudent decisions, and a few where the motivation of management has been questionable, at best.

As the financial world becomes ever more complex, the need for informed regulatory judgement will be more and more apparent. It will always be part of the regulators' job to set minimum standards, and for many banks that will involve a more straightforward, and perhaps more formulaic, approach. But in institutions where the highest standards prevail the regulator will want to be satisfied that the internally designed solution reaches the required standard rather than trying to find a single solution that works for everyone.

This new edition of the *Handbook of Banking Regulation and Supervision in the United Kingdom* is a timely and welcome addition to the literature. Its review of the major events in the history of supervision provide a context for our current system and its clear explanation of how banking supervisors currently go about their work is valuable to anybody with an interest in financial supervision.

Preface

Since publication of the second edition of this handbook in 1993, a number of significant developments have occurred to fundamentally alter the conduct of banking supervision in the UK. On the international front, risk-based capital adequacy assessment has been formally extended to embrace market risk; and other multilateral initiatives have focused on interest rate risk, settlement risk, internal risk management and control, and the prerequisites of effective banking supervision. On top of this, the member states of the European Economic Area have formally adopted a range of Directives designed to complete the Single Market in financial services by the end of 1996. Closer to home, we have witnessed continuing developments in the Bank of Credit and Commerce International saga, the collapse of the Barings Group and the transfer of responsibility for banking supervision from the Bank of England to a new super-regulator, the Financial Services Authority. All of these events receive detailed coverage in this updated and completely revised text which, as before, charts the evolution of banking supervisory practice in the UK as well as providing an in-depth analysis of the various components of UK supervisory policy.

Given its up-to-date and comprehensive treatment of the subject matter, its policy orientation and the depth of analysis provided, the book should appeal to both students of banking and finance and practitioners (i.e. commercial and central bankers, lawyers, accountants, etc.) alike.

Acknowledgements

I am indebted to the Bank of England for granting me permission to reproduce some of its published works as Exhibits in the text, and to Gloria Brentnall for her expert assistance in producing the final text in a presentable form. My thanks are also extended to Edward Elgar for so willingly taking on board the publication of a third edition of this text following the withdrawal of the previous publisher from the 'handbook' market.

Abbreviations

AA	Arthur Andersen
AFBD	Association of Futures Brokers and Dealers
ALCO	Asset and Liability Management Committee
APB	Auditing Practices Board
B&C	British and Commonwealth Holdings
BAH	Banco Ambrosiano Holdings
The Bank	Bank of England
BB&Co.	Baring Brothers and Company Ltd
BCCI	Bank of Credit and Commerce International
BCMB	British and Commonwealth Merchant Bank
BFS	Baring Futures (Singapore) Pte Ltd
BIB	Baring Investment Bank
BIS	Bank for International Settlements
BSD	Banking Supervision Division of the Bank of England
BSL	Baring Securities Limited
C&L	Coopers and Lybrand
CACA	Chartered Association of Certified Accountants
CAD	Capital Adequacy Directive
CCC	Competition and Credit Control
CDs	Certificates of deposit
CGO	Central Gilts Office
CLSS	CLS Services
CPSS	Committee on Payment and Settlement Systems
CHAPS	Clearing House Automated Payments System
CSD	(Second) Consolidated Supervision Directive
DTI	Department of Trade and Industry
DVP	delivery versus payment
EAI	European authorized institution
EC	European Community
ECGD	Export Credit Guarantee Department
ECU	European Currency Unit
EEA	European Economic Area
EEC	European Economic Community
EIB	European Investment Bank

EU	European Union
FIMBRA	The Financial Intermediaries, Managers and Brokers Regulatory Association
FRAs	Forward rate agreements
FSA	Financial Services Act
FSAu	Financial Services Authority
G7	'Group of Seven' countries
G10	'Group of Ten' countries
G30	'Group of Thirty' countries
GEMM	Gilt-edged market-maker
IBRD	International Bank for Reconstruction and Development
ICAEW	Institute of Chartered Accountants of England and Wales
ICBS	International Conference of Banking Supervisors
IIF	Institute of International Finance
IMF	International Monetary Fund
IMRO	The Investment Management Regulatory Organization
ING	Internationale Nederlanden Group
IOSCO	International Organization of Securities Commissions
JGB	Japanese Government Bond
JMB	Johnson Matthey Bankers
LAUTRO	The Life Assurance and Unit Trust Regulatory Organization
LDCs	Less developed countries
LIFFE	London International Financial Futures Exchange
NCB	National Commercial Bank of Saudi Arabia
NGR	net to gross ratio
NIFs	Note-issuance facilities
NK	Nikkei Index
OECD	Organization for Economic Co-operation and Development
OSE	Osaka Stock Exchange
PIA	Personal Investment Authority
RAR	Risk asset ratio
RATE	Risk Assessment, Tools of Supervision and Evaluation
RTGS	Real time gross settlement
RUFs	Revolving underwriting facilities
S&S	Supervision and Surveillance Division of the Bank of England
SA	The Securities Association
SBCD	Second Banking Co-ordination Directive
SCALE	Schedule 3 Compliance Assessment, Liaison, Evaluation
SFA	The Securities and Futures Authority
SFO	Serious Fraud Office
SIB	Securities and Investments Board
SIMEX	Singapore Monetary Exchange

SRO	Self-Regulatory Organization
TOWRA	Total of weighted risk assets
TSE	Tokyo Stock Exchange
UAE	United Arab Emirates
UBS	Union Bank of Switzerland
VAR	Value at risk
WMSD	Wholesale Markets Supervision Division of the Bank of England

PART I

The evolution of supervisory practice

1.   Regulation and supervision in the early post-war years (1945–73)

Until the implementation of the Banking Act 1979, statutory regulation played a relatively minor role in the prudential control of banks operating in the United Kingdom. Rather, the Bank of England (henceforth termed the 'Bank') was happy to continue the long-standing tradition of allowing the banking industry a high degree of self-regulation. In this manner, the bulk of supervisory costs was borne by the industry itself and supervision was exercised by those most fully acquainted with its far-reaching ramifications. Moreover, minimal damage was done to the industry's international competitiveness and to its ability to adapt to market change because of the resultant light supervisory touch. As for the effectiveness of such an approach, the threat of public censure by a self-regulatory body or, ultimately, expulsion from any of the various banking 'associations'[1] was seen as a sufficient deterrent to ensure prudent behaviour.

Despite the adoption of this fairly *laissez faire* approach to the prudential regulation and supervision of banks, a back-up statutory framework nevertheless existed. First and foremost, the Bank of England Act 1946 vested the Bank with a range of powers with respect to the domestic banking system (as defined under Section 4(6)). With Treasury approval, this allowed the Bank to issue *directions* to bankers thought to be in need of such corrective action although, in practice, informal guidance from the Bank sufficed, obviating the need for the former course of action. Beyond this, the statutory element of control embraced the Exchange Control Act 1947, the Companies Acts 1948 (Schedule 8) and 1967 (Section 123), and the Protection of Depositors Act 1963 (as amended by Section 127 of the Companies Act 1967).

The contribution made by the Exchange Control Act 1947 was to confine the provision of a full range of foreign exchange services to a select group known as *authorised dealers*. In this way, the requirements of integrity, competence and expertise in foreign exchange dealing were, in part, assured.

The role performed by Schedule 8 (later revised in Schedule 2 of the Companies Act 1967) of the Companies Act 1948 was to confer privileged status upon further categories of institution – *recognized banks* or *discount companies* – by exempting them from certain disclosure provisions, notably in respect of hidden reserves, pertaining to the drafting of a company's balance sheet.[2] Again, this selection process presumably involved some form of objective

3

assessment of the competence and/or integrity of the officers of the institution in question.

More explicit protection, at least in theory, was afforded to the consumer of financial services with the passing of the Protection of Depositors Act in 1963. Under this Act, the advertising activities of deposit-taking intermediaries not exempted by the Board of Trade under Section 127 of the Companies Act 1967[3] were restricted.

The final piece of legislation, Section 123 of the Companies Act 1967, again conferred a form of status upon certain institutions in the form of the granting of certificates to those deemed *bona fide* carrying on the business of banking for the purpose of the Moneylenders Acts 1900 to 1927.[4]

The practical effect of the above legislation was to establish a 'status ladder' which could be climbed by banks as their reputation grew and their expertise developed. Although this provided a degree of reassurance to the investing public about the standing of those institutions holding particular 'recognitions', the complexity of the legal provisions and the potentially conflicting criteria used in determining such recognitions left much to be desired.

Nor did the supervisory system inspire overwhelming confidence as a result of the adoption of a perverse policy which resulted in those having achieved the highest recognitions (i.e. those classified as 'recognized banks' by the Bank) receiving the closest attention. Accordingly, many small and less well-known deposit-taking intermediaries escaped the Bank's supervisory net almost entirely, while the likes of discount and accepting houses were obliged to engage in annual discussions of past performance (involving balance-sheet evaluation) and future business plans. And for the clearing banks, at the top of the tree, close relationships were developed with senior management and regular contact made, although discussions did not necessarily focus specifically on the balance sheet. Those UK-registered banks lying within the extremes of the status spectrum were usually required to submit their annual balance sheets to the Bank; these then formed the basis for subsequent discussions in management interviews.

In spite of these limitations, little pressure emerged during the 1960s for movement towards either an enlarged or more formalized and integrated supervisory system. The main reasons for this would appear to be the lack of any politically damaging bank collapse during this period, the simplicity of deposit-taking intermediaries' balance sheets, which facilitated basic ratio analysis, and the contribution made by monetary controls to the limitation of banking risk.

On the subject of balance-sheet ratio analysis, the practice during the 1950s and 1960s was to concentrate upon assessment of both capital and liquidity adequacy. Within the former assessment process, the quantitative measure adopted was the 'gearing' ratio or the ratio of the (adjusted) capital base to total deposits.[5] And within the assessment of liquidity adequacy, attention was focused on the 'quick-assets' ratio, or the ratio of short-term assets to deposits, for the purposes of providing a quantitative measure. In both cases, however, it should be stressed that the ratio analysis was used to complement other pieces of information to allow for an overall, subjective evaluation to be made by the Bank. The analysis did, nevertheless, facilitate objective assessment on a peer group basis, perhaps its main intended purpose.

As for monetary controls, the various measures applied throughout most of the period (*see* Hall, 1983, Chapters 1 and 2, for a more detailed discussion) certainly played an indirect part in prudential control, albeit at the cost of reduced efficiency (*see* Hall, 1987a, Appendix, for further discussion). For example, credit risks for both primary and some secondary banks[6] were reduced by the application of lending ceilings and hire purchase terms control, both of which improved the quality of loans by inducing institutions to favour the lowest-risk borrowers by accommodating them first from the queue of potential borrowers. The operation of the clearing banks' interest rate cartel (until 1971) provided further assistance to the supervisory authorities by ensuring healthy profit margins, with concomitant effects for stability, capital adequacy, and so on (*see* Part II). And finally, the application of a minimum liquid assets ratio (replaced by the minimum reserve assets ratio in 1971) served to enhance both liquidity[7] and asset quality by enforcing a minimum level of holdings of prime liquid assets (mainly short-term public sector debt).

The first event to change the climate of opinion favouring a high degree of non-statutory regulation, in the guise of self-regulation, was the introduction of new monetary control measures in 1971 under the Competition and Credit Control (CCC) banner. At one and the same time, lending ceilings, hire-purchase terms control and the clearing banks' interest rate cartel were all abolished in a government drive to increase competition and efficiency dramatically within the financial system (*see* Hall, 1983, Chapter 2).[8] From a prudential perspective, the implications were potentially very serious although, to the extent that business returned to the primary sector of the deposit-taking industry – the so-called reintermediation process – the threats to financial stability might be ameliorated. The reasons for concern were self-evident. The prudential safeguards provided by the previous monetary control regime had been removed overnight in the active promotion of competition as the means of improving resource allocation, the efficiency of the financial system and consumer welfare. The potential for structural (and, as it later transpired, monetary) destabilization was high, requiring the exercise of a more vigilant, watchful eye by the Bank over its charges. The inevitable cracks (some might say fissures) were not long in surfacing.

2. The UK 'secondary banking crisis' (1973–75)

In the winter of 1973, London and County Securities, a Section 123 certificate holder, was the first of a number of 'fringe' (or secondary) banks to experience difficulties in renewing deposits from the money markets, its main source of funds. The difficulties soon escalated into a crisis, threatening both secondary and fully recognized banks, and a 'lifeboat' was promptly launched by the Bank.[9] In the words of the Bank:

> the Bank felt it essential to meet their responsibility for fully-recognised banks by mounting a rescue operation for the benefit of the depositors of a group of institutions which were not fully-recognised banks, but whose otherwise inevitable collapse would have threatened the well-being of some recognised banks. (Bank of England, June 1978, p. 233)

The immediate causes of the crisis were readily identifiable: banks' over-exposure in property as an investment; too great a reliance on wholesale money markets as a funding source; the adoption of an imprudent degree of balance-sheet maturity mismatching; and abrupt changes in, and uncertainty associated with, government policy towards monetary control and rent controls (*see* Reid, 1982, for a full discussion).

The event that triggered the crisis was the government's switch to a tight money policy in the latter part of 1973 in an attempt to rein back the explosive growth in monetary aggregates that had materialized after the introduction of CCC. This resulted in a doubling of nominal interest rates during the second half of 1973, the intensity of the squeeze peaking in November, the month London and County Securities experienced its funding difficulties. The sudden and sustained rise in (nominal) interest rates caught many institutions unawares, with those running maturity-mismatched books and funding at variable rates yet lending at fixed rates incurring running losses as well as declining asset values. Uncertainty over government intentions on rent controls and land-development taxes induced a collapse in property values the following spring, intensifying the pressures on those heavily invested in property or involved in property-related lending. And to cap it all, the stock market subsequently slumped, depressing the market valuation of investment portfolios still further. Given this juxtaposition of events, it is hardly surprising that a full-scale liquidity crisis evolved as 'primary' banks and others sought to reduce exposure to the fringe operators affected.[10] As indicated above, however, imprudent bank business behaviour was, in part, to blame, calling into question the merits of the existing supervisory framework and methods.

The immediate outcome of the official *post mortem* on the crisis was the implementation of an enlarged and more intensive supervisory system in the summer of 1974. First and foremost, reporting requirements were stiffened. Apart from clearing banks and British overseas banks, all UK-registered banks and large non-bank deposit-taking intermediaries, including members of the Finance Houses Association, were required in future to submit returns in a standard format to the Bank at quarterly intervals and to attend a subsequent interview at the Bank to discuss the returns. The information required in the return embraced the following:

1. Identification of balance-sheet components.
2. Details of the maturity structure of assets and liabilities in both sterling and other currencies.
3. Identification of large deposits and loans and deposits/loans made by or to others with whom the company or directors are connected.
4. Details on bad debt provisions and the geographical spread and purpose of international loans.
5. Profitability figures.

This wealth of data became the subject of analysis at the Bank, which concerned itself particularly with the assessment of liquidity and capital adequacy and the appropriateness or otherwise of the degree of maturity transformation undertaken. Such analysis formed the basis of the subsequent discussions held during the management interviews, the interviews themselves being viewed by the Bank as the cornerstone of the whole supervisory process. In particular, the interviews were used by the Bank to form an overall impression of managerial competence rather than to lay down any hard and fast rules as to the observance of any particular balance-sheet ratio. This is not to deny, however, the valuable contribution made by the continuation of peer group assessment based upon ratio analysis.

For the clearing banks and British overseas banks, the new system meant annual reviews, the provision of a more detailed set of returns than for other banks, and several visits to the Bank each year to explain, in detail, any particular aspects of their business operations about which the Bank was particularly concerned. Beyond this, the Bank determined to place greater emphasis on the examination of control systems and reporting and auditing procedures.

Finally, for foreign institutions operating in the UK, letters of comfort were to be sought from their parent companies as a means of securing moral commitments, additional to any legal obligations, to support their associates and/or subsidiaries operating in the UK should the need ever materialize. In order to improve its understanding of their operations in the UK, the Bank also initiated discussions with the management of the London branches of foreign banks. The previous reporting requirements, relating to transactions in both the London foreign exchange and Eurocurrency markets, were also continued.

Following these adjustments to supervisory practice, it soon became clear that a more radical overhaul would eventually be required. Indeed, in so far as there remained the need to end the confusion over what actually constitutes a 'bank', the Bank was a willing partner in the demand for statutory reform. But the pressure for reform did not end there. In particular, UK membership of the European Economic Community (EEC) obliged the government to observe the proposals for harmonizing banking law throughout the Community – the First Banking Directive was adopted in December 1977 – which would require the formal licensing of deposit-taking companies operating in the UK. And finally, the voice of the consumer protection lobby, which called for the enhancement of depositor protection, could not be ignored for ever if political damage was not to be sustained by the incumbent administration. In the light of these pressures, a White Paper on the Licensing and Supervision of Deposit-taking Institutions was published in 1976, paving the way for the enactment of a new Banking Act in 1979, which became operational from October of that year.

3. The Basle *Concordat*

The other major event of the 1970s which forced a reassessment of existing supervisory practice was the collapse of Bankhaus I.D. Herstatt in June 1974. The collapse of this German bank resulted from the incursion of heavy losses on foreign exchange speculation, most especially in the forward market, and led to a virtual standstill in foreign exchange and Eurocurrency trading around the world as a result of the uncertainty created by the Bundesbank's handling of the situation (*see* Hall, 1987a, note 31, p. 201). Currency traders, in particular, were concerned about the lack of a formal 'lender of last resort' for the Eurocurrency markets, and the 'flight to quality' by interbank depositors created interest rate tiering in the market as well as starving some potential borrowers of funds. Supervisors around the world reacted by raising reporting requirements and intensifying their monitoring arrangements for banks' foreign exchange transactions. The Bank was no exception, announcing in the aftermath of the collapse that it would extend the range of information it required relating to foreign exchange dealing for all banks operating in London. And later that year (December) it sent all banks a guide as to the type of checklist that they should use in reviewing their internal controls and regulations (Exhibit 1.1).

Apart from initiating reviews of the supervisory arrangements applied by national regulatory bodies to foreign exchange dealing, the event led directly to the first major attempt to harmonize, at the international level, the prudential regulation and supervision of banks operating across national boundaries. For, following the reassurance given by European central bank governors to Eurocurrency market operators in September 1974 that liquidity support would be provided to the market on an informal basis, should the need ever arise, a standing committee of bank supervisors from the 'Group of Ten' (G10) countries, plus Switzerland and Luxembourg, was established to effect the co-ordination of prudential supervision of banks operating within their territorial domain. It was hoped that the harmonization net could be extended further through the encouragement of other supervisory bodies around the world to adopt the principles and practices established by the committee.

Operating under the auspices of the Bank for International Settlements (BIS), this committee – the Committee on Banking Regulations and Supervisory Practices, to give it its proper title[11] – first addressed the problem of how to improve early warning systems with a view to identifying incipient problems

Exhibit 1.1   Control of foreign exchange dealing in the UK[1]

Reports of the losses suffered this year, by banks in a number of countries, as a result of operations in foreign exchange markets, will undoubtedly have caused many banks to undertake a rigorous review of their internal regulations governing procedures for foreign exchange dealings by, and dealing and overnight and forward credit limits imposed on, individual branches and wholly owned subsidiaries at home and abroad. Any banks which have not yet done so are urged to undertake such a review as soon as possible and to ensure in particular that authorities to deal are specific and are confined to strictly selected staff and branches.

The list that follows is not intended as an exhaustive check for conducting such a review; it merely covers points which have risen from the Bank's discussions in a number of centres about the losses:

1. Some general managements seem to have placed their dealers in an exposed position by looking well beyond the service element of the dealing function and imposing ambitious profit targets upon them.
2. In some overseas offices, managements do not appear to have paid sufficient attention to the relations between dealers and brokers; in London, the Foreign Exchange and Currency Deposit Brokers' Association has exercised a beneficial influence in this area.
3. Dealers should never write their own outgoing confirmations or receive incoming confirmations.
4. Forward deals should always be confirmed at once; in particular, confirmations should not be delayed until instructions are passed just prior to maturity.
5. There should be snap checks of dealing activities between regular internal audits or inspections.
6. Central management should from time to time, on a random basis, seek from correspondent banks independent second confirmation of outstanding forward contracts.
7. A bank should check with its correspondent's head or main dealing office if it notices that a branch of that bank has suddenly or appreciably expanded its operations in the forward market.

Note: 1. Extract from the Bank of England circular of December 1974.

Source: Bank of England, 1981, p. 37.

at an early stage. Largely on the grounds of practicality, the Committee decided against the establishment of a supranational supervisory body for this and other purposes. Rather, it promoted the idea of making parent and host supervisors jointly responsible for all matters of international banking supervision and drew up principles to be used as a basis for determining the division of supervisory responsibility. These principles were spelt out in a document which became known as the 'Basle *Concordat*' and which served as a cornerstone of international supervisory co-operation. Given the importance of this historic document, its principal guidelines are worth spelling out in full:

1. The supervision of foreign banking establishments should be the joint responsibility of host and parent authorities.
2. No foreign banking establishment should escape supervision; each country should ensure that foreign banking establishments are supervised and supervision should be adequate as judged by both host and parent authorities.
3. The supervision of liquidity should be the primary responsibility of host authorities since foreign establishments generally have to conform to local practices for their liquidity management and must comply with local regulations. Home authorities, nevertheless, should monitor the liquidity of their international banks.
4. The supervision of solvency of foreign branches should be essentially a matter for the parent authority. In the case of subsidiaries, while primary responsibility lies with the host authority, parent authorities should take account of the exposure of their domestic banks' foreign subsidiaries and joint ventures because of the parent banks' moral commitment in this regard.
5. Practical co-operation would be facilitated by transfers of information between host and parent authorities and by the granting of permission for inspections by or on behalf of parent authorities on the territory of the host authority. Every effort should be made to remove any legal restraints (particularly in the field of professional secrecy or national sovereignty) which might hinder those forms of co-operation.

The *Concordat* survived in its original form until June 1983, when a revised edition was issued. The revision was designed to incorporate agreements reached since 1975 on the principle of 'consolidation'[12] and to clarify and amplify some of the original points in the light of experience – most notably the collapse of the Luxembourg-based Banco Ambrosiano Holdings (BAH) in 1982, which raised issues about the treatment of intermediate institutions such as bank holding companies (which BAH was) and joint ventures.[13]

While the Committee reaffirmed its line that the question of responsibility for the lender-of-last resort function was outside its remit, it sought, nevertheless, to clarify the position of other supervisory responsibilities with respect to such intermediate institutions. For example, in the case where a foreign company is classified as a bank by the parent supervisor but not by the host – as was the case for BAH – the Committee asserted that responsibility lies with the parent authority to ensure that adequate supervision is being exercised. However, the host authority is charged with the responsibility of informing the parent supervisor when it feels unable to effect adequate supervision. In the reverse situation, where the host authority has reason to doubt the adequacy of supervision being exercised by the parent authority over the parent of the foreign company operating on its soil, the Committee argued that the host authority should either discourage or prohibit the operation of that company or, otherwise, impose conditions on the conduct of its business. As for the treatment of holding companies and non-banking companies within banking groups, the Committee called for increased co-ordination and co-operation between the relevant supervisory bodies. In circumstances where bank supervisors feel that the non-banking activities of the group are, for whatever reason, inadequately supervised, they are advised to take formal steps to minimize the risks for the banking business.[14]

More generally, the revised *Concordat* stressed more than the original document the need for close co-operation between host and parent authorities, emphasizing the overlapping nature of supervisory responsibilities. As to the specific treatment of joint ventures, the Committee argued that, normally, supervision should be the primary responsibility of the authorities in the country of incorporation, although it cautioned that the parent authorities of the shareholder banks should become involved in cases where dominant shareholdings prevail. Finally, in connection with the supervision of foreign exchange operations – an area not touched upon by the original document – the need for joint, co-ordinated supervision was stressed. Parent supervisors need to satisfy themselves as to the adequacy of the monitoring systems used by parent banks to assess group exposure, and host supervisors need to ensure the adequacy of their arrangements for monitoring the exposures of foreign companies operating on their soil and to acquaint themselves fully with the supervisory procedures adopted by the parent supervisors in this respect.

The final adjustment to the *Concordat* occurred in 1992 as a response to the Bank of Credit and Commerce International (BCCI) affair (*see* Chapter 11). Agreed proposals for the introduction of minimum standards, which have to be applied in the supervision of international banking groups and their cross-border establishments, appeared in the form of a press release on 6 July 1992. This document, which represented the Basle Committee's first public response to the BCCI affair, had been endorsed by the G10 group of bank supervisors and circulated to supervisory authorities throughout the world in an attempt to widen the spread of best practice. The minimum standards, which represent a reformulation of certain principles already enshrined within the *Concordat*, are designed to reinforce the *Concordat* in the light of continued rapid growth of international banking activities and, more importantly, in the light of experience gained in the supervision of seriously troubled institutions such as BCCI. In essence, the new agreed proposals are designed to provide greater assurances that in the future no international bank can operate without being subject to effective consolidated supervision (Basle Committee, 1992).

The principal features of the minimum standards may be summarized as follows:

1. 'All international banking groups and international banks should be supervised by a home country authority that capably performs consolidated supervision.'
2. 'The creation of a cross-border banking establishment should receive the prior consent of both the host country supervisory authority and the bank's, and if different, the banking group's home country supervisory authority.'
3. 'Supervisory authorities should possess the right to gather information from the cross-border banking establishments of the banks or banking groups for which they are the home-country supervisor.'
4. 'If a host country authority determines that any one of the foregoing minimum standards is not met to its satisfaction that authority could impose restrictive measures necessary to satisfy its prudential concerns consistent with these minimum standards, including the prohibition of the creation of banking establishments.'

Further clarification of the implications of each of these minimum standards is provided in the document. For example, in seeking to satisfy the first minimum standard, home supervisory authorities have received clear guidance as to what 'capably' means. Among other things, they are expected to do the following:

1. 'Receive consolidated financial and prudential information on the bank's or banking group's global operations, have the reliability of this information confirmed to its own satisfaction through on-site communication or other means, and assess the information as it may bear on the safety and soundness of the bank or banking group.'
2. 'Have the capability to prevent corporate affiliations or structures that either undermine efforts to maintain consolidated financial information or otherwise hinder effective supervision of the bank or banking group.'
3. 'Have the capability to prevent the bank or banking group from creating foreign banking establishments in particular jurisdictions.'

In connection with the second minimum standard, host and home supervisory authorities are asked to consider, *inter alia*, both the strength of the bank's and banking group's capital and the 'appropriateness' of the bank's and banking group's organization and operating procedures for ensuring the effective management of risks (on both a local and consolidated basis, respectively) when reviewing proposals for inward and outward expansion. The host authority is also asked to concern itself in particular with the level of support that the parent is capable of providing to the proposed establishment. Before giving consent to the creation of cross-border establishments, the home and host supervisory authorities are each expected to review the allocation of supervisory responsibilities recommended in the *Concordat* in order to determine whether its application to the proposed establishment is appropriate. If either authority concludes that it is not appropriate, then that authority has responsibility for initiating discussions with the other authority with a view to reaching an explicit understanding on an alternative sharing of responsibilities. A similar review is also expected to be undertaken if there is a significant change in the bank's or banking group's activities or structure.

As for the third minimum standard, concerned with information gathering, a supervisory authority is expected, as a condition for giving either inward or outward consent for the creation of a cross-border banking establishment, formally to establish an understanding with the other authority that they may each gather information to the extent necessary for effective home country supervision.

Under the final proposal, which is concerned with the appropriate response of host authorities to non-attainment of the standards, the host authority is generally expected to ban the operation of cross-border establishments on its territory if any of the standards are not met and appear unlikely to be met in the near future. At its discretion, however, the host authority may alternatively choose to permit the creation of local establishments in such instances, albeit on a restricted basis, provided *it* is willing to assume responsibility for supervising (consistent with satisfying the minimum standards) the bank or banking group on a stand-alone basis.

The Basle Committee's attempts to raise supervisory standards and to plug the gaps in international supervisory arrangements so successfully exploited by BCCI are clearly to be applauded, although a number of concerns remain. Looking on the positive side, the effectiveness of international banking supervision should certainly be enhanced as a result of the further clarification of the respective roles of home and host supervisory authorities, which includes the allocation of responsibility for lead regulation of banking groups (i.e. responsibility for ensuring effective consolidated supervision) to the *home* supervisory authority. Moreover, home supervisors (especially in the G10 area) will be under greater pressure than before to devote adequate resources to supervising international banks and banking groups by virtue of the following:

1. The setting of minimum standards of supervision which they are obliged to observe.
2. The involvement of the host authorities in the assessment of the supervisory capabilities of home authorities when banks incorporated in the latter's jurisdiction operate, or plan to operate, on the territories of the former.
3. The Basle Committee's decision to monitor for itself implementation of the agreed minimum standards (especially in the G10 arena).

Further comfort can be derived from the granting of additional powers to home authorities in respect of the gathering of information on the overseas activities of banks and banking groups – information exchanges are likely to be extended through the development of closer bilateral links with bank supervisors overseas – which should also serve to enhance the effectiveness of consolidated supervision. (Within the European Community (EC) arena, this is also provided for in the Consolidated Supervision Directive – *see* Chapter 9.) The greater involvement of *host* authorities in the supervisory process should also be viewed in a positive light. As noted above, their formal consent has now to be obtained before overseas-incorporated banks can start operations on their soil, and they are also allowed to implement whatever restrictive measures they deem appropriate to enhance the effectiveness of host supervision in instances where they doubt the effectiveness of consolidated supervision, as exercised by the home authority – this should also be viewed in a positive light. And finally, the eschewal of 'grandfathering' clauses is to be welcomed as, in principle (practical problems clearly abound), it subjects both existing and new cross-border banking operations to the same tougher supervisory regime.

Concerns surrounding the package centred on the Basle Committee's failure to clarify the lead regulation position for banking groups with non-bank parents (BCCI represented such a case); its failure to tackle the problems still posed by bank secrecy provisions; the apparent conflict with the EC's approach to the selection of lead regulator for banking groups where parent holding companies are incorporated in countries other than the banks' countries of incorporation (another BCCI feature); and the difficulties EC host authorities faced from 1 January 1993 in meeting the fourth minimum standard by virtue of their limited ability to challenge the supervisory capabilities of home country authorities based in the EC.

The first two omissions, which are surprising in the light of BCCI revelations, are self-explanatory, and require no further comment bar noting that the EC's

Consolidated Supervision Directive attempts to deal with both issues for the benefit of member states.

The apparent lack of consistency with the EC approach to allocating lead regulation responsibilities for banking groups of the kind described above – under the Consolidated Supervision Directive responsibility resides with the supervisory authority of the country in which the bulk of the group's banking business is conducted and *not* with the parent's home supervisor – is also a worry as it could potentially lead to uncertainty and confusion. Finally, the obligations assumed by member states under the Second Banking Co-ordination Directive, which adopts the 'single passport' principle, would appear to preclude the kind of action the Basle Committee anticipates host authorities taking in the face of perceived deficiencies in home supervision.

Problems experienced in the implementation of the "minimum standards" were subsequently reviewed by a working group, comprising members of the Basle Committee on Banking Supervision and the Offshore Group of Banking Supervisors, set up at the end of 1994. The group's findings were presented at the International Conference of Banking Supervisors (ICBS) held in Stockholm in June 1996. A report, endorsed by the banking supervisors of the 140 countries represented at the conference, duly emerged in October 1996 (Basle Committee on Banking Supervision, 1996a). It contained 29 recommendations (*see* Exhibit 1.2) aimed at improving and facilitating prudential supervision of banking risks with a view to ensuring the soundness of individual credit institutions and the stability of the financial system as a whole. Individual countries' compliance with the recommendations will be reviewed in time to allow for a report to be submitted to the next ICBS in October 1998. Where the recommendations are in conflict with bank secrecy or similar legislation, supervisors are expected to use their best endeavours to have the conflicting legislation amended.

As is evident from Exhibit 1.2, the report is focused in particular on how to improve the access of home supervisors to the information necessary to allow them to conduct effective consolidated supervision (i.e. the third of the minimum standards) and on how to improve the access of host supervisors to the information necessary for effective host supervision (as required under the fourth minimum standard). In addition to tackling the problems associated with gaining access to information, the report addresses the more general issue of how to ensure that all cross-border banking operations are subject to effective home and host supervision. The lack of common standards by which host supervisors can judge what constitutes 'effective consolidated supervision' by home supervisors and home supervisors can judge the standards of supervision exercised by host supervisors was seen as a particular source of concern, as were continuing 'gaps' in supervision which threatened achievement of the *Concordat* principle that no banking establishment should escape supervision.

Exhibit 1.2   Recommendations of the working group

---

1. Improving the access of home supervisors to the information necessary for effective consolidated supervision

(i)   In order to exercise comprehensive consolidated supervision of the global activities of their banking organizations, home supervisors must be able to make an assessment of all significant aspects of their banks' operations that bear on safety and soundness, wherever those operations are conducted and using whatever evaluative techniques are central to their supervisory process.

(ii)   Home supervisors need to be able to verify that quantitative information received from banking organizations in respect of subsidiaries and branches in other jurisdictions is accurate and to reassure themselves that there are no supervisory gaps.

(iii)   While recognizing that there are legitimate reasons for protecting customer privacy, the working group believes that secrecy laws should not impede the ability of supervisors to ensure safety and soundness in the international banking system.

(iv)   If the home supervisor needs information about non-deposit operations, host supervisors are encouraged to assist in providing the requisite information to home supervisors if this is not provided through other supervisory means. The working group believes it is essential that national legislation that in any way obstructs the passage of non-deposit supervisory information be amended.

(v)   Where the liabilities side of the balance sheet is concerned, home supervisors do not routinely need to know the identity of individual depositors. However, in certain well-defined circumstances, home supervisors would need access to individual depositors' names and to deposit account information.

(vi)   It should not normally be necessary for the home supervisor to know the identity of investors for whom a bank in a host country is managing investments at the customer's risk. However, in certain exceptional circumstances, home supervisors would need access to individual investors' names and to investment account information subject to the safeguards in paragraph (x).

(vii)   The working group recommends that host supervisors whose legislation does not allow a home supervisor to have access to depositor information use their best endeavours to have their legislation reviewed, and if necessary amended, to provide for a mechanism whereby in exceptional cases a home supervisor, with the consent of the host supervisor, will gain access to depositor information subject to the same conditions as outlined in (viii) below.

(viii)   In order to provide legitimate protection for bank customers, it is important that the information obtained by home supervisors, especially that relating to depositors' or investors' names, is subject to strict confidentiality. The working group recommends that those host jurisdictions whose legislation

Exhibit 1.2   (continued)

allows foreign supervisors to have access to banks' depositor or investor information should subject such access (at the host country's discretion) to the following conditions:

- the purpose for which the information is sought should be specific and supervisory in nature;
- information received should be restricted solely to officials engaged in prudential supervision and not be passed to third parties without the host supervisor's prior consent;[1]
- there is assurance that all possible steps will be taken to preserve the confidentiality of information received by a home supervisor in the absence of the explicit consent of the customer;
- there should be a two-way flow of information between the host and home supervisors, though perfect reciprocity should not be demanded;
- before taking consequential action, those receiving information will undertake to consult with those supplying it.

(ix)   If a host supervisor has good cause to doubt a home supervisor's ability to limit the use of information obtained in confidence solely for supervisory purposes, the host would retain the right not to provide such information.

(x)   Subject to appropriate protection of the identity of customers, home supervisors should be able at their discretion, and following consultation with the host supervisor, to carry out on-site inspections in other jurisdictions for the purposes of carrying out effective comprehensive consolidated supervision. This ability should include, with the consent of the host supervisor and within the laws of the host country, the right to look at individual depositors' names and relevant deposit account information if the home supervisor suspects serious crime as defined in section (d). If a host supervisor has reason to believe that the visit is for non-supervisory purposes, it should have the right to prevent the visit taking place or to terminate the inspection.

(xi)   It would avoid potential misunderstandings if a standard routine were laid down for conducting cross-border inspections along the lines recommended in Annex A.

(xii)   In those countries where laws do not allow for on-site inspections by supervisors from other jurisdictions, the working group advocates that host supervisors use their best endeavours to have their legislation amended. In the meantime, host supervisors should, within the limits of their laws, be willing to co-operate with any home supervisor that wishes to make an inspection. The working group believes that the host supervisor should have the option to accompany the home supervisor throughout the inspection.

(xiii)   It is important that the confidentiality of information obtained during the course of an inspection be maintained. Home supervisors should use their best endeavours to have their legislation modified if it does not offer sufficient protection that information obtained for the purposes of effective consolidated supervision is limited to that use.

(xiv)   In the event that a home supervisor, during an on-site inspection in a host country, detects a serious criminal violation of home country law, the home supervisor may be under a strict legal obligation to pass the information immediately to the appropriate law enforcement authorities in its home country. In these circumstances, the home supervisor should inform the host supervisor of the action it intends to take.[2]

(xv)   In order to carry out effective comprehensive consolidated supervision, home supervisors also need information on certain *qualitative* aspects of the business undertaken in other jurisdictions by branches and subsidiaries of banking organizations for which they are the home supervisor. All members of the working group agree that it is essential for effective consolidated supervision that there are no impediments to the passing of such qualitative information to the home supervisor.

2.   Improving the access of host supervisors to information necessary for effective host supervision

(xvi)   In the case of information which is *specific to the local entity*, an early sharing of information may be important in enabling a potential problem to be resolved before it becomes serious. The home supervisor should therefore consult the host supervisor in such cases and the latter should report back on its findings. In particular, it is essential that the home supervisor inform the host supervisor immediately if the former has reason to suspect the integrity of the local operation, the quality of its management or the quality of internal controls being exercised by the parent bank.

(xvii)   A home supervisor should have on its regular mailing list for relevant material all foreign supervisors which act as hosts to its banks.

(xviii)   While the working group agrees that home supervisors should endeavour to keep host supervisors appraised of material adverse changes in the global condition of banking groups, the group recognizes that this will typically be a highly sensitive issue and that decisions on information-sharing necessarily will have to be made on a case-by-case basis.

3.   Ensuring that all cross-border banking operations are subject to effective home and host supervision

(xix)   The working group has formulated a set of principles of effective consolidated supervision (see Annex B) which could be used by host supervisors as a checklist to assist in determining whether a home supervisor is meeting the minimum standards.

Exhibit 1.2   (continued)

(xx)   Regional group procedures might be used to support the implementation of the minimum standards, as the Offshore Group of Banking supervisors is now doing.

(xxi)   The working group recommends that other regional groups consider the possibility of using a checklist similar to that used by the Offshore Group (see Annex C) as a means of establishing which of their members might be certified as meeting certain general criteria.

(xxii)   The Basle Committee encourages its member countries to assist the Offshore Group or any other regional group in the fact-finding verification process, but any decision-making regarding membership of a regional group should be left to that group alone. The Committee has asked its Secretariat to maintain a list of competent persons (e.g. retired supervisors) who are available to undertake exercises of this nature.

(xxiii)   The supervisor that licenses a so-called 'shell branch' has responsibility for ensuring that there is effective supervision of that shell branch. No banking operation should be permitted without a licence, and no shell office should be licensed without ascertaining that it will be subject to effective supervision. In the event that any host supervisor receives an application to license a new shell branch that will be managed in another jurisdiction, that supervisor should take steps to notify both the home supervisor and the appropriate host supervisor in the other jurisdiction in order to establish that there will be appropriate supervision of the branch before approving the application.

(xxiv)   Home supervisors should not authorize their banks to establish or acquire offices in any host jurisdiction without satisfying themselves in advance that such offices will be subject to appropriate supervision.

(xxv)   Where the home authority wishes to inspect on site, it should be permitted to examine the books of the shell branch wherever they are kept. The working group believes that in no case should access to these books be protected by secrecy requirements in the country that licenses the shell branch.

(xxvi)   The working group recommends that home or host supervision be vigilant to ensure that parallel-owned banks (where a bank in one jurisdiction has the same ownership as a bank in another jurisdiction, where one is not a subsidiary of the other) become subject to consolidated supervision, if necessary by enforcing a change in group structure as indicated by the minimum standards.

(xxvii)   Any home supervisor that licenses a banking entity has a responsibility to monitor its operations on a worldwide basis.

(xxviii)   No entity should be allowed to use the word 'bank' in its name if it is not conducting banking activities and being supervised as a bank.

(xxiv)   The working group believes that the Basle Committee should advise all host countries to be extremely cautious about approving the establishment of cross-border operations by banks incorporated in under-regulated financial centres, and even more cautious about accepting other financial institutions conducting banking activities from those centres.

Notes:
1. Except in the circumstances described in paragraphs 11 and 26.
2. Some members of the working group strongly believe, as is required by their laws, that the home supervisor should be expected to obtain approval from the host country supervisor before informing the home country law enforcement authorities of any suspected violations of home country law.

Source: Basle Committee (1996a).

ANNEX A

Standard Procedures for Cross-border Inspections

The working group recommends that the following routine should be followed in cases where the home supervisor wishes to undertake a cross-border inspection:

1. the home supervisor should contact the host supervisor to let the latter know of an intention to make a visit to a specified branch/subsidiary within the host supervisor's jurisdiction;
2. the home supervisor should be prepared to explain to the host supervisor the purpose of the visit and what aspects of the branch or subsidiary it wishes to explore;
3. the host supervisor should be able to obtain an undertaking from the home supervisor that information obtained in the course of the visit will be used for specific and supervisory purposes and, to the maximum extent possible under applicable laws, will not be passed to third parties without the host supervisor's prior consent. The disclosure of information to third parties would be subject to those conditions outlined in paragraphs 10 and 11 of the main text;
4. the host supervisor should identify to the home supervisor any areas where access to information is normally restricted (e.g. information on individual customers), and the home supervisor should indicate where exceptions are needed;
5. the host supervisor should have the option, but not the duty, to accompany the home supervisor during the inspections;
6. where relevant, the host supervisor should advise the home supervisor of procedures necessary to comply with local/host country legislation and, where necessary or appropriate, assist in ensuring that these procedures are correctly followed to expedite the examination.

ANNEX B

Effective Consolidated Supervision

1.   Under the first of the four minimum standards, it is required that all international banks be supervised by a home country authority that capably performs consolidated supervision. The purpose of this Annexe, and in particular the checklist in paragraphs 6 and 7 below, is to provide examples of some of the principles and factors that could be taken into account in making a judgement about effective consolidated supervision.

2.   There can be no single set of criteria to determine whether or not a home supervisor is performing 'effective consolidated supervision', since supervisory techniques differ from country to country, due to institutional, historical, legal or other factors. The concepts of consolidated supervision can, however, be defined, namely as a group-wide approach to supervision whereby all the risks run by a banking group are taken into account, wherever they are booked. In other words, it is a process whereby a supervisor can satisfy itself about the totality of a banking group's activities, which may include non-bank companies and financial affiliates, as well as direct branches and subsidiaries.

3.   One of the prime reasons why consolidated supervision is critical is the risk of a damaging loss of confidence if an associated enterprise gets into difficulties. This so-called 'risk of contagion' goes well beyond legal liability. Consolidated supervision helps to protect the integrity of, and confidence in, the group – both supervised and unsupervised elements. More directly, the purpose of consolidated supervision is essentially threefold:

- to support the principle that no banking operation, wherever located, should escape supervision altogether;
- to prevent double-leveraging of capital;
- to ensure that all the risks incurred by a banking group, no matter where they are booked, are evaluated and controlled on a global basis.

4.   It is important to draw a distinction between accounting consolidation, which is a mechanical process, and the concept of consolidated supervision, which is qualitative as well as quantitative. The drawing up of consolidated accounts facilitates consolidated supervision but is not necessarily sufficient. Consolidated accounting may, for example, be inappropriate when the nature of the business or the nature of the risks are markedly different, but that does not mean that the risks should be ignored. Moreover, some risks need to be monitored at local level too. Liquidity concerns, for one, can be considered on a market-by-market (or currency-by-currency) basis, though a group liquidity spectrum would need to include at least the main funding centres. Market risk is another risk that the

supervisor may decide should not necessarily be consolidated: that decision would depend on whether the bank manages its market risks centrally or regionally. Moreover, if a bank is operating in jurisdictions subject to controls on capital flows, offsetting of market (and other) risks through consolidation would not necessarily be prudent.

5.   In reaching a decision as to the effectiveness of the consolidated supervision conducted by a home supervisor, the host supervisor will also need to take account of its own supervisory capabilities. If it has limited resources, greater demands will be placed on the home supervisor than if host supervision is strong. The host also has to judge the extent to which its supervision complements that of the home supervisor, or whether there are potential gaps. Accordingly, one host supervisor may decide that a given country is conducting effective consolidated supervision, whereas another host supervisor with different capabilities may decide that it is not. Nonetheless, there are certain common factors on which host supervisors will base their decisions. The checklist below is designed to assist in that decision-making process.

Checklist of Principles for Effective Consolidated Supervision

A.   Power to exercise global oversight
6.   Does the home country supervisor have adequate powers to enable it to obtain the information needed to exercise consolidated supervision; for example:

- Does the bank in question have its own routine for collecting and validating financial information from all its foreign affiliates, as well as for evaluating and controlling its risks on a global basis?
- Does the home supervisor receive regular financial information relating both to the whole of the group and to the material entities in the group (including the head office) individually?
- Is the home supervisor able to verify that information (e.g. through inspection, auditors' reports or information received from the host authority)?
- Is there access to information on intra-group transactions, not only with downward affiliates but also, if appropriate, with sister companies or non-bank affiliates?
- Does the home supervisor have the power to prohibit corporate structures that deliberately impede consolidated supervision?

B.   Exercise of consolidated supervision
7.   Which of the following procedures does the home country supervisor have in place to demonstrate its ability to capably perform consolidated supervision:

- adequate control of authorization, both at the entry stage and on changes of ownership;
- adequate prudential standards for capital, credit concentration, asset quality (i.e. provisioning or classification requirements), liquidity, market risk, management controls, and so on;
- off-site capability, that is, systems for statistical reporting of risks on a consolidated basis and the ability to verify or to have the reports verified;
- the capability to inspect or examine entities in foreign locations;
- arrangements for a frequent dialogue with the management of the supervised entity;
- a track record of taking effective remedial action when problems arise?

ANNEX C

Offshore Group of Banking Supervisors' On-site Examination Checklist

1.   What number and types of bank, and so on are licensed in the jurisdiction? Is there any differentiation in the type of banking licence issued or the conditions imposed and, if so, why? What legislation is in place, when was it last updated and does it provide for the Basle Committee's minimum standards to be met?

2.   What resources are available to the supervisory authority, with regard to the background and experience of the supervisory team, and what training programme is in place?

3.   What are the requirements which banks/banking groups have to fulfil in order to become authorized in the jurisdiction? What measures are in place to ensure that banks/banking groups are managed and controlled by fit and proper persons?

4.   What is the process of authorization – what objective criteria and what types of background check are used? What arrangements are in place to ensure the approval of the home supervisor? What regular links are there to other supervisory authorities?

5.   What steps are taken to ensure that banks/banking groups are subject to effective consolidated supervision?

6.   What financial and prudential information is collected from banks/banking groups in the jurisdiction and how frequently is the information collected? By what means is the reliability of this information confirmed?

7.   Are on-site inspections of banks/banking groups undertaken? If not, what are the alternative arrangements? If so, who carries them out, what is their scope and what is their frequency? Is the home supervisory authority informed of examination findings?

8. What measures are taken to supervise the overseas operations of any banks/banking groups for which the supervisory authority is the home supervisor? Are financial conglomerates allowed? If so, what are the arrangements for supervising the operations of non-bank subsidiaries?

9. What limits are applied with regard to the extent to which a bank or banking group can lend to:

- any one customer (including any arrangements for treating groups of borrowers as one risk);
- companies or persons connected with the bank/banking group itself;
- particular sectors (e.g. real estate)?

10. What rules are in place to monitor:

- solvency;
- asset quality;
- country risk exposure;
- liquidity control systems;
- foreign exchange positions;
- off-balance-sheet activity;
- ownership and organization structure;
- derivatives activities?

What is the frequency of report on each of the above?

11. What arrangements are in place to ensure that banks/banking groups maintain adequate accounting and other records, and adequate systems of control?

12. What measures and actions can be taken if the banks/banking groups in the jurisdiction fail to comply with prudential requirements or any other factors that are a cause for concern?

13. Are internal auditors from the parent bank or head office entitled to inspect the banks in the jurisdiction? Are internal auditors required to meet with/report to the host/home supervisor?

14. Are the home supervisory authorities of banks/banking groups entitled to conduct on-site inspections?

15. What powers does the supervisory authority have to provide or share information with other supervisory authorities? What kind of information may be provided or shared? What restrictions or constraints are there (if any) on the provision or sharing of information with other supervisory authorities? What statutory or other protection is available for information passed to the supervisory authorities by other authorities?

16. Have the Basle Committee's capital convergence proposals been adopted?

17.   What legislation, rules, and so on are in place to control money-laundering activities and to provide for the implementation of the 40 recommendations of the Financial Action Task Force on Money Laundering (FATF)?

18.   Are locally incorporated subsidiaries required to publish annual audited accounts? Are all banks subject to external audit and, if so, in what form? What are the criteria for appointing/approving external auditors and do they have to be the same as the auditors of the parent/group?

4. Supervision under the Banking Act 1979

The key component of the Banking Act 1979 was the introduction of new authorization procedures whereby any company desiring to operate as a deposit-taker[15] in the UK had first to secure authorization from the Bank unless it was specifically exempted from the Act, as was then the case for building societies, local authorities, the Bank of England, the National Girobank, and the National and Trustee Savings Banks.[16] Under the authorization procedures, the Bank drew a distinction (but not in status) between what it termed *recognised banks* and *licensed deposit-taking institutions*, largely on the basis of the range of services offered. Only those companies that had enjoyed a high reputation and standing in the financial community for a reasonable period of time could hope to have the former status conferred upon them. In reaching a decision, the Bank was required to review the information it received from applicants[17] regarding the planned provision of services according to the five categories identified in Schedule 2 of the Act. These embraced the provision of the following:

1. Current or deposit account facilities or the acceptance of wholesale money-market funds.
2. Overdraft or loan facilities or the lending of funds in the wholesale money markets.
3. Foreign exchange services.
4. Finance through the discounting of bills of exchange and promissory notes and for foreign trade.
5. Financial advice or investment management services and general securities market services.

In most cases, a recognized bank would be required to provide an 'adequate' level of service in each category, although this requirement could be waived in exceptional circumstances. Additionally, those deemed to provide a necessary and highly specialized banking service – such as the discount houses – might qualify. Despite the existence of statutory criteria to be used at the authorization stage, it can thus be seen that the Bank retained a considerable degree of discretion in interpreting and applying them. By way of offering a deeper insight into the Bank's decision-taking process, however, prospective applicants were advised to read the 'Guide for Intending Applicants' issued by the Bank and further useful information was later published by the Bank in its annual report for 1984 (pp. 41–4).

To qualify as a licensed deposit-taker, a company had again to satisfy the Bank that it could match the requirements and standards implied by a different set of criteria laid down by the Act. This required, *inter alia*, that directors, controllers and managers be 'fit and proper persons', that at least two individuals effectively direct the business and that the business be conducted in a 'prudent manner'.[18] To satisfy the Bank on the last front, institutions would be required to meet specific demands relating to capital and liquidity adequacy and provisions for bad and doubtful debts as well as any obligations of a contingent nature.

Finally, under Section 11 of the Act, grievance procedures were established whereby those companies refused authorization were given the right of appeal to the Chancellor of the Exchequer, who, in turn, was required to refer them to three persons appointed by him who heard the appeal. The Chancellor decided the appeal after taking into account the recommendation of the appointed persons.

Once over the authorization hurdle, a bank (henceforth taken to embrace both recognized banks and licensed deposit-takers) then became subject to the supervisory procedures adopted by the Bank. The management interviews that followed statistical analysis at the Bank of the prudential returns made by the banks remained the centrepiece of the system. The frequency of such meetings varied according to the type of bank. During 1985, for example, meetings with clearing banks and UK branches of overseas companies were held at intervals of approximately six and nine months,[19] respectively; but for other UK-incorporated companies they normally took place every quarter.

Aside from the assessment of the management itself, supervision was centred on the measurement and assessment of capital and liquidity adequacy and foreign currency exposure. As explained in Part II, this involved, in the first two cases, an element of quantitative assessment through the use of balance-sheet ratio analysis and 'maturity ladders', respectively; but, at the end of the day, an overall subjective evaluation was reached on each front after due consultation at the interview stage. Other important areas scrutinized by the Bank included large loan exposures (including country risk), provisioning for bad and doubtful debts, and the operations of banking groups. Views had also to be formulated about the question of bank ownership.[20] Finally (apart from the imposition of rigorous reporting requirements), the Bank was responsible for the administration of the Deposit Protection Scheme according to the Banking Act 1979, which required the establishment of a Deposit Protection Board chaired by the Governor of the Bank of England. Under the Scheme, which took effect from February 1982, 75 per cent of the first £10,000 (later raised to £20,000 – *see* p. 360) of a sterling deposit with an initial maturity of less than five years, made by a non-bank customer with any institution covered by the Banking Act, was guaranteed. To make this guarantee effective, all institutions covered by the Act[21] had to pay a levy, the amount of which was in proportion to the size of their deposit bases. Initially, the contributions were limited to a minimum and maximum of £2500 and £300,000, respectively.

5. The Johnson Matthey Bankers affair and its aftermath

The failings revealed at Johnson Matthey Bankers (JMB), the banking arm of Johnson Matthey plc, which necessitated a Bank-orchestrated rescue (*see* Hall, 1987b for a full analysis) in the autumn of 1984, was the catalyst for the reform of the 1979 Banking Act. This reform culminated in a new Banking Act, which took effect in October 1987.

To appreciate the nature of this reform fully, it is necessary to review the shortcomings in banking supervision exposed by the JMB affair. (The ensuing discussion rests heavily on Hall, 1987c.) This is best done by grouping points under a number of different headings, starting with the role of *auditors*.

AUDITORS

Prior to the introduction of the new Banking Act in 1987, auditors occupied a particularly awkward position within the supervisory process. Under the Companies Act they were required to report to shareholders whether or not the accounts prepared by a bank's directors provided the required 'true and fair view'. If, after exhausting the consultative process with the directors, the auditors failed to form such an opinion, two courses of action were open to them: either to resign or, alternatively, to qualify the accounts. In practice, both courses of action risked precipitating a run on the bank. Unlike in other countries, a third option of taking one's fears to a supervisory body (in this case the Bank), was not available to UK bank auditors without the express permission of their client banks. Without receiving the latter, such action would have represented a breach of confidentiality.

In the light of the above and the subsequent litigation that arose out of the JMB case – the Bank, JMB and Johnson Matthey plc all sued Arthur Young, the auditors of JMB, for alleged negligence while Arthur Young, in turn, sued the Bank (for negligence) and the Chancellor of the Exchequer (for defamation)[22] – it obviously seemed desirable to introduce new procedures, through legislation if necessary, to allow for a regular dialogue between bank auditor and supervisor. Moreover, it was clear that more exacting reporting requirements would have to be imposed on auditors if a repeat of a JMB-style collapse, which went undetected by the auditors, were to be avoided.

AUTHORIZATION PROCEDURES

The merits of the two-tier authorization process, whereby the upper-tier institutions (i.e. authorized banks) receive a lighter supervisory touch than the lower-tier intermediaries (i.e. licensed deposit-takers) were also called into question by the JMB affair. For here was an upper-tier institution, indeed a member of the august Accepting Houses Committee, which, in the words of the Bank, had presided over a situation where

> the controls and systems were inadequate; ... the organisation and management of the commercial banking and credit monitoring activities had serious shortcomings; ... insufficient attention had been given to the concentration of risks involved. Security was not required from borrowers ... and even when security was required the steps necessary to give the bank title to the security were not always taken properly. The need for provisions against bad and doubtful debts was not assessed with the proper degree of caution and the judgement of management in approving so many loans which have required substantial provisions was clearly defective' (Bank of England, 1985, pp. 34–5)

If one eliminates the possibility of fraud and corruption,[23] one is left with the impression of gross managerial incompetence in virtually every facet of commercial banking, a situation presided over by the Bank which had positively vetted the same individuals for the very purpose of running a banking operation. Not only was the two-tier system of authorization shown to be inadvisable but the authorization process itself, depending on the Bank's subjective interpretation and application of statutory criteria, could be called into question. Did the criteria need changing or was more vigilance required of the Bank? In practice, both remedies were applied.

SUPERVISORY PRACTICE

As far as the Bank was concerned, its immediate reaction was to introduce a number of amendments to supervisory practice. Even before the Banking Bill came to fruition, the Bank had embarked upon an intensification of its programme of supervisory visits, and increased the number of staff in its supervision department (which itself was restructured) and extended the scope of their training. These measures were designed to give the Bank a better understanding of the business operations undertaken by individual banks and to improve the capacity of Bank staff to reach informal judgements on the banks they were supervising. The new reporting requirements imposed on auditors, and the formal establishment of the Board of Banking Supervision (*see* p. 34) further assisted Bank staff in this capacity by providing them with access to additional information and professional expertise.

The existing frequency of management interviews and reviews of statistical returns – roughly every six and three months respectively for UK-incorporated institutions – was retained, although larger and more complex banks and banking groups were subjected to more frequent visits. Additionally, the proportion of interviews taking place on the institutions' own premises, rather than, as before, at the Bank, was increased with a view to providing the Bank with more detailed knowledge of the activities and control systems of the institutions it supervises. Increasingly (75 were carried out during 1986/87), informal, on-the-spot reviews are being used to supplement the routine prudential interviews, although the Bank is keen to rebut ideas that this represents a move towards a system of formal inspection, as is applied in the US and elsewhere.

The range of issues covered during visits was also extended to include more detailed discussion of a bank's corporate plans and future strategies and its financial budgets and forecasts. This contrasted with the previous position, where discussions concentrated on the statistical returns which contained, *inter alia*, information covering balance-sheet composition, profit and loss accounts, the maturity structure of assets and liabilities, country and sectoral analysis of business, and details of concentrations of risk in assets and deposits. In this way, the Bank hoped to obtain a clearer view of the basis of the bank's decision-taking process and increasingly to direct supervision towards the future.

Finally, the Bank sought new statutory powers[24] to extend the range of institutions and individuals from which it could require information and to increase the powers of any special investigators appointed. Additionally, it sought to make misreporting and failure to provide adequate information to the Bank for prudential purposes a criminal offence. This last move proved necessary in the wake of JMB's 'misreporting' of its two largest exposures and its failure to report certain other large exposures. On the former point, the Bank had claimed in its Annual Report for 1985 that the reported figures for the two exposures at end-June 1983 were 15 per cent and 12 per cent of capital compared with the 'true' figures of 26 per cent and 17 per cent, respectively; and that at end-June 1984 the reported figures were 38 per cent and 34 per cent compared with the 'true' figures of 76 per cent and 39 per cent respectively.

LARGE EXPOSURES

This leads conveniently to the final issue arising from the JMB affair, namely the treatment of large exposures. Given the significance of the over-concentration of risks in the collapse of JMB, it was clear that arrangements would have to be tightened. Under the regime ruling at that time, UK incorporated banks were expected, but not statutorily required, to inform the Bank of any exposure to a non-bank exceeding 10 per cent of the bank's capital base. In considering the acceptability of exposures, the Bank took into account the standing of the borrower, the nature of the bank's relationship with the borrower, the nature and extent of security taken, and the bank's expertise in the area of lending undertaken. Exposures to borrowers connected with the bank received particularly close attention and, generally speaking, the greater the number of large exposures the greater the level of capital required to back them. For individual large exposures, higher capital coverage would generally be demanded where the risks were conspicuously high or where there was a high concentration of large exposures. Limits were not placed on interbank, country or sectoral exposures, although, again, they were subject to the same reporting requests. Significantly, no standardized guidelines were specified, the Bank preferring to ensure that adequate internal assessment, control and monitoring systems existed, aiding this process through the dissemination of relevant information (e.g. relating to the credit-worthiness of debtor nations).

In the light of JMB's failure to report certain large exposures and its persistent understatement of the size of its two largest exposures, the need to move towards statutory reporting of large non-bank exposures, both single and connected, and to make misreporting or failure to report a criminal offence, was evident. More contentious were the issues of whether or not to raise the reporting threshold or to impose a statutory ceiling on single or connected non-bank exposures. As it transpired, neither was implemented – *see* below.

THE OFFICIAL RESPONSE

An important consequence of the JMB affair was the establishment by the Chancellor of the Exchequer in 1984 of a committee (the *Review Committee*), under the Chairmanship of the Governor of the Bank and comprising Treasury and Bank officials, to review banking supervisory procedures. In particular, the Committee was asked to consider the relationship between bank auditor and supervisor, the handling of risk concentration and assessment of asset quality, the statistical requirements imposed upon authorized institutions, and the adequacy of existing staff resources and training programmes in the Bank's supervision department.

The Review Committee duly reported (the Leigh-Pemberton Report) in June 1985 (HMSO, 1985a), making the following recommendations:

1. That the two-tier system of authorization be replaced with a single, Bank authorization to take deposits.

2. That legislative steps be taken to dismantle the barriers preventing discussions taking place between auditors and supervisors.
3. That exposure to a single non-bank borrower or interconnected group of borrowers should not exceed 25 per cent of a bank's capital.
4. That banks should set up audit committees and appoint finance directors.
5. That internal control systems be more carefully monitored by the Bank and that reporting requirements be strengthened (this was to include measures to ensure that statistical returns are lodged with the Bank on the due dates).[25]
6. That the number of staff (especially accountants) engaged in the supervision department at the Bank be increased and given commercial banking experience.
7. That the ceiling for the deposit protection granted under the Deposit Protection Scheme be raised from £10,000 to £20,000.

Following publication of the Report, the Bank issued three consultative papers on issues raised therein[26] and, after extensive consultations with the principal banking and accountancy associations and other interested parties, the government issued a White Paper on Banking Supervision in December 1985 (HMSO, 1985b). This document (see Exhibit 1.3 for a review of its main proposals) outlined the government's intentions, endorsing most of the proposals in the consultative documents. In addition, however, it proposed the establishment within the Bank of a Board of Banking Supervision to assist the Bank in exercising its supervisory responsibilities by providing it with direct access to senior practitioners in the fields of law, accountancy and commercial banking. Those proposals requiring implementation through legislation duly formed the basis of the Banking Bill, which received Royal Assent in May 1987. The main provisions took effect from October 1987.

Exhibit 1.3   The White Paper on Banking Supervision (Cmnd 9695, 17 December 1985)

Major proposals
1. The establishment of a Board of Banking Supervision to advise the Governor on supervisory matters and oversee the implementation of the (reformed) Banking Act.
2. An end to the two-tier system of authorization by applying a single set of criteria to all banks.
3. Auditors should be brought more fully into the supervisory process, preferably according to agreed guidelines but, if necessary, according to statute. The Bank is keen that, in exceptional circumstances (e.g. when fraud is suspected),

auditors will contact the supervisors directly without informing the client bank's management or directors.

4. Misreporting to the Bank should become a criminal offence.
5. The Bank should have wider statutory powers to obtain information.
6. Banks should be obliged by law to report large (i.e. more than 10 per cent of the capital base) exposures to the Bank and provide prior notification of those in excess of 25 per cent of the capital base.
7. Institutions should have paid-up share capital of at least £5 million before they can call themselves 'banks'.
8. The definition of 'deposits' should be amended to take account of new banking instruments.
9. The Bank should be allowed to pass on information obtained in its supervisory capacity to other government departments (except the Inland Revenue) where the public interest is at stake or when it would best serve the interests of depositors.

Source: HMSO, 1985b.

6. Reforms instituted under the Banking Act 1987

AN EXTENDED ROLE FOR AUDITORS

Under the new Banking Act, each authorized institution is required to commission an independent firm of accountants (preferably UK-based) to produce two separate reports, both of which are to be made available to the Bank.[27] These comprise an annual report on the bank's internal control systems and accounting and other records and, as and when requested by the Bank, a report on the statistical returns made to the Bank on prudential matters (*see* Bank of England, 1987a). The requirement to furnish the first report is part of the new minimum authorization criteria (*see* p. 37) and the second requirement represents an attempt by the Bank to check the accuracy of prudential returns by allowing for sampling on a spot-check basis.[28]

To facilitate the working of the new reporting system (a consultative paper had been issued by the Bank in November 1986 on the reporting requirements it intended to impose on banks), the Act enables accountants to disclose information, through the medium of *ad hoc* reports, to the Bank without contravening a duty of confidentiality to their clients and, in certain circumstances, enables the Bank to disclose information to accountants.[29] Additionally, UK-incorporated authorized institutions are required to notify the Bank of any change in their auditors and auditors will have to notify the Bank if they resign, qualify the accounts or do not seek reappointment.

On the subject of dialogue between auditors and the Bank, the Bank envisages that, in all bar exceptional circumstances (e.g. when fraud is suspected or the bank is thought to be in imminent danger of collapse), direct contact between itself and auditors will take place at trilateral meetings – to be held at least once a year – where the client banks are also present. Auditors, however, have been given a *right* (not a *duty*)[30] to consult with supervisors without informing their client, in which instances they will be immune from legal action by their clients provided the disclosures are made in good faith and the information is relevant to the supervisory process.

Given the precarious legal position they were still left, auditors quite naturally sought further guidance from the Bank on the circumstances in which they should report directly to the Bank without their clients' knowledge.[31] Interim guidance[32] was subsequently issued by the Bank and the Consultative Committee of Accountancy bodies in July 1987,[33] three months before the Act took effect. After months of discussion, it was eventually decided that the scope of the requirement was limited to the reporting of information uncovered during an audit. The Bank could not reasonably expect auditors to act on suspicions unsubstantiated in this way.

The final measure adopted by the Bank which affects the accountancy profession is approval of the appointment of reporting accountants. Only in exceptional circumstances will the appointment of a firm which does not qualify as auditors under the Companies Act 1985 be approved, and even then the Bank will seek to ensure that the firm is familiar with the Bank's supervisory approach and practice and has appropriate professional skills and resources as well as experience in undertaking similar work.

NEW AUTHORIZATION PROCEDURES

As foreshadowed in the Leigh-Pemberton Report and the Banking Bill, the two-tier authorization process was replaced by a single authorization to take deposits. Additionally, the minimum authorization criteria previously applied were extended to include a requirement that all UK incorporated institutions have as many non-executive directors as the Bank deems appropriate and that business is carried on with integrity and the appropriate professional skills. Finally, a minimum net asset requirement of £1 million[34] is applied at the time of authorization (though not afterwards) and more emphasis is now laid, as explained earlier, on institutions keeping adequate accounting and other records and maintaining appropriate internal controls. The new set of criteria and the Bank's approach to interpreting and applying them are dealt with more fully in Part II.

THE NEW TREATMENT OF LARGE EXPOSURES

As proposed in the Banking Bill, the new Act, as from 1 April 1988, requires all UK-incorporated banks to notify the Bank of any exposure to a single non-bank party or group of 'closely related' non-bank parties which exceeds 10 per cent of the bank's capital base, and to give prior notification of any exposures in excess of 25 per cent.[35] The Bank's view is that exposures should not normally exceed 10 per cent of the capital base – those that do receive thorough examination and require justification – and that, apart from the most exceptional circumstances, no exposure should exceed 25 per cent.[36] In the interests of flexibility and to maintain the international competitiveness of UK-incorporated banks, the Bank held out against the application of a statutory ceiling.

NEW CRIMINAL SANCTIONS

Under the Act it is a criminal offence to provide to the Bank for supervisory purposes knowingly or recklessly information which is false or misleading in a material particular; and for an authorized institution to fail to provide information in its possession which it knows or has reasonable cause to believe is relevant to the Bank's supervision of it (HMSO, 1987, Part VI, Section 94). A maximum two-year prison sentence also applies where people obstruct Bank investigations by destroying or concealing evidence.

NEW BANK POWERS

The 1987 Act gives the Bank the power to require a bank to provide a report by suitably qualified persons (reporting accountants) on any aspects of its business. The Bank's powers to require information were also extended to cover holding companies, subsidiaries, sister subsidiaries, directors, controllers, significant shareholders and managers of authorized institutions. Finally, under Schedule 3 of the Act, the Bank is given wide discretion in determining whether or not an institution should have: (1) non-executive directors on its board – it also has the power to determine the appropriate number; and (2) an audit committee. In reaching such decisions the Bank will take into account the size of the bank,[37] the nature and complexity of its business, and the group structure within which it operates.

FORMAL ESTABLISHMENT OF THE BOARD OF BANKING SUPERVISION

As called for under the 1987 Act, the Board of Banking Supervision was formally established in November 1987, having operated on a non-statutory basis since May 1986. On its inauguration, the Board comprised eight members: the Governor of the Bank, his deputy, the Bank's senior supervision executive and five independents appointed by the Governor with the agreement of the Chancellor of the Exchequer. In November 1987, however, the independent contingent was increased by one, raising the number to that proposed in the Banking Bill.

Although the Board is there to provide the Bank with practitioner-based advice on all aspects of bank supervision, the Governor is not obliged to accept the advice given. However, if the Governor chooses to ignore the advice of the Board he or she has to explain why to the Chancellor. The independent reporting to Parliament, through the medium of the Bank's annual report, reinforces the Board's power and independence of the Bank.

AMENDMENTS TO THE DEPOSIT PROTECTION SCHEME

The last major[38] statutory amendment introduced under the Act involves changes in the deposit insurance arrangements applying to bank depositors under the Deposit Protection Scheme. As called for by the Review Committee, although it is not clear that it was of any direct relevance to the JMB affair, the insurance cover for depositors holding sterling deposits with the UK offices of an authorized institution was doubled to 75 per cent of the first £20,000. Additionally, the Scheme was extended to cover all authorized institutions, including the offices of overseas banks previously exempt; and the minimum contribution for authorized institutions was raised from £2500 to £10,000.

7. International harmonization of banking supervision

Since the establishment of the Basle Committee of Supervisors in 1975, the Bank has played a leading role in promoting, at the international level, the harmonization of (or at least convergence in) bank supervisory practice. This has been achieved not just through participation in the work of the Basle Committee, although the Bank's contribution in this area has been considerable, but also through bilateral contact with its counterparts in other countries and through the dissemination of ideas at international forums.[39]

HARMONIZATION OF CAPITAL ADEQUACY REQUIREMENTS

Leaving EC developments, and the Bank's involvement in and reaction to them, aside for the time being (they are covered in Chapter 9), the first major breakthrough in the quest for convergence occurred with the signing of the US/UK 'accord' on capital adequacy in January 1987 (Bank of England, 1987c). The desire for convergence was based upon identification of the following needs:

1. To ensure all institutions are caught within the supervisory net.
2. To eliminate the possibility of regulation drifting towards the lowest common denominator as a result of 'competition in laxity'.[40]
3. To remove the incentive for banks to shift business between locations on the basis of the differential 'costs' imposed by supervision.
4. To ensure competitive equity between banks operating internationally.

Given the strength of feeling of international bankers on the last point when related to the question of capital adequacy assessment (Group of Thirty, 1982), the authorities in the two countries concerned – the Bank in the UK and the Board of Governors of the Federal Reserve System, the Office of the Comptroller of the Currency and the Federal Deposit Insurance Corporation of the US – could not have chosen a better place from which to begin their convergence exercise.

Under the accord, a common approach was to be adopted in the US and UK towards both the measurement of capital and the assessment of capital adequacy. On the former front, agreement was reached to adopt a definition of capital termed *primary capital*[41] which is supposed to represent the highest quality form of capital (*see* Exhibit 1.4); on the latter front, it was agreed that the risk-weighted approach pioneered in the UK (*see* Chapter 17) and recommended for adoption by the US regulatory authorities in January 1986 be used as the basis for assessment. The assignment of risk weights proposed (*see* Exhibit 1.5) largely reflected perception of the degree of credit risk inherent in the holding of certain types of asset, but the intention was, at some stage in the future, to take both position risk and interest rate risk into account. (In the event, only the former was accommodated – *see* below.) Nor were off-balance-sheet items overlooked. The nominal amounts of contracts have first to be converted into on-balance-sheet loan equivalents (the 'deemed credit risk equivalents') by the application of conversion factors (*see* Exhibit 1.6) before being slotted into the basic risk-weighting framework according to the type of counterparties involved. (The treatment of off-balance-sheet items is more fully analysed in Chapter 17.) For business involving the provision of undrawn commitments, the contracts were to be distinguished according to their original maturity, with longer-term obligations getting a higher risk weight.

Exhibit 1.4   Components of primary capital under the US/UK accord

---

A.   Funds included *without* limit

1. Common stock/equity and premium (UK), surplus (US).
2. Retained earnings (including current year earnings).
3. Minority interest in consolidated subsidiaries.
4. General reserves for losses resulting from charges to earnings.
5. Hidden reserves (comprising undisclosed retained earnings) – not applicable in US, to be phased out in UK.

B.   Funds included *with* limits – items included in this category must not exceed 50 per cent of the total items included in A above less intangible assets

1. Preferred shares that:
    (a) do not mature; or
    (b) mature on a fixed date *and* have an original maturity of at least 25 years. (Amount included in primary capital would be discounted for prudential purposes as the instrument approaches maturity.)
2. Subordinated debt that:
    (a) can only be converted into primary capital instruments;

Exhibit 1.4   (continued)

(b) is available at all times to absorb losses;

(c) provides that interest payments may be deferred if the issuer does not make a profit in the preceding period and/or pay dividends on common and perpetual preferred stock.

This is intended to include perpetual debt.

Notes:
(a) Existing mandatory convertible securities which do not meet the criteria in IB2 (for US banks) and existing property revaluation reserves (for UK banks) are to be 'grandfathered'.

(b) For bank holding companies in the United States, perpetual debt issued by the parent company need not be subordinated. It must, however, be unsecured.

Source: Bank of England, 1987c, p. 92.

Exhibit 1.5   Risk weights for on-balance-sheet items proposed under the US/UK accord

---

0 per cent
1. Vault cash – domestic and foreign.
2. All balances with, and claims on, domestic central banks.
3. Domestic national government guaranteed export and shipbuilding loans (UK only).

10 per cent
4. For the US, short-term (remaining maturity of one year or less) claims on the US government (Treasury) and on US government agencies (for the US, national government agencies are defined as those agencies whose debt obligations are backed by the full faith and credit of the US government). For the UK, short-term (one year or less) claims on the UK and Northern Ireland governments.
5. Short-term (one year or less) claims on discount houses, gilt-edged market makers (GEMMs) and stock exchange money brokers (UK only).

25 per cent
6. Cash items in the process of collection – foreign and domestic.
7. Short-term (one year or less) claims on domestic depository institutions and foreign banks.
8. All claims on domestic local authorities (UK only).
9. Long-term (over one year) claims on domestic national governments (including, for the UK, Northern Ireland) and all long-term claims on domestic national government agencies. For the UK, this includes all claims on UK public corporations and on the rest of the public sector.

10. All claims (including repurchase agreements) fully collateralized by domestic national government debt and (for the US) debt of US government agencies. Also, all claims collateralized by cash on deposit in the lending institution.
11. Federal Reserve Bank stock (US only).
12. Portions of loans guaranteed by domestic national government or (for the US) domestic national government agencies.
13. All local currency claims on foreign central governments to the extent funded by local currency liabilities in that foreign country.

50 per cent
14. All claims on domestic national government-sponsored agencies (US government-sponsored agencies are defined as agencies whose debt obligations are not guaranteed by the full faith and credit of the US government).
15. All claims (including repurchase agreements) that are fully collateralized by domestic national government-sponsored agency debt (US only).
16. All general obligation claims on domestic state and local governments (US only).
17. Claims on multinational development institutions in which the domestic government is a shareholder or contributing member.

100 per cent
18. Long-term (over one year) claims on domestic depository institutions and foreign banks.
19. All claims on foreign governments other than local currency claims on foreign central governments funded by local currency liabilities in that foreign country.
20. The customer liability on acceptances outstanding involving standard risk obligators (US only).
21. Domestic state and local government revenue bonds and industrial development bonds (US only).
22. All other assets.
23. Net open position in foreign exchange (UK only).

Source: Bank of England, 1987c, pp. 92–3.

Exhibit 1.6 Conversion factors for off-balance-sheet items under the US/UK accord[1]

10 per cent
1. Overdrafts, revolving underwriting facilities (e.g. NIFs/RUFs), underwriting commitments, and commercial and consumer credit lines with an original maturity[2] of up to one year.

Exhibit 1.6   (continued)

25 per cent
1. Overdrafts, revolving underwriting facilities (e.g. NIFs/RUFs), underwriting commitments, and commercial and consumer credit lines with an original maturity of over one year and up to five years.

50 per cent
1. Overdrafts, revolving underwriting facilities (e.g. NIFs/RUFs), underwriting commitments, and commercial and consumer credit lines with an original maturity of over five years.
2, Trading contingencies (e.g. commercial letters of credit, bid and performance bonds, and performance standby letters of credit).

100 per cent
1. Direct credit substitutes (e.g. financial guarantees and standby letters of credit serving the same purpose and, in the UK, acceptances outstanding).
2. Sale and repurchase agreements and asset sales with recourse, if not already included on the balance sheet.

To be determined[3]
1. Conversion factors for: interest rate swaps and other interest rate contracts; foreign exchange rate contracts

---

Notes:
1. Not all off-balance-sheet obligations need to be considered within the capital adequacy assessment process (e.g. indemnities for lost share certificates and bill endorsements, and 'holders in due course' obligations can be ignored).
2. Defined as the earliest possible time at which the bank may unconditionally cancel the commitment.
3. Proposals were issued in May 1987 for discussion.

Source: Bank of England, 1987c, p. 93.

Finally, and most importantly from the perspective of banks seeking equitable treatment, the regulatory bodies agreed to impose a common minimum primary capital ratio (i.e. the ratio of adjusted primary capital (see Exhibit 1.7) to the total of weighted risk assets, which is calculated by summing the nominal values of the individual balance-sheet items multiplied by their risk weights and adding this number to the sum of the weighted loan equivalents arising from off-balance-sheet activities) on all internationally active banks operating in the two countries. Beyond prescribing this minimum ratio (which would be published), the regulatory bodies were to be allowed to retain the freedom to set, on a confidential basis, minimum ratios for each institution falling within their jurisdiction. For most banks, the latter ratio would most likely have been significantly higher than the prescribed minimum. Perhaps of more ideological concern, however, was the damage done to the principle of establishing a 'level playing field', since national regulators would undoubtedly have exercised their freedoms in different ways. For example, it soon became clear that the Bank would take a tougher line than the majority of its international counterparts in the imposition of capital requirements in the run-up to 1992.

Exhibit 1.7   Adjustments to be made to primary capital for calculation of the risk asset ratio (RAR) under the US/UK accord

---

A. Deduction of all intangible assets. (Existing intangibles currently allowed by US regulatory authorities will be 'grandfathered'.)
B. Deduction of investments in unconsolidated subsidiaries and associated companies including, but not limited to, unconsolidated joint ventures. For the US, this could include certain consolidated subsidiaries as determined by US regulatory authorities; for the UK this also includes related securities companies.
C. Deduction of bank holdings of capital instruments of other banking organizations. (In the US these would be monitored and deducted on a case-by-case basis.)

Source: Bank of England, 1987c, p. 92.

Although the UK and US authorities were the only signatories to the agreed proposals for capital adequacy assessment, it was hoped that other supervisory bodies would be won over. Encouragingly, and despite the formidable problems encountered (even the US supervisors had to deal with the problem of the exclusion of specific reserves from 'primary capital', which at that time ranked as capital in the US), others soon indicated their willingness to abide by at least the spirit of the accord. Thus Japan was brought into the fold in June 1987, although the problem remained of how to treat Japanese banks' hidden reserves in the form of unrealized gains on securities holdings;[42] and, in September 1987, it was rumoured that the G10[43] central banks were close to accepting the accord, subject to agreement on a phasing-in period.

In December 1987, however, the convergence process initiated by the accord was superseded by an initiative launched by the Basle Committee of Supervisors under the auspices of the BIS. The new approach was based on the accord and therefore, not surprisingly, embraced a similar methodology in the shape of establishing a common system of risk weights and measure of capital to be used in the calculation of a risk assets ratio, for which a minimum would be set.

Differences, however, lay in the specification of the set of risk weights and conversion factors[44] to be applied to both on- and off-balance-sheet transactions respectively (*see* Exhibits 1.9–1.11) and in the definition of capital. The 'primary capital' definition was replaced with the twin concepts of 'Tier 1' (or core) and 'Tier 2' (or supplementary) capital (*see* Exhibit 1.8), with the capital base comprising the sum of Tier 1 and Tier 2 elements, subject to certain limits and restrictions.[45]

Exhibit 1.8   Definition of capital included in the capital base under the BIS proposals (to apply at end-1992 – see Exhibit 1.11 for transitional arrangements)

A.   Capital elements
Tier 1   (a)   Ordinary paid-up share capital/common stock.
        (b)   Disclosed reserves.
Tier 2   (a)   Undisclosed reserves.
        (b)   Asset revaluation reserves.
        (c)   General provisions/general loan loss reserves.
        (d)   Hybrid (debt/equity) capital instruments.
        (e)   Subordinated term debt.
The sum of Tier 1 and Tier 2 elements will be eligible for inclusion in the capital base, subject to the following limits.

B.   Limits and restrictions
1.   The total of Tier 2 (supplementary) elements will be limited to a maximum of 100 per cent of the total of Tier 1 elements, that is, at least 50 per cent of the capital base must comprise Tier 1 elements.
2.   Subordinated term debt will be limited to a maximum of 50 per cent of Tier 1 elements, that is, to 25 per cent of the capital base.
3.   Where general provisions/general loan loss reserves include amounts reflecting lower valuations of assets or latent but unidentified losses present in the balance sheet, the amount of such provisions or reserves will be limited to a maximum of 1.25 percentage points, or exceptionally and temporarily up to 2.0 percentage points, of risk assets.[1]
4.   Asset revaluation reserves which take the form of latent gains on unrealized securities (*see* below) will be subject to a discount of 55 per cent.

C.   Adjustments made to the capital base for calculation of the risk asset ratio under the BIS proposals
1.   Deductions from Tier 1: goodwill.
2.   Deductions from total capital:

(a) investment in unconsolidated banking and financial subsidiary companies (N.B. The presumption is that the framework would be applied on a consolidated basis to banking groups);

(b) investments in the capital of other banks and financial institutions (at the discretion of national authorities).

Note: 1. This limit would only apply in the event that no agreement is reached on a consistent basis for including unencumbered provisions or reserves in capital.

Source: BIS, 1987.

Exhibit 1.9   Risk weights by category of on-balance-sheet assets under the BIS proposals

---

0 per cent
(a) Cash.
(b) Balances at, and claims on, domestic central bank.
(c) Loans to domestic central governments.
(d) Loans and other assets fully collateralised by cash or domestic central government securities[1] or fully guaranteed by domestic central governments.

0 or 20 per cent
(a) Claims on International Bank for Reconstruction and Development and regional development banks (at national discretion) (EC countries would treat EC institutions consistently).

20 per cent
(a) Claims on domestic and foreign banks with an original maturity of under one year.
(b) Claims on domestic banks with an original maturity of one year and over and loans guaranteed by domestic banks.
(c) Claims on foreign central governments in local currency financed by local currency liabilities.
(d) Cash items in process of collection.

0, 20 or 50 per cent
(a) Claims on the domestic public sector, excluding central government (at national discretion) and loans guaranteed by such institutions.

50 per cent
(a) Loans to owner-occupiers for residential house purchase fully secured by mortgage.

100 per cent

(a) Claims on the private sector.

(b) Cross-border claims on foreign banks with an original maturity of one year and over.

(c) Claims on foreign central governments (unless 20 per cent).

(d) Claims on commercial companies owned by the public sector.

(e) Premises, plant and equipment and other fixed assets.

(f) Real estate and other investments (including non-consolidated investment participations in other companies).

(g) Capital instruments issued by other banks (unless deducted from capital).

(h) All other assets.

Note: 1. National supervisors have the discretion to prescribe non-zero weights (e.g. 10 per cent or 20 per cent) if they attempt to take account of the investment risk on securities issued to their domestic central governments.

Source: BIS, 1987.

Exhibit 1.10   Credit conversion factors for off-balance-sheet items under the BIS proposals

---

Instrument	Credit conversion factor (%)
1. Direct credit substitutes, for example, general guarantees of indebtedness (including standby letters of credit serving as financial guarantees for loans and securities) and acceptances (including endorsements with the character of acceptances)	100
2. Certain transaction-related contingent items (e.g. performance bonds, bid bonds, warranties and standby letters of credit related to particular transactions)	50
3. Short-term self-liquidating trade-related contingencies (such as documentary credits collateralized by the underlying shipments)	20
4. Sale and repurchase agreements and asset sales with recourse,[1] where the credit risk remains with the bank	100
5. Forward purchases, forward forward deposits and partly paid shares and securities, which represent commitments with certain drawdown	100
6. Note issuance facilities and revolving underwriting facilities	50

7. Other commitments (e.g. formal standby facilities and credit
   lines with an original maturity exceeding one year)   50
8. Similar commitments with an original maturity of less than
   one year, or which can be cancelled at any time   0
9. Foreign exchange – and interest rate-related items   Treated separately

---

N.B. Member countries will have some limited discretion to allocate particular instruments into items 1 to 8 above according to the characteristics of the instrument in the national market.

Note: 1. These items are to be weighted according to the type of asset and not according to the type of counterparty with whom the transaction has been entered into.

Source: BIS, 1987.

Exhibit 1.11 *Credit conversion factors for interest rate- and exchange rate-related activities under the BIS proposals*

A. If the 'current exposure' method is adopted the following conversion factors have to be used in the calculation of potential future credit exposures:

Residual maturity	Interest rate contracts	Exchange rate contracts
	(% of notional principal amount)	
Less than one year	Nil	1.0
One year and over	0.5	5.0

B. If the 'original exposure' method is adopted, the following conversion factors have to be applied to calculate the 'deemed credit risk equivalents':

Original[1] maturity	Interest rate contracts	Exchange rate contracts
	(% of notional principal amount)	
Less than one year	0.5	2.0
Over one year and less than two years	1.0	5.0 (i e. 2 + 3)
For each additional year	1.0	3.0

Note: 1. In the case of interest rate contracts, banks may, subject to the consent of their supervisory authorities, choose to use either original or residual maturity.

Source: BIS, 1987.

Finally, the Basle Committee at last put a number on the standard minimum level of (adjusted) capital which international banks would have to hold against their risk-adjusted assets and off-balance-sheet business: a 'risk asset ratio' (*see* Exhibit 1.12) of 8 per cent would have to be observed by the end of 1992. Transitional arrangements (*see* Exhibit 1.13) allowed for the gradual build-up of this ratio and, as under the accord, national regulators will retain the discretion to apply the standard to all banks and to require higher levels where this is judged appropriate. Although the proposals were recommended for adoption by all the G10 countries plus Luxembourg, it was hoped that other countries would eventually decide to abide by the spirit, if not the letter, of the document, as later refined.

Exhibit 1.12   The risk asset ratio methodology to be employed by banking regulators under the G10 capital accord of 1988

Under the accord, all internationally active banks authorized in G10 countries have to observe a minimum RAR of 8 per cent. The RAR is calculated as follows:

$$RAR(\%) = \frac{ACB}{TOWRA}$$

where *ACB* is the adjusted capital base and *TOWRA* (the total of weighted risk assets)

$$= \sum_{i=1}^{s}\sum_{j=1}^{t}\left(A_{ij}W_j\right)$$

$$+ \sum_{i=1}^{u}\sum_{j=1}^{v}\sum_{k=1}^{w}\left(B_{ijk}X_kW_j\right)$$

$$+ \sum_{i=1}^{x}\sum_{j=1}^{y}\sum_{k=1}^{z}\left[\left(C_{ijk}X_k + M\right)W_j\right]^{*}$$

where A_{ij} is the value of the ith asset with risk weight, W_j;
$\quad\quad\quad B_{ijk}$ is the notional principal amount of off-balance-sheet activity i with risk weight W_j and conversion factor X_k;

C_{ijk} is the notional principal amount of the interest- or exchange-rate related activity i with risk weight W_j and conversion factor X_k;

s is the number of different asset components;

u is the number of distinct off-balance-sheet activities (excluding interest rate- and exchange rate-related activities),

x is the number of distinct interest- and exchange rate-related off-balance-sheet instruments;

M is the 'mark-to-market' value of the underlying contract,

where $x < u < s$; $v \le t = 5$; $y \le t = 5$; $w = 4$; and $z = 4$.

* 'Current exposure' assessment method employed.

Source: Hall, 1994a.

The adoption of the refined Basle proposals[46] by most of the world's main supervisory bodies would certainly be a major step forward in raising prudential standards, at least in terms of capital adequacy assessment, to an acceptable minimum. The discretion allowed national regulators, however, militated against the establishment of a regulatory 'level playing field' (*see* Hall, 1992a), and further harmonization of not only supervisory practice but also accounting practice and legal and fiscal systems will be needed if the other goals of convergence (spelt out on p. 40) are to be met.

Since the Basle capital accord (as it became known) took effect in January 1993, it has been amended in two major ways. First, it has been amended to recognize 'netting' arrangements (and the treatment of potential exposure for off-balance-sheet items updated); and, second, it has been revised to accommodate market risk alongside credit risk. Each of these amendments will now be addressed in turn.

RECOGNITION OF NETTING UNDER THE BASLE CAPITAL ACCORD

Supervisory recognition of netting arrangements has been forthcoming in respect of both bilateral and multilateral netting schemes. As regards *bilateral netting* schemes (Hall, 1996a), under the accord only 'netting by novation' for the same currency and same value was recognized for supervisory purposes, whereby risk weights could be applied to the net rather than the gross claims arising from swaps and similar off-balance-sheet contracts with the same counterparties. This position was subsequently reviewed by the Basle Committee,

Exhibit 1.13   Transitional arrangements under the BIS proposals

	Initial	End-1990	End-1992
1. Minimum standard (for the RAR)	The level prevailing at end-1987	7.25%	8.0%
2. Measurement formula for the capital base	Core elements plus 100%	Core elements plus 100% (3.625% plus 3.625%)	Core elements plus 100% (4% plus 4%)
3. Supplementary elements included in core	Maximum 25% of total core	Maximum 10% of total core (i.e. 0.36%)	None
4. Limit on general loan loss reserves in supplementary elements[1]	No limit	1.5 percentage points, or exceptionally up to 2.0 percentage points of risk assets	1.25 percentage points, or exceptionally and temporarily up to 2.0 percentage points of risk assets
5. Limit on subordinated debt in supplementary elements	No limit (at discretion)	No limit (at discretion)	Maximum of 50% of Tier 1
6. Deduction for goodwill	Deducted from Tier 1 (at discretion)	Deducted from Tier 1 (at discretion)	Deducted from Tier 1

N.B. The Committee as a whole had not endorsed any precise standard figure at this stage. The figures given in line 1 are those proposed by the ten member countries wishing to announce indicative levels as a basis for consultation on the framework.

Note: 1. This limit would only apply in the event that no agreement is reached on a consistent basis for including unencumbered provisions or reserves in capital.

Source: BIS, 1987.

which produced a consultative paper in April 1993 (Basle Committee, 1993a) proposing an amended treatment of the netting of credit risks which would result in banks enjoying reductions in capital charges to the extent that they have legally valid netting arrangements governing their trading in certain instruments. Specifically, the consultative paper did three things: (1) it laid down new conditions,[47] consistent with the principles espoused in the Lamfalussy Report[48] (BIS, 1990) – *see* Exhibit 1.14 – which have to be satisfied before netting arrangements can be recognized for capital adequacy assessment purposes; (2) it proposed an amendment of the accord to allow for recognition of bilateral netting arrangements, other than netting by novation, where such arrangements are effective under relevant laws (and national supervisors are mutually satisfied that agreed minimum legal requirements are met) and comply with the other minimum standards set out in the Lamfalussy Report;[49] and (3) it indicated the Committee's preliminary thinking on the conditions under which *multilateral* netting might be recognized for capital measurement purposes at some future date.

Exhibit 1.14   Minimum standards for netting schemes set out in the Lamfalussy Report

---

1. Netting schemes should have a well-founded legal basis under all relevant jurisdictions.
2. Netting scheme participants should have a clear understanding of the impact of the particular scheme on each of the financial risks affected by the netting process.
3. Multilateral netting systems should have clearly defined procedures for the management of credit risks and liquidity risks which specify the respective responsibilities of the netting provider and the participants. These procedures should also ensure that all parties have both the incentives and the capabilities to manage and contain each of the risks they bear and that limits are placed on the maximum level of credit exposure that can be produced by each participant.
4. Multilateral netting systems should, at a minimum, be capable of ensuring the timely completion of daily settlements in the event of an inability to settle by the participant with the largest single net-debit position.
5. Multilateral netting schemes should have objective and publicly disclosed criteria for admission which permit fair and open access.
6. All netting schemes should ensure the operational reliability of technical systems and the availability of back-up facilities capable of completing daily processing requirements.

Source: BIS, 1990.

More formally, under the amended accord banks may now net transactions subject to novation, or subject to any other legally valid form of bilateral netting including other forms of novation, under which any obligation between a bank and its counterparty to deliver a given currency on a given value date is automatically amalgamated with all other obligations for the same currency and value date, legally substituting one single amount for the previous gross obligations, provided that the bank's supervisor is satisfied that the bank has:[50]

(1) a netting contract or agreement with the counterparty which creates a single legal obligation, covering all included transactions, such that the bank would have either a claim to receive or obligation to pay only the net sum of the positive and negative mark-to-market values of included individual transactions in the event a counterparty fails to perform due to any of the following: default, bankruptcy, liquidation or similar circumstances;

(2) written and reasoned legal opinions that, in the event of a legal challenge, the relevant courts and administrative authorities would find the bank's exposure to be such a net amount under:
- the law of the jurisdiction in which the counterparty is chartered and, if the foreign branch of a counterparty is involved, then also under the law of the jurisdiction in which the branch is located;
- the law that governs the individual transactions; and
- the law that governs any contract or agreement necessary to effect the netting. The national supervisor, after consultation when necessary with other relevant supervisors, must be satisfied that the netting is enforceable under the laws of each of the relevant jurisdictions;

(3) procedures in place to ensure that the legal characteristics of netting arrangements are kept under review in the light of possible changes in relevant law (Basle Committee, 1993a, Annex 2, p. 2.)

Contracts containing walkaway clauses[51] will not be eligible for netting for the purpose of calculating capital requirements under the accord.

For banks using the *current exposure* method – *see* Exhibit 1.12 – the Committee recommended that the credit exposure on bilaterally netted forward transactions be calculated in exactly the same way as for non-netted forward transactions, that is, by adding the net marked-to-market replacement cost, if positive, to an 'add-on' based on the notional underlying principal.[52] Moreover, it was proposed that the scale of add-ons (i.e. 'conversion factors' – *see* Exhibit 1.11A) used, at least for the time being, be the same as those for non-netted transactions although, as explained in the next section, this was changed at the end of 1995.[53] Finally, it was proposed that the weights used to weight the 'loan equivalents' be of the same scale and be applied in the same manner (i.e. usually according to the category of counterparty) as those used for non-netted transactions. The concessionary weightings given in respect of exposures backed by eligible guarantees and collateral would thus also apply, as would the concessionary weight – 50 per cent – applicable, at national discretion, in respect of counterparties which would otherwise attract a 100 per cent risk weight under the original accord.[54]

For banks using the *original exposure* method, which was allowed until market risk-related capital requirements were implemented (i.e. the end of 1997 for non-EU G10 nations – *see* Hall, 1995a), a concessionary set of conversion factors can be used when calculating the credit exposure of bilaterally netted transactions. These factors – *see* Exhibit 1.15 – represent a reduction of approximately 25 per cent from those applicable under the original accord (compare Exhibit 1.11B).[55] As for banks using the current exposure method, the weighting system employed under the original accord is also carried forward.

Exhibit 1.15   *Concessionary conversion factors which may be (temporarily) employed by banks adopting the original exposure method to calculate the loan equivalents arising from netted off-balance-sheet transactions*

Maturity	Interest rate contracts	Exchange rate contracts
	(% of notional principal amount)	
Less than one year	0.35	1.5
One year and less than two years	0.75	3.75 (i.e. 1.5 + 2.25)
For each additional year	0.75	2.25

Source: Basle Committee, 1993a.

As for the *new treatment of potential exposure for off-balance-sheet items*, from the end of 1995 the scale of 'add-ons' (i.e. conversion factors) to be used in the calculation of credit risk equivalents for legally valid bilaterally *netted* forward transactions was reduced from the previous levels. In addition, an expanded matrix of add-on factors applied to off-balance-sheet transactions. Both policy changes were confirmed in a Basle Committee document dated April 1995 (Basle Committee, 1995a), which followed an earlier (July 1994) consultation paper on the subject.[56]

As can be seen from Exhibit 1.16, the expanded matrix covers contracts in gold, other precious metals, equities and 'other commodities', as well as the traditional interest rate- and exchange rate-related contracts (*see* Exhibit 1.11A). Gold contracts are to be treated in the same way as exchange rate contracts except that contracts with an original maturity of 14 calendar days or less are to be included. Forwards, swaps, purchased options and similar contracts in precious metals other than gold (e.g. silver, platinum and palladium) are to receive separate treatment, as are such contracts in 'other commodities' (e.g. energy contracts, agricultural contracts, contracts in base metals such as aluminium, copper and zinc, and commodity contracts in other non-precious metals). The equity contracts to be covered also embrace forwards, swaps, purchased options and similar derivative contracts based on individual equities or on equity indices. Forwards, swaps, purchased options and similar derivative contracts not covered by any of the columns in the matrix are to be treated as contracts in 'other commodities'.

Exhibit 1.16   The expanded matrix of add-ons used from the end of 1995 by banks adopting the current exposure method to calculate the loan equivalents arising from non-netted off-balance-sheet transactions

Residual maturity	Type of contract				
	Interest rate	Exchange rate and gold	Equity	Precious metals except gold	Other commodities
One year or less	0.0	1.0	6.0	7.0	10.0
Over one year and up to five years	0.5	5.0	8.0	7.0	12.0
Over five years	1.5	7.5	10.0	8.0	15.0

Source: Basle Committee, 1995a.

Turning to the recognition of the effects of netting in the calculation of add-ons, for banks using the current exposure method[57] the add-ons for netted transactions may be calculated in accordance with the following formula:

$$A_{net} = (0.4 \times A_{gross}) + 0.6 \times NGR \times A_{gross}$$

where: A_{net} = the add-on for netted transactions;
            A_{gross} = the sum of individual add-on amounts (calculated by multiplying the notional principal amounts by the appropriate add-on factors set out in Exhibit 1.16)
            NGR = the ratio of net current replacement cost to gross current replacement cost for transactions subject to legally enforceable netting arrangements.[58]

For banks using the original exposure method,[59] the concessionary add-ons set out in Exhibit 1.15 could be applied.[60]

With respect to the supervisory treatment of *multilateral netting*, the Committee's provisional thinking on the subject focused on the use of a clearing house as the medium through which all transactions originating bilaterally between members of a specific group of counterparties could be netted (Basle Committee, 1993a, Annex 3). The clearing house would be interposed as the common legal counterparty to each clearing house member, with the members having no legal obligations towards each other. For each member, the clearing house would maintain a running, legally binding net position in each currency and each value date eligible for netting, all subject to a binding netting agreement between the member and the clearing house. As a result, multiple transactions originating with a range of counterparties could be amalgamated and netted, thereby substantially reducing exposures, and thus capital charges to cover replacement costs, compared with what they would be in a non-netting environment.[61]

Under the clearing house arrangements, if a clearing house member defaulted the clearing house would have to replace the cash flows that the defaulting member's portfolio of foreign exchange contracts would have produced. Payment to, or a claim on, the defaulting member would represent the replacement value of the member's portfolio. Given the likely limited resources of the clearing house, mechanisms would clearly need to exist to allow for any shortfall to be covered in the event of a claim being made on defaulters. This might involve the clearing house in recovering losses through a 'defaulter pays' scheme (whereby each member would be obliged to post collateral equal to its own net debt with the clearing house which could be seized in the event of default), through a 'survivors pay' scheme (whereby losses are somehow allocated to the surviving, non-defaulting members)[62] or through a hybrid of the two models. In the last-mentioned case, members would be obliged to reimburse the clearing house according to a predetermined loss allocation rule, but losses to be allocated to survivors would be reduced by the value of the collateral posted by the defaulting member.

Whatever the nature of the loss recovery arrangements, the Committee was keen to ensure that the minimum standards for netting schemes outlined in the Lamfalussy Report are adhered to. Accordingly, multilateral netting arrangements should incorporate, *inter alia*, safeguards to address settlement risk in a responsible manner, including risk controls such as internal limits, adequate and reliable liquidity support, and appropriate technical back-up facilities. Adherence to the minimum standards would have to be monitored by central banks and other relevant parties, and national supervisors whose banks belong to a multilateral netting arrangement would have to satisfy themselves that the standards were met before extending supervisory recognition to the netting performed under the scheme.

As for the level of *capital requirements* that should be imposed under any multilateral netting arrangement, the Committee had not reached any firm conclusions; it instead welcomed suggestions from interested parties. It was agreed, however, that capital charges should be levied to cover both current exposure and potential future exposure. The current exposure for each member would be represented by its exposure to the clearing house in the event of another member defaulting, determined in accordance with the rules applying under the prevailing loss allocation scheme. A bank's current exposure might thus be the sum of the loss shares that it would be allocated in the event of a default (or close-out) of each member to which it had a notional bilateral exposure, after allowing for any collateral available to the clearing house.[63] In contrast, a bank's *potential future exposure* would be determined by a combination of the underlying rates and prices, the changing pattern of clearing house exposure to other members and the loss allocation procedure in place. A simplified approximation would be required to determine the 'add-ons' needed to cover the resulting exposure.

Finally, *risk weights* would have to be applied to take account of banks' exposures to the clearing house arising from the funding and liquidity back-up arrangements employed. In line with the accord, the weight applicable to claims on a clearing house would be the usual 100 per cent private sector weighting, unless the clearing house is incorporated as a bank and becomes subject to bank supervisors' rules (in which case a 20 per cent weight would apply), or the host government or central bank has given a clear and unequivocal guarantee for all of its obligations (in which case a zero weight would be justified).

In April 1996, the Committee finally published its 'interpretation' of how the multilateral netting of forward-value foreign exchange transactions should be treated under the accord (Basle Committee, 1996b). The Committee's interpretation was based upon a belief that a well-constructed multilateral netting system could reduce forward credit exposure for the participants. Consistent with the framework of the accord, it focused only on forward replacement risk (i.e. the potential cost of replacing the cash flows on outstanding contracts in the case of counterparty default) and not on settlement risk (Hall, 1997a). It also assumed that the multilateral system had received approval from the relevant authority responsible for its oversight, and that it therefore satisfied certain standards concerning, at a minimum, the legal soundness of the netting arrangements, the sound design and operation of the system, the sufficiency of the liquidity arrangements, and the mechanisms for managing collateral.

Focusing on how best to capture the economic effects of multilateral netting through the imposition of capital requirements on participants, the Committee noted that the primary risk of loss for a participant arises from the possibility of another participant's default and not from a default by the clearing house itself.[64] Accordingly, it recommended that a participant's capital requirements for current credit exposure should be determined on the basis of the primary loss allocations[65] of the clearing house (i.e. the participant's *pro rata* share of the clearing house exposure). Since a defaulter cannot be identified in advance, a participant's total net current exposure is the sum of the primary loss allocations it could be required to absorb from a default by every other participant, individually, in the clearing system.

By way of illustration, the Committee's document included an example of how such a system might operate for a simple clearing house structure where clearing house losses are allocated in proportion to the surviving participants' exposures to the defaulting participant. Using the figures set out in Exhibit 1.17, it can be seen that participant B owes the clearing house the net amount of $250, the loss that the clearing house would incur if participant B were to default. This loss would be allocated to those survivors which have bilateral net claims on participant B, that is, to participants C and D. These participants have claims of $100 and $400 respectively, totalling $500. Of this amount, C is owed 20 per cent and D 80 per cent.

Exhibit 1.17   Net replacement values ($)

Position of	With respect to				
	A	B	C	D	Clearing house
A	–	–250	50	0	–200
B	250	–	–100	–400	–250
C	–50	100	–	500	550
D	0	400	–500	–	–100

Source: Basle Committee, 1996b, p. 4.

As indicated in Exhibit 1.18, C's primary loss allocation *vis-à-vis* B would be $50 (i.e. 20 per cent of $250) and D's primary loss allocation would be $200 (i.e. 80 per cent of $250). The other primary loss allocations can be derived in a similar manner. It can be seen that the sum of the primary loss allocations for participant A, and thus its current credit exposure, is zero, while the current exposures for participants B, C and D are $200, $150 and $200, respectively. The example also illustrates why current exposures should not be based on the net bilateral exposures of participants *vis-à-vis* the clearing house. For example, Exhibit 1.17 indicates that participant D's net bilateral exposure to the clearing house is zero (because the market value of the net exposure is negative – it actually equals minus $100), whereas its loss allocation exposure, and therefore real credit risk, is $200, as shown in Exhibit 1.18.

Under the Committee's 'interpretation', the capital charge for the *potential future exposure* of a bank participating in a multilateral netting arrangement for forward-value contracts continues to be calculated on the basis of the notional bilateral relationships with each of the other clearing house participants. In other words, the add-on under multilateral netting has to be calculated as if netting occurred bilaterally with the same set of counterparties, applying the bilateral netting formula noted above, that is, $A_{net} = 0.4 (A_{gross}) + 0.6 (NGR \times A_{gross})$. The '$A_{nets}$' with respect to each of the bilateral counterparties must therefore be summed to arrive at the figure for the total add-on for potential future exposure. This, of course, requires that each participant and/or the clearing house has to keep track of its gross potential future exposure, gross current exposure and bilaterally netted current exposure to each of the participants in the multilateral system.

Exhibit 1.18   Primary loss allocations ($)

Default of			Loss allocation to		
	Total	A	B	C	D
A	200	–	200 (100%)	0	0
B	250	0	–	50 (20%)	200 (80%)
C	0	0	0	–	0
D	100	0	0	100 (100%)	–
Total	550	0	200	150	100

Source: Basle Committee, 1996b, p. 5.

While accepting that its approach was relatively conservative and pragmatic, reflecting the difficulties of approximating a multilateral netting participant's potential future exposure (which depends on the transactions across all participants of the clearing house and the loss-sharing arrangements operated by the clearing house in the event of a default by a participant), the Committee felt that further study was necessary before it could allow a more 'permissive' approach to be taken.[66]

As explained earlier, under the accord off-balance-sheet contracts have to be converted into credit equivalent amounts and then risk weighted according to the identity of the obligor or counterparty. If a guarantee is associated with the transaction or if qualifying collateral has been posted, the portion of the credit equivalent amount that is covered by the guarantee or collateral may be risk weighted according to the identity of the guarantor or the nature of the collateral. For forward-value foreign exchange transactions subject to multilateral netting, a given participant has to add each primary loss allocation amount to the corresponding add-on for potential future exposure to derive a total credit equivalent amount with respect to each of the other participants in the clearing house. These credit equivalent amounts must then be assigned to the appropriate risk category according to the identity of the other participants[67] or the nature of the collateral.

As is the case for other types of transaction, a participant in a multilateral netting arrangement is able to assign the portion of its credit equivalent amount that is supported by collateral in the form of cash or OECD government securities to the 0 per cent risk category. However, this will only be allowed where that portion is clearly identifiable. If collateral has been posted by all banks participating in the multilateral system but an individual bank cannot identify what percentage of the collateral, if any, it would be entitled to recover to satisfy its losses in the event of a default by another participant, employment of a reduced risk weight will not be permitted.

To clarify the situation of the *treatment of collateralized transactions*, the Committee drafted a number of guidelines. First, for a supervisor to recognize a reduction in current exposure for a clearing house participant which has posted collateral, the following criteria have to be satisfied:

1. The collateral carries a 0 per cent risk weight under the accord.
2. The collateral is only available to cover forward replacement risk.
3. A participant can determine how much of the collateral pool posted with the clearing house is available to reduce current exposure.

To the extent that participants fully collateralize the exposure they present to the clearing house and all of the above criteria are met, then participants may risk weight the current exposure portion of the credit equivalent amounts at 0 per cent.

Second, if all participants *fully collateralize* on a daily basis the exposure they present to the clearing house, the calculation of potential future credit exposure can be waived if, in addition to those listed immediately above, the following criteria are satisfied:

1. The market value of the collateral held by the clearing house is sufficient to cover potential increases in its exposure to each of the participants on an on-going basis and at a high level of probability.
2. The market value of the collateral is also sufficient to cover a build-up of potential losses to the clearing house resulting from the inability quickly to replace or close out the positions of defaulting participants.
3. The collateral is sufficient to cover potential losses over a sufficiently long holding period to account for the settlement cycle associated with the receipt of collateral.
4. The adequacy of the amount of collateral posted is reviewed and, if necessary, adjusted on at least a daily basis.

Third, in a *partially collateralized* system, the criteria set out above have to be applied to that portion of potential future exposure that is covered by collateral. For example, if the clearing house requires participants to maintain collateral in a fixed proportion to the exposure they present to the clearing house, and the full set of criteria noted immediately above is satisfied, a reduction in the capital requirement for potential future exposure proportional to the level of collateralization is appropriate. If, however, participants are required to maintain an absolute level[68] of collateral, which is independent of the fluctuation of the exposure that they present to the clearing house, it is suggested that the full capital charge for potential future exposure be maintained, although a reduction in the charge for current exposure may be justified.

Finally, the Committee considered *'second round effects'*. It acknowledged that, in the absence of full collateralization of the exposures that participants present to the clearing house, the default of one participant could trigger the default of one or more other participants, propagated through the loss allocation mechanism of the clearing house. In addition, it is possible that two or more independent defaults could occur simultaneously. In either scenario, problems arise in the multilateral netting case because the loss to a participant as a result of the default of two or more of the other participants could exceed the sum of the corresponding primary loss allocations.

Notwithstanding the dangers associated with such 'second round effects', the Committee believes that its relatively conservative treatment of potential future exposure provides, to some extent, a cushion against such risks. It has not, however, ruled out the possibility of imposing an additional capital charge at some future date to cover such risks, if further study suggests the need for it. Moreover, this interpretation does not represent the Committee's last word on the subject of multilateral netting arrangements, and further refinements, if not a formal 'amendment' to the accord, may be forthcoming in the not-too-distant future.

THE AMENDMENT TO THE BASLE CAPITAL ACCORD TO ACCOMMODATE MARKET RISK

Switching attention away from the supervisory recognition of netting and towards the accommodation of *market risk*, it should be realized that ever since its success, in July 1988, in securing agreement on the prescription of minimum capital charges to cover the credit risks of 'internationally active' banks, the Basle Committee had been working on ways of widening the agreement to take account of banks' market risks. Such activity reflected concerns with developments, such as the deregulation of interest rates, the dismantling of capital controls, the relaxation of constraints on banks' permitted range of activities, the erosion of the traditional distinction between 'banks' and 'securities firms', and the rapid growth in banks' trading in derivatives, foreign exchange and securities, which had both allowed for, and led to, a dramatic increase in the market risks faced by banks, risks which were not captured by the credit risk-based assessment methodology of the accord. The outcome of this work was the publication in April 1993 of consultative proposals for the measurement and assessment of the market risks facing banks and for the extension of capital requirements to cover banks' open positions in debt and equity securities (including their derivatives) in 'trading' portfolios and in foreign exchange (Basle Committee, 1993b). A revised version of this document, accommodating the banking industry's reactions to the initial proposals, was issued in April 1995 (Basle Committee, 1995b; *see* Hall, 1995a, for a review). The consultation period for this document lasted until the end of July 1995, with a definitive statement emerging in January 1996 (Basle Committee, 1996c). The final set of agreed proposals (reviewed in Hall, 1996b) had to be implemented by all G10 nations by the end of 1997 at the latest. As far as banks' trading books are concerned, the new risk-based requirements will substitute for the existing credit risk requirements, the overall impact on a bank's total capital requirement depending on its risk profile.

In developing a framework for integrating market risk-based capital requirements into the accord, the Basle Committee was guided by a number of considerations. First, it was determined to design proposals that would ultimately apply to institutions (i.e. securities firms) beyond its immediate sphere of influence, namely internationally active banks. Thus although eager to secure the support of banking regulators, it was willing to run the risk of upsetting some in the interests of securing a degree of harmonization between the approaches adopted by banking and securities regulators.

Second, in developing its approach, it was seeking to satisfy two principal objectives: to promulgate capital requirements that would constitute minimum prudential standards for regulators to adopt; and to establish a set of capital charges to cover the market risks arising from position-taking in debt, equities, commodities (including their derivatives) and foreign exchange that would not artificially distort the use of one class of instrument.

Third, the minimum capital charges suggested for debt and equities (and their derivatives) would only apply to trading book positions, expressed in market value terms, where trading positions were defined as

the banks' proprietary positions in financial instruments (including positions in derivative products and interest rate instruments) which are taken on with the intention of benefiting in the short term from actual or expected differences between their buying and selling prices or of hedging other elements of the trading book, or which are held for short-term resale, or in order to execute a trade with a customer. (Basle Committee,

1993b, p. 6, para.8; a similar definition is provided in Basle Committee, 1995b, at p. 1, para.2)

Inclusion or exclusion of items from the trading book should also be in accordance with the adoption of 'objective procedures', such procedures and their implementation being subject to regulatory review for legitimacy and consistency. The proposed capital charges for foreign exchange and commodities risk would, in contrast, be applied to *all* the business activities undertaken by an intermediary, some of which are likely to be in book value terms.

Fourth, the Committee was concerned that the capital charges, to be applied on a worldwide consolidated basis, be statistically valid and objectively determined, and accordingly subjected them to the test that 'the capital required should cover adequately a high proportion of the losses that would have been experienced in any two-week holding period in a range of representative portfolios over the last five years' (Basle Committee, 1993b, p. 5, para.4).

Fifth, the Committee favoured capital requirements over limits as the appropriate means through which harmonization of the treatment of market risk should be secured because the former enable bank managements to retain flexibility in managing such risks, while encouraging risk management activities (e.g. hedging and risk-based capital allocation) designed to improve capital allocation and the risk-adjusted rates of return on the overall portfolio.[69] Notwithstanding this, however, national supervisors are encouraged to maintain limits where they judge it appropriate to do so, perhaps as a means of capping banks' exposures or of reinforcing internal controls.

Sixth, the Committee continued to promote the use of the 'building block' approach to risk assessment by splitting total position risk arising from exposures in debt and equities into 'specific' and 'general risk' components because it believed 'it provides a sound conceptual and practical basis for permitting offsetting of matched (i.e. long and short) positions' (Basle Committee, 1993b, p. 7). While such an approach undoubtedly facilitates such offsetting activities, it is less clear, however, that it is soundly based – *see* Dimson and Marsh, 1995 – a criticism taken on board in its revised proposals (*see* below).

Finally, the Committee was concerned to consult as widely as possible with market practitioners before finalizing its plans. A consultation period, lasting from the date of publication of the proposals – April 1993 – until end-December 1993 was duly established for the original set of proposals, with a somewhat shorter time period (i.e. three and a half months) applicable to the revised proposals.

As for the implications of implementation of the new proposals for the capital accord, it is worth emphasizing that, in the case of debt securities and equities held in the trading book, the proposed market risk capital charges would *substitute* for the credit risk-weighted requirements previously applied to balance-sheet assets. Items not falling within the trading book (e.g. derivative products taken on to hedge positions in the banking book, the loan book and the investment book) would, however, continue to be subject to the credit risk-based requirements of the accord. If national regulators sanction the inclusion of short-term subordinated debt within regulatory capital – *see* below – this can only be used to meet the market risk-based capital charges discussed below (i.e. it cannot be used to meet credit or counterparty risk, including that arising in respect of derivatives in either the trading or banking books).

The Committee's revised proposals of 1995[70] were designed, *inter alia*, to address some of the comments and criticisms received during the first consultation period. In particular, the Committee was responding to the criticisms that: (1) the initial proposals did not recognize best market practice in risk measurement techniques and thus failed to provide a sufficiently strong incentive for institutions to improve risk management systems; (2) the proposed risk assessment methodology failed to take account of correlations and portfolio effects across instruments and markets, and generally did not sufficiently reward risk diversification; and (3) the initial proposals were not sufficiently compatible with banks' own, often far more sophisticated, measurement systems, implying unnecessarily high compliance costs.

Eager to encourage the development of sound management practices and to minimize the creation of perverse incentives, the Committee duly set about investigating the possibility of allowing banks to use their own proprietary *internal models*, often termed 'value-at-risk' models, to generate capital charges to handle their exposures to market risk as an alternative to adopting the (slightly amended) standardized measurement framework originally proposed (*see* Hall, 1995a). (Such a development had, indeed, been foreshadowed in the Committee's original sanctioning of the use of simulation techniques to generate capital charges to cover foreign exchange risk.) To balance the need to preserve the integrity and flexibility of banks' internal models against the need to ensure the transparency and consistency of capital requirements across banks, however, the Committee decided, after conducting a series of tests with the industry during the second half of 1994, to sanction such a development (still subject to national discretion) provided that six sets of conditions were met. These conditions relate to the following: (1) general criteria concerning the adequacy of the risk management system; (2) qualitative standards for internal oversight of the use of the models, notably by management; (3) guidelines for specifying an appropriate set of market risk factors (i.e. the market rates and prices which affect the value of banks' positions); (4) quantitative standards setting out the use of common minimum statistical parameters for measuring risk; (5) validation procedures for external oversight of the use of models; and (6) rules for banks which use a mixture of models and the standardized approach. Given the significance of this supervisory development, it is worthwhile elaborating on some of these conditions further. (For full details *see* Part B, Sections B.1 to B.6 of the Basle Committee's 'Planned Supplement to the Capital Accord to Incorporate Market Risks', itself a part of the Basle Committee's document, 1995b.)

Under the general criteria, a supervisory authority has to be satisfied with at least the following aspects of a bank's operations before granting approval for the use of internal models to generate market risk capital charges: its risk management system; the number of skilled staff employed in the trading, risk control and audit areas and, if necessary, in back office areas also; the track record of the models in predicting losses with reasonable accuracy; and its conduct in the area of 'stress-testing'.

To meet *qualitative criteria* which banks have to satisfy before being allowed to employ a models-based approach to generating market risk capital requirements, a bank is required to do the following: operate an independent risk control unit, ensuring the active involvement of senior management in the process; ensure that the model is closely integrated into day-to-day risk management and that a routine and rigorous programme of 'stress-testing' is in place; adopt a routine for ensuring compliance; ensure that an independent review of both risk management and risk measurement procedures is carried out at regular intervals; and prescribe procedures for internal (involving the use of 'backtesting' – *see* Basle Committee, 1996d) and external validation of the risk measurement process. In summary, the qualitative standards are designed to ensure that banks' management systems are conceptionally sound and that the process of managing market risks is carried out with integrity. In this context, it is also thought necessary to define the risks that need to be covered, to establish appropriate guidelines for the conduct of stress tests (for further details *see* Section V of 'An Internal Model-Based Approach to Market Risk Capital Requirements', Basle Committee, 1995b) and to provide guidance on validation procedures for examiners and auditors charged with independently reviewing and validating banks' internal models (for further details *see* Part B, section B.5 of the Basle Committee's 'Planned Supplement to the Capital Accord ...', Basle Committee, 1995b).

The *quantitative standards*, which are designed to address supervisors' prudential concerns and to ensure that the dispersion between the results of different models for a uniform set of positions is confined to a relatively narrow range, are expressed as a number of broad risk measurement parameters for banks' internal models, together with a simple rule for converting the models-based measure of exposure into a supervisory capital requirement. Accordingly, the 'value-at-risk' has to be computed daily using a 99th percentile, one-tailed confidence interval and a minimum holding period of ten working days (i.e. two weeks). The historical observation period is subject to a minimum length of one year, although the Committee is investigating the possibility of a dual observation period. Banks will have discretion to recognize empirical correlations *within* broad risk categories (e.g. interest rates, exchange rates, equity prices, etc.), but value-at-risk *across* these risk categories has to be aggregated on a simple sum basis. (The 1996 proposals now allow for recognition of empirical correlations *across* risk factor categories.) Models must also accurately capture the unique risks associated with options. At a minimum this means that banks' internal risk measurement systems should incorporate option price behaviour through a non-linear approximation approach involving higher-order risk factor sensitivities.

The general market risk capital charge is to be computed as the higher of: the previous day's 'value-at-risk' calculated according to the established parameters; and an average of the daily 'value-at-risk' on each of the preceding 60 business days, multiplied by a 'multiplication factor' to account for extreme market conditions – *see* Exhibit 1.19. This factor is to be set by the national supervisor on the basis of its assessment of the quality of each bank's risk management system, subject to an absolute minimum of three. It will, however, at least for the time being, also be subject to a 'plus' which is directly related to the *ex-post* performance of the model. This is designed to provide banks with a positive incentive to raise or keep high the predictive quality of the model as a plus of zero might apply where the *ex-post* performance is excellent.

Exhibit 1.19 *The calculation of the capital charge for market risk under the internal models approach allowed, at national discretion, by the Basle Committee*

Under the Basle Committee's internal models approach, banks have to apply the following formula to calculate their market risk capital charge:

$$CMR_t = \text{Max}\left[\frac{SM_t}{60} \sum_{i=1}^{60} VaR_{t-i}, VaR_{t-1} \right] + SR_{t-1}$$

where CMR_t = bank's market risk capital requirement at time t;
         VaR_{t-i} = bank's market risk exposure estimate at date $t–i$;
         SM_t = supervisory-determined factor $[3 \leq SM_t]$;
         SR_{t-1} = additional capital charge for the *specific risk* of trading book positions ($SR_{t-1} \geq 0.5$ times the specific risk capital charge generated by the application of the standardized methodology).

Source: Kupiec and O'Brien, 1996.

Finally, banks using internal models – no particular type of model is prescribed, the only requirement is that they capture all the material risks run by the bank – will be subject to a separate capital charge to cover the *specific risk* of traded debt and equity securities to the extent that this risk is not incorporated into their models. In such circumstances, however, the total specific risk charge applied to debt or equity securities should in no case be less than half the specific risk charges calculated according to the standardized methodology. (This requirement was eventually dropped in October 1997 for banks satisfying certain criteria.)

In establishing a set of guidelines for the specification of an appropriate set of market risk factors, the Committee is trying to ensure that the risk factors contained in a bank's market risk measurement system are sufficient to capture the risks inherent in the bank's portfolio of on- and off-balance-sheet trading positions. Although banks will retain some discretion in this area, the guidelines have to be fulfilled. For *interest rates*, this involves specifying a set of risk factors which corresponds to interest rates in each currency in which the bank has interest rate sensitive on- or off-balance-sheet positions. Additionally, the risk measurement system should model the yield curve using one of a number of generally accepted approaches, dividing the yield curve into various maturity segments in order to capture variation in the volatility of rates along the yield curve. For material exposures to interest rate movements in the major currencies and markets, banks must model the yield curve using a minimum of six risk factors (typically one for each maturity segment of the yield curve). Ultimately, however, the number of risk factors used should be determined by the nature of the bank's trading strategies. The risk measurement system must also incorporate separate risk factors to capture spread risk (e.g. between bonds and swaps), with the sophistication of approach being a function of the nature and scope of the bank's exposure to interest rates.

For *exchange rates*, the risk measurement system should incorporate risk factors corresponding to the individual foreign currencies in which the bank's positions are denominated.

For *equity prices*, there should be risk factors corresponding to each of the equity markets in which the bank holds significant positions. At a minimum, there should be a risk factor that is designed to capture market-wide movements in equity prices (e.g. a market index), while the sophistication and nature of the modelling technique employed in respect of a given market should correspond to the bank's exposure to the overall market as well as its concentration in individual equity issues in that market.

Similarly, for *commodity prices*, there should be risk factors corresponding to each of the commodity markets in which the bank holds significant positions, with the sophistication of the modelling techniques employed being linked to the size of positions run and scale of trading activity engaged in.

Finally, when handling the volatilities related to *options positions*, where the risks are particularly complex, the relevant quantitative standards outlined above have to be adhered to.

The final set of conditions, concerning the rules governing the *mixed use of internal models and standardized approaches*, is designed to cover the period during which banks which use models extend them to cover all their market risks. The Committee is keen to ensure that banks which start to use models for one or more risk factor categories will, eventually – no time limit has been set – extend the models to all their market risks. Accordingly, a bank which has developed one or more models will not be able to revert to measuring the risk measured by those models according to the standardized methodology (unless the supervisor withdraws approval for that model). For those using combinations during this 'transitional phase', the following conditions apply: (1) each broad risk factor category must be assessed using a single approach (either internal models or the standardized approach); (2) the models used must comply with the six sets of conditions described above; (3) banks may not modify the combination of the two approaches they use without supervisory consent; (4) all market risk exposures must be captured; and (5) the capital charges assessed under the two approaches are to be aggregated according to the simple sum method.

In respect of the *standardized measurement method*, the two main changes to the original proposals made in the 1995 document concerned the introduction of a separate framework for measuring *commodities risk* and amended proposals for the treatment of *options* (for full details *see* Section A.5 of Part A of the Basle Committee's 'Planned Supplement to the Capital Accord to Incorporate Market Risks', 1995b). Under the original proposals, the Committee envisaged banks being allowed, at national discretion, a choice of two or more methods for the treatment of options, some of which would be incompatible with the espoused building-block methodology (*see* Basle Committee, 1993b, Annexe 5). In its revised proposals, the Committee suggests that banks, again subject to national discretion, be allowed to choose from a number – three are described in its document – of different alternatives within the standardized methodology, although banks which use significant trades in options will be expected over time to move to a comprehensive options risk management model and thus become subject to the relevant restrictions associated with the use of in-house models, as outlined earlier. Generally, supervisors are expected to apply the principle that the greater a bank's involvement in writing options, the more sophisticated its measurement method should be.

Other, fairly minor, changes made to the proposed standardized measurement method involved: the movement of the provisions governing the use of comprehensive risk factor models for foreign exchange (referred to as the 'simulation method' in the original proposals) to the models section, to ensure that all banks using comprehensive models will be subject to the same qualitative and quantitative standards; and, in order to improve accuracy in the measurement of general market risk for traded debt securities, those employing the so-called 'duration' method would now have 'vertical disallowances' of half the size of the 'maturity' method (*see* below).

Finally, if banks, subject to local supervisory approval, use the 'duration-based' method for calculating capital charges to cover the general market risk on debt securities – *see* below – they no longer have to ensure that the capital charges so generated are 'broadly equivalent' with the results produced using the standard 'maturity' method. In taking this line, which is now also adopted in respect of the use of internal models to generate capital charges to cover foreign exchange risk, the Committee further demonstrated its willingness to recognize and encourage the use of sophisticated risk assessment techniques.

The only other changes of note related to the definition of regulatory capital. As noted earlier, 'Tier 3' capital can now be used to satisfy all market risk requirements, including those relating to foreign exchange and commodities exposures. In the original proposals, the use of Tier 3 capital to satisfy foreign exchange capital charges (a commodities charge was not, at that time, contemplated) was explicitly ruled out. Second, and sticking with the use of Tier 3 capital, the new 'lock-in' clause – *see* below – preventing payment of interest and principal is less severe than the original, as it becomes operative when such payment would reduce a bank's overall capital to an amount less than its minimum risk-based capital requirement rather than the original specified threshold of 20 per cent above required capital.

We are now in a position to explain precisely what the new capital requirements will entail.

The Definition of Capital

In meeting its market risk-based capital requirements, a bank must use the definition of capital currently employed within the accord unless its supervisors allow the inclusion of short-term subordinated debt ('Tier 3' capital). If the latter is the case, the new form of subordinated debt can only be used in satisfaction of the market risk-based requirements, including those relating to foreign exchange and commodities risk, and cannot be used to satisfy the capital requirements levied against the 'banking' book. Moreover, its inclusion is subject to a number of limitations and restrictions.[71]

First, to be eligible for inclusion, the subordinated debt must satisfy the following:[72]

1. It must be unsecured, subordinated and fully paid up.
2. It must have an original maturity of at least two years.
3. It may not be repayable before the agreed repayment date without the agreement of the supervisors.
4. It must be subject to a 'lock-in' clause which stipulates that neither interest nor principal may be paid (even at maturity) if such payment would mean that the bank's overall capital would then amount to less than its minimum capital requirement.

And, second, the following limitations would apply to its use:

1. It would be limited, in aggregate, to 250 per cent of the Tier 1 capital allocated to support market risks.
2. Tier 2 capital can be substituted for Tier 3 capital up to the same limit of 250 per cent as long as the overall limits in the accord are not breached (i.e. aggregate Tier 2 capital does not exceed total Tier 1 capital, and long-term subordinated debt does not exceed 50 per cent of Tier 1 capital).

Overall Minimum Capital Requirement

The combination of the capital accord of 1988 and the new market risk-based requirements will mean that banks will have to satisfy the following overall minimum capital requirement:

1. The credit risk requirements arising from application of the current accord's provisions to the 'banking' book (i.e. excluding debt and equity securities in the trading book and all positions in commodities, but including the credit counterparty risk on all over-the-counter derivatives, whether in the trading or banking books).
2. The capital charge for market risks arising from the application of the market risk-based requirements.

The latter is derived *either* by summing the individual capital charges for market risks derived by applying the 'standardized measurement methods' *or* by using the figures deriving from the use of internal models (as explained below) *or* by using a mixture of the two, summed arithmetically.

This overall minimum capital requirement has to be met on a continuous basis, that is, at the end of each business day, and banks are expected to ensure that intra-day exposures are not 'excessive'. Supervisors, in turn, are asked to ensure that banks do not 'window dress' on reporting dates.

Calculation of the Capital Ratio

To ensure consistency in the calculation of capital requirements to cover both credit and market risks, the RAR methodology adopted in the original accord – *see* Exhibit 1.12 – must be adapted to accommodate market risk. This is to be done by expressing the new capital ratio as the ratio of 'eligible capital' (i.e. the sum of a bank's aggregate Tier 1 capital plus eligible Tier 2 capital, subject to the limitations and restrictions applied under the original accord, plus (subject to national discretion) eligible Tier 3 capital used to meet market risk requirements, subject to the limitations and restrictions noted above) to the sum of risk-weighted assets compiled for credit risk purposes and the market risk capital charge multiplied by 12.5 (the reciprocal of the 8 per cent minimum ratio). (The latter transformation gives a figure for notional risk-weighted assets on the trading book.) This is illustrated in Exhibit 1.20.

Exhibit 1.20　　The new RAR methodology to be employed under the Basle capital accord to accommodate market risk

$$\text{RAR} (\geq 8\%) = \left[\frac{\text{Adjusted* eligible capital}}{\substack{\text{Banking book risk-weighted assets +} \\ \text{Notional trading book risk-weighted assets}}} \right] \times 100$$

where 'eligible capital' = Tier 1 capital plus eligible Tier 2 capital, subject to the limitations and restrictions applied under the original accord (*see* Exhibit 1.8) plus, at national discretion, Tier 3 capital, subject to the limitations and restrictions noted in the text;
'Banking book risk-weighted assets' are represented by the '*TOWRA*' expression in Exhibit 1.12;
'notional trading book risk-weighted assets' = 12.5 × ('Market risk capital charge');
the 'market risk capital charge' equals the sum of the individual minimum capital charges derived under the standardized methodology (to cover position risk in debt, equities, derivatives, foreign exchange and commodities) or, at national discretion, the capital charge generated by the use of internal models (*see* Exhibit 1.19).

Note: *　For the necessary adjustments *see* Exhibit 1.8, Part C.

MARKET RISK-BASED CAPITAL REQUIREMENTS UNDER THE STANDARDIZED MEASUREMENT METHODS

For Equities

The Basle Committee's proposals for a minimum capital standard to cover the position risk arising from equities trading,[73] which might be modified in the light of further discussions with securities regulators, embrace the building-block approach referred to earlier. Accordingly, the overall capital charge is derived by summing the 'specific risk' and 'general risk' capital requirements.[74]

The (minimum) *specific* risk requirement proposed is 8 per cent of an institution's 'gross equity positions' (i.e. the sum of all long and of all short equity positions) unless the portfolio is both 'liquid' and 'well diversified' (as interpreted by national regulators), in which case the capital charges may be reduced to a figure as low as 4 per cent, but no lower. The proposed (minimum) *general* risk requirement, which applies to an institution's 'overall net position' (i.e. the difference between the sum of the longs and the sum of the shorts), is also set at 8 per cent.[75]

In principle, all *derivatives* held inside the trading book must be converted into (notional) positions in the relevant underlying and be subjected to the measures outlined above. Where the underlying is an index representing a 'well-diversified' portfolio of equities, the specific risk requirement may be reduced from 8 per cent to 2 per cent of the net position in the index. For options, a range of treatments is permissible, embracing both a 'simplified approach' and 'intermediate approaches' (covering both the 'delta-plus' method and 'scenario analysis'). (for full details *see* Basle Committee, 1995b, Section A.5 of the 'Planned Supplement to the Capital Accord to Incorporate Market Risks').

In calculating the capital charges, matched positions in each identical equity in each market (separate calculations have to be carried out for each national market in which the equities are held) may be fully offset, thereby allowing for the application of the minimum percentage charge to a single short or long position. Dispensation, in the form of lower than normal specific risk charges or, perhaps, the removal of such positions from the building-block methodology, may also be given for certain hedging and arbitrage strategies – *see* Basle Committee, 1995b, pp. 20–21 of the 'Planned Supplement to the Capital Accord to Incorporate Market Risks'.

For Debt Securities

As for equities, the overall minimum capital requirements are expressed in terms of two separately calculated charges, one to cover 'specific risk' and one to cover 'general market risk' (or the interest rate risk in the portfolio). Once again, long and short positions may be offset in the calculation of the latter requirement, but offsetting in the calculation of the former is restricted to matched positions (including positions in derivatives) in the *identical* issue.

In establishing the appropriate capital charges for *specific risk*, the Committee classifies debt securities into five broad categories. Accordingly, government securities[76] receive a risk weighting of 0 per cent,[77] 'qualifying items'[78] attract a risk weight of either 0.25, 1.00 or 1.60 per cent, according to the residual maturity of the issue (the lower figure applying to issues with residual maturity of up to six months, the middle figure to maturities of between 6 and 24 months, and the highest figure to maturities exceeding 24 months), and the 'other' items attract a risk weight of 8 per cent. Finally, for 'high-yield' debt securities, either a higher than 8 per cent specific risk charge is applied and/or offsetting within the calculation of general market risk is not allowed between such securities and other debt securities. The specific risk capital requirement is then derived by summing all the 'weighted positions' (short or long) for the different instruments, where the 'weighted position' of a given instrument is the 'net position' (i.e. the difference between the firm's long and short positions, converted daily at spot rates into the firm's reporting currency) multiplied by the relevant risk weighting.

In calculating charges for *general market risk*, designed to capture the risk of loss arising from changes in market interest rates, a choice of two assessment methodologies is available: the 'maturity' method and a 'duration-based' method.[79] The latter, however, may only be adopted with the consent of national supervisors, must be used on a continuous basis (unless a change in method is approved by the national authority), and is subject to supervisory monitoring.

Under the 'maturity' method, long or short positions in debt securities (and their derivatives)[80] are slotted into a 'maturity ladder' comprising 13 maturity bands (15 for low coupon instruments). Fixed rate instruments are allocated on the basis of residual time to maturity, and floating rate instruments according to the next repricing date. The positions are then weighted to reflect their price sensitivity to changes in interest rates. The weights have two components: the 'modified duration'[81] of a bond with a maturity equal to the mid-point of the respective time band, assuming an 8 per cent interest rate environment and an 8 per cent coupon;[82] and an assumed change in yield which is designed to cover about two standard deviations of one month's yield volatility in most major markets. The product of the two components provides the weighting factor for each time band. (The weighting factors and maturity ladder used are presented in Exhibit 1.21.)

Exhibit 1.21   *Weighting factors to be employed in the calculation of general market risk capital charges for debt securities under the 'maturity' method*

Zone	Maturity band		Weighting (%)	Assumed interest rate change (%)
	Coupon of 3% or more	Coupon of less than 3%		
1	0 ≤ 1 month	0 ≤ 1 month	0.00	–
	> 1 ≤ 3 months	> 1 ≤ 3 months	0.20	1.00
	> 3 ≤ 6 months	> 3 ≤ 6 months	0.40	1.00
	> 6 ≤ 12 months	> 6 ≤ 12 months	0.70	1.00
2	> 1 ≤ 2 years	> 1.0 ≤ 1.9 years	1.25	0.90
	> 2 ≤ 3 years	> 1.9 ≤ 2.8 years	1.75	0.80
	> 3 ≤ 4 years	> 2.8 ≤ 3.6 years	2.25	0.75
3	> 4 ≤ 5 years	> 3.6 ≤ 4.3 years	2.75	0.75
	> 5 ≤ 7 years	> 4.3 ≤ 5.7 years	3.25	0.70
	> 7 ≤ 10 years	> 5.7 ≤ 7.3 years	3.75	0.65
	> 10 ≤ 15 years	> 7.3 ≤ 9.3 years	4.50	0.60
	> 15 ≤ 20 years	> 9.3 ≤ 10.6 years	5.25	0.60
	> 20 years	> 10.6 ≤ 12.0 years	6.00	0.60
		> 12.0 ≤ 20.0 years	8.00	0.60
		> 20 years	12.50	0.60

Source: Basle Committee, 1996c.

Having weighted the positions in this fashion, various netting arrangements are then applied before calculating the capital charge. This involves first offsetting the weighted longs and shorts in each time band ('vertical offsetting'), leaving a single short or long position for each band as a residual. A capital charge, known as a 'vertical disallowance', of 10 per cent of the sum of the 'matched weighted positions' (i.e. the amounts of the vertical offsetting) in all maturity bands is prescribed to reflect the fact that, because each band would include positions whose maturities are not identical as well as different instruments with the same maturity, full vertical offsetting within the band would not reduce general risk to zero.

Second, the Basle Committee proposes that two rounds of partial 'horizontal offsetting' also be allowed to reflect the fact that interest rates at different points in the maturity spectrum tend to move together. Accordingly, the capital charges prescribed reflect the 'disallowances'[83] applied to the horizontal offsetting undertaken between the net (i.e. 'residual') positions (the 'unmatched weighted positions') in each of the three time zones and, subsequently, between the net positions in the different zones.[84] These have to be added to the disallowances prescribed for the vertical offsetting and to the absolute amount of the residual net short or long position to arrive at the general market risk charge.

The (minimum) general market risk requirement is therefore equal to:

10 per cent of the sum of the 'matched weighted positions' in all maturity bands
plus 40 per cent of the *matched weighted position in Zone 1*
plus 30 per cent of the *matched weighted position in Zone 2*
plus 30 per cent of the *matched weighted position in Zone 3*
plus 40 per cent of the *matched weighted position between Zones 1 and 2*
plus 40 per cent of the *matched weighted position between Zones 2 and 3*
plus 100 per cent[85] of the *matched weighted position between Zones 1 and 3*
plus 100 per cent of the *residual unmatched weighted position.*

Adding to this sum the specific risk charge, calculated as shown above, yields the overall *minimum* capital charge to be met by an institution to cover the position risk arising from trading debt securities.[86]

Derivatives

In principle, all derivatives held inside the trading book are to be converted into (notional) positions in the relevant underlying which then become subject to the assessment procedures outlined above.[87] Alternative treatments for options, however, are available, as noted earlier – *see* Section A.5 of Basle Committee, 1995b. The amounts reported would be the market value of the principal amount of the underlying or notional underlying.

Futures and forward contracts, including FRAs, are to be treated as a combination of a long and a short position in a notional government security (i.e. with a zero specific risk requirement),[88] the maturity of a future or FRA being the period until delivery or exercise of the contract, plus – where applicable – the life of the underlying security. Where a range of deliverable instruments may be delivered to fulfil the contract, the institution is free to choose which deliverable security goes into the maturity ladder. Swaps, in turn, are to be treated as two notional positions in government securities with relevant maturities, that is, residual maturities for fixed rate instruments and the period until the next interest-fixing for floating rate instruments.

To Cover Foreign Exchange Risk

Under the Committee's proposals for dealing with foreign exchange (including gold) risk, institutions can either use the 'shorthand' method or internal models (subject to supervisory approval and satisfying the minimum standards outlined earlier).[89]

If the *shorthand method* is adopted, the Committee proposes a minimum capital charge (subject to a *de minimis* exemption)[90] of 8 per cent of the 'net open position', which is calculated by adding the sum of the short currency positions or the sum of the long positions, whichever is the greater, to the total of the net position (short or long) in gold, regardless of sign. In order to evaluate its capital charges, a bank has therefore first to calculate its net position in each currency and gold, converting the nominal amounts of the net positions at spot rates into the reporting currency. The net open position in any currency is, in turn, derived by summing the following:

1. The net spot position (i.e. all asset items less all liability items, including accrued interest, denominated in the currency in question).
2. The net forward position (i.e. all amounts to be received less all amounts to be paid under forward foreign exchange transactions, including currency futures and the principal on currency swaps not included in the spot position).[91]
3. Guarantees (and similar instruments) that are certain to be called and are likely to be irrecoverable.
4. Net future income/expenses not yet accrued but already fully hedged (at the discretion of the reporting institution).
5. The net delta (or delta-based) equivalent of the total book of foreign currency options.[92]
6. Any other items representing a profit or loss in foreign currencies (this depends on the accounting conventions applicable in different countries).

For measurement purposes, positions in composite currencies may be treated either as a currency in their own right or split into their component parts (on a consistent basis). Any positions taken deliberately to hedge (partially or totally) against the adverse effect of exchange rate movements on the capital adequacy ratio can be excluded from the calculation or net open currency position if the following conditions are met:[93]

1. Such positions are of a 'structural' (i.e. of a non-dealing) nature (as defined by national supervisors).
2. National supervisors are satisfied that the structural positions excluded do no more than protect the bank's capital adequacy ratio.
3. Any exclusion of positions is applied consistently, with the treatment of the hedges remaining the same for the life of the assets or other items.

To Cover Commodities Risk

Under the Committee's proposals for handling commodities risk, banks can either use models to measure position risk – subject, of course, to local supervisory approval and to satisfying the set of safeguards applicable to the use of any model for market risk assessment purposes – or a 'standardized approach'. If the latter route is adopted banks have a further choice. They may either adopt a 'simplified approach' or a more complex approach involving the use of maturity ladders. Each of these approaches is explained in more detail in Exhibit 1.22.

Exhibit 1.22   The Basle Committee's proposed capital requirements for dealing with commodities risk

---

As for the other categories of market risk, banks may use internal models to generate capital charges to cover commodities risk as long as they are subject to the 'safeguards' outlined in the text (indeed, major traders are expected over time to adopt such an approach). In the context of commodities risk, the methodology adopted must encompass 'directional risk' (to capture the exposure from changes in spot prices arising from net open positions), 'forward gap' and 'interest rate risk' (to capture the exposure to changes in forward prices arising from maturity mismatches), and 'basis risk' (to capture the exposure to changes in the price relationships between two similar, but not identical, commodities). Moreover, it is essential that the models used take proper account of market characteristics, notably delivery dates and the scope traders have for closing out positions.

For those banks not using a models-based approach, the Committee has proposed two possible measurement frameworks for adoption under the 'standardized approach': a simplified approach and a more complex approach.

Under the *complex* approach, a bank must first convert, at current spot rates, its net positions (spot plus forwards) in commodities, as expressed in standard units of measurement, into the national currency. Positions in the separate commodities must then be entered into a maturity ladder – a separate one for each commodity (excluding gold, which is treated as a foreign currency) – with physical stocks being allocated to the first time band. For each time band, the sum of short and long positions (in national currency terms) which are matched must then be multiplied by the appropriate 'spread rate' for that band – see the table below – to give the relevant capital charges to cover curvature/spread risk (i.e. the forward gap and interest rate risk arising within a given time band).

Time band	Spread rate (%)
0–1 month	1.5
1–3 months	1.5
3–6 months	1.5
6–12 months	1.5
1–2 years	1.5
2–3 years	1.5
Over 3 years	1.5

The residual net positions from the nearer time bands may then be carried forward to offset exposures in time bands further out, although a surcharge equal to 0.6 per cent of the net position carried forward would have to be added in respect of each time-band that the net position is carried forward from to recognize the lack of perfect hedging that would result. The capital charge for each matched amount created by carrying forward positions would then be calculated in accordance with the procedures outlined above. At the end of this process, a bank will have either only long or only short positions, to which a capital charge of 15 per cent must be applied.

All commodity *derivatives* (and off-balance-sheet positions) which are affected by changes in commodity prices must also be included in the measurement framework (although options subject to risk measurement approaches other than the 'delta-plus' basis should be handled in accordance with the models-based approach). *Futures and forward contracts* relating to individual commodities should be incorporated as notional amounts of the standard unit of measurement and should be assigned a maturity determined in accordance with the expiry date. *Commodity swaps* where one leg is a fixed price and the other a current market price should be incorporated as a series of positions equal to the notional amount of the contract, with one position corresponding to each payment on the swap and slotted into the maturity ladder accordingly. (The positions will be 'long' if the bank is paying fixed and receiving floating, and 'short' if it is receiving fixed and paying floating.) Finally, commodity swaps where the legs are in different commodities must be reported in the relevant reporting ladder. No offsetting will be allowed in this regard except where the commodities belong to the same subcategory.

Under the *simplified* approach, the same procedure described above is used to derive the capital charge to cover directional risk. Accordingly, the net position, long or short, in each commodity will attract a capital charge of 15 per cent. In order to protect the bank against basis risk, interest rate risk and forward gap risk, however, the capital charge for each commodity derived in accordance with the procedures adopted in respect of the complex approach must be subject to an additional capital charge equivalent to 3 per cent of the bank's

Exhibit 1.22 (continued)

gross positions, long plus short, in that particular commodity. Banks should use the current spot price in valuing the gross positions in commodity derivatives for this purpose.

Source: Basle Committee, 1996c.

OTHER AREAS OF HARMONIZATION

Apart from the harmonization of capital adequacy requirements, other (non-European Union (EU)) international initiatives have focused on interest rate risk, settlement risk, the need for an international standard on banking supervision to help strengthen the prudential supervision of banks (especially in emerging markets) and the case for allowing global institutions to develop their own standards for risk management and control. (For a discussion of derivatives-related initiatives, *see* Dale, 1995 and Barcroft, 1998.)

With regard to *interest rate risk*, the Basle Committee again took the lead by publishing a consultative document setting out 12 principles for the sound management of interest rate risk (Basle Committee, 1997a). These principles – *see* Exhibit 1.23 – were grouped into five broad categories: the role of the board and senior management; policies and procedures; measurement and monitoring systems; independent controls; and information for supervisory authorities. This document, which includes annexes on techniques for interest rate risk management and monitoring systems which supervisors might adopt in respect of interest rate risk exposures, is a follow-up to an earlier document on the subject (Basle Committee, 1993c) and accommodates industry reaction to that earlier document as well as the principles enshrined in the guidance issued by the Committee for derivatives activities (Basle Committee, 1994). Interested parties were asked to respond by 15 April 1997.

Exhibit 1.23 The Basle Committee's principles for interest rate risk management

A. The role of the board and senior management
Principle 1:
In order to carry out its responsibilities, the board of directors in a bank should approve interest rate risk management policies and procedures, and should be informed regularly of the interest rate risk exposure of the bank.
Principle 2:

Senior management must ensure that the structure of the bank's business and the level of interest rate risk it assumes are effectively managed, that appropriate policies and procedures are established to control and limit these risks, and that resources are available for evaluating and controlling interest rate risk.

Principle 3:

Banks should have a risk management function with clearly defined duties that reports risk exposures directly to senior management and the board of directors and is sufficiently independent of the business lines of the bank. Larger or more complex banks should have units responsible for the design and administration of the bank's interest rate risk management system.

B.   Policies and procedures

Principle 4:

It is essential that a bank's interest rate risk policies and procedures be clearly defined and consistent with the nature and complexity of their activities. These policies should address the bank's exposures on a consolidated basis and, as appropriate, also at the level of individual affiliates.

Principle 5:

It is important that banks identify the risks inherent in new products and activities and ensure that these are subject to adequate procedures and controls before being introduced or undertaken. Major hedging or risk management initiatives should be approved in advance by the board or its appropriate delegated committee.

C.   Measurement and monitoring system

Principle 6:

It is essential that banks have interest rate risk measurement systems that capture all material sources of interest rate risk and that assess the effect of interest rate changes in ways which are consistent with the scope of their activities. The assumptions underlying the system should be clearly understood by risk managers and bank management.

Principle 7:

Banks must establish and enforce operating limits and other practices that maintain exposures within levels consistent with their internal policies.

Principle 8:

Banks should measure their vulnerability to loss under stressful market conditions – including the breakdown of key assumptions – and consider those results when establishing and reviewing their policies and limits for interest rate risk.

Principle 9:

Banks must have adequate information systems for monitoring and reporting interest rate exposures to senior management and boards of directors on a timely basis.

Exhibit 1.23   (continued)

D.   Independent controls

Principle 10:

Banks must have adequate internal controls for their interest rate risk management process and should evaluate the adequacy and integrity of those controls periodically. Individuals responsible for evaluating control procedures must be independent of the function they are assigned to review.

Principle 11:

Banks should periodically conduct an independent review of the adequacy and integrity of their risk management processes. Such reviews should be available to relevant supervisory authorities.

E.   Information for supervisory authorities

Principle 12:

The G10 supervisory authorities will obtain from banks sufficient and timely information with which to evaluate their level of interest rate risk. This information should take appropriate account of the range of maturities and currencies in each bank's portfolio, as well as other relevant factors, such as the distinction between trading and non-trading activities. Other supervisory authorities are recommended to obtain similar information.

Source: Basle Committee, 1997a.

As regards *settlement risk*, the main focus of attention at the international level has been on foreign exchange transactions (i.e. 'Herstatt risk' – *see* Chapter 3). A report produced by the Committee on Payment and Settlement Systems (CPSS) of the central banks of the G10 countries (BIS, 1996) recommended a three-pronged strategy for addressing foreign exchange settlement risk:

- action by individual banks to control their foreign exchange settlement exposures (e.g. by measuring and managing such exposures properly, and by reducing excessive exposures);
- action by industry groups to provide risk-reducing multi-currency services (i.e. bilateral and multilateral obligatory netting arrangements – examples of the latter are the 'ECHO' (Exchange Clearing House) system introduced in London in 1995 and the 'Multinet' system introduced in the US in 1996);
- action by central banks to induce rapid private sector progress (e.g. by increasing private sector understanding of the problems and possible solutions and by working with industry groups to develop appropriate solutions).

At the time of publication of this report, the commercial banks of the so-called 'Group of 20' (embracing most of the world's major banks) were already engaged in developing a form of 'payment versus payment' system whereby settlement in the foreign exchange markets would be instantaneous (i.e. payment by one bank is immediately offset by a matching payment from another bank, a process called 'continuous linked settlement'). The ideal system would be to link the various national 'real-time gross settlement' (RTGS) systems operating in different countries but a formidable array of difficulties would first have to be overcome. In June 1996, the Group of 20 began work on developing a fully operational central clearing house, linked to national RTGS systems. A UK company, CLS Services (CLSS), was set up to develop the real-time settlement system, and other participants in the foreign exchange market were invited to become shareholders. In July 1998, CLSS announced that it had raised sufficient capital ($150 million) to allow for the completion of its plans for the establishment of a settlement bank (to operate out of New York) in the year 2000. Initially, the bank will be connected to the central bank settlement systems of eight countries but, eventually, it hopes to effect settlement for around 50 per cent of the foreign exchange (forex) market.

More recently, the focus of concern has shifted to the fragility of the global payment systems following a warning by the BIS, in its 1996 annual report, that liberalized banking markets (e.g. in Japan, the US and the EU) posed a greater threat to payments stability than the growth in the use of derivatives. The spread of RTGS systems, such as that introduced in the UK in April 1996 in respect of large value cash payments and the TARGET system – which will link national RTGS payment systems, denominated in the Euro – planned for introduction in the EU, should help to contain the risks, however.

Finally, on the securities front, national regulators around the globe are still working towards 'delivery versus payment' (DVP), and clearing house facilities are widely available in respect of the settlement of derivatives transactions, at least for exchange-traded products. Moreover, cross-border securities settlement is guaranteed through such systems as Euroclear and Cedel, while the CPSS and IOSCO are jointly developing a disclosure framework for securities settlement systems for adoption by relevant bodies.

The last area of study, the development of an *international standard* for banking supervision (Goldstein, 1996), is related to a desire to strengthen prudential supervision in developing countries. Increasingly, both the IMF and the World Bank pay attention to the soundness of national banking systems when prescribing remedial action for borrower nations and, following discussions with these institutions, the Basle Committee decided to produce a list of 'core principles for effective banking supervision'. Building on the work of the 'Tripartite Group' (*see* Chapter 25), a consultative paper on the subject was first issued in April 1997 (Basle Committee, 1997b). It was developed in close consultation with non-G10 supervisory authorities, endorsed by the G10 central bank governors and submitted to the G7 and G10 finance ministers in preparation for the Denver Summit. Interested parties, particularly non-G10 supervisory authorities, were invited to comment by 16 June. The final version of the document, which materialized in September 1997, contained minor modifications to the definition of capital to be used in capital adequacy assessment and to the application of consolidated supervision to diversified banking groups.

Apart from promulgating the set of core principles which, for the first time, address the conduct of banking supervision in general rather than particular aspects of supervision, the focus of the Committee's previous concerns under the *Concordat* and the capital accord, the Committee also aimed to gain the support of the regional supervisory group for its initiative and to monitor the progress made by individual countries in implementing the principles, which were designed to be verifiable by both supervisors and the market at large. More formally, implementation will be reviewed at the ICBS in October 1998 and bi-annually thereafter. The Committee hopes that, eventually, all supervisory authorities around the world will formally endorse the principles.

The core principles, of which there are 25 in total – *see* Exhibit 1.24 – are grouped under the following headings: 'preconditions for effective banking supervision' (Principle 1); 'licensing and structure' (2–5); 'prudential regulations and requirements' (6–15); 'methods of ongoing banking supervision' (16–20); 'information requirements' (21); 'formal powers of supervisors' (22); and 'cross-border banking' (23–25). The principles are to be regarded as minimum requirements, to be supplemented where necessary (e.g. to address particular conditions and risks in the financial systems of individual countries) by other measures, and should be applied in respect of the supervision of all banks.

Exhibit 1.24   List of core principles for effective banking supervision

---

Preconditions for effective banking supervision
 1. An effective system of banking supervision will have clear responsibilities and objectives for each agency involved in the supervision of banks. Each such agency should possess operational independence and adequate resources. A suitable legal framework for banking supervision is also necessary, including provisions relating to authorization of banking establishments and their on-going supervision; powers to address compliance with laws as well as safety and soundness concerns; and legal protection for supervisors. Arrangements for sharing information between supervisors and protecting the confidentiality of such information should be in place.

Licensing and structure

2. The permissible activities of institutions that are licensed and subject to supervision as banks must be clearly defined, and the use of the word 'bank' in names should be controlled as far as possible.

3. The licensing authority must have the right to set criteria and reject applications for establishments that do not meet the standards set. The licensing process, at a minimum, should consist of an assessment of the bank's ownership structure, directors and senior management, its operating plan and internal controls, and its projected financial condition, including its capital base. Where the proposed owner or parent organization is a foreign bank, the prior consent of its home country supervisor should be obtained.

4. Banking supervisors must have the authority to review and reject any proposals to transfer significant ownership or controlling interests in existing banks to other parties.

5. Banking supervisors must have the authority to establish criteria for reviewing major acquisitions or investments by a bank and ensuring that corporate affiliations or structures do not expose the bank to undue risks or hinder effective supervision.

Prudential regulations and requirements

6. Banking supervisors must set minimum capital requirements for banks that reflect the risks that the banks undertake, and must define the components of capital, bearing in mind its ability to absorb losses. For internationally active banks, these requirements must not be less than those established in the Basle capital accord.

7. An essential part of any supervisory system is the independent evaluation of a bank's policies, practices and procedures related to the granting of loans and making of investments, and the on-going management of the loan and investment portfolios.

8. Banking supervisors must be satisfied that banks establish and adhere to adequate policies, practices and procedures for evaluating the quality of assets and the adequacy of loan loss provisions and reserves.

9. Banking supervisors must be satisfied that banks have management information systems that enable management to identify concentrations within the portfolio. Supervisors must set prudential limits to restrict bank exposures to single borrowers or groups of related borrowers.

10. In order to prevent abuses arising from connected lending, banking supervisors must have in place requirements that banks lend to related companies and individuals on an arm's-length basis, and ensure that such extensions of credit are effectively monitored, and that other appropriate steps are taken to control or mitigate the risks.

Exhibit 1.24 (continued)

11. Banking supervisors must be satisfied that banks have adequate policies and procedures for identifying, monitoring and controlling country risk and transfer risk in their international lending and investment activities, and for maintaining adequate reserves against such risks.
12. Banking supervisors must be satisfied that banks have in place systems that accurately measure, monitor and adequately control market risks; supervisors should have powers to impose specific limits and/or a specific capital charge on market risk exposures, if warranted.
13. Banking supervisors must be satisfied that banks have in place a comprehensive risk management process (including appropriate board and senior management oversight) to identify, measure, monitor and control all other material risks and, where appropriate, to hold capital against these risks.
14. Banking supervisors must determine that banks have in place internal controls that are adequate for the nature and scale of their business. These should include clear arrangements for delegating authority and responsibility; separation of the functions that involve committing the bank, paying away its funds, and accounting for its assets and liabilities; reconciliation of these processes; safeguarding its assets; and appropriate independent internal or external audit and compliance functions to test adherence to these controls as well as applicable laws and regulations.
15. Banking supervisors must determine that banks have adequate policies, practices and procedures in place, including strict 'know your customer' rules, that promote high ethical and professional standards in the financial sector and prevent the bank being used, intentionally or unintentionally, by criminal elements.

Methods of on-going banking supervision
16. An effective banking supervisory system should consist of some form of both on- and off-site supervision.
17. Banking supervisors must have regular contact with bank management and a thorough understanding of the institution's operations.
18. Banking supervisors must have a means of collecting, reviewing and analysing prudential reports and statistical returns from banks on a solo and consolidated basis.
19. Banking supervisors must have a means of independent validation of supervisory information either through on-site examinations or use of external auditors.
20. An essential element of banking supervision is the ability of the supervisors to supervise the banking organization on a consolidated basis.

Information requirements

21. Banking supervisors must be satisfied that each bank maintains adequate records drawn up in accordance with consistent accounting policies and practices that enable the supervisor to obtain a true and fair view of the financial condition of the bank and the profitability of its business, and that the bank publishes on a regular basis financial statements that fairly reflect its condition.

Formal powers of supervisors

22. Banking supervisors must have at their disposal adequate supervisory measures to bring about corrective action when banks fail to meet prudential requirements (such as minimum capital adequacy ratios), when there are regulatory violations, or where depositors are threatened in any other way.

Cross-border banking

23. Banking supervisors must practise global consolidated supervision, adequately monitoring and applying appropriate prudential norms to all aspects of the business conducted by banking organizations worldwide, primarily at their foreign branches and subsidiaries.

24. A key component of consolidated supervision is establishing contact and information exchange with the various other supervisors involved, primarily host country supervisory authorities.

25. Banking supervisors must require the local operations of foreign banks to be conducted to the same high standards as are required of domestic institutions, and must have powers to share information needed by the home country supervisors of those banks for the purpose of carrying out consolidated supervision.

Source: Basle Committee, 1997b.

In drafting the core principles, the Committee adopted a number of fundamental precepts, which are worth repeating as they help to clarify the Committee's views on what constitutes effective banking supervision:

- the key objective of supervision is to reduce the risk of loss to depositors and other creditors, and to maintain confidence in the financial system;
- supervisors should encourage and pursue market discipline by encouraging good corporate governance (through an appropriate structure and set of responsibilities for a bank's board of directors and senior management) and enhancing market transparency and surveillance;
- in order to carry out its tasks effectively, a supervisor must have operational independence, the means and powers to gather information both on and off site, and the authority to enforce its decisions;

- supervisors must understand the nature of the business undertaken by banks and ensure to the extent possible that the risks incurred by banks are being adequately managed;
- effective banking supervision requires that the risk profile of individual banks be assessed and supervisory resources allocated accordingly;
- supervisors must ensure that banks have the resources appropriate to undertake risks, including adequate capital, sound management, and effective control systems and accounting records;
- close co-operation with other supervisors is essential and particularly so where the operations of banks cross national boundaries.

Having set out the core principles, the remainder of the document put flesh on the raw principles, indicating what adoption of each should mean, in practice, for the supervisory authority. In this way, a blueprint for the operational procedures to be adopted by banking supervisors around the world has been established, as well as a checklist of the minimum essential components (licensing, assessment of the adequacy of capital, liquidity, provisions, internal controls and risk management systems, control of asset concentrations, internal/external audit, monitoring, deposit insurance, etc.) which should feature in an optimal supervisory framework. Notwithstanding its willingness to produce such a blueprint, the Committee, quite rightly, noted that sound banking supervision alone cannot guarantee financial stability; other arrangements, including, *inter alia*, sound and sustainable macro-economic policies, a well-developed public infrastructure, effective market discipline, procedures for the efficient resolution of problems in banks and mechanisms for providing an appropriate level of systemic protection, are also required. This serves as a reminder of the limitations of banking supervision and the need for governments to do more to ensure that financial stability prevails at both the local and international level.

The main responsibility for ensuring implementation and monitoring compliance with the core principles resides with the IMF and the World Bank, although the Basle Committee is to conduct a worldwide self-assessment survey.

The only other development of note at the international level is the pressure building up for an industry initiative to promote consistently high standards of risk management and control for *global institutions*. The issue assumed even greater significance after the Barings and Sumitomo scandals and was the subject of a G30 report in July 1997 (Heimann and Lord Alexander of Weedon, 1997). The latter called for action on six main fronts:

- a standing committee to be established to decide on guidelines for managing and controlling risks in leading international banks;

- increased disclosure and greater use of external audits to ensure compliance with agreed standards;
- investment in risk measurement systems to be increased and pay scales to put compliance officers closer to front-office bankers;
- steps to be taken to ensure risk reduction measures, such as netting schemes, are legally binding in the event of bankruptcy;
- national supervisors to agree on a co-ordinator to take the lead in overseeing large multinational banks;
- risk control in the infrastructure of the financial system (e.g. exchanges and settlement systems) to be stepped up.

Not everyone, however, is totally happy with such developments. The Institute of International Finance (IIF), for example, recommends a special supervisory regime for globally active institutions that incorporates supervisors from more than one country and focuses on evaluating management of comparable risk types in a comparable manner in order to evaluate a firm's global risk management. Moreover, it believes a risk-based supervisory framework, concerned less with corporate structure and more with market globalization, should 'focus on explicitly addressing global systemic safety and soundness, and should seek to harness market discipline for supervisory purposes' (IIF, 1997).

To implement the conclusions of its report, the Task Force makes four recommendations (IIF, 1997):

- 'Financial supervisors should consider creating a special supervisory arrangement for globally active financial institutions whose key goal is to foster the safety and soundness of the global financial system.'
- 'This arrangement should initially focus on collecting information on common risk types present in the financial business (e.g. credit risk, contingent credit risk, market risk, interest-rate risk).' A corollary recommendation is that supervisors should avoid collecting information or creating new rules based exclusively on corporate structure. The Task Force calls this new approach a 'risk-based supervisory framework'.
- 'The Home Country supervisor for each globally active financial group should receive information on common risk types and should use it to generate an assessment of the financial group's global risk profile. This assessment should be communicated to supervisors for individual entities in the group, although the Home supervisor should not be expected to share the detailed information it receives from other supervisors.' This implies that supervisors will have to upgrade their internal ability to assess risk-based data sets and become more willing to rely on other supervisors' judgements. It also implies that regulatory reporting requirements should

be rationalized, at least for globally-active financial institutions, providing risk-based data sets to their supervisors on a confidential basis.
- 'Financial firms should expand their public disclosures (and confidential regulatory reporting) to increase understanding of their risk management approach among supervisors, analysts, counterparties, and investors.'

Others are less concerned with the detail of the G30 report than with its general thrust, which promotes 'self-regulation' of global institutions through the establishment of the standards-setting standing committee and the voluntary adoption of its recommendations. (A similar framework was developed by the Derivatives Policy Group in 1995 in respect of over-the-counter derivatives.) The alternative, of binding international standards, as currently feature in EU directives – *see* Chapter 9 – is viewed as being inflexible, ineffective and likely to lull supervisors into a false sense of security by creating an illusion of security which does not exist. Dissenters, however, question whether recalcitrant institutions can be 'brought to heel' effectively, presumably through the sanctions of the market place, and are unhappy about the power wielded by such a private sector 'club'. Yet others doubt that the big accounting firms, as auditors, would be willing to 'police' the adoption of the agreed industry standards by individual global players at a 'reasonable' price, not least because of the hazards and potential financial risks involved. At the end of the day, it will be down to national supervisors to decide whether the agreed industry standards which emerge are sufficient to allow them to discharge their national supervisory responsibilities, and to decide what comfort to attach to external validation of procedures adopted by individual firms. To this extent, the G30 initiative should be seen as complementing, rather than displacing, the continuing supervision of global institutions at the national level. National supervisors, after all, cannot escape from their legal responsibilities in respect of institutions operating within their jurisdictions and hence have to have a continuing concern with corporate structure, even if this bears little resemblance to management reality.

8. Implications of the Financial Services Act 1986

The Financial Services Act of 1986 represented the first attempt in the UK to put the regulation of all 'investment business' on a common statutory footing. At the heart of this comprehensive piece of legislation was the provision making engagement in investment business without appropriate prior authorization a criminal offence.

Authorization could be acquired in one of two ways: either direct from the Securities and Investments Board (SIB), the designated agency to which the Secretary of State for Trade and Industry had delegated his supervisory powers; or from the appropriate self-regulatory organization (SRO) – *see* Exhibit 1.25 – which was held responsible for day-to-day supervision of its members. (The full regulatory structure is depicted in Exhibit 1.26 and described in Hall, 1987d, Chapter 4. For recent developments *see* Hall, 1990, 1992b, 1994b.)

Exhibit 1.25   SRO structure under the Financial Services Act 1986

SROs and the areas of investment business covered	
The Securities Association (SA)[1]	Firms dealing and broking in securities, investment management, forward agreements and related futures and options, and international money-market instruments.
The Association of Futures Brokers and Dealers (AFBD)[1]	Firms dealing and broking in futures and options; investment management and advice incidental to this business.
The Financial Intermediaries, Managers and Brokers Regulatory Association (FIMBRA)[2]	Firms dealing and broking in securities and collective investment products; investment managers and advisers.
The Investment Management Regulatory Organization (IMRO)	Investment managers and advisers, including managers and trustees of collective investment schemes and in-house pension fund managers.

Exhibit 1.25　(continued)

The Life Assurance and Unit Trust Regulatory Organization (LAUTRO)[2]	Life companies and unit trust managers and trustees, for the management and selling of insurance-linked investments or units in a collective scheme by themselves and their tied sales forces.

Notes:
1. The SA and AFBD later merged to form the Securities and Futures Authority (SFA).
2. The FIMBRA and LAUTRO later merged to form the Personal Investment Authority (PIA) (*see* Hall, 1994b).

Apart from its authorization powers, the SIB was also empowered to recognize investment exchanges and professional bodies, to draw up 'conduct of business' rules (to govern the operations of those investment businesses authorized directly by itself and to act as a standard for the equivalent SRO rule books), to establish compensation schemes,[94] and to discipline firms and individuals where necessary.[95]

Although their deposit-taking function is exempted from the Act[96] – because it is regulated by the Bank[97] under the Banking Act 1987 – banks, nevertheless, fall within the purview of the Act by virtue of the investment business in which they engage. This obliges them, like other investment businesses, to acquire separate authorization for each category of business engaged in and to abide by the relevant conduct of business rule books.[98] As envisaged under the Act, however, attempts were made to reduce the degree of supervisory overlap between the Bank and the SIB/SROs according to the so-called 'lead regulator' approach, whereby the supervisory body responsible for overseeing the bulk of an investment business' operations is required to co-ordinate the supervision exercised by itself and other supervisory bodies. (It should be noted, however, that implementation of the EC's Second Banking Co-ordination Directive (*see* Chapter 9) necessitated both the Bank and the SIB (or SRO) being involved in the supervision of a bank's investment business.)

The approach to be taken towards the supervision of UK-incorporated[99] banks' investment business operations was formalized with the agreement, in March 1988, between the Bank, on the one hand, and the SIB, the SA (now the SFA) and IMRO (*see* Exhibit 1.25) on the other, on *Memoranda of Understanding*. According to the Memoranda, the Bank, at least initially, would act as 'lead regulator', with the financial services supervisor being required to monitor an institution's compliance with 'conduct of business' rules (other than those relating to wholesale market activities, which will be monitored by the Bank). A similar Memorandum was agreed between the Bank and the AFBD and FIMBRA later in 1988.

Exhibit 1.26   The Financial Services Act 1986

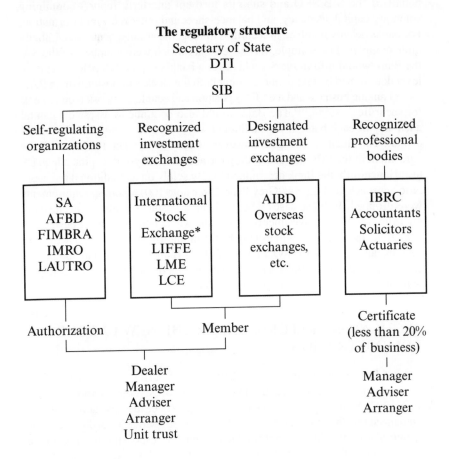

The regulatory structure

Secretary of State
DTI

SIB

Self-regulating organizations	Recognized investment exchanges	Designated investment exchanges	Recognized professional bodies
SA AFBD FIMBRA IMRO LAUTRO	International Stock Exchange* LIFFE LME LCE	AIBD Overseas stock exchanges, etc.	IBRC Accountants Solicitors Actuaries

Authorization   Member

Dealer
Manager
Adviser
Arranger
Unit trust

Certificate
(less than 20% of business)

Manager
Adviser
Arranger

Abbreviations:

AIBD	Association of International Bond Dealers
DTI	Department of Trade and Industry
IBRC	Insurance Brokers Registration Council
LCE	London Commodities Exchange
LIFFE	London International Financial Futures Exchange
LME	London Metal Exchange
RIE	Recognised Investment Exchange
RPB	Recognised Professional Body
SRO	Self-Regulating Organization

* Now the London Stock Exchange.

As lead regulator, the Bank monitors the capital adequacy of a bank on behalf of the SIB/SRO and submits to them quarterly reports containing summary capital adequacy, and balance-sheet and other relevant information. For banks heavily involved in securities trading, the arrangements were initially quite complex. For example, for those banks which were members of the SA, the Bank would inform the SA whenever a bank's capital fell below a certain level determined by taking into account both the Bank's imposition of an RAR on its banking business and the SFA's position and counterparty risk requirements for securities trading.[100] The Bank would also continue to assess the capital adequacy of each bank in the traditional way, using its standard definition of capital. The situation changed, however, in July 1990 when the SA, with the agreement of the SIB, decided to drop the additional 'hybrid' capital adequacy test. Henceforth, the Bank determined to rely solely on its traditional risk asset ratio approach, and the SA/'Grey Paper' (*see* note 100) reporting requirements were dropped. In those cases where a bank's business is almost exclusively securities trading- or investment-related, and where non-investment business is negligible, the SIB/SRO will usually be the monitoring supervisor, however. In such instances, the SIB/SRO, on behalf of the Bank, will calculate the bank's capital ratio, using the Bank's standard definition of capital and in accordance with rules agreed between itself and the Bank.

REGULATORY REFORM UNDER THE NEW LABOUR ADMINISTRATION

Apart from the mergers between SROs noted earlier, these institutional arrangements remained intact until the new Labour government took power in May 1997. Within a few weeks of assuming office, the new administration announced that the Financial Services Act would be overhauled and that a single, statutory body would be established to assume the responsibilities imposed at that time upon the SIB and SROs. Moreover, the Bank would be stripped of its supervisory functions, although it would be given 'operational independence' in respect of the conduct of monetary policy (Hall, 1997b).

A new super-regulator, the Financial Services Authority (FSAu), duly emerged on 28 October 1997. This body replaced the old SIB. It became responsible for banking supervision (as well as for the supervision of listed money-market institutions and related clearing houses) once the Bank of England Bill, also introduced on 28 October, became law, which occurred on 1 June 1998. Although the process of integration of staff from the old SROs, along with staff from the Supervision and Surveillance Division of the Bank, began in the spring of 1998 (HM Treasury, 1998a), full integration is unlikely to be complete until around October 1998, when the FSAu moves to new headquarters at Canary Wharf in London's docklands. The three SROs will keep their statutory responsibilities until a Regulatory Reform Bill, published in draft form in July 1998, becomes law (replacing the old Financial Services Act), which is not anticipated before the year 2000. In the meantime, SRO staff will technically become employed by the FSAu but will be contracted out to the SROs. The FSAu will thus eventually become responsible for the authorization and supervision of individual banks, building societies, investment houses, insurance companies (including the Lloyd's of London insurance market – the FSAu will authorize managing agents, Members' agents and, should it be deemed appropriate, Members of Lloyd's, as well as overseeing the operation of the emerging market in syndicate capacity) and professionals, such as solicitors, accountants and actuaries (the 'recognized professional bodies' – *see* Exhibit 1.26 – will lose their supervisory responsibilities), as well as for the supervision of financial markets (the Bank also lost responsibility for the regulation of 'wholesale' market institutions) and clearing and settlement systems. In this way, the institutional framework governing the regulation of the UK financial services industry will change from that outlined in Exhibit 1.27 to the much simpler (at least on paper) structure set out in Exhibit 1.28. Moreover, the FSAu is to be given the power to impose civil sanctions, including unlimited fines, to deal with instances of market abuse such as insider trading and market manipulation. Uncertainty, however, surrounds the future treatment of general insurance (although motor and home insurance are unlikely to fall within the purview of the FSAu, as they are not investment products (long-term health care insurance may be so classified), the FSAu has indicated its willingness to act if the industry's proposals for a new, all-embracing, self-regulatory framework – the Insurance Brokers' Registration Council, the statutory body currently responsible for the registration and discipline of brokers, is to be abolished – fail to satisfy) and mortgages (not currently defined as an investment product although the government may change this if the voluntary Code of Conduct fails to provide adequate consumer protection). Deposits, too, at least for the time being, will remain outside the scope of the legislation. What is clear, however, is that other government departments and regulatory bodies will continue to play a part in the new regulatory regime. Major fraud/theft will remain the preserve of the Serious Fraud Office (SFO) (liaising with police forces). Company malpractice and insider dealing will continue to involve the DTI. The recently established Occupational Pensions Regulatory Authority will retain responsibility for the regulation of occupational pensions. Matters arising from consumer credit, hire purchase, loan sharking and pawn broking will continue to be dealt with by the Office of Fair Trading. And, at least for the time being (European Commission allowing), the Takeover Panel will continue to regulate, in a non-statutory fashion, mergers and takeovers. Moreover, the London Stock Exchange will continue, for the time being, to act as the 'competent authority' for the listing of UK companies, and will be given the power to impose statutory fines for breaches of its rules.

Exhibit 1.27   The structure of UK financial regulation pre-June 1998: a simplified model[1]

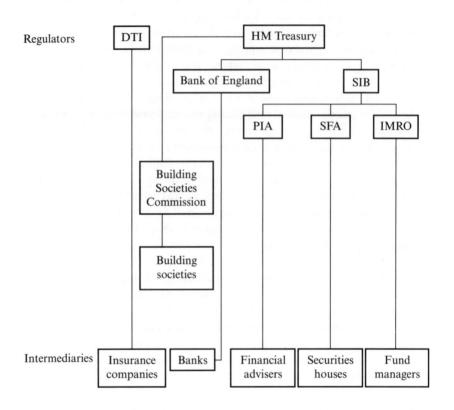

Note: 1. Pension funds, for example, are ignored, as are friendly societies.

Source: adapted from Bank of England, 1997a, p. 215.

As far as the style of *banking* supervision is concerned, little is likely to change, not least because the front-line troops will be represented primarily by those previously employed in the Supervision and Surveillance Division at the Bank, and the new Head of Financial Supervision at the FSAu is Michael Foot,

Exhibit 1.28   The structure of UK financial regulation under the new Financial Services Act

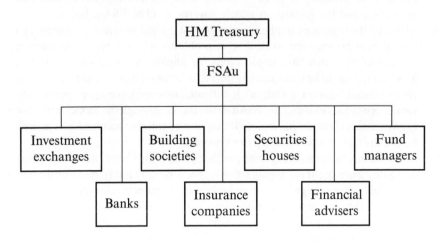

Source: Hall, 1997b.

previously in charge of banking supervision at the Bank. Accordingly, the changes introduced in the wake of the Barings saga and the subsequent 'Arthur Andersen Review' (*see* Chapter 12) are likely to proceed as planned, with the Board of Banking Supervision remaining in place as a Committee, advising the FSAu board.

Finally, it is important to appreciate that, although it has lost responsibility for banking supervision, the Bank retains responsibility for ensuring the overall stability of the financial system and for the integration of the payments system (alongside its monetary policy function).[101] To avoid confusion and uncertainty over how this would work in practice, the Bank, HM Treasury and the FSAu have drawn up a 'Memorandum of Understanding' (October 1997) setting out a clear delineation of responsibilities (*see* Bank of England, 1998, Annexe). As noted above, the Bank will be responsible for maintaining overall financial stability and, in 'exceptional circumstances', can provide financial support to individual firms to prevent problems spreading from one institution to another (i.e. to limit the spread of contagion) following consultation with the FSAu and the Treasury. This reflects the Bank's continuing concern with so-called 'systemic risk'. The Bank will also oversee the efficiency and effectiveness of the financial sector, particularly its international competitiveness. Much of this work will be directed towards improving the infrastructure. The FSAu, in contrast, will be responsible for the authorization and supervision of financial firms and professionals engaged in investment business, as well as for the supervision of financial markets, clearing and settlement systems. It will also be the first port of call for any financial firm which gets into difficulties. Finally, the Treasury is to be responsible for the institutional structure of regulation and the legislation which governs it. (The FSAu, however, will advise on the regulatory implications of domestic legislation and EU directives.) It will also be required to deal with problems which threaten 'economic disruption' or which have implications for 'diplomatic or foreign relations'. Moreover, it has to be consulted (by the FSAu/Bank) if there is a perceived need for an official 'support operation'. It will not, however, have any responsibility for the operations of either the FSAu or the Bank, although the former will have to answer to it via an annual report. (It may also be called to account for its actions before the Commons' Treasury Committee.)

To put this 'understanding' into practice, a Standing Committee, comprising delegates from the three organizations, meets on a monthly basis to discuss individual cases of significance and other developments relevant to financial stability. The first test of its effectiveness came in the wake of the turmoil experienced in the financial markets in the Far East (notably in Japan and South Korea) during the last quarter of 1997. An emergency action plan was drawn up by the three bodies to deal with any fallout which might hit UK markets/institutions. In the event, it would appear that action proved unnecessary, as London clearing mechanisms and counterparties to foreign defaulters (e.g. Yamaichi Securities of Japan) weathered the storm successfully.

9. Requirements arising from membership of the European Community

Relationships between the Bank (and the British government) and the Community's supervisory bodies have not always been happy. To understand fully the nature of the disagreements that have arisen, it is necessary to appreciate the functions of the Community supervisors and their advisory committees.

The first advisory body to be set up (in 1972) was the Contact Group of EC Supervisory Authorities (Groupe de Contact), an informal club comprising the supervisory authorities of the member states. Its role is to provide a forum for the exchange of views by national supervisors so as to achieve closer understanding of supervisory practices and promote practical co-operation. It commissions its own research studies and submits reports to the Banking Advisory Committee and the EC Commission. The Commission also receives advice from the Banking Advisory Committee, which comprises representatives (not more than three) from each member state and the Commission. Set up in 1979, as required by the First Banking Co-ordination Directive of 1977; EC, 1977 (77/780/EEC), this Committee is responsible, along with the Commission, for determining general policy guidelines for the Community in respect of supervisory co-ordination. Technical assistance is available from the Contact Group, if needed. Finally, close contact with both the Basle Committee of Supervisors and individual national regulators is also maintained by the Commission.

Having taken advice from all these sources, the Commission can then proceed by issuing either *Recommendations* or *Directives*, the latter alone carrying legal force. (The Commission can also make decisions or propose legally binding regulations.) Given the disappointing results achieved by early Recommendations, albeit in the non-financial sector, and the mixed results that followed the issue of a recommended Code of Conduct for Security Markets the Commission determined to proceed by way of issuing Directives.

The first initiative was taken with the publication, in 1972, of a draft Directive on the harmonization of the regulation of Community banks and credit institutions (see Revell, 1975, Chapter 6). Closely based on West German banking law, it was strongly resisted by the British authorities and was subsequently withdrawn in favour of a step-by-step approach to harmonization. A revised Directive, however, dealing with only part of the ground covered in the earlier draft, was issued in January 1975 and duly adopted by member states in December 1977.

The First Banking Co-ordination Directive (EC, 1977), as it was termed, provided for the introduction of minimum authorization criteria, the establishment of common prudential ratios[102] and the setting up of the Banking Advisory Committee. To obtain authorization, an intermediary must have separate capital from the resources of its proprietors; meet an unspecified initial capital requirement test; be directed by at least two persons; and be directed by persons of 'sufficient repute' and of 'sufficient experience'.

The Directive also allowed for the establishment of credit institutions of member states in other parts of the Community on a non-discriminatory basis, and made provision for co-operation between national supervisory authorities (i.e. in the form of information exchanges on matters of prudential supervision and authorization in general, and on the monitoring of liquidity, solvency and large exposures in particular).

In broad terms, the Directive sought to pave the way for the gradual shift of effective prudential supervision from the host to the parent supervisory authority – the 'home country control' objective – a move not entirely in keeping with the approach to allocating supervisory responsibility adumbrated within the Basle *Concordat* (*see* Chapter 3), and the integration of Community banking through liberalization of the right of establishment. It was recognized, however, that these objectives could only be secured if further harmonization steps were taken:

> Authorisation procedures for a credit institution should allow banks access to the entire common market, necessitating either the harmonisation of licensing conditions throughout the community or mutual recognition of national authorisation procedures; secondly, if branches are to be exempt from local supervision rules such as solvency requirements through the principle of home country rule, control and supervision techniques must be coordinated so as to avoid distortions of competition. (EC, 1977)

Given the apparent divergence in course taken by the Commission and the Basle Committee to the development of supervisory co-operation, and the differences in approach adumbrated by the Bank and the Commission to specific supervisory issues (e.g. the assessment of capital and liquidity adequacy), it is perhaps not too surprising that differences of opinion were eventually aired in public. The Chairman of the Basle Committee (who was also a senior Bank employee) set the ball rolling with what certainly appeared to be a wide-ranging condemnation of Community supervisory initiatives. In a presentation to the British Bankers' Association in January 1982 the following observations were made:

1. There are more serious impediments to cross-border competitive equality than differences in supervisory practice, and these obstacles should be tackled first.

2. Care must be taken to ensure that harmonization does not lead to over-regulation, damage innovative zeal, unduly interfere with commercial judgement, impair the freedom of action of national authorities or wider attempts to secure the soundness of international banking, or damage the competitive position of Community banks active in Eurocurrency markets.
3. A less juridically based attitude to the implementation of Community initiatives is desirable.
4. Continued efforts[103] should be made to find a consensus between the banking and credit industries and the regulatory authorities at both the national and Community level (Cooke, 1982).

Moving from the general to the specific, the 'desirability, practicality and relevance' of seeking to establish normative (*observation*) ratios is questioned, the wisdom of including specific aspects of the consolidation principle in any future Directive was challenged, and reservations were expressed concerning the harmonization of prudential returns, the establishment of a Community credit information exchange and the necessity of standardized statutory winding-up procedures for banks. And finally, to round off the attack, the Basle Committee Chairman cautioned against transferring supervisory powers from national authorities to a supranational Community body and cast doubt on the need for a second Co-ordination Directive.

In response to the above attack and other criticisms, a vigorous defence of the Commission's approach was mounted by the EEC Director General for Financial Institutions and Taxation. Seeking to refute the charges and allay the fears of the Commission's critics, he maintained that the Commission:

- 'does not pursue harmonisation for its own sake'[104] and 'given a choice will put emphasis on co-ordination of national practices rather than on legal harmonisation';
- 'has no intention, or even ambition, of setting up supranational supervisory authorities';
- 'has no particular preference for one banking structure over another. It is up to the markets ... We endeavour to put forward proposals that are neutral in this respect';
- seeks to ensure that co-ordination of banking supervision does not lead to 'a monotonous increase in the administrative burden for European credit institutions and authorities';
- believes that 'the framework for a common market in banking in Europe must be flexible in order to meet the challenges' presented by technological advance in data processing;
- takes an interest in the working conditions of Community banks operating or trying to operate in third countries 'and is fully aware that we cannot

create a banking market among the Ten which turns its back on the rest of the world' (Henriksen, 1983).

Since this public airing of their differences, little has emerged within the public domain to indicate any continuing rift between the Basle Committee (and the Bank) and the Commission over the latter's supervisory initiatives. This is just as well since, as is explained below, the completion of the Community's internal market by 1992 required very close contact being maintained between Brussels and Basle, on the one hand, and between Brussels and national supervisory bodies, on the other, if the scope for inconsistency were to be minimized.

Apart from the initiatives associated with the completion of the internal market, the Commission, following the adoption of the First Banking Co-ordination Directive, issued two further Directives and two Recommendations of relevance to banking supervision. The first of these, the Consolidated Supervision Directive (83/350/EEC; EC, 1983), obliged member states to supervise credit institutions with financial subsidiaries on a consolidated basis.[105] It was adopted in June 1983. The Bank Accounts Directive (86/635/EEC; EC, 1986a) came next – it was adopted in December 1986 and took effect from 31 December 1990 – requiring standardization of the presentation of the annual accounts and consolidated accounts of credit institutions.[106] This in turn was followed by two Recommendations, both adopted in 1986, relating to large exposures (87/62/EEC; EC, 1986b) and deposit protection arrangements (87/63/EEC; EC, 1986c). As far as the UK was concerned, neither posed any problems since the large exposure policy adopted by the Bank (*see* page 35) was, in several respects, stricter than the former Recommendation (e.g. a maximum exposure level of 40 per cent of own funds was suggested for individual exposures), while the existence of the Deposit Protection Scheme fulfilled the provisions of the latter Recommendation, which simply called on member states to satisfy themselves that their own schemes were adequate; those without one were asked to consider establishing one.

The remaining banking supervisory initiatives taken by the Commission all related to the completion of an internal market in financial services, as provided for in the Treaty of Rome[107] and the Single European Act of July 1987 which revised it. To achieve this end, the Commission secured agreement on eight key new Directives: the Second Banking Co-ordination Directive, the Own Funds Directive, the Solvency Ratio Directive, the Second Consolidated Supervision Directive, the Large Exposures Directive, the Investment Services Directive, the Capital Adequacy Directive and the Deposit Guarantee Directive.

The draft *Second Banking Co-ordination Directive*, which was issued in February 1988, was seen as the centrepiece of the Commissions proposals for the banking sector (Bank of England, 1988b) which, together with the liberalization of capital movements,[108] sought to eliminate the remaining barriers (such as host country authorization of branches and the imposition of an earmarked endowment capital requirement on foreign bank branches) to freedom of establishment in the banking sector and to afford full freedom to provide banking services without establishment.

Building on the First Banking Co-ordination Directive, this Directive (89/646/EEC; EC, 1989b), taken together with the Own Funds and Solvency Ratio Directives (*see* below), established the conditions on which a credit institution authorized in one member state may establish a branch in, or provide a range of banking services into, another member state on the strength of its home country authorization. The services covered by this single passport currently comprise, at national discretion:[109] deposit-taking; lending (including trade financing, factoring, consumer credit and mortgage credit); money transmission; leasing; participation in securities issues and related activities; the issuing and administering of credit cards, travellers cheques and other means of payment; securities trading (as both agent and/or principal); portfolio management; guarantees and commitments; the provision of financial advice; money broking; safekeeping of securities; safe custody; and credit reference services.[110]

The Directive, which was adopted in December 1989 and took effect from 1 January 1993, prescribes minimum standards of authorization and prudential supervision to be adopted throughout the Community. These comprise, *inter alia*, a minimum (initial and continuing) capital base of ECU 5 million (lower for certain categories of credit institutions);[111] administrative, accounting and internal control mechanisms; supervisory control over major shareholders;[112] and limitations on a bank's holdings in non-financial companies.[113] The Directive also provides for co-ordination and consultation between national supervisory authorities (e.g. the division of supervisory responsibilities between parent and host supervisor is clearly set out – *see* below)[114] and covers relations with third countries.[115]

The harmonization of authorization criteria secured by the above was deemed necessary in the light of the intended application of the concepts of mutual recognition (of supervisory standards) and home country control.[116] Under the latter, *home* supervisors would be responsible for authorizing and supervising the EC-branching operations of their credit institutions in respect of the permitted activities, although *host* authorities would retain exclusive control over the implementation of monetary policy and, pending further co-ordination of EC standards, primary responsibility for supervising liquidity and position risk and the securities activities of the branches of EC credit institutions.

The *Own Funds Directive* (89/299/EEC EC, 1989c) as amended by 91/633/EEC), which was adopted in April 1989 and had to be implemented by 1 January 1993 at the latest, established a common definition for the capital base

of credit institutions which can be used as a basis for setting minimum levels
of capital adequacy.

Under the Directive, a distinction is drawn between original own funds and
additional own funds, the former alone being eligible for inclusion in 'own funds'
(i.e. the capital base) without limit. 'Own funds' are defined to comprise the
following elements:

1. Paid-up share capital plus share premium accounts.
2. Eligible disclosed reserves plus published interim retained profits (net of
   foreseeable charges and dividends) which have been verified by (external)
   auditors.
3. Eligible revaluation reserves.
4. Funds for general banking risks.
5. Allowable value adjustments.
6. Certain other funds and securities which satisfy the requirements of Article 3.
7. Commitments of the members of credit institutions set up as co-operative
   societies and of the borrowers of certain institutions organized as funds.
8. Fixed term cumulative preference shares and subordinated loan capital
   which satisfy the requirements of Article 4(3).

Of these elements, items 1, 2 and 4 are classified as 'original own funds' and
items 3 and 5–8 as 'additional own funds'.

The limits imposed on additional own funds comprise the following:

1. The total amount of additional own funds may not exceed 100 per cent of
   the total of original own funds (excluding funds for general banking risks
   but including holdings of own shares at book value, intangible assets and
   current year losses).
2. The total of items 7 and 8 above may not exceed 50 per cent of original own
   funds (excluding funds for general banking risks, holdings of own shares at
   book value, intangible assets and current year losses).

Finally, the following items have to be deducted from the total of own funds
to arrive at the definition of the capital base to be used in the assessment of capital
adequacy:

1. Holdings in other credit and financial institutions amounting to more than
   10 per cent of the equity of the institutions in which the investments are made
   (full deduction is required).
2. Such holdings which constitute less than 10 per cent of the equity of the
   institutions in which the investment is made but which, in aggregate, exceed

10 per cent of the own funds of the reporting institution (the excess amount only must be deducted).

Although the Directive specifies which items of capital may be recognized as own funds and establishes qualifying criteria for the inclusion of some and limits for the inclusion of others, member states are allowed the discretion to adopt a more restrictive approach. This may take the form of specifying tougher qualifying criteria, adopting harsher limits to the inclusion of additional own funds, refusing to recognize some elements of additional own funds, or insisting upon additional deductions from total own funds before arriving at a figure for the (adjusted) capital base. (For a contrast with the G10 approach to defining bank capital see item 5 of Exhibit 1.29.)

Exhibit 1.29   Differences between the Basle agreement on capital adequacy assessment and the EC Directives on own funds and solvency ratios

---

The major differences between the Basle agreement and the EC framework comprise the following:

1. The EC Directives establish legally binding rules for member states whereas the Basle framework consists of a 'gentleman's agreement' concerning the implementation of guidelines within G10 nations (plus Luxembourg) and any other countries which decide to participate on a voluntary basis.
2. The EC Directives apply to all credit institutions within the EU (now the European Economic Area (EEA)), whereas the Basle framework applies solely to internationally active banks unless national authorities deem otherwise.
3. The EC Directives have to be applied on an unconsolidated basis (as well as on a consolidated basis) where subsidiaries are authorized in a member state which is different from that in which the parent is authorized; application on an unconsolidated basis is otherwise at the discretion of the national authorities, as is always the case under the Basle agreement.
4. No transitional arrangements were specified within the EC framework, although credit institutions had to ensure that in the run-up to January 1993 their RAR did not fall below the levels ruling on 1 January 1991.
5. On the definition of capital a number of differences arise:
    (a) The Own Funds Directive does not refer to 'Tier 1' and 'Tier 2' capital, the terms used by the Basle Committee, but rather to 'original' and 'additional' capital. (However, the limits introduced under Article 6 effectively create a tiering of capital very similar to that adopted within

Exhibit 1.29   (continued)

the Basle framework, thereby facilitating comparison of the two systems. The terms 'Tier 1' and 'Tier 2' are thus adopted below.)

(b) Under the EC rules, *current year profits* can only be included within Tier 1 capital if they have been verified by external auditors under the EC rules, whereas all current year profits are eligible for inclusion, at national discretion, under the Basle guidelines.

(c) *Latent revaluation reserves* are not eligible for inclusion within the capital base, whereas under the Basle guidelines they may be included within Tier 2 capital, albeit subject to a discount of 55 per cent.

(d) *Unpublished profits* are eligible for inclusion within Tier 2 capital only if they have been verified by (eventually, external) auditors, whereas under the Basle agreement all unpublished profits are eligible for inclusion, at national discretion.

(e) A new separate category of Tier 1 capital was (temporarily) created under the EC rules in the shape of *funds for general banking risks* (see Annexe 2.2, para.10), although, initially, it did not rank as Tier 1 capital for the purpose of calculating the upper limits on Tier 2 capital. (Eventually, such funds were included in Tier 1 capital under the heading of 'disclosed reserves'.)

(f) Under the EC rules, *holdings of the capital of other credit institutions* need only be deducted from capital when in excess of 10 per cent of the investee institution's capital (when the whole investment must be deducted) or in excess of 10 per cent of the reporting institution's own funds (when only the excess amount must be deducted (at national discretion) or otherwise weighted at 100 per cent in the risk weight framework).

(g) General provisions are eligible for inclusion in Tier 2 capital without limit, in contrast to the Basle guidelines, which limit their inclusion to a maximum of 1.25 percentage points of risk assets (temporarily and exceptionally, a limit of 2.0 percentage points of risk assets may be applied, but the lower limit is likely to apply from the end of 1993 at the latest).

6. In respect of the risk weightings applied, the following major differences emerge (for a full list of differences, see Price Waterhouse, 1991, pp. 128–30):

(a) Member states may, at national discretion, apply a 10 per cent weighting to claims on institutions specializing in the interbank and public debt markets under the EC rules (under the Basle framework, these assets are not separately distinguished).

(b) Under the EC rules, a more extensive allowance for collateral applies than under the Basle guidelines, thereby allowing for risk weight reductions on certain balance-sheet items.

Completing the Commission's proposals for the credit risk-based assessment of bank capital adequacy, the *Solvency Ratio Directive* (89/647/EEC; EC, 1989a) was adopted in December 1989 and had to be complied with by 1 January 1991 at the latest (although the 8 per cent minimum solvency ratio requirement did not have to be met until 1 January 1993). Its purpose is to establish minimum standards for the assessment of the capital adequacy of EC credit institutions through the imposition of a harmonized minimum RAR requirement.

Under the Directive, all EC credit institutions had to comply with a minimum 8 per cent RAR requirement (which has to be calculated at least twice a year) by 1 January 1993 at the latest. The RAR is to be derived by expressing the capital base of the institution (as defined in the Own Funds Directive) as a proportion of the total of risk-adjusted on- and off-balance-sheet items (*see* Exhibit 1.12). The (minimum) risk weights[117] and conversion factors[118] used to adjust the nominal on- and off-balance-sheet exposures are to reflect credit risk primarily. Interest rate and foreign exchange rate-related items may be treated, at national discretion, in accordance with either the current exposure or original exposure approaches.[119]

Further discretion is accorded national authorities in the following areas:

1. In the decision on whether or not to apply the Directive on a solo or solo-consolidated basis as well as on a consolidated basis (which is mandatory).
2. In the determination of those institutions which may be exempted (in accordance with Article 1(4)).
3. In the approach to be adopted towards the deduction from capital of credit institutions' holdings of the capital of other credit institutions (Article 6(1)(d)(6) allows a 100 per cent weighting in certain circumstances).
4. In the allocation of certain items within the risk-weight framework (e.g. as provided for in Articles 2, 7, 8 and 11).
5. In the decision on whether or not to delegate the responsibility for supervising the solvency of locally incorporated institutions to supervisory authorities of parent undertakings (as provided for in Article 3(6)).

(For a comparison with the GIO's approach to the assessment of a bank's capital adequacy *see* Exhibit 1.29.)

The *Second Consolidated Supervision Directive* (92/30/EEC; EC, 1992a), which was adopted on 6 April 1992 and took effect from 1 January 1993, replaced the earlier Directive (83/350/EEC; EC, 1983) on the subject adopted in 1983. It extends the range of circumstances under which credit institutions have to be supervised on a consolidated basis.

Under the earlier Directive, consolidation of banking groups, or parts of banking groups, was required for those which had a credit institution as their parent. The new Directive extends the requirement to those credit institutions which have a financial holding company as their parent, where a financial holding company is defined as a financial institution whose subsidiaries are either exclusively or mainly banks or financial institutions and which comprise at least one credit institution. For credit institutions with mixed-activity holding companies as parents, the Directive provides for banking supervisors to be given power to require the holding company and its subsidiaries to provide the information deemed necessary to judge the soundness of the credit institutions. Finally, the replacement Directive reduces the ownership threshold in the definition of 'participation' from 25 per cent to 20 per cent.

The identity of the member state responsible for exercising consolidated supervision over financial holding companies should be determined according to the following rules:

1. Where the parent undertaking of a credit institution is a financial holding company, consolidated supervision shall be exercised by the member state responsible for authorizing the credit institution.
2. Where a financial holding company has credit institution subsidiaries in more than one member state, including the member state where the financial company has been set up, consolidated supervision shall be undertaken by the member state where the financial holding company has been set up.
3. If there is no credit institution subsidiary in the member state where the financial holding company has been set up, the member states concerned will have to reach agreement as to which member state shall exercise consolidated supervision. In the absence of such an agreement, the supervising member state is selected on the basis of the largest balance sheet of the first date of authorization of the credit institution subsidiaries.

The required form of consolidation differs from case to case. Full consolidation is required of credit institutions and financial institutions which are subsidiaries of the parent undertaking or over which the latter effectively exercises a dominant influence. *Pro rata* consolidation may be prescribed in cases where the responsibility of the undertaking holding the participation is limited to its part of the capital, because of the responsibilities of other shareholders whose solvency is considered satisfactory. In other cases, or where a significant influence is exercised, the competent authorities shall determine whether and how consolidation is to be carried out.

The final 'banking' Directive agreed to before the end of 1992 was the *Large Exposures Directive* (91/121/EEC; EC, 1992b). Adopted in December 1992 for implementation by June 1994, the Directive established an absolute limit of 25 per cent (20 per cent for exposures to associated non-financial institutions) of own funds for exposures to a single (non-bank) client or group of associated clients, with 'large exposures' (i.e. those amounting to 10 per cent or more of own funds) being limited in aggregate to 800 per cent of own funds. The limits have to be observed at all times. Provisions allowed for the phasing in of the requirements, with the possibility of a further three-year extension.[120]

Notwithstanding the introduction of new exposure limits, a range of exemptions (full or partial) are provided for in the Directive. These cover:

- exposures to parent undertakings which are credit institutions and which are subject either to supervision on a consolidated basis or, if located in a third country, to equivalent supervision;
- exposures incurred by subsidiaries which are credit institutions, financial institutions or undertakings providing 'ancillary banking services' and which are included in the consolidated supervision of the parent undertaking;
- exposures incurred directly or indirectly to Zone A (i.e. OECD) central governments (as defined in the Solvency Ratio Directive) and central banks and to the European Communities;
- cases where the risk may be considered negligible or even zero;
- claims on other credit institutions with a maturity of up to one year.

Apart from establishing exposure limits, the Directive also requires member states to introduce reporting requirements entailing *either* notification of all large exposures at least once a year, backed up by communication during the year of any modifications to the annual notification, *or* notification of all large exposures at least four times a year, *or* both. Finally, the Directive sets out the conditions under which consolidated and non-consolidated supervision should be exercised.

The *Investment Services Directive* and the *Capital Adequacy Directive* (CAD), taken together, establish the conditions under which an intermediary – bank or investment firm – authorized in one European member state may provide 'investment' services cross-border into another member state on the strength of its home country authorization, in accordance with the 'single passport' principle. They thus do for firms engaged in investment business what the Second Banking Co-ordination Directive, the Own Funds Directive, the Solvency Ratio Directive and the Large Exposures Directive did for credit institutions, by way of opening up Europe's securities markets and establishing the terms on which the securities passport will be made available (Hall, 1995b).

The Investment Services Directive (93/22/EEC; EC, 1993a), which was adopted by member states in May 1993 and had to be implemented by the end of 1995 at the latest, is concerned with the definition of 'investment business' (*see* Exhibit 1.30) and the establishment of minimum standards with which firms[121] wishing to engage in such activities must comply before being granted authorization.[122] These minimum standards comprise, *inter alia*: holding sufficient initial (and continuing) capital, as specified in the CAD – *see* below; directors being 'of sufficiently good repute and experience'; and persons holding 10 per cent or more of the firm's capital or voting rights or otherwise exercising significant influence over the firm being classified as 'suitable'.

Exhibit 1.30   The services covered by the 'single passport' under the Investment Services Directive[1]

Brokerage
Dealing for one's own account
Market-making
Portfolio management
Underwriting
Safekeeping and administration[2]
Safe custody services[2]
Advisory services (e.g. in connection with mergers and acquisitions, capital structures, industrial strategy, etc.)
Credit extensions to investors to finance transactions in eligible instruments[1] by firms involved in the transactions[2]
Investment advice[2]
Services related to underwriting[2]
Foreign exchange services related to the provision of investment services[2]

Notes:
1. The services must relate to the following instruments: transferable securities; units of collective investment undertakings; money-market instruments; financial options and futures contracts; forward interest rate agreements; and interest rate, currency and equity swaps.
2. These so-called 'non-core' services may be authorized at the discretion of national competent authorities but authorization cannot be related exclusively to these services.

Source: EC, 1993a.

Apart from these functions, the Investment Services Directive is also concerned with the division of supervisory responsibilities between home and host supervisory authorities. Home authorities are held responsible for authorization, the monitoring of capital positions and prudential supervision in general, while host authorities are, at least for the foreseeable future, to be held responsible for the setting and supervision of 'conduct of business' rules including, at the host authorities' option, those relating to compensation funds, pending formal agreement of a Directive on the subject.

Finally, the Investment Services Directive also contains provisions on the following: relations with third countries (the familiar demands for 'national treatment reciprocity' and 'effective market access' are made); arrangements for the separation of clients' money and securities from the firms'; the establishment of ('sound') administrative and accounting procedures, and ('adequate') internal control mechanisms and records; compensation; information exchanges between supervisors; the handling of conflicts of interest; liberalizing access to Community stock exchanges and regulated markets and clearing and settlement systems; supervisory control of major shareholders and controllers; and the establishment of branches in other member states.

The CAD (93/6/EEC; EC, 1993b), which was formally adopted by member states in March 1993 and, like the ISD, had to be implemented by the end of 1995 at the latest,[123] was designed to secure two objectives: (1) to help stabilize the international financial system by seeking to ensure that all EU credit institutions and investment firms exposed to 'market' risks (i.e. position risks, foreign exchange risk, settlement risk, counterparty risk and large exposures risk) hold sufficient capital to cover such risk exposures adequately; and (2) to help level the playing field for those engaged in investment business by removing or reducing competitive imbalances caused by differences in the regulatory approaches adopted in different countries and/or by the differential treatment of market risk undertaken by banking and securities regulators. (For a discussion of whether or not these objectives are likely to be attained *see* Hall, 1995c.)

To meet these objectives, the CAD prescribes minimum capital requirements for intermediaries exposed to market risks, establishes a common framework for the measurement, assessment and monitoring of market-related risks, and sets out a common approach to defining capital for regulatory purposes. It also does for investment firms what the Second Banking Co-ordination Directive did for credit institutions by way of establishing minimum initial (and continuing) capital requirements. Each of these subject areas will now be addressed in turn, but in reverse order.

On the subject of *minimum initial capital requirements*, investment firms have to comply with figures ranging from ECU 50,000 to ECU 730,000, depending on the nature of the investment business undertaken. A minimum requirement of ECU 125,000, for example, applies to those firms which hold clients' money and/or securities and which offer one or more of the following services: 'the reception and transmission of investors' orders for financial instruments; the execution of investors' orders for financial instruments; and the management of individual portfolios of investments in financial instruments' (EC, 1993b, Article 3). This is subject to the proviso, however, that the investment firms 'do not deal in any financial instruments for their own account or underwrite issues of financial instruments on a firm commitment basis' (ibid.). At the discretion of member states, this amount may be reduced to ECU 50,000 for investment firms which are not authorized to hold clients' money or securities, nor to deal for their own account, nor to underwrite issues on a firm commitment basis.

'Locals' and 'order-takers'[124] which benefit from the opportunities afforded by the Investment Services Directive are also subject to the lower figure of ECU 50,000. All other investment firms, unless exempt from the provisions of the CAD,[125] must comply with a minimum initial capital requirement of ECU 730,000. The requirements will be reviewed in the light of experience by 1 January 1999, and only paid-up share capital (or its equivalent), retained earnings and audited profits may be used to satisfy them.

In respect of the *definition of capital* to be used for regulatory purposes, the starting point is the definition of town funds' established under the Own Funds Directive (*see* p. 104). It is this definition of capital which has to be used in satisfaction of the CAD's risk-based requirements (*see* below) unless a firm's national supervisor dictates otherwise. The ability, however, of national supervisors to accommodate alternative approaches is severely constrained. As Exhibit 1.31 shows, an alternative definition allowing, *inter alia*, for the inclusion of a limited amount of short-term subordinated debt and for the exercise of national discretion in a small number of other ways, may be approved by national supervisors for both investment firms and credit institutions engaged in investment business, but only in respect of satisfying the CAD's risk-based requirements arising from *trading book* activities (*see* below). Accordingly, the risks arising from investment firms' non-trading book activities, like banks' lending activities, have to be covered by capital of the form permitted under the Own Funds Directive.

As for the CAD's *risk measurement and assessment regime*, which applies to all EU credit institutions and investment firms unless they are specifically exempted,[126] a variety of market risks – arising from the firms' trading activities in debt, equities, foreign exchange and derivatives – are separately identified. These embrace position risk, settlement risk, counterparty risk, large exposures risk and foreign exchange risk. Minimum capital charges are prescribed to deal with each type of risk exposure, and the minimum risk-based capital requirement is derived by summing the following: (1) the minimum capital charges prescribed to account for position risk, settlement risk, counterparty risk and large exposures risk[127] arising from 'trading book'[128] activities; (2) the minimum charge prescribed to account for the foreign exchange risk arising from the totality of business operations; (3) the amount of own funds held (they must be 'adequate') to take account of the risks arising from business which is outside the scope of both the CAD and the Solvency Ratio Directive; and (4) the minimum capital requirement arising from the application of the Solvency Ratio Directive to non-trading book business. (For a detailed discussion of the methodologies employed to measure position risk, settlement risk, counterparty risk, large exposures risk and foreign exchange risk *see* the appendices to Hall, 1995a.)

Exhibit 1.31   Alternative definition of own funds allowed, at national discretion, under the CAD

Own funds (as defined in Directive 89/299/EEC)[1] (EC, 1989c).

Plus   Net trading book profits (net of any foreseeable charges or dividends) less net losses on other business

Plus   Subordinated loan capital[2]

Less[3]   Illiquid assets[4]

Notes:

1. But excluding items (12) and (13) of Article 2(1) of Directive 89/299/EEC for those investment firms required to deduct 'illiquid assets' from own funds in accordance with Annexe V, para.2 of the CAD.

2. Provided that: (a) it has an initial maturity of at least two years; (b) it is fully paid up; (c) the debt cannot be repaid, other than on the winding-up of the institution, before the agreed repayment date without the approval of the competent authorities; and (d) the subordinated loan capital may not exceed a maximum of 150 per cent of the original own funds left to meet the requirements laid down in Annexes I to IV and VI of the CAD, and may approach that maximum only in particular circumstances acceptable to the relevant authorities. (Exceptions to this rule for investment firms and credit institutions are specified in paras 6 and 7 of Annexe V of the CAD, respectively.) Neither the principal nor the interest on such subordinated loan capital may be repaid if such repayment would mean that the own funds of the institution in question would then amount to less than 100 per cent of the institution's overall requirements. In addition, an institution is required to notify the competent authority of all such repayments as soon as its own funds fall below 120 per cent of its overall requirements.

    The competent authorities may permit institutions to replace this with items (3) and (5) to (8) of Article 2(1) of Directive 89/299/EEC if they so choose.

3. The deduction is at the discretion of the competent authorities.

4. As defined in para.8 of Annexe V of the CAD.

Source: EC, 1993b.

In this way, a degree of equality of treatment ('regulatory neutrality') between banks and securities houses is secured, although the amount of discretion residing with national regulators[129] and likely differences in interpretation and implementation of the provisions – not least in respect of the interpretation of the meaning of the trading book – militate against the achievement of wider benefits in this area.

Finally, in respect of the promulgation of *overall minimum capital requirements*, different regimes are prescribed for investment firms and credit institutions. For EU *credit institutions* the minimum capital requirement which has to be observed is the higher of the minimum initial capital requirement specified in the Second Banking Co-ordination Directive (ECU 5 million for most) and the sum of the minimum risk-based capital charges deriving from the application of the CAD. (As explained above, the latter incorporates the application of the Solvency Ratio Directive to the banking book and the CAD's market risk requirements to the trading book, with 'add-ons' to account for foreign exchange risk and risks arising from business outside the scope of the CAD and the Solvency Ratio Directive – *see* Exhibit 1.32.) By way of contrast, the (overall) minimum capital requirement which has to be observed by EU *investment firms* is the higher of: (1) the minimum initial capital requirement imposed under the CAD; (2) the minimum risk-based own funds requirement deriving from the application of the CAD; and (3) a quarter of the firm's fixed overheads in the previous year (or a quarter of the projected figure for fixed overheads for start-up firms). (The last requirement is imposed under the CAD to account for the 'other' risks to which firms are exposed.) (For differences between the EC and Basle Committee approaches to measuring and assessing market risk for firms engaged in investment business *see* Exhibit 1.33.)

Exhibit 1.32   The RAR methodology employed by EU banking regulators since the implementation of the CAD on 1 January 1996

Under the CAD, all EU credit institutions have to observe, continuously, a minimum capital requirement which is the higher of ECU 5 million and the sum of the minimum risk-based capital charges deriving from the application of the Directive. For comparative purposes, and to ensure consistency in the calculation of capital requirements to cover both credit and market risks, the RAR methodology employed in the Solvency Ratio Directive must be adapted to accommodate market risk in the following fashion:

$$RAR(\%)^1 = \frac{ACB^2}{TOWRA^3 + [12.5 \times \text{Market risk capital charge}]^4}$$

Notes:
1. This remains subject to a minimum of 8 per cent.
2. The capital items which may be included in the adjusted capital base (ACB) are the same as those which were eligible for inclusion (subject to limits and deductions) within the capital base under the Own Funds Directive. However, national regulators are empowered to permit credit institutions to adopt an alternative definition of capital (*see* Exhibit 1.31), subject to limits and restrictions, but only in respect of satisfying the CAD's risk-based capital requirements arising from *trading book* activities.
3. This now represents the 'total of weighted risk assets' arising from *banking book* activities only. (Note, however, that although the CAD's market risk-based requirements substitute for the Solvency Ratio Directive's credit risk-based requirements as far as a credit institution's trading book is concerned, credit counterparty risk on all over-the-counter derivatives, whether or not they are included on the trading book, remains subject to the credit risk-based assessment of the Solvency Ratio Directive.)
4. This represents notional risk-weighted assets on the trading book.

Exhibit 1.33 *Differences between the EC and Basle Committee approaches to measuring and assessing market risk for firms engaged in investment business*

Area of concern	EC approach	Basle Committee approach
1. Institutions subject to the provisions	Investment firms and credit institutions in the EU and those European Free Trade Area countries covered by the EEA Agreement of May 1992	Banks in the G10 area and elsewhere where national supervisors mandate compliance
2. Legal status of the provisions	The CAD is legally binding on member states of the EU	A 'gentleman's agreement' between G10 bank supervisors
3. Group supervision	Consolidated supervision is the norm for financial groups, although national supervisors have the discretion to waive it for investment (but not banking) groups which satisfy certain criteria (*see* Article 7 of the CAD, paras 4 to 7)	'Banking' groups must be supervised on a consolidated basis for market risk
4. Date of implementation	From end of 1995	From end of 1997
5. Scope of coverage	Apart from position risk, covers underwriting exposures, settlement risk, counterparty risk and large exposures risk arising from trading book positions in debt and equities[1] (foreign exchange risk is assessed on all business activities); sets capital requirements to cover 'other' risks (for investment firms only) and risks not covered by the CAD or the Solvency Ratio Directive	Only covers position risk and foreign exchange risk arising from transactions in debt, equities, commodities and foreign exchange; does not prescribe capital charges to cover risks not already covered by the above-mentioned capital charges
6. Definition of capital for regulatory purposes	'Qualifying' criteria for eligibility of short-term subordinated debt for inclusion in regulatory capital do not include a provision that it must	Short-term subordinated debt needs to be unsecured if it is to be eligible for inclusion in Tier 3 capital; the

Exhibit 1.33   (continued)

	be unsecured; the limitations imposed on the use of such debt are more restrictive than those applying under the Basle Committee's approach; alternative definition of own funds allowed. at national discretion, includes net trading book profits (less net losses on other business); short-term subordinated term debt and net trading book profits can be used to satisfy counterparty risk requirements arising from trading activities	limitations on its usage are less restrictive than those applicable under the CAD; net trading book profits not eligible for inclusion in Tier 3 capital; Tier 3 capital cannot be used to cover any counterparty risk arising from trading activities
7. Choice of assessment methodologies available	Under the CAD, EU institutions do not have the option of adopting an internal modelling approach as an alternative to the prescriptive standardized approaches[2]	At national discretion and subject to satisfying six sets of conditions, banks may adopt an internal modelling approach as an alternative to the standardized approaches
8. Assessment of position risk on equities under the standardized approach	Minimum specific risk capital charge is set at 4% (reducing to 2% for 'highly liquid' and 'well-diversified' portfolios) of a firm's overall gross positions	Minimum specific risk capital charge set at 8% (reducing to 4% for liquid and well-diversified portfolios) of a bank's gross equity positions
9. Assessment of foreign exchange risk under the standardized approach	Capital charge set at 8% of the excess of an institution's net open position over 2% of own funds; precious metals not subject to the provisions; 'dispensations' available for positions in currencies subject to legally binding intergovernmental agreements limiting variability *vis-à-vis* other currencies, participants in the second stage of European Monetary Union, and for 'closely correlated' currencies; no *de minimis* exemption; foreign currency options treated on a net delta valuation basis	Sets the capital charge under its basic approach at 8% of a bank's net open position; gold subject to the assessment procedures as well as foreign currencies; 'dispensations' available under the CAD are not available; a *de minimis* exemption applies; a wide range of treatments for foreign currency options is available

Notes:
1. A revised CAD ('CAD II') will extend the coverage to embrace commodities and commodity derivatives (on both the trading and non-trading book). It is unlikely to become operational, however, until well into 1998.
2. 'CAD II', however, will rectify this anomaly and allow national supervisors to permit their banks and investment firms to use an internal modelling approach to calculate market risk capital requirements. Prior to implementation of CAD II, competent authorities of member states can still allow institutions to use a modelling approach – provided that it results in a level of capital being held to meet market risks which is at least as high as that resulting from the application of the CAD's prescriptive approach – but this is open to challenge in the European Court.

Source: Hall, 1995a.

In addition to observing the above capital requirements, which have to be applied on a consolidated basis to any institution which has a financial institution as a subsidiary or a financial holding company as a parent, intermediaries engaged in investment business are asked to set up systems to monitor and control interest rate risk, such systems being subject to approval by their national supervisors. They are also obliged to adhere to prescribed reporting requirements.

The final Directive to be considered,[130] the Deposit Guarantee Directive (94/19/EEC; EC, 1994), was adopted in May 1994 and implemented on 1 January 1995. The Directive obliges member states to offer a minimum level of protection to qualifying depositors of ECU 20,000.[131] This figure will be reviewed by 31 December 2004. For those wishing to enforce the principle of 'co-insurance' (i.e. forcing depositors to bear some of the risk on all their deposits), a minimum level of protection of 90 per cent of the nominal value of protected deposits has to be offered on sums up to ECU 20,000.

An important principle employed in the Directive is that of 'home country responsibility'. Accordingly, the member state responsible for authorizing a credit institution is also held responsible for protecting the deposits of all depositors of that bank, no matter where in the Community the deposits are placed – in branches in the home country or overseas. By 'internalizing' the costs of licensing, the policy should help to prevent a recurrence of the BCCI fiasco which saw the Luxembourg authorities, responsible for licensing both the parent holding company and a major banking arm of the group, openly admitting their inability to supervise the sprawling international financial services group effectively (see Hall, 1994c).

Other important features of the Deposit Guarantee Directive concern the arrangements for opting into and out of host country deposit protection schemes. Branches of banks authorized in other EU countries have to be given access to host state schemes if the latter are more generous – the so-called 'topping-up' principle – while branches of banks whose home country schemes are more generous must 'level down' to the scope/level of protection offered by host country schemes, at least until 31 December 1999. The latter requirement is deemed necessary to avoid potentially destabilizing deposit flows that might arise from competitive action in this area. (For a discussion of the limitations of the internal market programme *see* Hall, 1997c.)

Since the completion of the internal market at the end of 1996, a number of Directives have been modified to accommodate market developments. In particular, the Solvency Ratio Directive (Annexe II) has been amended to allow for a widening of the supervisory recognition of (bilateral) netting to include, for example, bilateral close-out netting (*see* Clarotti, 1997). The so-called 'Netting Directive' which secured this (96/10/EC; EC, 1996) was adopted by member states in March 1996 and took effect from 1 July 1996. In addition, in March 1996 the Commission proposed another Directive to the Council of Ministers and the European Parliament that would further amend the Solvency Ratio Directive by expanding the matrix of 'add-ons' used by banks to calculate the loan equivalents arising from (non-netted) off-balance-sheet transactions. When implemented (the Council of Ministers adopted a common position on the subject in March 1998), the new capital requirements will bring the EU into line with the Basle Committee 'rules', which took effect in the (non-EEA) G10 region at the end of 1995 (*see* Chapter 7, p. 55). Finally, on the netting front, the Commission has indicated its intention to issue a similar 'interpretation note' to that issued by the Basle Committee (*see* Chapter 7, p. 58) on the subject of multilateral netting of forward-value foreign exchange transactions. If necessary, an (amending) Directive might be considered at a later stage.

Outside these areas, the Commission's recent initiatives in the financial services arena have focused on three separate proposals. The first would amend the CAD to allow for the use of internal models by EEA firms to generate market risk capital requirements (as catered for in the 1996 amendment to the Basle capital accord (*see* Chapter 7, p. 65) and to extend the coverage of the CAD to embrace commodities and commodity derivatives. A common position on the subject was adopted by the Council of Ministers in March 1998. Second, the Commission has proposed that the Solvency Ratio Directive be amended (yet again) to allow mortgage-backed securities to be treated in the same way as the mortgage loans referred to in Article 6(1)(c)(1) and in Article 11(4), and to extend to property leasing transactions the option given to member states, until 31 December 2006, to apply a 50 per cent risk weighting. A common position on this issue was also adopted by the Council of Ministers in March 1998. And finally, the Commission adopted in December 1997 a proposal to replace the 19 (7 basic and 12 amending) banking Directives with one consolidating 'banking code' as part of its 'SLIM' (Simpler Legislation for the Single Market) exercise. Member states will be expected, in due course, to simplify their national laws accordingly in a way which does not change the substance of the Directives establishing the Single Market for banking services.

10. The British and Commonwealth Bank affair

On 17 April 1990, the UK financial services company, British and Commonwealth Holdings (B&C) announced that it was to write off almost £550 million against its investment in its computer-leasing subsidiary, Atlantic Computers, which would be placed in the hands of administrators. B&C also asked for its shares to be suspended on the London Stock Exchange. On 1 June 1990, the SIB removed B&C's merchant bank – the British and Commonwealth Merchant Bank (BCMB) – from the list of banks with which authorized investment firms can place clients' money, a decision which precipitated the collapse of B&C two days later, the company itself being put into the hands of administrators. Finally, on 4 June 1990, BCMB's £300 million of deposits were frozen by the administrators.

The collapse of BCMB, which had suffered a drain of liquidity prior to the move by the SIB, raised a number of important points for UK banking supervision. First, it highlighted the dangers of allowing financial services groups to become so diversified – B&C had 40 subsidiaries spread across six countries – given the speed with which the failure of non-financial arms (Atlantic Computers in B&C's case) can bring down the whole group, including any banking operations. (Apart from BCMB, B&C owned two other licensed banks and was also heavily involved in money broking – Exco was the 'jewel in the crown' – stockbroking and funds management.) Second, it served to demonstrate the Bank's willingness to allow banks (albeit small) to fail,[132] a message the market may have needed in the light of the rescue of JMB (*see* Chapter 5), although one which the depositors and shareholders of BCMB may have found difficult to comprehend on the grounds of equity alone. Third, it vindicated the Bank's approach to 'ring fencing' the capital of the finance subsidiaries to stop the parent of a diversified group from sucking such subsidiaries dry in times of difficulty.[133] Fourth, it demonstrated the need for close supervisory co-operation between interested parties, both at the domestic and international level, when diversified international financial services groups are concerned.[134] Fifth, the affair highlighted the inadvisability of allowing banking arms of diversified groups to depend so heavily for their deposit resources on the rest of the group.[135] And, finally, the plight of the depositors of B&C's banking operations – although they were fully reimbursed, with interest, they had to wait until the end of 1993 for full compensation – indicates the substantial liquidity losses which the UK's deposit protection arrangements can impose on bank customers.

11. The Bank of Credit and Commerce International affair

On 5 July 1991, under an operation orchestrated by the Bank, co-ordinated action was taken in more than 60 countries around the world to close down the activities of the banking group Bank of Credit and Commerce International (BCCI). The action followed the Bank's receipt, in June 1991, of a report commissioned from the auditors to the bank, Price Waterhouse, which alleged that the then existing management, board members and representatives of the majority shareholders were all party to fraud which comprised, *inter alia*, the making of fictitious loans, the non-recording of deposits and dealings in the group's own shares through nominees to manufacture profits. This action was followed in January 1992 by the issuing of compulsory winding-up orders by both British and Luxembourg courts against the Luxembourg and Cayman Islands-based subsidiaries of the group – BCCI SA and BCCI (Overseas) Ltd, respectively – presaging the liquidation of most of the banking group.

The full BCCI story has been reviewed in depth by both the Treasury and Civil Service Committee (HMSO, 1992a) and Lord Justice Bingham, who chaired the official inquiry into the affair (HMSO, 1992b). A chronological summary of the major events is presented in Exhibit 1.34. Of more importance for this text, however, is a consideration of the changes in domestic supervisory practice which the affair has prompted. (Possible changes to international supervisory practice – apart from those covered in Chapter 3 – are presented in Exhibit 1.35 (Parts B and C) and discussed in more detail in Hall, 1993a and HMSO, 1992b.)

Exhibit 1.34   BCCI: timetable of events 1972–98

1972	BCCI SA (owned directly by its shareholders) incorporated in Luxembourg.
1974	Structure of BCCI (a number of subsidiaries below a Luxembourg holding company) created.
1976	New York regulators turn down BCCI's attempt to buy a US bank using an intermediary because of BCCI's lack of a lead regulator.
1978	US court affidavit shows Bank of America (30 per cent shareholder in BCCI) critical of BCCI's lending. Bank of America decides to dispose of its shareholding in BCCI. (Divestment completed in 1980.)

Exhibit 1.34   (continued)

1978	UK branch expansion blocked by Bank.
1980	Bank turns down BCCI's request for recognized status under Banking Act 1979. Instead accorded licensed deposit-taker status.
1985	Huge losses in BCCI's Treasury Division (legally part of BCCI (Overseas) Ltd, the Cayman Islands Company). This division transferred to Abu Dhabi.
1985	Bank discourages Luxembourg's suggestion that BCCI sets up separately incorporated company in UK so that Bank takes on role of lead regulator.
1986	Ernst & Whinney (predecessor of accountants Ernst & Young) writes to BCCI complaining about excessive management power and weakness of BCCI's accounting controls.
1986	BCCI's Treasury Division losses (see 1985 above) revealed to Bank.
1987	Price Waterhouse appointed sole auditor.
1987	Establishment of College of Regulators for BCCI agreed.
1987	BCCI, as licensed deposit-taker recognized under Banking Act 1979, is automatically authorized under Banking Act 1987.
June 1988	First meeting of College of Regulators.
October 1988	Drug indictment against BCCI (relating to Tampa branch) issued in USA. BCCI's UK management sets up investigation. Bank kept informed. Bank insists on daily balances and liquidity statistics, and on weekly meetings.
February 1989	Bank's meetings with BCCI become monthly and figures weekly.
January 1990	Bank institutes formal review of UK operations of BCCI in respect of drug money laundering.
Early 1990	Bank becomes aware of terrorist finance accounts at BCCI.
March 1990	Evidence of poor banking emerges from Price Waterhouse's work on BCCI's 1989 report and accounts. Section 39 report commissioned by Bank from Price Waterhouse on adequacy of BCCI's accounting systems to detect drug money laundering. Under pressure from Price Waterhouse, BCCI sets up task force to review bad loans and related transactions, using Price Waterhouse's report of 14 March as briefing note.
April 1990	Price Waterhouse's report to the board of BCCI (received by Bank on 18 April) sets out task force findings, including confirmation of previously identified problem loans, but also finds evidence of accounting transactions and statements, mainly offshore, being 'either false or deceitful'. Recommends contingency provisions. Bank later argues this report contained no evidence of systematic fraud.
4 April 1990	Governor briefs the Chancellor of the Exchequer on aftermath of Tampa.
20 April 1990	College of Regulators meets. Considers Price Waterhouse's report. Leads to injection of capital (in mid 1990) by Abu Dhabi, which gives it shareholding of over 75 per cent.
30 April 1990	College of Regulators meets. Still not satisfied by current provisions, wants $600 million. Reported to College that in-house committee

has been set up to reorganize BCCI. Headquarters to be moved to Abu Dhabi.

16 May 1990   Governor briefs the Chancellor on BCCI's reconstruction plans.

June 1990   Luxembourg gives BCCI a year to move its operations. Price Waterhouse's Section 39 report shows BCCI's systems and controls are satisfactory.

October 1990   Follow-up to Price Waterhouse's April report shows need for additional financial support of $1.5 billion to cover potential losses. Says previous management may have colluded with customers to misstate transactions. Abu Dhabi agrees to meet liabilities and make management changes. Mr Naqvi, former Chief Executive of BCCI, and Mr Abedi, BCCI's founder, step down. Bank later says it still had no evidence of fraud to justify revocation at this stage.

December 1990   In last week of December, BCCI executive tells Price Waterhouse of substantial unrecorded deposits.

January 1991   In first week of January, Bank is told of these unrecorded deposits. Abu Dhabi agrees to make good any shortfall in respect of these deposits. Price Waterhouse informs Bank that some irregular transactions may have gone through UK branches and investigates, keeping Bank informed.

25 January 1991   Bank of France bans BCCI from taking new deposits because of inadequate capital requirements.

4 March 1991   Price Waterhouse commissioned to investigate BCCI under Section 41 of Banking Act (1987).

April 1991   Bank briefs the Chancellor that BCCI's UK branches in 'pretty sound shape'.

May 1991   Financial package signed by BCCI's shareholders.

24 June 1991   Bank receives Price Waterhouse's draft Section 41 report. Report reveals 'massive and widespread fraud' going back a number of years and involving not only past but existing management, even after the reconstruction. Uses evidence provided by Mr Naqvi's 6000 personal files, previously concealed from Price Waterhouse.

29 June 1991   Governor of Bank receives Section 41 report.

1 July 1991   Bank alerts Serious Fraud Office (SFO).

2 July 1991   College of Regulators meets. Abu Dhabi not informed.

4 July 1991   Governor informs Prime Minister and Chancellor of decision to close BCCI.

5 July 1991   Co-ordinated closure of BCCI.

22 July 1991   Bank petitions the High Court in London for a winding up of BCCI SA. High Court adjourns the application for eight days but orders the freezing of BCCI's assets and appoints provisional liquidators.

23 July 1991   Governor of Bank gives oral testimony to the Treasury and Civil Service Committee. Describes the banking group's culture as 'criminal'.

30 July 1991   High Court in London reconvenes to reconsider Bank's winding-up petition. Further adjournment granted until 2 December 1991 to allow time for further talks on a possible compensation package for creditors.

July 1991   Terms of reference for Lord Justice Bingham's independent inquiry announced. Federal Reserve Board and a New York grand jury

Exhibit 1.34   (continued)

	initiate legal proceedings against BCCI and some of its employees, past and present. US House of Representatives' Banking Committee attempts to obtain from the Federal Reserve Board confidential information disclosed to it during information exchanges on BCCI with the Bank.
August 1991	Mr Clark Clifford and Mr Robert Altman resign their positions as Chairman and President of First American Bankshares respectively.
8 September 1991	Thirty-six senior BCCI executives (including Mr Naqvi and Mr Iqbal, his replacement), detained by the Abu Dhabi police.
September/ October 1991	Further US indictments made against senior BCCI officials, past and present.
October 1991	Majority shareholders announce that they have abandoned hope of restructuring the bank's UK operations.
November 1991	New bank supervisory measures passed by US Congress to plug the 'loopholes' revealed by the BCCI affair.
2 December 1991	High Court in London grants a further adjournment – until 14 January 1992 – to the Bank's petition for a winding up of BCCI SA.
16 December 1991	The Treasury and Civil Service Committee's report on the role of local authorities and money brokers in the BCCI affair is published.
December 1991	High Court in London rules that Price Waterhouse is free to comply with official requests for information concerning BCCI's financial affairs.
3 January 1992	Luxembourg District Court orders the liquidation of BCCI SA.
14 January 1992	High Court in London issues a compulsory winding-up order against BCCI SA.
24 January 1992	New York Judge Joyce Green approves the plea bargain agreement struck between the liquidators of BCCI (acting on the latter's behalf) and the US regulatory authorities.
January 1992	The Independence Bank of Encino, California, is seized by US regulatory authorities and its accounts transferred to the First Interstate Bank of California.
February 1992	Details of the compensation package agreed between the majority shareholders of BCCI and the liquidators are announced. Attempts to save the Hong Kong banking subsidiary (BCCHK) of BCCI from liquidation are abandoned.
4 March 1992	Report of the Treasury and Civil Service Committee (*Banking Supervision and BCCI: International and National Regulation*) is published (HMSO, 1992a).
6 March 1992	Liquidators of BCCI announce that they are to sue Ernst & Young accounting partnership for damages, alleging breach of contract, breach of duty and negligence in Ernst & Whinney's audit of BCCI's 1986 accounts.
12 March 1992	Liquidators of BCCI announce that they will also sue Price Waterhouse and others (including Ernst & Whinney) for damages alleging negligence, breach of duty and breach of contract in the audits for BCCI's 1985 and 1986 accounts.

8 April 1992	High Court in London adjourns hearing into the compensation package negotiated by the liquidators Touche Ross with the majority shareholders of BCCI to allow the English Creditors Committee more time to examine the proposals.
24 April 1992	Announcement that Price Waterhouse and Ernst & Whinney are to face a disciplinary inquiry into their performances as auditors to BCCI. (The hearings, instituted by the Institute of Chartered Accountants of England and Wales (ICAEW) under the Joint Disciplinary Scheme, are to be held in private but the findings will be published.)
11 May 1992	High Court in London grants a further adjournment of the hearing into the compensation package negotiated by the liquidators to allow creditors further time to clarify the terms of the proposed settlement.
30 May 1992	In response to the Treasury and Civil Service Committee's December 1991 report on the BCCI affair, the Bank announces that it is to 'strongly recommend' the tape-recording of telephone calls by money-market brokers and dealers. It also agrees to revise the London Code to make clear that local authorities and other principals operating in the market are entirely responsible for their own actions and cannot rely on the views of brokers. It declines, however, to institute disciplinary proceedings against the broking firm R.P. Martin, claiming that the evidence was 'still ... conflicting and insufficient to find the allegations ... proven'.
12 June 1992	The Vice Chancellor in the London High Court finally approves the compensation package negotiated by the liquidators of BCCI with the majority shareholders, despite opposition from the English Creditors Committee.
18 June 1992	A court in Grand Cayman approves the compensation package negotiated by the liquidators of BCCI with the majority shareholders.
1 July 1992	Sheikh Khalid Bin Mahfouz, Chief Operating Officer of the National Commercial Bank of Saudi Arabia (NCB), the largest commercial bank in that country, indicted in New York on charges of scheming with another to defraud the depositors, regulators and auditors of BCCI of over $300 million.
6 July 1992	The Basle Committee of Supervisors, in its first public response to the BCCI affair, issues a set of 'minimum standards' which members have agreed to adopt in their supervision of international banking groups. The minimum standards are designed to reinforce the Basle *Concordat*, first issued in 1975, which governs the division of supervisory responsibilities between parent and host bank supervisors.
8 July 1992	The Bank published its response to the Second Treasury and Civil Service Committee Report (HMSO, 1992a) on the BCCI affair.
9 July 1992	NCB ordered by US Federal banking authorities to close its New York branch within 30 days because of the bank's violation of 'significant provisions' of US banking laws.
20 July 1992	Luxembourg court judge delays consideration of the negotiated compensation package until 7 October to allow time for further consultation with BCCI's unsecured creditors.

Exhibit 1.34   (continued)

29 July 1992   Courts in New York and Washington charge Mr Clark Clifford and
                      Mr Robert Altman with receiving bribes, conspiracy and fraud.
                      Similar charges also brought against Mr Abedi, Mr Naqvi and Mr
                      Pharaon, a Saudi Arabian financier.

30 September 1992   An accountant working on the SFO's BCCI inquiry is jailed for three
                      years after being convicted of conspiracy to pervert the course of
                      justice. (He tried to sell confidential material from the inquiry to a
                      solicitor acting on behalf of a suspect.) His accomplice is also
                      convicted of the same offence and jailed for a similar term.

1 October 1992   Findings of a US Senate investigation into the BCCI affair are
                      published (the Kerry Report; Kerry and Brown, 1992). The report
                      strongly criticizes the roles played by the Bank, the UK government,
                      the Abu Dhabi government and the auditors Price Waterhouse in
                      the affair.

20 October 1992   The SFO clears three Bank officials accused of corruption in
                      connection with BCCI.

22 October 1992   The findings of Lord Justice Bingham's inquiry into the supervision
                      of BCCI are published (the 'Bingham Report', HMSO, 1992b). The
                      Bank's supervision of BCCI is strongly criticized. A Luxembourg
                      court approves the $1.7 billion compensation package worked out
                      between BCCI's liquidators and the Abu Dhabi majority
                      shareholders. In a ballot on the agreed package, about 90 per cent
                      of those creditors who vote are in favour of the scheme.

20 November 1992   Mr Virani, the former Chairman of Control Securities, is charged
                      with a further 14 offences in connection with his dealings with BCCI.
                      A warrant is also issued for the arrest of Mr Mohammed Moizul
                      Haque, a former member of the Central Credit Division of BCCI's
                      London office.

1 December 1992   Five former BCCI officials who have been held on suspicion of fraud
                      in the United Arab Emirates (UAE) since September 1991 released.
                      Thirteen other former officials, however, remain in custody.

11 December 1992   Liquidators of BCCI file a $10.5 billion civil lawsuit against Sheikh
                      Khalid Bin Mahfouz and the NCB.

24 December 1992   Three BCCI creditors file an appeal in Luxembourg against the
                      court's approval of the compensation package.

23 March 1993   Liquidators estimate the size of the 'black hole' of unrealizable assets
                      in BCCI's global accounts to be $12.4 billion.

24 May 1993   In an action co-ordinated by the liquidators, a small group of BCCI
                      depositors issue a writ against the Bank for allegedly failing to
                      regulate BCCI properly in accordance with the 1979 and 1987
                      Banking Acts.

13 July 1993   Thirteen former officers of BCCI, held in Abu Dhabi since July 1991,
                      are charged. The charges include, *inter alia*, forgery and false
                      accounting. Among those charged is Mr Naqvi. Charges also
                      brought against Mr Iqbal, Mr Abedi and Mr Akbar (Head of
                      Treasury), although the last named has been remanded in the UK
                      on charges laid by the SFO, while Mr Abedi remains beyond the
                      reach of the law in Pakistan.

27 July 1993	Price Waterhouse fails in its High Court attempt to halt a disciplinary inquiry launched by the ICAEW into its performance as auditors to BCCI. Price Waterhouse argues that the inquiry should not proceed while legal actions against it were still pending.
28 July 1993	European Commission announces proposals to strengthen the powers of EC banking supervisory authorities in the wake of the BCCI scandal.
29 July 1993	Four of the eight criminal charges, including that of bribery, brought against the Washington lawyer, Mr Robert Altman, are dismissed by a New York judge. (Mr Clark Clifford, who had been indicted on the same charges in 1992, had earlier been deemed too ill to stand trial and the charges against him were deferred.)
August 1993	BCCI's liquidators confirm that they are to pursue legal action (for £500 million) against the Bank after more than 5000 depositors agree to assign claims to the liquidators.
14 August 1993	Mr Robert Altman acquitted in a New York state court of charges that he helped BCCI to gain secret control illegally of the Washington-based banking group First American.
27 October 1993	Appeal court in Luxembourg upholds the appeal made by the three BCCI creditors in December 1992 against the Luxembourg Court's October 1991 approval of the $1.7 million compensation package.
December 1993	The Court of Appeal overturns the July 1993 High Court ruling against Price Waterhouse, thereby delaying the start of the disciplinary inquiry.
10 January 1994	Deal is struck between the US parties and the Abu Dhabi government whereby, in return for the Americans dropping the civil law suit against Sheikh Zayed Bin Sultan, the ruler of Abu Dhabi and BCCI's majority shareholder, and agreeing not to pursue any criminal charges against the Sheikh or any Abu Dhabi officials, Abu Dhabi agrees to give up claims on $400 million invested in First American, its 28 per cent stake in the bank, and to make available to US prosecutors Mr Naqvi, held under house arrest in Abu Dhabi since 1991. Abu Dhabi also agrees to grant the US prosecutors complete access to documents (including the 'Naqvi files') held in the country relating to the bank and to those detained in the country since the collapse of BCCI. The Abu Dhabi criminal court issues a summons ordering Mr Abedi to appear before a hearing on 22 January 1994. (There is little expectation that he will attend, however, given the lack of an extradition treaty between the UAE and Pakistan.)
January 1994	The Joint Disciplinary Scheme of the accountancy profession announces that it is to petition against the Court of Appeal's December 1993 ruling in favour of Price Waterhouse.
February 1994	Mr Mohammed Baqi, the former Managing Director of Attock Oil, is convicted in the UK of conspiring fraudulently to inflate BCCI's profits. He is fined £120,000, plus costs.
10 March 1994	A new 'deal' between BCCI's liquidators and the Abu Dhabi authorities is announced, whereby Abu Dhabi agrees to hand over $1.8 billion ($200 million immediately) to the liquidators and to waive its own extensive claims against BCCI. The agreement,

Exhibit 1.34   (continued)

	however, has to be approved by courts in Britain, the Cayman Islands and Luxembourg before it can be put to creditors.
May 1994	Mr Virani, former head of Control Securities, is jailed in the UK for 2 and a half years for fraud relating to his business dealings with BCCI.
14 June 1994	Twelve former senior BCCI executives are sentenced in Abu Dhabi to serve a combined total of 61 years in prison and ordered to pay $9 billion to cover monies stolen and costs. Mr Naqvi, on trial in the US, to where he had earlier been extradited, receives the heaviest sentence of 14 years. Mr Abedi is sentenced in his absence to eight years' imprisonment. One defendant, out on bail, is acquitted; Mr Akbar, currently serving six years in an English jail on counts of false accounting, is given a three-year sentence; and Mr Iqbal received six years in jail.
July 1994	Mr Abbas Gokal, head of the Gulf Group shipping and trade conglomerate which was BCCI's largest customer, is arrested at Frankfurt airport. Proceedings are initiated to seek his extradition to the UK.
9 July 1994	A 'plea bargain' is struck between the US Justice Department and Mr Naqvi, securing the latter's co-operation in continuing investigations by US authorities. Under the deal, Mr Naqvi pleads guilty in Washington to charges of fraud, conspiracy and racketeering.
29 July 1994	Mr Imran Imam, a former BCCI accounts officer based in London, is convicted at the Old Bailey of helping dishonestly to boost BCCI's profits.
3 August 1994	Mr Imran Iman is jailed for three years at the Old Bailey in London, despite pleas for clemency from US prosecutors, with whom Mr Iman had co-operated.
19 October 1994	Mr Naqvi is sentenced by a federal court in Washington to 11 years and 3 months' imprisonment in the US for his role in the BCCI affair.
19 December 1994	The High Court in London approves the latest settlement plan agreed between the liquidators and Abu Dhabi.
31 January 1995	A Luxembourg court approves the latest settlement plan agreed between BCCI's liquidators and Abu Dhabi, finally paving the way for payouts to the creditors of BCCI. (The deal was approved in the Cayman Islands earlier in the month.)
April 1995	Four former employees of BCCI appeal against the Luxembourg court's decision to approve the settlement plan.
3 July 1995	The liquidators scale down their legal claim against the auditors to BCCI from $11 billion to no more than $4 billion.
6 October 1995	BCCI's liquidators yet again scale down the size of their claim against the auditors to BCCI – from between $3 billion and $4 billion to $250 million
16 November 1995	The four former employees of BCCI who had blocked the settlement plan withdraw their appeal.

20 December 1995	Following the withdrawal of the appeal by the former employees of BCCI, a Luxembourg court finally allows the settlement plan to proceed. Payments of up to 40 per cent of claims (more if outstanding legal actions prove successful) are expected, with a first dividend of at least 20 per cent promised during 1996.
18 July 1996	The final date for the implementation of the post-BCCI Directive in the EU (EC, 1995). The implementing legislation in the UK is 'The Financial Institutions (Prudential Supervision) Regulations 1996'.
10 December 1996	Liquidators make the first payment, of 24.5 per cent of valid claims, to creditors of BCCI under the agreed settlement plan.
3 April 1997	Mr Abbas Gokal convicted by an Old Bailey jury of the largest single fraud ($1.2 billion) in British history.
8 May 1997	Mr Gokal is sentenced to 14 years in prison for fraud. A confiscation order is also issued compelling him to repay £2.94 million or otherwise face a further three years in jail.
30 July 1997	High Court throws out a (£550 million) claim from the liquidators of BCCI alleging 'misfeasance in public office' by the Bank. Liquidators announce they will appeal.
19 November 1997	Mr Abdul Chiragh, a chartered accountant, is convicted at the Old Bailey of fraud and false accounting.
20 November 1997	Mr Chiragh sentenced at the Old Bailey to 5 and a half years in prison for false accounting, conspiracy to defraud and perverting the course of justice.
13 February 1997	A $1.8 billion claim brought by the liquidators against Ernst & Whinney is reinstated by the Court of Appeal.
7 May 1998	Liquidators recommend that a second dividend, equal to 18.4 per cent of claims, be paid to worldwide creditors of BCCI.
4 June 1998	Liquidators apply to a Luxembourg court for approval of payment of a second dividend, now put at 21.5 per cent of valid claims. Further dividends are expected to raise the final returns to creditors to between 50 and 55 per cent, well above the levels originally anticipated.

Sources: HMSO, 1992a, Annexe, pp. xxxi–xxxiii; Hall, 1991a, 1991b, 1991c, 1992c, 1992d; press reports (various).

The recommendations for domestic reform made by myself and the two bodies referred to above are contrasted in Exhibit 1.35 and the Bank's response is depicted in Exhibit 1.37.[136] As can be seen, the Bank (along with the government) accepted Bingham's recommendations (reproduced in full in Exhibit 1.36) in their entirety. Accordingly, the Bank strengthened its investigative function by establishing a new, in-house Special Investigations Unit and by extending, on a discretionary basis, its on-site examination of banks operating in the UK. Both moves should help in the early detection of fraud. A new legal unit was also established in the Bank to advise the latter on its powers and responsibilities under the Banking Act 1987. Strengthened communication, both within the Bank (i.e. between junior and senior Bank staff and between Bank

Exhibit 1.35   BCCI: a comparison of suggested supervisory reforms

Reform measure	Advocated/supported by		
	Bingham	Treasury and Civil Service Committee	Hall
A. UK supervisory arrangements			
1. The Bank to extend on-site supervision	Yes[1]	Yes	Yes
2. The Bank to devote more resources to searching for fraud	Yes	Yes[1]	Yes
3. A duty to be imposed on auditors to report suspicions of fraud or malpractice to the Bank.	Yes	Yes	Yes
4. Overseas banks to be subject to a full-scope review by reporting accountants on an annual basis.	Yes[2]	Yes	Yes
5. 'Minimum criteria for authorization' to be strictly interpreted	Yes[1]	Yes	Yes
6. The Bank, if necessary, to be given an explicit power to refuse or revoke authorization on the grounds that the applicant or bank cannot be effectively supervised because of the group's structure	Yes[3]	Yes[1]	Yes
7. Co-operation and co-ordination between the Bank, other UK supervisory authorities and non-regulatory UK public bodies to be enhanced	Yes	Yes[1]	Yes
8. 'Single-firm' system of bank audits to be introduced	No	Yes[4]	Yes
9. The Bank to be given an explicit power to allow it to enforce local incorporation of (non-EC) overseas incorporated banks' UK branch operations when deemed necessary	No[5]	Maybe[6]	Yes
10. The Deposit Protection Scheme to be amended	–[7]	–[8]	Yes
11. An auditor to a bank not to be allowed to act as a reporting accountant under Section 41 of the Banking Act 1987	No	Yes	Yes
12. Audit firms to be forcibly rotated	No	–[8]	Yes
13. Limitations to be placed on an auditing firm's non-audit work for the same client	–[8]	–[8]	YES
14. Banking supervision to be hived off to an independent agency	No	–[8]	Maybe

B. EC supervisory arrangements

1. A Deposit Guarantee Directive, embracing the principle of home country responsibility, to be implemented as soon as possible	Yes	–[8]	Yes
2. Explicit powers to be conferred on EC supervisors, allowing them to refuse or revoke authorization in instances where group structures or other factors prevent the exercise of effective consolidated supervision	Yes	Yes[1]	Yes

C. Other international supervisory arrangements

1. Supervisory standards to be subject to independent monitoring	Yes	Yes[9]	Yes
2. International supervisory co-operation to be enhanced	Yes	Yes	Yes
3. The problem of bank secrecy provisions to be tackled	Yes	Yes[1]	Yes[1]

Notes:
1. Implied.
2. All 'small' banks to be so treated.
3. Or because of other factors.
4. Thought desirable (as by Bingham) although not recommended.
5. Bingham, although in favour of the principle of discretionary use of such a power, does not believe new powers are necessary.
6. Bank asked to consider the case for mandatory incorporation of UK operations of overseas banks.
7. Deemed outside his terms of reference.
8. Subject not addressed.
9. By the BIS.

Sources: HMSO, 1992a, 1992b; Hall, 1991a, 1991b, 1992d.

staff and the Board of Banking Supervision) and with outside parties[137] will also assist in the co-ordinated fight against fraud. Finally, small or potentially vulnerable overseas institutions are now usually subject to a full-scope review by reporting accountants on an annual basis, as opposed to the previous four- to five-year rolling basis.

Exhibit 1.36   A summary of Lord Justice Bingham's recommendations

---

A.   UK supervisory arrangements

- The Bank should develop a high degree of alertness and inquisitiveness in its supervisory staff.
- The Bank should improve its internal communications.
- The Bank should ensure that the Board is better informed.
- The Bank should proceed with its plans to enhance the efficacy of its investigation function through the establishment of a Special Investigations Unit within the Banking Supervision Division.
- The Bank should proceed with its plans to strengthen the Banking Supervision Division's legal unit.
- The Bank should, if necessary, be given an explicit power to refuse or revoke authorization on the grounds that the applicant or bank cannot be effectively supervised.
- The Bank should, if necessary, be given an explicit power to require banks to locate their effective head office in the country of incorporation.
- A duty should be imposed on auditors of financial institutions to report suspicions of fraud or malpractice to the relevant supervisory authority.
- There should be a review of the circumstances in which public bodies – regulators and others – may and should pass information to each other about a bank's activities.
- All 'small' banks should be subject to a full-scope review by reporting accountants on an annual basis.
- The Bank should give consideration to the imposition of a specific duty on a bank's management to disclose and provide information on any organization under common control.
- The Bank should be given the power to require separate audits for the UK branches of non-EC banks.
- All companies in a banking group should have the same accounting dates.

B.   EC supervisory arrangements

- The principles that EC member states should stop supervisory 'forum-shopping', that a credit institution's place of incorporation should be regarded as its home state, and that a credit institution's head office should be in the same member state as its registered office should be enshrined as articles in the Second Banking Co-ordination Directive.

- The Second Consolidated Supervision Directive should explicitly confer powers on all EC supervisors allowing them to refuse or revoke authorization in instances where group structures or other factors prevent the exercise of effective supervision.
- The proposed Deposit Guarantee Directive, embracing the principle of home country responsibility, should be implemented as soon as possible.

C.   Other international supervisory arrangements

- There should be some independent monitoring of supervisory standards. Banks operating in financial centres offering 'impenetrable secrecy' should generally be refused authorization or otherwise have it revoked.
- The arrangements governing the exchange of information between international supervisors should be improved.
- An international database listing those individuals deemed by national supervisors not to be 'fit and proper' for the purpose of operating as a director, manager or controller of a bank should be established.
- All payment instructions passing through a correspondent bank should show the name of both the originator and the beneficiary.

Source: HMSO, 1992b.

Exhibit 1.37   The Bank's response to the Bingham Report

To implement the Bingham Report recommendations:

- The Bank is creating a new Special Investigations Unit, to be headed by Ian Watt, FCA, who joins the Bank from KPMG Peat Marwick. This will be specifically responsible for pursuing any indication of fraud or malpractice affecting banks.
- The Bank will extend its on-site examination of banks in the UK.
- The Bank is creating a new specialized Legal Unit, to be headed by Peter Peddie, formerly a partner in Freshfields.
- The Bank has strengthened systems for internal communication and for communication with the Treasury.
- The Bank will strengthen procedures for involving the Board.
- The Bank will continue to press for adoption of the new minimum standards of supervision by overseas regulators; the Treasury is taking steps to encourage better exchanges of information with overseas supervisors.

Exhibit 1.37   (continued)

- At the Bank's request, the Treasury will introduce a change in the Banking Act to give the Bank an explicit power to refuse or revoke authorization of banks with group structures that cannot be properly supervised.
- At the Bank's request, the Treasury will introduce a change in the Banking Act to place auditors of banks under a duty to pass relevant information to the Bank.
- The Bank will be actively involved in the new machinery announced by the Chancellor to co-ordinate action against fraud.

Source: Bank of England press release, 22 October 1992.

As for the Banking Act 1987 itself, two changes were proposed to Parliament. The first would transform into a *duty* the previous *right* given to bank auditors to pass on suspicions of fraud or malpractice to the Bank without informing their client banks (the Banking Act was amended accordingly in February 1994). The second would give the Bank an explicit power to refuse or revoke a bank's authorization on the grounds that the bank cannot be effectively supervised (the Banking Act was amended accordingly in July 1996 under the so-called 'post-BCCI Directive' (see Hall, 1998)). This might be, as in BCCI's case, because of the opacity of the group's structure or, possibly, because of the bank's operation in a jurisdiction offering impenetrable secrecy.[138]

Taken together, these measures[139] should help to prevent a repetition of a BCCI-style fiasco, and enhance the Bank's ability to detect fraud in a timely fashion should the occasion demand it in the future. Whether or not the Bank has gone far enough, however, remains to be seen (*see* Exhibit 1.35 and Hall 1993a, for details of other remedial action which might have been taken). To this day, the Bank asserts that it should not have acted to close down BCCI earlier[140] – depositors' interests, actual and potential, being protected through an agreed programme for restructuring and recapitalizing the bank – that it was not inhibited from taking decisive action by the appeals procedures available to aggrieved parties under the Banking Act 1987 and that, in certain circumstances (i.e. when depositors' interests, actual and potential, are best served), it may have to tolerate non-fulfilment of the minimum criteria for authorization (*see* Chapter 15). The controversy continues.

12. The Barings affair

On 26 February 1995, much of the UK merchant banking group, Barings, was placed in administration following a failed attempt by the Bank to find a buyer in the wake of massive losses incurred on unauthorized derivatives trades. The Board of Banking Supervision of the Bank (the 'Board') was duly asked by the Chancellor of the Exchequer to conduct an investigation into the events leading up to the crash. The Board's report, which was published on 18 July 1995 (HMSO, 1995a), concluded that the Barings Group was brought down by the losses incurred on unauthorized and concealed trades undertaken by a Mr Nick Leeson in Singapore. Management failings and a lack of internal controls within Barings were held to be mainly responsible for allowing this situation to develop, although contributory factors were seen to be weaknesses in external audit and supervision (*see* Hall, 1995d). These findings were confirmed by the official Singapore report into the affair (Singapore Ministry of Finance, 1995), which went on to outline details of a 'cover-up' allegedly perpetrated by senior Barings staff (*see* Hall, 1995f).

While recognizing that many parties contributed, directly or indirectly, to the collapse of Barings, the rest of this chapter focuses on the role played by the Bank as the main UK supervisor of the Barings Group. The approach it adopted in respect of the Barings Group will be scrutinized to highlight areas of concern. The various recommendations for reform of UK banking supervision made in the wake of the *post mortems* on Barings will be assessed in the light of these revealed deficiencies.[141] The Bank's response to these recommendations will also be addressed.

THE BACKGROUND TO THE COLLAPSE OF BARINGS

The major events in the life of Baring Futures (Singapore) Pte Ltd (BFS) – the indirect securities subsidiary of the UK-incorporated merchant bank Baring Brothers & Co. Ltd (BB&Co.), where Mr Leeson worked from July 1992 – are charted in Exhibit 1.38, as are the major developments in the Barings saga, pre- and post-collapse in February 1995. Accordingly, Exhibit 1.38 provides a useful summary of the following: who, within Barings, was responsible for what; who knew what and when; Leeson's operation of the error account '88888', his forging of documents and his trading positions; the roles played by the Bank, the Singapore Monetary Exchange (SIMEX), and internal and external auditors; the details of the alleged 'cover-up' operation; and the 'aftermath'.

Exhibit 1.38   The collapse of BFS and the Barings Group and its aftermath: a chronology of events 1986–98

17 September 1986	BFS incorporated. Mr Paul Hitchcock, Mr Christopher Heath and Mr Alexander Phillips appointed as the first Directors.
15 October 1986	Deloitte Haskins & Sells (now known as Deloitte & Touche) appointed as auditors.
31 October 1986	BFS applies for corporate non-clearing membership of SIMEX.
1 June 1988	Mr Bax appointed Director of BFS.
July 1989	Mr Nick Leeson joins Barings Securities Ltd (BSL) as a settlements clerk.
18 May 1990	Mr Jones appointed Director of BFS.
30 June 1990	Mr Hitchcock resigns as Director of BFS.
February 1992	BSL submits an application to the SFA to have Mr Leeson recognized as a registered representative. Mr Leeson states in the application form that there is no unsatisfied judgement debt against him. It is subsequently discovered that this is untrue.
21 February 1992	BFS applies for clearing membership of SIMEX.
13 April 1992	Mr Leeson appointed Derivatives Operations Manager of BFS.
28 May 1992	BFS purchases three seats on SIMEX. Mr Phillips resigns as a Director of BFS.
26 June 1992	Mr Leeson sits for the Institute of Banking and Finance, Futures Trading Test which he passes.
1 July 1992	Mr Leeson registered as a seatholder for BFS. BFS begins trading on SIMEX. Mr Leeson and Mr Eric Chang are the only two traders.
3 July 1992	Mr Leeson opens account 88888. This is reflected within BFS records as an error account.
9 July 1992	Ms Fu Ya-Yin appointed Director of BFS.
21 July 1992	Mr Leeson submits his Application for Registration as an Associated Person to SIMEX. He makes a false statement that he has not had any civil judgements entered against him. BFS confirmed that the information stated in the form is correct notwithstanding that the SFA has already informed BSL that Mr Leeson lied in his application form to the SFA in a similar manner.
12 August 1992	Mr Leeson's application to be registered as an Associated Person on SIMEX is approved and he is registered shortly thereafter.
September 1992	BSL withdraw Mr Leeson's application to the SFA.
October–November 1992	Mr Leeson forges an audit confirmation purportedly by Mr Bowser to resolve an audit point raised by the external auditors, Deloittes.
	The forged confirmation is dated 30 September 1992.
4 December 1992	Mr Killian appointed Director of BFS.

1993	Bank grants an 'informal concession' to Barings allowing the Group's exposure to the Osaka Stock Exchange (OSE) to exceed the 25 per cent of capital base 'large exposures' limit.
24 March 1993	Mr Heath resigned as Director of BFS.
25 May 1993	Mr Norris and Mr Roy Johnson appointed Directors of BFS.
28 June 1993	Mr Leeson appointed Assistant Director and General Manager of BFS.
Last quarter of 1993	Mr Baker becomes Head of FPG (Financial Planning Group). The proprietary trading activities of Mr Leeson came within his purview.
November 1993	Bank decides to solo consolidate BSL and Baring Brothers and Co. Ltd for supervisory purposes.
January 1994	Mr Bowser relinquishes his role as Derivatives Controller. Ms Granger assumes his duties in respect of BFS settlements.
11 July 1994	Deloittes resign as auditors of BFS. Coopers & Lybrand (C&L) Singapore are appointed in their place.
19 July 1994– 1 August 1994	An internal audit of BFS is conducted.
August 1994	Baring Brothers and Co. Ltd and BSL merge to form the Baring Investment Banking Group.
October 1994	The BFS internal audit report is circulated to Barings senior management.
11 January 1995	SIMEX writes to BFS querying margin requirements for account 88888. *Nikkei Index; NK (2408), Japanese Government Board; JGB (412)* (The figures in italics show the daily volumes of proprietary positions in Nikkei and JGB futures that Mr Leeson reported he maintained on SIMEX. Mr Leeson reported that these were hedged by matching positions on the Tokyo Stock Exchange or OSE.) Mr Hawes sends the terms of reference for the Singapore Project to Mr Hopkins.
12 January 1995	On the instructions of Mr Hopkins, Mr Hawes sends to Mr Bax a copy of the terms of reference for the Singapore Project and asks for his comments. *NK (2402) JGB (1948)*
14 January 1995	C&L Singapore Ltd identifies a discrepancy in its audit. (This is later identified as the SLK (Spear, Leeds and Kellogg) Receivable.) C&L Singapore tries over the next two weeks to obtain an explanation from Mr Leeson.
16 January 1995	SIMEX informs BFS that during its audit, SIMEX auditors noted BFS had violated SIMEX Rules and the Futures Trading Act and Regulations. *NK (5002), JGB (1502)*
17 January 1995	The Kobe earthquake takes place. *NK (1002), JGB (204)*
24 January 1995	The Asset and Liability Management Committee (ALCO) decides that Mr Leeson should be asked to reduce the Baring Group's positions because of funding pressure. Mr Hawes informs ALCO that without a booking error Barings would have broken its Citibank daylight margin facility limit. ALCO also notes the general lack of accuracy about margin calls received from

Exhibit 1.38   (continued)

	Singapore. Mr Barnett, Mr Broadhurst, Mr Hawes and Mr Katz were present at the meeting.
	NK (6240), JGB (9178)
	Mr Hawes informs Mr Leeson, Mr Jones and Ms Walz that ALCO has discussed the large size of margin calls.
25 January 1995	Mr Leeson and Mr Jones reply to the letter from SIMEX dated 11 January 1995.
	NK (16,958), JGB (12,578)
	ALCO holds further discussions on funding pressure. Mr Broadhurst, Mr Hawes, Mr Katz, Mr Blyth and Ms Smith were present at the meeting. Mr Broadhurst, Mr Hawes and Mr Sacranie meet Mr Norris to update him on BFS's positions and suggest the need for urgent action. Mr Norris tells Mr Baker to instruct Mr Leeson to reduce his positions.
26 January 1995	Mr Norris prepared an agenda of points for discussion at the ALCO meeting to be held later that day. In particular, he singles out the risk issues arising from the Baring Group's positions on SIMEX.
	NK (32,820) JGB (450)
	Mr Baker, who is in New York, participates in the ALCO meeting by telephone. He explains that Mr Leeson did not reduce the Nikkei positions because of a misunderstanding. In fact, the positions had increased although the JGB positions had decreased. Mr Baker (in New York), Mr Barnett, Mr Broadhurst, Mr Hawes, Mr Katz, Mr Maclean, Mr Norris, Mr Blyth, Ms Smith and Ms Walz were present at the meeting.
	Mr Gamby, Ms Granger, Mr Jones and Mr Leeson participate in a telephone conversation about settlements problems and the need to get someone from BSL Settlements to come to Singapore to address these issues.
27 January 1995	Mr Hawes informs Mr Leeson and Mr Jones that there appears to be improper reporting of customer and house positions from BFS. He asks for a true reflection of the house positions.
	Mr Leeson informs Mr Norris of the house positions as at 27 January 1995.
	NK (32,820) JGB (4086)
	ALCO takes note of the Baring Group's positions on the OSE. ALCO decides that Mr Leeson should be advised not to increase his Nikkei positions and, if the market is favourable, to decrease his positions. Mr Barnett, Mr Broadhurst, Mr Hawes, Mr Katz, Mr Maclean, Mr Norris, Mr Blyth, Ms Smith and Ms Walz are present at the meeting.
	C&L Singapore raises a discrepancy between the balances in the individual trading accounts and those shown on SIMEX transactions with Mr Leeson.
	Mr Khoo of C&L Singapore sends the 'Baring Group (Singapore) Status Report' to Mr Turner of C&L London, conveying to him the explanation offered by Mr Leeson for the discrepancy in the

balances in individual trading accounts and those shown on
SIMEX transactions, which was that it related to the SLK
Receivable. C&L Singapore also states that the contracting party
with SLK was BSL, and that they had been told that the SLK's
creditworthiness had been discussed with BSL.

Mr Leeson and Mr Jones send a response to Mr Hopkins and Mr
Hawes on the Singapore Project. Mr Bax insists that Mr Jones
countersign the fax.

SIMEX writes to BFS questioning the adequacy of funds to meet
potential losses or margin calls.

Barings receives a telephone call from the BIS concerning market
rumours that Barings cannot meet its margin calls.

28 January 1995   C&L Singapore meets with Mr Jones, Mr Leeson and Ms Yong
on the SLK Receivable. They ask for various audit confirmations.

30 January 1995   BSL asks Mr Leeson for a correct statement of the house positions
as at 31 December 1994. The request is urgent because returns have
to be submitted to the Bank by the next day and the reports
submitted previously by Mr Leeson were thought to be wrong.
NK (26, 774), JGB (5086)

Mr Norris and Mr Bax have a conversation concerning SIMEX
correspondence. Mr Bax later says that it is possible that the
SLK Receivable was mentioned during this conversation although
he cannot be sure.

Mr Broadhurst receives C&L Singapore's fax dated 27 January
1995. He does not know about SLK Receivable. He speaks to Mr
Gamby and Mr Hughes among others about it. He also tries to
speak to Mr Norris and Ms Walz but he is unable to reach them.

Mr Broadhurst and Mr Sacranie discuss the SLK Receivable.

Mr Broadhurst calls Ms Granger and asks her whether Mr Leeson
had entered into an over-the-counter Nikkei transaction on behalf
of BSL with SLK. Ms Granger checks her records and confirms
that there is no record of such a transaction. She offers to call SLK
but Mr Broadhurst tells her not do so.

31 January 1995   Mr Hawes questions Mr Leeson and Mr Jones on the SLK
transaction. He informs them that Mr Broadhurst has passed to him
a copy of C&L Singapore's comments and that he cannot
understand these comments. He asks Mr Leeson and Mr Jones to
telephone him to discuss the matter.
NK (26, 278), JGB (5486)

Mr Leeson informs Mr Hawes and Mr Jones that he will revert to
BSL after speaking to C&L Singapore and that this will be after
the Chinese New Year holidays.

The SIMEX letter of 27 January 1995 is discussed at ALCO.

Mr Hawes is asked to draft a reply. Mr Hawes asks Mr Leeson and
Mr Jones for information to draft a reply.

c.31 January 1995   Mr Maclean finds out about the SLK Receivable from Mr Hawes.

31 January 1995   By this date, Mr Sacranie and Mr Broadhurst have informed Mr
Norris about the SLK transaction. Mr Broadhurst asks Mr Norris
whether he should raise the SLK Receivable at the ALCO meeting.
Mr Norris tells him not to do so.

Exhibit 1.38   (continued)

1 February 1995   Mr Leeson prepares a handwritten explanation on the SLK
                       Receivable for Mr Jones and Mr Bax. He informs Mr Jones that
                       the Receivable arose from an unauthorized transaction. Mr Jones
                       informs Mr Bax about this.
                       NK (27,360), JGB (5486)
                       Mr Hawes speaks to Mr Leeson about the SLK transaction.
                       Mr Leeson tells him that he is addressing the issue and that there
                       is no cause for worry.
                       Bank decides that the 'informal concession' granted in respect of
                       compliance with the large exposures limit should be withdrawn.
2 February 1995   C&L Singapore meet Ms Yong, Mr Jones and Mr Leeson to
                       discuss the SLK Receivable. They press for the audit confirmations
                       which they have yet to receive.
                       NK (27,7040), JGB (13,486)
                       Mr Leeson presents various forged documents to C&L Singapore
                       to support his explanation on the SLK transaction.
                       Mr Gamby informs Ms Granger and Mr Railton that Mr Leeson
                       has apparently done an unauthorized trade. Mr Railton is instructed
                       not to look into the SLK trade when he goes to Singapore. They
                       are told that their discussion should be kept among themselves and
                       that the issue is being handled at the highest levels.
                       C&L London meet Mr Broadhurst and Ms Seal. The SLK
                       Receivable is discussed.
3 February 1995   C&L Singapore write to C&L London clearing BFS's financial
                       statements. The letter states that BSL was the counterparty to the
                       transaction. It also states that BSL had confirmed the transaction.
                       NK (27, 053), JGB (6052)
                       Mr Bax sends a fax to Mr Norris, Mr Broadhurst, Mr Baker, Mr
                       Hopkins and Mr Gamby on control weaknesses in BFS. He states
                       that Mr Leeson will immediately relinquish his settlement functions
                       and that Mr Jones will become responsible for all support functions
                       of BFS.
                       Mr Railton arrives in Singapore, *inter alia*, to understand the
                       flow of funds into and out of BFS.
6 February 1995   Mr Hawes arrived in Singapore. His visit was prompted by various
                       factors, including the need to make inquiries into the SLK
                       transaction. Mr Bax suggested to Mr Hawes that he (Mr Bax)
                       should speak to Mr Leeson directly about SLK. Mr Railton started
                       his work at BFS.
                       NK (25,837), JGB (6722)
                       Mr Hopkins finds out about the SLK Receivable. He asks Mr
                       Broadhurst about it and is told that the money has been repaid and
                       it is no longer a problem. Mr Norris speaks to Mr Baker and Ms
                       Walz about the SLK Receivable. Mr Norris tells Mr Baker that
                       it has arisen from an accounting error.
7 February 1995   Mr Hawes presents Mr Bax with a list of audit points to clarify
                       with Mr Leeson in connection with SLK.
                       NK (27,628), JGB (11,272)

Mr Baker speaks to Mr Bax about the SLK transaction. Mr Bax informs him that it is a non-transaction and that Mr Baker need not be concerned.

8 February 1995   The SLK Receivable is discussed at the ALCO meeting. It is reported as an operational error. Mr Norris informs the meeting that he has spoken to Mr Bax about it and Mr Bax will prepare a report on it. Mr Norris instructs Ms Smith to keep the minutes brief and not to minute further discussions on SLK. Mr Baker, Mr Barnett, Mr Broadhurst, Mr Hopkins, Mr Maclean, Mr Norris, Mr Blyth, Ms Walz and Ms Smith are present at the meeting.
NK (30,116), JGB (10,212)

Mr Hawes and Mr Jones meet with SIMEX and give SIMEX verbal assurances of the Baring Group's ability to meet its financial obligations.

9 February 1995   A meeting is held between Mr Jones, Mr Leeson and Mr Hawes on the SLK transaction. Mr Leeson explains to Mr Hawes that he has been asked by BNP and SLK, who are both clients of the Baring Group, to assist them by brokering an over-the-counter transaction between them. He tells Mr Hawes that ¥7.7 billion was paid as settlement due on maturity rather than as premium. Mr Hawes asked Mr Leeson for documents evidencing the transaction. Mr Leeson leaves to retrieve the documentation but does not return that day.
NK (28,566), JGB (11,612)

C&L London meet Ms Seal and Mr Broadhurst. Mr Duncan Fitzgerald of C&L London asks how the SLK issue arose. Mr Broadhurst explains that it was a booking error of a transaction between BNP and SLK. Mr Broadhurst makes a strong plea to omit mention of the SLK transaction in the audit management letter.

10 February 1995   Mr Hawes presents Mr Leeson and Mr Jones with a further list of audit points regarding SLK.
NK (28,566), JGB (11,612)

Mr Hopkins prepares a report on SLK for the Barings Investment Bank (BIB) management committee. He records the transaction as being between BNP and SLK.

BFS replies to the letter dated 27 January 1995 from SIMEX, reassuring SIMEX that the assets of the Baring Group are available to meet the obligations of BFS. This reply is approved by ALCO.

13 February 1995   The SLK transaction is mentioned again at the ALCO meeting but this is not minuted.
NK (30,316), JGB (13,212)

14 February 1995   Mr Hawes writes to inquire as to the progress on the SLK audit points. He suggests a meeting on 25 February 1995 with Mr Leeson, Mr Jones and Mr Railton to resolve this among other issues.
NK (31,188), JGB (13,212)

15 February 1995   Mr Jones agrees to meet Mr Hawes with Mr Leeson on 25 February 1995.
NK (30,488), JGB (16,708)

Mr Bax read Mr Hawes's memo of 14 February 1995 on the SLK audit points. On his copy of the memo, he writes that Mr Jones

Exhibit 1.38   (continued)

	is to 'get Nick out of this loop' and to 'take on' Mr Hawes himself. Mr Railton sends Mr Hawes some notes and information on BFS's margin cash flow, together with a sample spreadsheet.
16 February 1995	Mr Norris arrives in Singapore. He meets Mr Bax for six hours and Mr Leeson for more than an hour.

NK (33,588), JGB (19,004)

ALCO decides that Mr Leeson is not to increase his positions any further. Mr Baker, Mr Hawes, Mr Hopkins, Mr Maclean and Ms Smith were present at the meeting.

17 February l995   ALCO directs Mr Baker to inform Mr Leeson to reduce his positions. Mr Baker, Mr Hawes, Mr Hopkins and Mr Maclean are present at the meeting.

NK (38,188), JGB (18,402)

Mr Baker leaves London for his vacation.

Mr Railton informs Ms Granger and Mr Gamby that he is unable to reconcile funds remitted to BFS from other Barings companies with money in BFS's bank account or deposited with SIMEX. The discrepancy is ¥14 billion. Mr Railton tries to talk to Mr Leeson about this later that day, but Mr Leeson says that he is too busy. He suggests a meeting on 19 February 1995. This meeting does not materialize.

19 February 1995   Mr Baker calls Mr Leeson from Switzerland and orders him to reduce his positions.

20 February 1995   Mr Norris informs ALCO that after talking to Mr Leeson in Singapore the previous week, he has decided that the positions in Singapore are not to be reduced and that it would be best to allow the positions to roll off at contract expiry within two weeks. Mr Barnett, Mr Broadhurst, Mr Hopkins, Mr Maclean, Mr Norris, Mr Platt, Ms Smith and Ms Walz are present at the meeting.

NK (34,388), JGB (18,402)

Mr Leeson informs Mr Hawes that following his conversation with Mr Norris, Mr Bax and Mr Jones he has been told that he should await the finalization of accounts before responding to Mr Hawes's audit points.

Mr Leeson claims that he is unwell and therefore unable to talk to Mr Railton about the ¥14 billion discrepancy.

21 February 1995   Mr Railton manages to meet with Mr Leeson for about 1 and a half hours. However, they do not discuss the ¥14 billion discrepancy. Instead, they discuss Mr Railton's plans to relocate to Singapore.

NK (27,098), JGB (19,402)

22 February 1995   Mr Leeson again avoids discussing the ¥14 billion discrepancy with Mr Railton.

NK (30,612), JGB (19,202)

Mr Hughes sends a memo to Mr Hawes in Japan raising further alarm about monies that cannot be reconciled. He says that the 22 February 1995 request for US$100 million of additional margin funds is totally incomprehensible given that Mr Leeson is supposed to be reducing his positions. This message is forwarded to Singapore on 23 February 1995.

23 February 1995   A meeting is organized between Mr Jones, Mr Leeson and Mr Railton to resolve the discrepancy of ¥14 billion. After ten minutes Mr Leeson says he has to go to the hospital to see his wife. He does not return. Mr and Mrs Leeson leave Singapore that night.
NK (30,112), JGB (15,940)

Mr Leeson sends a fax to the SIMEX trading floor to say that he has decided to celebrate his birthday in Phuket, Thailand. This fax is received on 24 February 1995.

In the evening, while waiting for Mr Leeson to return, Mr Jones, Ms Yong and Mr Railton scrutinize the documents handed to the auditors in connection with the SLK transaction. These, together with BFS's bank statement, suggest that Mr Leeson may have 'round-tripped' the sum of ¥7.7 billion that had been represented as payment by SLK.

Mr and Mrs Leeson check into the Regent Hotel, Kuala Lumpur. Mr Gamby is informed by Mr Railton, and in turn informs Mr Norris, that Mr Leeson has not kept his appointment. Mr Norris assembles a team of advisers in his office. By about 7.00 p.m. (London time), Mr Maclean, Mr Broadhurst, Mr Sacraine, Mr Hughes, Mr Gamby, Ms Granger and Ms Walz are gathered there.

24 February 1995   Mr Hawes arrives in Singapore at about 1.30 p.m. (Singapore time). *NK(30,112), JGB (15,940)*

Mr Bax receives a call from Ms Walz at about 2 p.m. (Singapore time). Ms Walz wants to know where Mr Leeson is. Mr Bax tells her that Mrs Leeson may be in hospital. He gives her the telephone numbers of a few hospitals. Mr Bax and Ms Walz inquire at several hospitals but Mr and Mrs Leeson cannot be found.

Mr Norris later telephones Mr Bax and tells him that Mr Leeson may have fled. He instructs Mr Bax to go into the office immediately. He also calls Mr Railton and Mr Hawes and instructs them to go to the office immediately. Soon after they arrive in the BFS office, they discover account 88888. They are joined by Mr Jones at about 6.00 p.m.

Later in the day, Mr Hawes prepares a report for ALCO on account 88888 and the outstanding positions as at the close of business on 23 February 1995.

Mr Leeson sends a fax to Mr Jones and Mr Bax from the Regent Hotel, Kuala Lumpur, apologizing for having fled and offering his resignation.

25/26 February 1995   Bank meets executives of leading UK clearing and merchant banks to try to agree a rescue package for Barings.

26 February 1995   Barings in London goes into administration when it fails to make a margin call.

27 February 1995   BFS is placed under interim judicial management.

Chancellor of the Exchequer announces that the Board of Banking Supervision of the Bank will conduct an investigation into the events leading to the collapse of Barings.

2 March 1995   Mr Leeson arrested at Frankfurt airport.

3 March 1995   SFO launches an inquiry into possible fraud at Barings.

Exhibit 1.38 (continued)

6 March 1995	High Court in London approves bid made for most of the Barings Group by Dutch financial services group, Internationale Nederlanden Group (ING).
9 March 1995	Messrs San and Kuang appointed as Inspectors by the Singapore Minister of Finance to investigate the affairs of BFS and to report thereon to the Minister.
13 March 1995	ING suspends, on full pay, 20 traders and backroom staff at BFS, pending the outcome of an internal inquiry. SFA bars former directors of Barings from becoming directors of the new Barings businesses created by ING, pending the outcome of its inquiry.
March 1995	Criminal investigation is launched by the Commercial Affairs Department of Singapore into the circumstances surrounding the collapse of BFS.
28 March 1995	Mr Watt appointed by the Bank to conduct an investigation under Section 41 of the Banking Act 1987 and to report to the Bank on certain aspects of the nature, conduct and state of the business of Baring Brothers Ltd.
3 April 1995	Chairman and Deputy Chairman of Barings plc, Mr Peter Baring and Mr Andrew Tuckey respectively, resign.
April 1995	Singapore authorities request the extradition of Leeson from Germany.
1 May 1995	Twenty-one Barings' bank executives (in London, Tokyo and Singapore) 'tainted' by the scandal are dismissed by ING.
17 May 1995	Securities industry regulators from 16 countries announce measures to strengthen the supervision of futures exchanges and improve information flows across international markets (the 'Windsor Declaration').
16 July 1995	Mr Christopher Thompson, senior Bank manager, responsible for supervising Barings since April 1991, resigns after learning of criticism of him in the Board of Banking Supervision report.
18 July 1995	Report of the Board of Banking Supervision inquiry into the collapse of Barings is published.
September 1995	The Bank and the SFA reveal joint tightening of supervision of UK investment banks. SFO interview Mr Leeson in his German cell.
4 October 1995	SFA begin questioning of former Barings executives.
6 October 1995	SFO moves to quash a private UK prosecution of Mr Leeson brought by Barings' bondholders by taking over the prosecution.
12 October 1995	British court approves the SFO's moves to have the bondholders' summonses withdrawn. (The SFO wants Mr Leeson to be tried in Germany.)
17 October 1995	Singapore Inspectors report into the collapse of BFS published.
October 1995	Singapore securities authorities fine Baring Futures £4.5 million for failing to follow correct procedures. Singapore authorities begin probing the link between Barings and Chicago-based First Continental Trading. BFS is wound up.

Bank reveals that it has already acted to establish a 'quality assurance function', with help from the accounting and consultancy firm, Arthur Andersen.

German courts decide to allow Mr Leeson's extradition to Singapore; Mr Leeson appeals against the decision to the German constitutional court.

29 October 1995	Mr Leeson drops appeal against Singapore extradition.
30 October 1995	SIMEX introduces new regulations to avoid a repetition of a Barings-style collapse and to prevent unauthorized trading.
9 November 1995	Bank announces it will examine the Singapore Inspectors' report to see if it was misled by Mr Norris in its earlier inquiries.
14 November 1995	Germany approves extradition request from Singapore.
23 November 1995	Mr Leeson arrives back in Singapore to face 11 charges of forgery and cheating.
1 December 1995	Mr Leeson pleads guilty to two charges of cheating – the other nine charges are 'stood down' – in a Singapore court.
2 December 1995	Mr Leeson is sentenced to six and a half years in jail by a Singapore court.
29 December 1995	Mr Norris, Mr Bax and the four other Directors of BFS are summoned to appear before a Singapore court to answer questions about the local derivatives trading which brought about the collapse of the Barings Group.
23 January 1996	The administrators to the Barings Group, from the accountancy firm Ernst & Young, issue writs against the three firms of accountants involved in the auditing of Barings accounts in the 1990s, that is, C&L in London, Deloitte Touche in Singapore, and C&L in Singapore.
15 March 1996	Forty-nine international exchanges and clearing houses announce that they have agreed to swap information about common members which appear to be building up risky or potentially excessive exposures.

Fourteen regulatory agencies agree to act as a conduit for the passing on of such information when legal constraints or commercial considerations preclude co-operation between exchanges.

SFA announces its intention to bar nine former Barings executives from working in the City (for between one and three years) for their share in the responsibility for the collapse of Barings. Each also to be fined £10,000. The two most senior executives – Peter Baring and Andrew Tuckey – are cleared, however, along with Richard Katz. Those to be barred are: Peter Norris, Ron Baker, James Bax, Geoffrey Broadhurst, Tony Gamby, Tony Hawes, Ian Hopkins, George Maclean and Mary Walz.

7 May 1996	SFA confirms that, following disciplinary proceedings, Peter Norris is to be removed from the SFA's register for managers/directors for a period of at least three years and fined £10,000.
20 May 1996	The Basle Committee and IOSCO issue a joint statement of principles designed to ensure closer co-operation between banking and securities regulators, as called for by the G7 nations at the Halifax Summit of June 1995. Eight principles are identified:

Exhibit 1.38   (continued)

- co-operation among supervisory authorities should be as free as possible from national and international impediments;
- all banks and securities firms should be subject to effective supervision, including supervision of capital;
- geographically and functionally diversified financial groups require special supervisory arrangements;
- all banks and securities firms should have adequate capital;
- all firms need to have proper risk management;
- adequate reporting and disclosure is needed to ensure the transparency and integrity of markets;
- markets must be able to survive the failure of individual firms;
- the supervisory process has to be constantly improved.

28 May 1996   SFA bans Geoffrey Broadhurst from working in the City as a director/manager for three years and fines him £10,000.

13 June 1996   Singapore's Commercial Affairs Department announces that it is taking no action against James Bax and Simon Jones because of insufficient grounds on which to bring criminal charges against them.

June 1996   G7 nations endorse the UK's proposal that a 'lead regulator' be given responsibility for co-ordinating the supervision of global financial conglomerates.

3 July 1996   Announcement that top officials from the Bank and SIB are to take seats on each other's boards in a bid to improve co-operation.

22 July 1996   SFA announces plans to make it easier to discipline senior directors of investment banks if internal controls are found to be inadequate. Member firms will have to designate a senior executive officer responsible for ensuring proper management control. This person will be held to account if firms suffer significant financial damage.

24 July 1996   Bank announces its intention to restructure its Supervision and Surveillance Divisions in line with the recommendations of the Arthur Andersen Review.

12 November 1996   A regulatory tribunal decides that Ron Baker should *not* be banned from working as a senior manager/director in the City for a period of at least three years (as the SFA had proposed), although he is reprimanded for failing fully to monitor Nick Leeson's trading activities. He is asked to pay £7500 of the £150,000 total costs of the case.

29 November 1996   C&L, auditors to the collapsed Barings Group, announces its intention to sue nine former directors and managers of Barings for their failure to prevent fraud at Barings. (The accounting firm itself faces legal action from the bank's administrators.)

10 December 1996   SFA retreats from its original intention to ban Mary Walz from the City for a period of time and, instead, merely reprimands her. She is also asked to pay a contribution to costs.

18 December 1996   House of Commons Treasury Committee publishes its report on 'Barings Bank and International Regulation'.

7 January 1997   Ron Baker appeals against the SFA tribunal's decision to reprimand him.

19 February 1997	Bank publishes a booklet containing three papers on the 'Objectives, Standards and Processes of Supervision', as called for by the Arthur Andersen Review. Bank proposes that the boards of directors of banks should be required to make written statements each year confirming that their banks have systems of internal controls to monitor risks and that their banks are in compliance with the minimum criteria for authorization.
21 February 1997	The DTI announces its intention to seek a ban on ten former Barings executives (including Andrew Tuckey) from serving as company directors for 10–15 years.
25 February 1997	SFA suspends (until end-1997) James Bax from acting as a director of a securities business.
3 March 1997	Bank publishes a study warning about the dangers associated with badly structured bonus systems.
11 March 1997	Ian Hopkins is struck off the SFA's register of managers/directors and banned from any financial management role until at least 2000. Following an SFA appeals tribunal hearing, he is also asked to pay £10,000 towards the costs of the case.
April 1997	Holders of bonds in Barings plc are offered £150 million compensation, funded by payments from Barings' auditors, former directors and brokers involved in issuing the capital.
11 June 1997	Ron Baker cleared by an SFA appeals tribunal of any blame for the collapse of Barings. This overturns an earlier decision to 'reprimand' him.
22 July 1997	SIB publishes its own proposals on how to ensure senior executives of financial firms are held to account for failures in internal controls. Its solution is to seek a clear division of responsibilities for risk management between the executives which all are required to acknowledge formally. It does not go as far as the SFA in suggesting that senior managers of failed firms should have to prove that they were not responsible for the collapse. In addition, it proposes that managers be required to assign a risk rating to each activity engaged in and that a designated manager be required to ensure that the risk levels are not exceeded. Entry into a new activity would require the assignment of a new manager to assess the risks involved.
29 July 1997	On the application of the DTI, the High Court disqualifies George Maclean from holding a directorship for four years.
September 1997	SFA issues a new consultation document on the responsibilities of senior management. In large part, it confirms the approach of its earlier document on the subject, but drops the controversial proposal that a senior executive officer be presumed responsible for any breakdown of controls leading to material damage to the firm unless he or she can prove otherwise.
21 February 1998	The High Court disqualifies Mary Walz from holding directorships for two years and Ian Hopkins for five years following DTI applications.
3 March 1998	The High Court disqualifies Peter Norris from holding directorships for four years and Tony Hawes for five years following applications from the DTI.

Exhibit 1.38   (continued)

2 April 1998	The High Court disqualifies James Bax from acting as a director for four years following an application for disqualification from the DTI.

Sources: Hall, 1996d, Annexe 1; press reports (various).

THE LESSONS TO BE LEARNT BY THE BANK

The Bank's supervisory 'performance' in respect of Barings is assessed below from a number of standpoints: its supervisory style and culture; the approach it adopts to the supervision of banking groups (and the issue of solo consolidation); implementation of its large exposures policy; and its relationships with other supervisors. Each of these issues will now be addressed in turn.

The Bank's Supervisory Style and Culture

The Bank's approach to banking supervision, which relies heavily on the management interview and analysis of prudential returns (*see* Chapter 13), remains in stark contrast with that adopted by its counterparties elsewhere in the world (e.g. by federal banking regulators in the US – for a comparison *see* Hall, 1993b, Chapter 9), notwithstanding its growing use of informal and formal on-site inspection since the collapse of BCCI (*see* Hall, 1993a for further details). Although the Board (HMSO, 1995a, paras.14.49 to 14.51) addressed the issue of whether or not it should move further down the road towards an inspection-based system, it concluded that, on the basis of the work done for the inquiry, a wholesale change to the Bank's style of supervision was unjustified, not least because of the 'very significant increase in the cost of supervision' (HMSO, 1995a, para.14.51) which would be involved and which would ultimately be passed on to the customer or taxpayer. While the Board was right to point out the concomitant increase in costs that would result from a further shift in this direction, a full cost–benefit style of analysis is necessary if a more considered decision is to be arrived at (who knows what an unannounced supervisory visit to Barings – no visits ever took place – might have unearthed?).

Whatever the case for continuing to eschew a more inspection-based approach, the Bank's supervisory culture continued to attract suspicions and doubts. Thus although the Governor vehemently argued (e.g. *see* HMSO, 1995b, para.10) that the Bank's supervisory culture had changed substantially in recent years, and especially since the collapse of BCCI (i.e. from being too aloof, too laid back and too trusting to being more inquisitive, adversarial, intrusive and alert – much of which was asked for by Lord Justice Bingham in his official inquiry (HMSO, 1992b)), the Barings' evidence suggested otherwise. Accordingly, the suspicion remained that the 'old boys' cosy club-like network' had not been totally swept aside in matters pertaining to UK banking supervision (HMSO, 1995b, paras 16, 21, 136, 143; House of Commons, 1996, paras 24, 29, 30).

The Supervision of Banking Groups

Some of the strongest criticism of the Bank's supervision of the Barings Group – it was consolidated supervisor of the Group and lead regulator of BB&Co. – was reserved for its failure to grasp fully what the Group's operations actually were and to appreciate fully the nature of the Group's management and control structures. Thus, for example, the independent members of the Board criticized the Bank for not having had 'a greater understanding of Barings' Far Eastern operations and a greater awareness of the degree of control of these operations as exercised by Barings in London' (HMSO, 1995a, para.13.61), while the Treasury and Civil Service Committee was 'dismayed that the Governor can on the one hand claim that London is one of the best regulated and supervised markets in the world and on the other have to concede that his supervisory staff actually have little real understanding of what its charges are up to' (HMSO, 1995c, para.67).

In carrying out its supervisory responsibilities in respect of banking groups, the Bank relies upon, *inter alia*, the group's management, auditors, reporting accountants and overseas supervisory authorities (*see* HMSO, 1995a, Appendix XIV, and pp. 205–7 of this text, for further details). Specifically, in the case of Barings, the Bank had confidence in the senior management of BB&Co., many of whom had been long-standing employees of Barings. Moreover, the senior management had told the Bank that BB&Co.'s standards of control, which were regarded by the Bank as informal but effective, would be applied to BSL in the course of the fusion to form BIB. Accordingly, the Bank (unfortunately) placed greater reliance on statements made to it by management than it would have done had this degree of confidence not existed. As far as Barings' overseas subsidiaries were concerned, the Bank undertook no reviews, relying on the reports and assurances given to it by Barings itself and by its auditors and reporting accountants, and on the supervision performed by the relevant overseas regulators, in accordance with recognized supervisory practice (i.e. according to the Basle *Concordat – see* Chapter 3 and HMSO, 1995c, Appendix 4). It did, however, impose a 'connected lending limit' (*see* below) on the solo-consolidated group's (i.e. BB&Co. and BSL) exposure to the overseas securities subsidiaries, as required by EU law (EC, 1992b), of 25 per cent of the solo-consolidated group's capital base. Thus while the Bank's supervision focused primarily on

BB&Co., the intermediary authorized to take deposits under the Banking Act 1987, it understood and accepted that its supervisory responsibilities also extended to the activities of other parts of the Group in so far as such activities were capable of affecting the financial soundness and reputation of BB&Co.

Although the independent members of the Board did not criticize the Bank for placing undue reliance on overseas regulators or on the explanations given by management or on the other information provided by Barings as to the nature, scale and profitability of Barings' overseas operations – it was thus not held to be at fault for being unaware of either Barings' non-compliance with the connected lending limit or its inaccurate reporting to the Bank – they did, nevertheless, make ten recommendations (*see* Exhibit 1.39) to enhance the Bank's ability to understand fully the nature of a banking group's operations and its management and control structures, and generally to improve the effectiveness of the supervision of banking groups. It is to be hoped that the future adoption of these recommendations will ensure that the Bank gets to grips with *all* banking groups falling within its jurisdiction. (For a critique of the Bank's traditional approach to supervising banking groups and an explanation of EU law in this area *see* Chapter 25.)

Exhibit 1.39   Barings: the lessons to be learnt by the Bank according to the (independent members of the) Board

---

1. In its role as *consolidated supervisor* of banking groups, it should go further than collecting and monitoring information on consolidated capital adequacy and consolidated large exposures. For example, (a) it should explore ways of increasing its understanding of the non-banking businesses (particularly financial services businesses) undertaken by such groups; (b) it should seek to obtain a more comprehensive understanding of how the risks in those businesses are controlled by the management of the group, in order to help determine which group companies or activities are likely to pose difficulties for the bank; (c) it should ensure that its relationship with other regulators is clearly defined; (d) it should ensure effective co-ordination with other regulators; (e) it should prepare internal guidelines to assist staff in identifying those parts or activities of a banking group which are capable of posing material risks to the bank and to advise them of the steps which they should take to assess and monitor such risks, and to ensure that safeguards are in place to protect depositors against such risks; (f) regular bilateral meetings with the management of significant overseas, and non-banking UK-based, businesses should be formally incorporated as a requirement in management guidelines and should include questioning, *inter alia*, the sources of profitability, sources of funding and control systems

within relevant parts of the group; (g) it should increase its dialogue with local regulators where a banking group has substantial operations overseas; (h) it should ensure that it understands the key elements of the management and control structures of banking groups; (i) it should receive prior notice of a significant reorganization within, and of significant new operations being commenced by, a banking group, together with reporting responsibilities; and (j) it should extend the scope of the current prudential returns (e.g. to include details of profitability by product line) to improve its understanding of the businesses of the institutions it supervises to enable it to ask relevant questions of management.

2. To improve the *accuracy of prudential returns*, it should require each bank to nominate a senior director previously notified to the Bank under Section 36(1) of the Banking Act 1987 to sign the most important returns (i.e. Banking Supervision Division (BSD) I and the large exposures (LE) return) on behalf of the board. Moreover, the nominated director should meet the Bank at least once each year (probably as part of a prudential meeting) to discuss the accuracy and timely completion of returns.

3. *Solo consolidation* of any active trading entity with a bank should require the formal approval of the Executive Director in charge of the Supervision and Surveillance Division of the Bank or of one of the Bank's Governors. Moreover, solo consolidation should only be proposed if, as a minimum, the following requirements are met (in addition to the criteria which the Bank already requires to be satisfied): (a) solo consolidation must result in supervision, to the satisfaction of the Bank, of every solo-consolidated entity and should only be contemplated where this is practicable; (b) the controls within all of the proposed solo-consolidated entities must be adequate to ensure that exposures to companies outside the solo-consolidated group can only be incurred in a controlled manner; and (c) the Bank must have the means to receive, on a continuing basis, suitable reassurance regarding such controls (e.g. through Section 39 reports into systems and controls across the solo-consolidated group). Finally, internal guidelines should be prepared to identify for Bank staff the procedures to be followed with respect to the granting of solo consolidation and the supervision of the solo-consolidated group thereafter. Such guidelines should include a requirement that once solo consolidation has been granted, a notice should be served under Section 38(3) of the Banking Act 1987 to ensure that the criminal sanction imposed by Section 38 applies to the solo-consolidated group.

4. It should review all of the existing Memoranda of Understanding between itself and other UK regulators with a view to accommodating the recommendations made above concerning the co-ordination of supervisory functions and solo consolidation.

Exhibit 1.39 (continued)

5. It should seek to agree formal Memoranda of Understanding with overseas regulators in order to provide a sound basis for the relationship and to set out what one regulator can reasonably expect the other to do.
6. It should seek to extend the process of removing legal impediments to the freeflow of information between supervisors to include non-banking regulators of financial services businesses, such as those involved in securities trading. Moreover, if there are legal obstacles to the Bank sharing information with other regulatory authorities, then appropriate legislative changes to the Banking Act 1987 should be made to remove them.
7. It should extend its current system of meeting with the internal audit departments of major UK banks to embrace other banks. Where the Bank acts as consolidated supervisor, the scope of these meetings should extend to include the group internal audit function. Moreover, for large UK-incorporated institutions, it should liaise regularly with the Chairman of the Audit Committee to provide the Bank with an opportunity to discuss internal audit, control and related issues with a non-executive director and to ask whether there are matters which should be brought to the attention of the Bank.
8. It should review its *human resources* in the shape of the number and skills of the people available for on-site visits and for general internal consultation on derivatives, other trading activities and banks' credit portfolios. Moreover, additional resources should be devoted to banking supervision, including the hiring of specialists with the required experience and expertise, to allow for the full implementation of the Board's proposals.
9. In appropriate circumstances, the scope of Section 39 reports should be extended and *reporting accountants* required to go outside the bank and, if necessary, outside the UK to perform their tasks. It should also periodically require authorized institutions to commission reports from reporting accountants on their systems of control, operating both domestically and overseas, over the accuracy of the information in their records and its transfer to returns. Finally, in respect of Section 39 reports, the Bank should initiate discussions with the accountancy profession with a view to ensuring that such reports indicate the extent of the work performed by the reporting accountants for the purposes of their preparation; and it should also be more flexible in its use of such reports (they are currently normally commissioned on an annual basis unless *ad hoc* work is required), commissioning reports more frequently in particular circumstances (e.g. where control systems or management structures materially change during the course of a year, where there is a plan to develop significantly or grow a specific aspect of the business, or where a previous Section 39 report has highlighted significant errors or weaknesses).

10. It should extend the guidelines given to management concerning the implementation of the *large exposures policy* so that existing concessions are formally reported to the relevant heads of division on an annual basis to ensure that he or she is content for them to continue. Repeated or significant breaches of the rules should be investigated promptly; heads of division should receive a summary of such breaches on a regular basis; and the Board should receive a regular report summarizing breaches of the rules.

11. It should urgently promote discussions between international regulators to try to get agreement on a common approach to the treatment of *guarantees* and *comfort letters* which properly takes into account the risks attendant upon the issuance of these instruments.

12. It should instigate an *independent quality assurance review* of its supervision of banks and report regularly to the Board on the results of such reviews.

Source: HMSO, 1995a.

Solo Consolidation

As noted in HMSO, 1995a (paras.13.67 to 13.70), the significance of the decision taken late in 1993 to solo consolidate BB&Co. and BSL – *see* Hall (1995d), Figure 1 – lay in its novelty (this was the first occasion on which the Bank had solo consolidated a bank with a substantial securities company) and in its unforeseen ramifications for the financing of the (concealed) trades undertaken at BFS by Mr Leeson. The Bank was duly criticized by the independent members of the Board for displaying a 'lack of rigour' in this respect (HMSO, 1995a, para.13.67). In particular, it was criticized for failing 'properly to address all the issues regarding the solo consolidation of BSL with BB&Co. or to finalise conclusions on points which had been raised' (HMSO, 1995a, para.13.67) – the decision to grant solo consolidation on a provisional basis in November 1993 was never reviewed – and for failing to refer the decision up to the highest level in the Bank and to the Board itself (HMSO, 1995a, para. 13.68).

The decision to allow solo consolidation[142] of BB&Co. and BSL – which, in effect, meant that BSL and BB&Co. would be treated as a single entity for capital adequacy and large exposures policies, and that BSL would be included in the unconsolidated prudential returns submitted by BB&Co. to the Bank – in the end resulted in BFS being provided with an unlimited supply of credit (*via* BSL). This was because, under solo consolidation, BSL was regarded as a branch of BB&Co. for funding purposes, thereby allowing it unconstrained access[143] to BB&Co. for loans (although access to external sources of borrowings was denied), funds which could then be lent to BFS. In principle, 'connected lending limits'[144] should have prevented the build-up of such large exposures[145] by the solo-consolidated entities (as noted by the Governor – HMSO, 1995b, para.108) but, in reality, they were ignored.

Given that the Bank is continuing to grant solo-consolidated status to banking groups – at least one such solo consolidation has been sanctioned since the collapse of Barings – it is to be hoped that the additional safeguards recommended for adoption by the Bank (*see* Exhibit 1.39, point 3) prevent further abuse of the supervisory technique.

Implementation of the Large Exposures Policy

Another source of criticism of the Bank was its implementation of its large exposures policy. Under Section 38(1) of the Banking Act 1987, all UK-authorized institutions (and UK banking groups) are required to submit returns to the Bank on a quarterly basis showing exposures to any single counterparty, or group of 'closely related' counterparties, which exceed 10 per cent of the bank's (group's) (adjusted) capital base. Moreover, such institutions (groups) are required to give the Bank prior notice of proposed transactions which would raise exposure to over 25 per cent of the (adjusted) capital base. These are the 'large exposures reporting requirements' (for further details *see* Chapter 5). In addition, the Bank has, more recently (i.e. since 1 January 1994) had to accommodate EU law in this area, in the guise of the Large Exposures Directive (EC, 1992b), which obliges the Bank to impose a limit of 25 per cent (20 per cent for exposures to associated non-financial companies) on such exposures at the individual level, with 'large' (i.e. exceeding 10 per cent of the capital base) exposures being limited in aggregate to 800 per cent of the capital base. The Directive, however, provides for a range of exemptions (full or partial) from the prescribed limits; for example, in the following cases: (1) in respect of exposures to parent undertakings which are credit institutions and which are subject either to supervision on a consolidated basis or, if located in a third country, to equivalent supervision; (2) in respect of subsidiaries which are credit institutions, financial institutions or undertakings providing ancillary banking services, and which are included in the consolidated supervision of the parent undertaking; (3) in respect of exposures incurred directly or indirectly to Zone A central governments (as defined in the Solvency Ratio Directive – *see* EC, 1989a)[146] and central banks and to the European Communities; (4) in respect of cases where the risk may be considered negligible or even zero; and (5) in respect of claims on other credit institutions with a maturity of up to one year.[147]

As noted earlier, these exemptions available under the Large Exposures Directive meant that loans made by BB&Co. to BSL were *not* subject to the large exposures reporting requirements and constraints (*see* category (2) above). Moreover, the Bank, presumably under the category (4) exemption, granted an 'informal concession' to Barings in 1993 allowing the Group's exposure to the

OSE to exceed the 25 per cent limit, without at any time imposing a limit on the concession, on the grounds that, because the exchange was backed by the Singapore government, the exposures were broadly equivalent to sovereign risk.[148] The Board concluded that the Bank made an 'error of judgement' in granting this informal concession, which facilitated the increasing transactions being undertaken by BFS, and was at fault in not imposing a limit on the concession nor clearing the decision to grant the concession with more senior management at the Bank, as required under an internal Bank guideline (HMSO, 1995a, para.13.63). Moreover, it condemned the Bank, which had been prompted by Barings for an answer in April 1994, for delaying the decision about whether or not to withdraw the 'informal concession' until 1 February 1995,[149] a delay which may have contributed to the collapse of Barings (HMSO, 1995a, para.13.66).

Once again, it is to be hoped that the trauma the Bank has suffered over this event and the implementation of the Board's recommendations in this area – *see* Exhibit 1.39, point 10 – will serve to prevent a repetition of such supervisory slackness.

Co-operation Between Supervisors

Much has been done in recent years, both unilaterally (e.g. through the establishment of formal *Memoranda of Understanding* between the Bank, on the one hand, and other financial services regulators in the UK, on the other) and multilaterally (e.g. through the G10 central bank governors' promotion of the Basle *Concordat* and *via* EU 'Single Market' legislation) to enhance co-operation and co-ordination between interested parties involved in the supervisory process. Yet whenever there is a major banking crisis, such as in the cases of BCCI and Barings, the *post mortems* inevitably reveal continuing difficulties being experienced in this area. Post-Barings, there have been a number of recommendations for improving the situation: (1) that the Bank review its existing Memoranda of Understanding with other UK regulators (HMSO, 1995a, para.14.44); (2) that the Bank should seek to agree formal Memoranda of Understanding with *overseas* regulators (HMSO, 1995a, para.14.45); (3) that the Bank should seek to extend the process of removing legal impediments to the free flow of information between supervisors to include *non-banking* regulators of financial services businesses, especially those involved in securities trading (HMSO, 1995a, para.14.46); (4) that the UK government should, if necessary, amend the Banking Act 1987 to remove any legal obstacles to the Bank sharing information with other (overseas) regulatory authorities[150] (HMSO, 1995a, para.14.61); (5) that the Bank should increase its dialogue with overseas regulators where a banking group has substantial operations overseas (HMSO, 1995a, para.14.36); (6) that a decision should be made as to which authority – home or host – should have responsibility for ensuring that internal control procedures operate effectively overseas (HMSO, 1995c, Volume III, Appendix 10, Section 5.3); (7) that an agreed international regulatory framework for securities business be developed along the lines of the various G10 initiatives (HMSO, 1995c, Volume III, Appendix 11, p. 47); and (8) that there be more co-ordination between the activities of banking and securities regulators worldwide (HMSO, 1995, Volume III, p. 45). It remains to be seen how effective such recommendations, if and when implemented, prove.

THE BANK'S RESPONSE

To the Board's Inquiry

The Bank's (first)[151] progress report on the implementation of the Board's recommendations was published in January 1996 (Bank of England, 1996a). It revealed that, of the 17 recommendations made by the Board, 15 had been reviewed in detail with the Board by end-December 1995, with two (including how a quality assurance function can be created) being considered as part of the review undertaken by Arthur Andersen (*see* note 151). All the required internal guidelines had been drafted and the recommendations had either been put into effect or were being carried forward in discussion with banks in the UK and with regulators in the UK or abroad. Accordingly:

- a framework had been established to define 'significant' risks in a banking group, combining both quantitative and qualitative yardsticks;
- all relevant banks had been asked to nominate a senior director to be responsible for the key returns;
- internal procedures for the approval of solo consolidation had been revised in July 1995 and the appropriateness of existing solo consolidation is to be reviewed on a regular basis;
- the existing programme of contact with regulators at home and abroad had been extended, with the Bank stepping up collaboration with the SFA and joining on-site visits to leading investment banks by securities regulators from the UK and the US;
- considerable progress had been made in extending the Bank's initiative of meeting the internal audit departments of banks, with the Bank concentrating initially on the major UK-incorporated entities;
- while the Bank had improved the training offered to supervisors and was in the process of building up the strength of its 'Traded Markets Team', Arthur Andersen was examining in detail the skills and use of staff in the capital markets area;

- the Bank had revised its instructions to reporting accountants to reflect the Board's view that the scope of Section 39 reports should be extended and used more flexibly and that reports should, if necessary, be commissioned outside the reporting institution itself (possibly including operations outside the UK) – the revised instructions had been sent to the major accountancy firms for comment;
- the Bank had rewritten its internal guidelines for the implementation of its large exposures policy, and was in the process of rewriting its Guidance Notes to banks on the completion of large exposures returns. (For full details *see* Bank of England, 1996a, or a review of this document in Hall, 1996c.)

To the Arthur Andersen Review

In its response to the Arthur Andersen review (Arthur Andersen, 1996), the Bank, on 24 July 1996 (Bank of England, 1996b), announced that it would reform the supervisory process and restructure its 'Supervision and Surveillance' (S&S) divisions in line with Arthur Andersen's recommendations – *see* Exhibits 1.40 and 1.41 – having accepted the proposals in their entirety (Hall, 1996e). Accordingly, the Bank agreed to: clarify the standards and processes of supervision; strengthen some of the key tools of supervision; restructure and expand its banking supervision divisions, recruiting more specialists and experienced bankers from outside; and develop further co-operation with other regulators at home and abroad. In doing so, the Bank aims to be at the leading edge of global best practice in banking supervision in all areas (Bank of England, 1996c, p. 1).

Exhibit 1.40   Arthur Andersen's summary of recommendations

---

1. The Bank should formalize and communicate a statement of objectives and standards of supervision.
2. S&S should maintain its style of supervision, characterized by its discretion, pragmatism and focus on institutions' management, systems and controls. At the same time it should increase its on-site activity and be on the 'front foot' in its relationship with institutions.
3. S&S should define a risk-based supervisory framework which provides for more consistent and better identification of the risks in an institution. Risks must then be prioritized. Supervisors' use of tools and supervisory actions should be linked more closely to the areas of material concern.
4. A number of changes should be made to enhance the consistency and usefulness of prudential information. Supervisors should supplement the

Exhibit 1.40   (continued)

information contained in prudential returns by the use of management information to support their understanding of the business, subject to procedures which confirm its accuracy.

5. The essential structure of the current Section 39 process, which addresses the adequacy of systems and controls, should be retained. A number of improvements should be made to the process immediately (e.g. in setting scopes, holding timely trilaterals and following up exceptions) while an internal review considers other measures (e.g. holding bilateral meetings, applying corporate governance provisions) which might enhance or operate in addition to the Section 39 regime.

6. Internal and external auditors should continue to be used as complementary sources of information to supervisors and should be particularly relevant in the risk assessment process. S&S should consider whether it would wish to make further, more formal, use of external auditors.

7. The efficiency and effectiveness of a number of other supervisory tools should be improved. In particular:

   • Prudential meetings should be focused on matters of significance and discussions should be forward-looking.
   • Review visits should use a more appropriate mix of line supervisors, specialists (e.g. Traded Markets Team members), and seconded accountants and bankers.
   • Supervisors should make more effective use of surveillance in their supervisory programmes.

8. The Policy Group needs to be able to achieve an optimal balance of long-term and short-term work, most significantly by reducing the volume of *ad hoc* queries from line supervisors.

9. The delegation of authority for supervisory decisions should be reviewed before being communicated in revised internal policy guidelines. Where appropriate, the guidance should reflect the risk and complexity of the institutions. In addition, the process whereby institutions' appeals against supervisory decisions are heard and resolved should be clearly defined.

10. The current approach and commitment to regulatory co-operation should be maintained.

11. The Bank's approach to supervising EEA and non-EEA banks with branches in the UK should be clarified and communicated, both internally and externally.

12. S&S should make more effective use of information technology to enhance the efficiency of supervision, in particular to capture, manage, analyse and present the wide range of supervisory information.

13. Training should be an integral part of supervisors' career and personal development. S&S should develop a core curriculum to ensure it has a good base level of knowledge and competence amongst its staff and the right mix of management, interpersonal and technical skills (both in supervision and in markets). It should also encourage informal and on-the-job learning.

14. S&S needs to create a more stimulating working environment. In particular, there needs to be a programme of cultural change, low-value tasks should be re-engineered to maximize the value of existing staff and increase job satisfaction, and the level of information-sharing across peer groups should be significantly improved.

15. The core skills within S&S need to be clearly defined and supplemented with the hire or inward secondment of specialists from outside the Bank.

16. Experience levels within S&S need to be significantly increased.

17. The organizational structure within S&S should be revised to expand the number of divisions and include the formation of an Operations Division which will have responsibility for data analysis, support management, training, administration and information technology.

18. The number of staff resources needs to be increased to implement successfully our recommendations. The increase in line resources needs to be carefully planned and allocated according to the size, complexity and risk of S&S's supervisory constituency.

19. A model for the operation of quality assurance as a management function has been defined and tested. It should be headed by an external recruit, reporting to the Director for S&S.

Source: Arthur Andersen, 1996, The 'Attachment'.

A significant move to accommodate one of Arthur Andersen's recommendations came in February 1997 when the Bank published a booklet containing three papers on the 'Objectives, Standards and Processes of Supervision' (Bank of England, 1997b). This met Arthur Andersen's demands for the development of a clear statement of objectives and standards of supervision, and clarification of how the standards and processes of supervision are linked to the objectives. (For an assessment of the paper on the 'Objectives of Supervision' *see* Taylor, 1997.) This followed earlier moves to review the 'Section 39' process (Bank of England, 1997c), to boost the number of staff employed on supervision,[152] to enhance their training (based around a 'core curriculum') and to allow them to spend more time in the supervisory wing of the Bank[153] and on secondment to outside institutions.[154] Moreover, spending on information technology had been substantially increased, and risk-based

Exhibit 1.41 The proposed new organizational structure for S&S

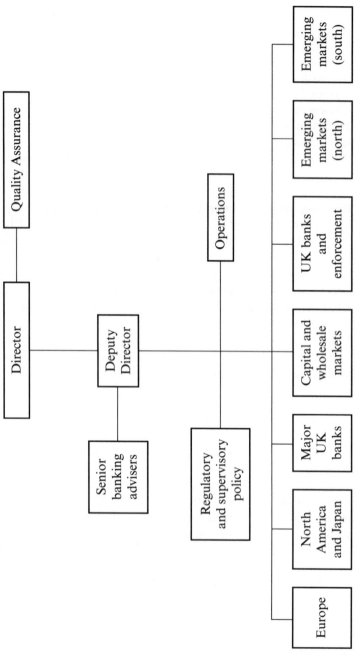

supervision enhanced using Arthur Andersen's 'RATE' (Risk, Assessment, Tools (of supervision) and Evaluation) model (*see* Hall, 1996e).

Then, in March 1997, the Bank announced that it had appointed two (later revised to three – four were planned) senior banking advisers – the so-called 'grey panthers' – to boost the number of experienced staff employed within supervision. They will be used as 'reference points' to assess, for example, whether the Bank's risk assessment findings are consistent with what they would expect given their knowledge of the banks' operations. 'Experienced hires', aged between 30 and 35 and with between five and seven years' experience, were also being sought. It was hoped that the expansion in size of the supervisory wing, and the increase in its standing, would boost overall morale in the supervisory wing of the Bank.

Later the same month, the Bank issued for consultation a paper outlining its plans for a new framework for banking supervision for UK-incorporated institutions (Bank of England, 1997d). Supervision is to become more risk-focused. Riskier banks will be reviewed more frequently. Banks will be assessed more systematically according to six different types of risk, including the inherent riskiness of their business. There will be more on-site visits, and talks will be held with a wider range of bank staff. Each business unit responsible for more than 5 per cent of a bank's revenue, pre-tax profits or capital, or any other unit posing significant risk to the group, will be studied in more detail. Stronger emphasis will be placed on the quality of internal controls. And greater efforts will be made to examine banking groups according to the way they are actually managed rather than according to their legal corporate structure. Many of these changes were recommended by Arthur Andersen.

The Bank's thinking on risk-based supervision was also taken a stage further when, in July 1997, it published a consultative paper on the approach it intended to take towards the supervision of non-EEA banks (Bank of England, 1997e). A 'SCALE' (SChedule 3 Compliance Assessment, Liaison and Evaluation) framework is developed in this paper to be used for assessing whether or not non-EEA banks meet the minimum criteria for authorization and whether their UK branches meet UK standards of practice. Increased communication with home supervisors is also anticipated.

Following testing of the RATE and SCALE frameworks on actual banks during 1997, the new frameworks were formally adopted for use with all banks in 1998.

Finally, in August 1997, the Bank revealed that it had appointed a head of the Quality Assurance Unit, set up on the recommendation of Arthur Andersen in 1996.

Notes: Part I

1. London and Scottish clearing banks, discount houses, finance houses and merchant banks were all represented by their own association.
2. The London and Scottish clearing banks, among others, had long since relinquished exemption and those still taking advantage of it, notably some accepting and discount houses, were forced to abandon the practice of maintaining hidden reserves under new EC legislation (*see* note 106).
3. Prior to 1967, exemption was confined to those banking and discount companies with Schedule 8 exemption under the Companies Act 1948.
4. The licensing provisions of the Moneylenders Acts were later repealed and replaced by provisions incorporated within the Consumer Credit Act 1974.
5. It is unnecessary at this juncture to elaborate further on capital adequacy assessment (e.g. to define the capital base) as current practice is covered in detail in Part II.
6. As defined in official statistics and usually taken to subsume overseas banks, consortium banks and other British banks.
7. Although the application of a *minimum* (rather than an average) requirement undermined somewhat its liquidity-enhancing role.
8. Hire-purchase terms control, however, resurfaced later in the 1970s, meeting its eventual demise in 1982.
9. The operation was co-ordinated by a Committee comprising senior representatives of the Bank of England and the English and Scottish clearing banks. The Chairmanship resided with the Deputy Governor of the Bank of England.
10. The recycling of funds to solvent institutions (the other criteria used in allocating lifeboat funds are set out in Bank of England 1978, pp. 233–9) was aided by the switch of non-bank wholesale depositors from the fringe banks to the clearing banks, the 'flight to quality' enhancing the latter group's ability to participate fully in the lifeboat.
11. Colloquially termed the 'Cooke Committee' after its first Chairman, Peter Cooke, of the Bank of England.
12. The principle of consolidation, whereby the risks undertaken by the banking group as a whole are assessed by the supervisor of the parent bank,

had been recommended by the Committee in 1976 and formally agreed by the G10 governors in 1978.

13. Following the collapse of BAH in July 1982, neither the parent nor host regulatory authority, the Bank of Italy and the Banking Commissioner in Luxembourg, respectively, were willing to offer restitution to creditors of BAH. The former authority took the view that the Vatican's bank, the Instituto per le Opere di Religione, was morally responsible as the alleged controller of a number of Panamanian companies which had received loans from BAH subsidiaries and having issued letters of comfort to the lenders. The Luxembourg authority similarly disclaimed responsibility on the grounds that BAH was not a bank as it did not take deposits from the general public.

14. This might involve outright prohibition of certain activities or a requirement that a 'dedicated capital' approach be adopted towards the allocation of capital. This latter approach is common in the field of securities operations, for example, in the UK primary gilt market.

15. Under Section 40 of the Act, overseas deposit-taking intermediaries were also allowed to establish representative offices in the UK, provided they notified the Bank within one month of their establishment; but such offices were not authorized to accept deposits. Rather, they were expected to act solely in the promotion of their parents' banking activities. Moreover, despite the wording of Section 40, the Bank expected to be consulted in advance of the establishment of a representative office and also sought assurance that the parent supervisory authority had been informed prior to the move.

16. The Trustee Savings Bank, following reorganization, and the National Girobank later lost this exemption on becoming 'fully fledged' banks.

17. All prospective applicants had to provide the Bank with completed questionnaires covering the nature of the applicant's business, or proposed business, and the detailed career histories of its managers, controllers and directors. (In the case of applicants from overseas institutions (i.e. branches of foreign banks), the Bank also sought reassurance from the parent supervisory body that the institution was financially sound and its management 'fit and proper'). In most cases, follow-up interviews were then held with senior management to obtain a deeper insight into the nature of the institutions' business operations.

   In the case of applications from foreign subsidiaries and consortium banks, the Bank sought letters of comfort, in an attempt to extend shareholder responsibility beyond that arising from limited liability status, from any institution or person controlling at least 15 per cent of the voting power of the bank. Similar assurances were also sometimes sought from controlling third parties.

18. These requirements also applied to recognized banks.

19. Prior to 1985, meetings with the managers of UK branches of overseas banks had been held on an annual basis but, following fears that some such branches were lending money to their home country effectively to finance balance of payments deficits, in June 1984 the Bank announced that, henceforth, discussions, focusing on liquidity, foreign exchange exposures, asset quality, and management control and information systems, would be held more frequently. Reporting requirements were also stiffened by extending the range of information required in statistical returns to include large deposits and exposures and branch profitability, as is demanded of UK-incorporated banks.

20. It took a Monopolies and Mergers Commission report to stop the proposed takeover of the Royal Bank of Scotland by the HongKong and Shanghai Banking Corporation in 1982 as the Bank of England's opposition to the takeover went unheeded by the foreign predator. Ironically, a tie-up between the same foreign bank and the ailing domestic Midland Bank received official approval, indeed encouragement, some years later (in 1987). This policy persisted until 1992, when the HongKong Bank successfully bid for Midland.

21. The National Girobank and Trustee Savings Banks were later brought into the Scheme on their transition to fully fledged banks. Overseas institutions, however, could gain exemption from the Scheme (this dispensation was ended in October 1987, when the new Banking Act took effect) if they could satisfy the Treasury that their home authorities provided at least as good a level of protection to the owners of the deposits made in their UK offices.

22. In the event, Arthur Young paid £25 million to the Bank in an out-of-court settlement in October 1988, at the same time dropping its claim against the Chancellor. (Its counter-claim against the Bank had been dismissed by the courts in July 1987 and, in February 1989, it paid a further £24.25 million to Johnson Matthey plc in another out-of-court settlement.)

    The payment to the Bank, together with the subsequent receipt of dividends from Minories Finance (the successor to JMB), allowed the Bank to retrieve its 'investment' and to reimburse fully the banks which participated in the rescue operation.

23. The Bank had not discovered any *prima facie* evidence of fraud, nevertheless, the City of London police were called in to investigate in July 1985. Since that date one former executive has been jailed for theft from JMB (but this had nothing to do with the collapse of the bank). Two businessmen have also been jailed for perpetrating fraud against JMB (the case against a former director of JMB was dropped on the advice of the Solicitor General in September 1988) and another for committing perjury.

24. This is not to say that the Bank was previously devoid of powers. Under Section 16 of the Banking Act 1979 the Bank could require a licensed institution to provide information and an accountant's report on that information or to produce its books and papers. Moreover, under Section 17 it could appoint qualified persons to investigate and report on a recognized bank or licensed institution when depositor interests appeared to warrant it. In the wake of the JMB affair, these powers were more frequently used – seven times during the 1985/86 financial year and on five occasions during 1986/87, for example.

25. The Committee suggested that late submissions prompt immediate action from the Bank in the form of a visitation or, perhaps, an inspection of the books. Partly as a result, in 1986 the Bank introduced computerized tracking of the reporting records of banks, which directly led to 74 institutions being asked to improve their reporting standards during 1986/87.

26. The first outlined the main changes to the Banking Act 1979 suggested or implied by the Committee and highlighted the areas in which the Bank's supervisory powers might be strengthened. The second covered the Bank's proposals for enhancing control over large credit exposures. The third contained proposals for establishing a regular dialogue between supervisors and bank auditors.

27. The Review Committee's suggestion that the Bank be given access to the auditor's 'management letter', which details the auditor's criticisms of the bank's controls and accounting records, was not taken on board.

28. An alternative option, involving the mandatory auditing of prudential returns, has been deemed 'cost-ineffective'.

29. To relax the confidentiality constraints on the Bank, amendments to Section 19 of the Banking Act 1979 were needed. And to deal with the problem of client confidentiality for auditors, legislation was required to override the express or implied terms in the contract between the bank and its auditors which might be taken to prevent a dialogue occurring between the auditors and the Bank.

30. The government acceded to the demands of the accountancy profession and dropped its earlier proposal to impose such a duty upon bank auditors. While the provision of a right rather than a duty helps to deal with the problem of the Bank being deluged with bits of paper as auditors seek to cover themselves against possible negligence claims by the Bank, and preserves, to a degree, the nature of the previous auditor/client relationship, auditors will nevertheless be susceptible to court action initiated by third parties. For example, depositors and other bank creditors may still be able to sue the auditor for damages if disclosures made to the Bank result in the former incurring financial loss. Moreover, it is still possible, though

unlikely, that the Bank could sue for negligence should auditors fail, erroneously in the eyes of the Bank, to exercise that right. (In the light of the BCCI affair – *see* Chapter 11 – the law was changed to transform the auditors' right into a duty.)

31. The accountancy profession also drew up guidelines on the audit of banks, the reports auditors have to produce and the relationship between auditors and reporting accountants under the new Act.

32. Pending the issue of a formal Exposure Draft on bank auditors. (This eventually materialized – 'Auditing Guideline, Banks in the UK' – in February 1988, being published in its final form in March 1989.)

33. The Bank also issued a 'notice' on the subject: *The Bank of England's Relationship with Auditors and Reporting Accountants* (BSD/1987/4) (Bank of England, 1987b).

34. This compares with the previous requirements of £250,000 for a licensed deposit-taker and £5 million for a recognized bank. To use the word 'bank' in its title, however, a UK-incorporated institution has to possess at least £5 million of paid-up share capital and/or undistributable reserves, unless it used a banking name immediately prior to the 1987 Act coming into force or unless it is among those institutions which were forced to drop their banking names following authorization under the 1979 Act. This latter group are now allowed to resurrect their previous names without being expected to satisfy the new requirement.

35. Special treatment is given to subsidiaries of UK banks and to UK branches of overseas banks; discount houses and money funds lie outside the scope of this policy. For full details *see* Chapter 20.

36. Exceptions to the general rule are covered in Part II.

37. Submissions to the Bank following the Leigh-Pemberton Report proposal to require all banks to establish audit committees and appoint finance directors had emphasized the very high costs that this would impose on the smallest banks. As a result, there is no legal requirement to do so. (An amendment to the Banking Bill making the establishment of audit committees with a majority of non-executive directors compulsory was, in fact, carried in February 1987 but subsequently withdrawn.) However, the Bank is committed to the principle that 'unless there are sound reasons to the contrary, *all* authorised institutions should appoint at least one non-executive director to undertake some audit committee functions'. The Bank's views were set out in a consultative paper issued in January 1987 – 'The role of audit committees in banks' – which, in brief, stressed the importance of audit committees (a subcommittee of the board of directors, usually chaired by a non-executive director) in ensuring that 'management is performing satisfactorily in the areas of accounts, records, controls, systems and compliance'. The Bank determines the appropriate number

of non-executive directors to sit on the committee on a case-by-case basis, paying due regard to the costs involved, most especially for small institutions.

38. The only other notable provision included in the Banking Bill was a proposal to allow the Treasury to block persons proposing to become shareholder controllers (i.e. to control 15 per cent or more of an institution's voting power) of UK-incorporated authorized institutions where such persons are from a country that does not offer reciprocal access to UK institutions. This was a sop to those banks, backed by the Bank, which had called for the Bank to be given a power of veto, on national interest grounds, over the ownership of (more than 5 per cent of) bank shares. Additionally, however, the Bill was amended to require persons becoming 'significant shareholders' (i.e. those entitled to exercise, or control the exercise of, between 5 and 15 per cent of an institution's voting power) to notify the Bank; the old notification point was at the 15 per cent level. The original version of the Bill only required those proposing to become shareholder controllers or those existing shareholder controllers proposing to raise their shareholdings over 50 per cent or over 75 per cent to give *advance* notice to the Bank. In the latter case, the Bank is empowered to object only on prudential grounds, that is, if the persons concerned are not deemed 'fit and proper'. (For developments since October 1987, *see* Chapter 23.)

39. In addition to the Basle Committee of Supervisors, a number of other agencies are involved in international supervisory co-operation. They include, *inter alia*, the G10's Standing Committee on Euromarkets, the Banking Advisory Committee to the European Commission, the Contact Group of Supervisors from the member states of the EC, the Committee on Financial Markets of the Organization for Economic Co-operation and Development (OECD), the Offshore Group of Supervisors and the Commission of Latin American and the Caribbean Supervisory and Inspection Organizations. And, where issues of securities business regulation are concerned, close liaison takes place between the European Commission, the Basle Committee and the International Organization of Securities Commissions (IOSCO).

40. Effective supervision on a consolidated basis, as proposed by the Basle Committee in 1976 and endorsed by the G10 governors in 1978, would also secure this objective.

41. Defined as one which can be used to meet current losses while leaving banks able to continue operating on a 'going concern' basis.

42. This problem was eventually resolved by allowing 45 per cent of such unrealized gains to rank as 'Tier 2' capital under the RIS proposals – *see* Exhibit 1.8.

43. This includes Belgium, Canada, France, Germany, Italy, Japan, the Netherlands, Switzerland, the UK, the US and Sweden.
44. Again, reflecting perceptions of relative credit risk only.
45. For the purposes of meeting the minimum capital standard, the total of supplementary elements should not exceed the total of core capital. Within supplementary capital, there are separate sublimits on general provisions and term debt – *see* Exhibit 1.8.
46. These materialized in July 1988. The final document incorporated the following major amendments to the original:

    1. To placate US banks in the main, perpetual preferred stock may be counted as core capital provided there is no obligation to make up for interrupted dividend payments.
    2. The risk weighting attached to debt instruments issued by the 24 full members of the OECD plus those countries (in effect, adding only Saudi Arabia) which have arrangements with the International Monetary Fund (IMF) through the General Agreement to Borrow was reduced – to zero.
    3. The reduced 50 per cent weighting applied to mortgages on owner-occupied buildings was extended to include non-owner-occupied buildings (including homes for rent) as well.

    Finally, to placate the West Germans, who had argued that the capital base should be confined to equity capital and disclosed reserves alone, the final communiqué included a statement saying that further work would be done on the issue of how to define capital.
47. Representing an extension and refinement of the old ones.
48. The Report argued that netting arrangements for both interbank payment orders and forward-value contractual commitments, such as foreign exchange contracts, have the potential to improve both the efficiency and stability of interbank settlements by not only reducing costs but also credit and liquidity risks, provided that certain conditions are met. It concluded, *inter alia*, that some form of bilateral netting was likely to be legally effective in each G10 country, and that multilateral netting of forward foreign exchange contracts through a central counterparty was likely to be legally enforceable in those countries.
49. It was expected that the proposals would be implemented fairly quickly after the expiry of the consultation period at the end of 1993. In the event, the accord was duly amended in July 1994 to accommodate the agreed recommendations. Under the accord, the new arrangements relate only to 'internationally active' banks; national supervisors retain the discretion as to whether or not to extend their application to other banks.

50. For those cases where netting arrangements had been recognized prior to adoption of the amended accord (i.e. prior to July 1994), supervisors must determine whether any additional steps, consistent with the new requirements, are necessary to enable them to be satisfied of the legal validity of the arrangements.

51. A 'walkaway clause' is a provision which permits a non-defaulting counterparty to make only limited payments, or no payment at all, to the estate of a defaulter, even if the defaulter is a net creditor.

52. Supervisors were asked to ensure that the add-ons are based on effective rather than apparent notional amounts.

53. For the purposes of calculating potential future credit exposure to a netting counterparty for forward foreign exchange contracts and other similar contracts in which notional principal is equivalent to cash flows, notional principal is defined as the net receipts falling due on each value date in each currency. The reason for this is that offsetting contracts in the same currency maturing on the same date will have lower potential future exposure as well as lower current exposure.

54. The concession was granted because most counterparties in these markets, particularly for long-term contracts, tend to be first class names. The Committee, however, keeps a close eye on the credit quality of participants in these markets and reserves the right to raise the weights if average credit quality deteriorates or if loss experience increases.

55. For the purposes of calculating the credit exposure to a netting counterparty for forward foreign exchange contracts and other similar contracts in which notional principal is equivalent to cash flows, the original credit conversion factors could be applied to the notional principal, which would be defined as the net receipts falling due on each value date in each currency. In no case, however, could the reduced factors be applied to net notional amounts.

56. The main differences between the proposals contained in the consultation document of July 1994 and the definitive statement of April 1995 are as follows:

    1. The Committee believes that neither approach is likely to systematically bias the results of the overall capital calculation; thus supervisors will have the discretion (on the condition that the method chosen by an institution is used on a consistent basis) to allow institutions to calculate the 'net to gross ratio' (NGR) – *see* the text – on either a counterparty-by-counterparty basis or on an aggregate basis.

    2. The Committee accepted the argument that the original proposal of an NGR weight of 0.5 in the formula – *see* the text – significantly

understated the reduction in potential exposure resulting from legally valid bilateral netting arrangements and, accordingly, raised the weight to 0.6.

3. Taking on board the view that the treatment of equity contracts with automatic zero value reset provisions first proposed should be extended to all contracts in the matrix, the Committee finally concluded that the residual maturity of contracts covered by the expanded matrix may be set equal to the time until the next reset date if the following conditions are met: (a) the contract is structured to settle outstanding exposure following specified payment dates; and (b) at these specified dates, the terms of the contract are reset such that the market value is zero. (However, in the case of *interest rate* contracts with remaining maturity of more than one year that meet the above criteria, the add-on factor will be subject to a floor of 0.5 per cent to ensure that the capital charge for such a contract is never zero.)

4. The Committee conceded that, based on additional work, it would be reasonable to reduce the add-ons for contracts in 'other commodities' of less than one year remaining to maturity from 12 per cent to 10 per cent.

5. Consistent with the approach adopted in the relevant EU legislation (i.e. in the Solvency Ratio Directive – EC (1989a)), the Committee decided to modify the residual maturity structure employed in the expanded matrix to include the last day of the year – the classifications to be used are thus 'one year or less', 'over one year and up to and including five years' and 'over five years'. (N.B. The same treatment is to be adopted in respect of the add-on matrix applicable to banks adopting the original exposure method.)

57. The current exposure method *has* to be employed in respect of forwards, swaps, purchased options and similar derivative contracts based on equities, precious metals except gold or other commodities. The original exposure method, if allowed, can only be adopted in respect of interest rate, exchange rate and gold contracts.

58. If the NGR is calculated on an aggregate basis, net negative current exposures to individual counterparties cannot be used to offset net positive current exposures to others: that is, for each counterparty, the net current exposure used in calculating the NGR is the maximum of the net replacement cost or zero. Also, the NGR must be applied individually to each legally enforceable netting arrangement so that the credit equivalent amount will be assigned to the appropriate counterparty risk weight category.

59. As noted earlier, this was only possible until the introduction of market risk-related capital requirements (although the Basle Committee also sanctioned an additional transitional period of up to 12 months if national supervisors so desired) and could only be adopted in respect of interest rate, exchange rate and gold contracts.
60. The only changes introduced in the Basle Committee's 1995a paper compared with its 1993a paper were that gold contracts could be treated in the same way as exchange rate contracts, and that the maturity classification system now adopted includes the last day of the year in each time band – *see* note 56, part (5).
61. Simulations conducted by market participants suggested that multilateral foreign exchange netting would reduce replacement costs by about 80–85 per cent for a given set of transactions conducted in the absence of netting.
62. For example, losses could be allocated in proportion to a measure – such as notional bilateral exposures – of the surviving members' bilateral relationships to the defaulting member.
63. For a clearing house that, on a daily basis, marks all outstanding contracts to market, collects from its members daily losses and pays out to its members daily gains (i.e. collects and pays variation margin), the capital treatment would be consistent with that of exchange-traded instruments – no capital charge would be levied. If, however, the clearing house requires its members to collateralize fully or partially potential losses but does *not* collect or pay variation margin, the standard treatment of collateral under the accord would apply.
64. A default by the clearing house, arising from its inability to meet a participant's net claims or its loss of some or all of the collateral posted by an out-of-the-money participant, is likely to be associated with operational risks, mismanagement or fraud. Such risks are not addressed by the accord, in either a multilateral or non-multilateral setting. Rather, in the case of the former, they should be addressed through the process of approval and oversight of the multilateral netting scheme and through an on-going adherence to sound risk management practices.
65. This involves the clearing house in determining, on a daily basis, the loss it would incur if a participant failed, allocating loss among the surviving participants according to a pre-established loss allocation formula, and notifying each participant of its exposure *vis-à-vis* every other participant in the system.
66. Such as allowing the clearing house to use its own simulations as the basis for setting the capital requirements for potential future exposure.
67. In practice, a risk weight of 20 per cent will normally apply – *see* Exhibit 1.9.

68. If, however, the participant's exposure to the clearing house is subject to a fixed limit (e.g. a net debit cap) and the absolute level of collateral is equal to or greater than this limit, then the capital charge for potential future exposure may be waived.

69. There is a danger, however, that (as for the accord) perverse outcomes, involving potentially destabilizing risk assumption, may result (*see* Hall, 1994a).

70. The final version, issued in January 1996, differed only to the extent that it allowed greater flexibility on the specification of model parameters for those banks allowed to use internal models – *see* the text – and gave greater recognition to diversified portfolios (*see* Hall, 1996b).

71. Apart from the limitations and restrictions applying to the use of such subordinated debt explained in the text below, the Committee also considered retaining the current rule in the accord that 'Tier 1' capital (*see* Hall, 1989), calculated on a consolidated basis, must account for at least half of the capital base. This would mean that the sum of 'Tier 2' and 'Tier 3' (the newly authorized type) capital would be restricted to the size of a bank's holdings of Tier 1 capital. In its proposals of April 1995, however, the Committee decided to leave the application of such a rule to national discretion. The rules limiting eligible Tier 2 capital to a maximum of 100 per cent of aggregate Tier 1 capital, and long-term subordinated debt to 50 per cent of aggregate Tier 1 capital, remain, however.

72. These conditions are designed to ensure that, if circumstances demand, such instruments are capable of becoming part of an institution's permanent capital, and thus would be available to absorb losses. As Dale (1994) has pointed out, however, the 'lock-in' clause preventing repayment of principal and interest is never likely to be activated because it would be tantamount to defaulting, a perilous course of action for any (deposit-taking) intermediary to take.

73. The treatment proposed would apply to equities and all instruments which exhibit market behaviour similar to equities, including equity warrants, convertibles, options on equities, commitments and other rights to buy or sell equity securities, derivative products, equity indices and index arbitrage. Non-convertible preference shares, however, are excluded and subject to the debt securities requirements – *see* the text.

74. However, if, in the future, wider convergence with securities regulators can be achieved, it is proposed that national authorities be allowed to retain the discretion to continue to apply a 'comprehensive approach' (i.e. one that combines specific and general market risks in a single risk charge), provided that the application of such an approach would produce, in all circumstances, capital charges which are at least as great

as those which would result from the application of the building-block methodology.

75. The figure reflects analysis of the price volatility of the principal equity indices in the major markets.

76. Although national regulators are empowered to apply a positive specific risk weight to securities issued by certain foreign governments, especially if the securities are denominated in a currency other than that of the issuing government.

77. Including, at national discretion, local and regional governments subject to a zero credit risk weight in the Basle accord.

78. To include securities issued by public sector entities and multilateral development banks, plus other securities that are:

    1. rated 'investment grade' by at least two credit-rating agencies specified by the relevant supervisors;
    2. rated 'investment grade' by one rating agency and not less than investment grade by any other rating agency specified by the supervisor (subject to supervisory oversight);
    3. unrated, but deemed to be of comparable investment quality by the bank, *and* the issuer has securities listed on a recognized stock exchange (subject to supervisory approval).

    The application of these qualifying criteria has to be monitored by supervisors.

    National authorities also have the discretion to include in this category debt securities issued by banks in countries which are implementing the accord, but subject to the proviso that they take prompt remedial action if an institution fails to meet such requirements.

79. This involves taking into account the exact coupon of each bond, rather than an assumed 8 per cent rate, and calculating duration according to the precise residual maturity of the instrument rather than the mid-point of a time band – for full details *see* Basle Committee, 1995b, 'Planned Supplement to the Capital Accord to Incorporate Market Risks', pp. 13–14.

80. Opposite positions of the same amount in the same issues, whether actual or nominal, can be omitted from the reporting framework because they incur no interest rate risk. Similarly, 'closely matched' swaps, forwards, futures and forward rate agreements (FRAs) can be excluded if they satisfy the conditions laid down in Basle Committee, 1995b, *ibid.*, paras 20–22, pp. 15–16.

81. 'Duration' is a concept designed to measure the price sensitivity of debt securities to changes in interest rates. In mathematical terms, it is derived as follows:

$$D = \frac{\sum_{t=1}^{m}\left(\dfrac{tCt}{(1+r)^{t}}\right)}{\sum_{t=1}^{m}\left(\dfrac{Ct}{(1+r)^{t}}\right)}$$

where r = yield to maturity;
         Ct = cash payment in time t;
         m = total maturity.

The 'modified duration' of a debt instrument = $\dfrac{D}{(1+r)}$.

82. The duration of a bond, although primarily influenced by its maturity, is also influenced by its coupon. As a result, adjustments need to be made before slotting bonds with high price volatility (e.g. zero coupon bonds and deep discount bonds) into the maturity ladder. The proposed treatment is to, in effect, convert low coupon bonds into the equivalent of 8 per cent bonds (with low coupon bonds being defined as bonds with a coupon of less than 3 per cent), with higher risk weights attaching to low coupon bonds of a comparable maturity to bonds with a coupon greater than 3 per cent, especially once residual maturities exceed 12 years.

83. Greater recognition is given to hedging for offsets taking place within the same time zone than for offsets between different zones.

84. Note, however, that no vertical or horizontal offsetting between 'high-yield' debt securities and other debt securities is allowed unless such high-yield debt securities are subjected to a specific risk weight in excess of 8 per cent.

85. The original Basle Committee proposal was 150 per cent.

86. Separate reporting ladders have to be used for each currency, except for those in which business is insignificant, and capital charges have to be calculated separately for each currency, with no offsetting between positions of opposite sign.

87. No offsetting is allowed between positions in different currencies. However, fully matched positions in identical instruments with exactly the same issuer, coupon, currency and maturity are excluded from the reporting framework. Moreover, 'closely matched' positions in the same

category of instrument may be exempt from the application of the disallowance factors if the following conditions hold:

1. the positions relate to the same underlying instruments;
2. the positions are of the same nominal value;
3. the positions are denominated in the same currency;
4. in the case of futures, the offsetting positions on the notional or underlying instruments to which the futures contract relates are for identical products and mature within seven days of each other;
5. in the case of swaps and FRAs, the reference rate (for floating rate positions) is identical and/or the coupon (for fixed rate positions) 'closely' matched (i.e. within 15 basis points);
6. in the case of swaps, FRAs and forwards, the next interest-fixing date or, for fixed coupon positions or forwards, the residual maturity, corresponds with the following limits:

   - less than one month hence: same day;
   - between one month and one year hence: within 7 days;
   - over 1 year hence: within 30 days.

88. Although the majority of interest rate-sensitive off-balance-sheet instruments (e.g. interest rate and currency swaps, FRAs, forward foreign exchange contracts and interest rate futures and options) relate to an underlying or notional underlying security which does not bear an identifiable specific risk, and hence do not incur a specific risk charge, this is not true of all such instruments. Accordingly, in the case of futures and options contracts where the underlying is a debt security, or an index representing a basket of debt securities, a specific risk charge would apply, based on the credit risk of the issuer (as explained in the text).
89. The more complex approach outlined in the Committee's first set of proposals was referred to as the 'simulation' method.
90. National supervisors have the discretion to exempt a bank from these capital requirements if:

1. The bank does not take foreign exchange positions for its own account.
2. Its foreign currency business (defined as the greater of the sum of its gross longs and the sum of its gross shorts in all foreign currencies) does not exceed 100 per cent of its 'eligible capital'.
3. The bank's 'net open position', as defined in the text, does not exceed 2 per cent of its 'eligible capital'.

91. Forward currency positions would normally be valued at current spot rates but banks are allowed to use net present values derived by discounting the cash flows.

92. Possible alternatives to the use of net delta values as the measure of exposure arising from options trading are discussed in section A.5 of Basle Committee, 1995b (*see* also Vlaar, 1996).

93. The same treatment can be applied to positions related to items that are deducted from a bank's capital when calculating its capital base.

94. Under the industry-wide scheme introduced on 27 August 1988, investors who suffer losses as a result of fraud or mismanagement by investment businesses operating with full authorization will be entitled to compensation of up to £48,000 – 100 per cent of the first £30,000 plus a maximum of 90 per cent on the next £20,000. The amount of compensation, however, may be scaled down if claims in any year exceed the £100 million ceiling on the fund set by the SIB.

95. Only the Secretary of State and the Department of Public Prosecutions possess prosecution powers.

96. Because of the existence of the Deposit Protection Scheme they also escape the requirements of the SIB's compensation scheme.

97. The Bank also retained supervisory responsibility for the wholesale money and foreign exchange markets.

98. Like building societies, banks are thus required, for example, to adopt the 'polarization rules' relating to the sale of life assurance, unit trust and pension products. Under these rules, a bank has to operate either as an independent intermediary, selling all but its own products, or as a company representative ('tied agent') in order to avoid obvious conflicts of interest. Both banks and building societies fought strongly for the withdrawal of the proposals, arguing that they would reduce competition for the consumer, but their efforts proved in vain. Most have, nevertheless, succeeded in evading the spirit, if not the letter, of the ruling by using their branch networks to sell their own products while their sales forces adopt the 'company representative' form of operation.

99. The SIB issued a consultation paper on the financial regulation of the capital adequacy of *overseas* institutions (including banks) with branches in the UK in October 1987. Following consultations with all interested parties, the SIB's proposals for the development of lead regulation arrangements with overseas supervisors were duly modified. The amended proposals were then commended by the Bank to the overseas banking supervisors concerned as a solution which avoided the need for overseas banks' investment businesses to be transferred to UK-incorporated subsidiaries.

Under the SIB's revised proposals, branches would be classified into three distinct groups:

1. Where the home supervisor is willing to share information and home supervision is adequate. On application from the institution concerned, the SIB would delegate financial regulation to the home supervisor.
2. Where the home supervisor is willing to share information but home supervision is evolving. Again, on application from the institution concerned, the SIB would disapply its financial regulation rules but, on this occasion, a local financial requirement (but not a branch capital requirement) would be applied to the UK branch.
3. Where the home supervisor is unwilling or unable to share information, or home supervision is inadequate, the SIB would not disapply its financial regulation rules. In most cases this would necessitate UK incorporation unless the company carried out all, or virtually all, of its business in the UK branch.

To allow time for discussion of its proposals, the SIB introduced a transitional provision, temporarily – until the end of August 1988 – exempting such overseas institutions from financial regulation. And to facilitate their acceptance, the Bank undertook to act as an intermediary in those cases where an overseas supervisor preferred, or was obliged, to report the required information to the Bank rather than direct to the SIB. Finally, the Bank agreed to the SIB's proposal that, in the case of a bank branch, the Bank should confirm to the SIB at regular reporting dates that neither the bank's liquidity nor other areas of operation gave cause for concern.

Despite the backing of the Bank, the response rate to the SIB's requests for signatures on Memoranda of Understanding calling for detailed financial information from home supervisors, and the response to its programme of visits undertaken during the second quarter of 1988, proved very disappointing. Indeed, agreement reached with many supervisors did little to change the *status quo* under which the Bank is assured at regular intervals by foreign supervisors that banks with branches in the UK are financially sound. In addition, the SIB faced defiance from the SA, which threatened unilaterally to authorize foreign banks for investment business. In the face of such hostility, the SIB relented and withdrew its threat to require the UK branches of banks whose home supervisors refused or were unable to meet its requirements to be restructured into UK-incorporated subsidiaries. Further, it extended the date at which interim authorization would cease to 1 November 1988 in the hope of receiving the outstanding Memoranda, duly signed. In the meantime, those operating with interim status did not benefit from the SIB's postponement, until October 1988, of Section 62 of the Financial Services Act – under which investors can sue firms for breaches of the rules – and were likely to lose business as a result of being excluded from the compensation scheme.

Subsequently, agreements, covering 60 firms, were secured with the US SEC (Securities and Exchange Commission), the Australian Stock Exchange and the German Federal Supervisory Office on 5 August 1988. And on 5 September, the SIB announced that it had reached agreement with eight more overseas regulatory bodies: the Reserve Bank of Australia, the Central Bank of Ireland, the Commission Bancaire of Belgium, the Nederlandsche Bank, the Canadian Superintendent of Financial Institutions, the Swiss Banking Commission, the Sydney Futures Exchange and the US Commodity Futures Trading Commission. These agreements meant that close on 150 additional firms moved to full authorization and others followed afterwards. (The EC's regulation of investment business under the Investment Services Directive and the associated Capital Adequacy Directive is discussed in Chapter 9.)

100. In certain cases, banks may alternatively choose to measure the capital requirement on their securities business in accordance with the Wholesale Markets Supervision Division's 'Grey Paper' on The Regulation of the Wholesale Markets in Sterling, Foreign Exchange and Bullion (Bank of England, 1988a). (For the changes necessitated by the EC's Investment Services Directive and Capital Adequacy Directive, *see* Chapter 9.)

101. Debt management operations were also lost to HM Treasury, which duly established a UK Debt Management Office (see HM Treasury, 1998b).

102. Initially, these were for observation purposes only, and covered the areas of solvency, profitability and liquidity (*see* Revell, 1975, Chapter 6).

103. The Committee of Credit Associations had, in fact, been established in 1980 for this purpose.

104. Commissioner Tugendhat (1985) has described the Commission's approach as 'negative harmonisation'.

105. The Directive establishes the principle that the home country authorities of banking groups must receive relevant information on the activities of all affiliates with a view to consolidating and centralizing supervision. This requirement is additional to the controls exercised by host country authorities over each local affiliate.

The Directive obliges member states to ensure that credit institutions which own, directly or indirectly, 25 per cent or more of the capital of another credit or financial institution (financial holding companies were added later under the Replacing Consolidation Directive – *see* the text) are supervised on a consolidated basis. Such supervision, which has to take place at least once a year, must be exercised by the competent authorities in the country where the head office of the credit institution owning the share capital is based. (In cases of participation in the 25–50 per cent range, there is discretion as to whether and how consolidation should be effected; beyond the 50 per cent level, however, consolidation is mandatory on either a full or *pro rata* basis.) The Directive also provides for the exchange of information between the relevant supervisory authorities to ensure the effectiveness of consolidated supervision. (Reciprocal bilateral agreements between the competent authorities of member states and non-EC countries are seen as the answer to participations in non-EC-domiciled institutions where impediments to the transfer of necessary information are encountered.)

The Directive was given effect in the UK with the publication by the Bank in March 1986 of the approach that it would adopt towards the consolidated supervision of banks (Bank of England, 1986a). Its general approach was described as follows:

> The Bank will seek to examine the capital adequacy and risk concentration of banks on a consolidated basis where this is appropriate. This will include large exposures to individual borrowers, countries and other sectoral risks. At this stage the measurement of liquidity and foreign exchange exposure on a consolidated basis for all banks is not contemplated.

The Bank's approach subsequently underwent minor amendment in March 1989 (Bank of England, 1989a) and December 1990 (Bank of England, 1990).

106. The issue of whether or not banks should be allowed to maintain hidden reserves was addressed under this Directive. The Commission concluded that, after 1 January 1993, undisclosed reserves would not be permitted, although member states were given the option of permitting certain assets to be stated at up to 4 per cent below the lower of cost and market value or, alternatively, permitting the creation of a fund for general banking risks.

107. Articles 52 and 53 provide for the rights of establishment in other member states and Articles 59 and 60 specifically endorse the principle of a free market for (financial) services.

108. The liberalization of capital movements in the Community was, of course, a prerequisite for the creation of a Single Market in financial services. The process started with the issuance of two Directives – in 1960 and 1962 – which secured a limited degree of liberalization through the enforced lifting of some restrictions on capital movements. Between 1962 and 1985, however, there were no further Directives, with some countries, such as Germany and the UK (which abolished controls completely in October 1979), relaxing controls while others tightened theirs. Then, in 1986, the

1960 Directive was amended to extend the range of capital transactions to be deregulated; and finally, in 1988, a further Directive was issued which provided for the progressive removal of the remaining capital controls by mid 1990. (Spain, Ireland, Greece and Portugal were, however, given an additional two years to effect their abolition, with Greece and Portugal being promised a further extension – until 1994/95 – should they desire it.)

Notwithstanding these developments, capital controls have not totally disappeared. This is because of the provision (Article 3) contained in the 1988 Directive (similar 'safeguards' are provided for under Article 73 of the Maastricht Treaty) which allows for the reintroduction of capital controls in a currency crisis. More precisely, currency movements adversely affecting exchange rate and monetary policies can be used to justify the imposition of temporary (i.e. up to 180 days) 'protective measures', although *prior* approval has to be obtained from the European Commission, the EC's Monetary Committee and EC central bank governors. The actions taken by Spain, Portugal and Ireland in the wake of the Exchange Rate Mechanism strains felt during September 1992, however, do not augur well for the future as *retrospective* endorsement proved to be the order of the day!

109. Member states can unilaterally widen or narrow the list of permitted activities. If they choose to narrow the list, however, they will disadvantage locally incorporated institutions, as the home country controls exercised in the more 'liberal' states will apply. (This would also be the case if home authorities exercise national discretion and apply stricter controls in areas such as capital adequacy assessment, the fitness and propriety of owners and the extent of participations by banks in non-financial businesses, etc.) Conversely, if they widen the list the new opportunities will apply to all institutions operating locally, irrespective of whether or not they are incorporated there, although host states may insist on supervising the new activities in accordance with local rules. Such credit institutions, however, would not automatically be allowed to engage in the wider range of services in other states; this would have to be sanctioned by the other states in question.

It should also be noted that, under Articles 52 and 59 of the Treaty of Rome (which deal with the freedom of establishment and provision of services), activities *not* included in the list of permitted activities may, nevertheless, be provided freely in a host country, without a new authorization or being subject to host country regulation, if the activities are duly licensed and properly supervised in the home country. Moreover, this applies to credit and non-credit institutions alike.

110. Because the Directive covers banks' securities operations, this proposal raised awkward problems for the SIB, responsible for overseeing the

regulation of investment business in the UK according to the Financial Services Act 1986. For, although agreement had been reached with the Bank on the allocation of supervisory responsibilities in respect of the investment business operations of UK-incorporated banks, the activities of the branches of overseas institutions banks and non-banks, remained subject to regulation by the SIB (*see* p. 92 for details).

The first problem arose because of the SIB's insistence (*see* note 99) that full authorization could only be granted once signed agreements – Memoranda of Understanding – had been reached with home supervisors on the basis on which prudential supervision of the branch's investment business would be exercised by the latter. Given the relative strictness of the SIB's requirements and the likely implementation of the Directive by the end of 1992, it is easy to understand the reticence of some European regulators to agree terms with the SIB.

A second set of problems also arose because of the parallel draft Directive on Investment Services in the Securities Field produced by the Commission in June 1988. Like the Second Banking Directive, it was founded on the principle that, once a firm is authorized by its home regulator, it should be free to operate throughout the EC. A major concern in the UK camp, with the largest number of non-bank securities firms out of all the European countries operating on its soil, was that implementation of the banking Directive in advance of the securities Directive would disadvantage the UK. Moreover, administration from Brussels of a reciprocity clause similar to that included in the banking Directive, possibly on a retrospective basis, again threatened the UK position. And finally, without prior agreement on the imposition of minimum standards, adoption of the home country regulation principle would, apart from putting British firms at a competitive disadvantage, threaten to undermine the stability of the financial system through 'competition in laxity'.

111. Credit institutions established before the Directive took effect had until 31 December 1996 to raise their own funds to this level.

112. The provisions cover: disclosure to the competent authorities, prior to the grant of authorization, of the identity and interests of shareholders (and members) who hold 10 per cent or more of the capital (or voting rights) of the credit institution, or who otherwise exert a significant influence over the credit institution; and prior reporting of the size of their prospective stakes to the competent authorities by shareholders and associates contemplating the acquisition of stakes in credit institutions (the same disclosure rules also cover those persons, natural or legal, intending to increase their qualified participations which would pass the 20 per cent, 33 per cent or 50 per cent of capital (or voting rights) thresholds, or which would result in the credit institution becoming their subsidiary). These

provisions ensure that supervisory authorities are informed, in timely fashion, of all major shareholdings and interests, actual and prospective, thereby allowing them time to assess the appropriateness of group structures and to ensure that major shareholders do not exercise their influence in an undesirable fashion (i.e. one which prejudices the safe and sound management of credit institutions). Supervisory authorities are able to enforce their wishes through the use of injunctions, sanctions against directors and managers, and/or suspension of voting rights.

113. The Banking Consolidated Supervision Directive (*see* above) addresses the issue of the appropriate level of participations in *financial* companies.

Under the Second Banking Co-ordination Directive: (1) a credit institution should not hold a qualifying participation (i.e. a direct or indirect holding in an undertaking representing 10 per cent or more of the capital or of the voting rights or making it possible to exercise significant influence over the undertaking's management) exceeding 15 per cent of its own funds in an undertaking which is neither a credit nor a financial institution; and (2) the total value of such participations should not exceed 60 per cent of its own funds. Exceptions to these limits are provided in stocks or shares temporarily held during a financial rescue operation, or in the course of the underwriting process, or in the institution's own name on behalf of others. If, however, the limits are exceeded in exceptional circumstances the competent authorities shall either require an increase in the volume of own funds or instruct the credit institution to take other equivalent remedial measures. Member states need not apply these limits if they require that own funds be increased to match 'excess' holdings and that such excess holdings are not included in the calculation of the solvency ratio.

114. Co-operation in respect of the establishment of branches and the free provision of services involves the imposition of a requirement that a credit institution wishing to establish a branch in another member state must first notify the authorities of its home state. Prior approval must be obtained from the home supervisor (which, in turn, will notify the host state of the institution's intentions) before such branching operations can commence. Host states can also halt such branching operations if they can demonstrate breaches of local legal provisions concerned with the protection of the 'general good'.

Supervisory co-operation is also facilitated by the provisions allowing for spot checks of branches by home authorities (host authorities, however, must be informed in advance) and for the exemption from professional secrecy obligations of information exchanges between supervisory authorities in the same or different countries.

115. Because it was planned to offer the 'single passport' benefits to all EC-incorporated banks, a problem arose in connection with third-country banks whose home supervisors did not offer reciprocal rights (on effective market access) to community banks. The Second Banking Co-ordination Directive's initial solution was to require member states to delay granting authorization (and the acquisition of participations) – even before the Directive came into effect – to subsidiaries of institutions from such countries until reciprocal arrangements were in place. (*Branches* of third-country banks operating in the EC do not enjoy the benefits of the single passport as they are not legal entities in their own right. They are subject to host country control.) In April 1989, however, it was confirmed that the Commission was only seeking so-called 'national treatment' reciprocity (i.e. that domestic and foreign firms are treated in a non-discriminatory fashion) rather than 'mirror image' reciprocity (which would require the application of identical rules in the two countries), although its desire for effective market access will still cause it to seek the elimination of non-legal barriers to entry and its commitment to further harmonization may lead it to champion the cause of deregulation in bilateral discussions with non-EC countries (especially Japan and the US). (N.B. The above reciprocity provisions are complementary to that contained in Article 58 of the Treaty of Rome which provides member states with the right to refuse recognition of an entity which is 'established' in another EC state if that entity has only a tenuous economic link with the state in which it claims to be established or if its shareholders or directors are resident outside the EC.)

116. Implementation of the provisions of the Directive was also delayed until the Directives on own funds and solvency were in operation, in recognition of the dangers that would be faced should the principle of home country control be adopted prior to the achievement of a 'levelling up' of supervisory standards in the EC.

117. The following *minimum* risk weightings are to be applied:

A. *Zero weighting*

1. Cash in hand and equivalent items.
2. Asset items constituting claims on Zone A central governments and central banks.
3. Asset items constituting claims on the European Communities.
4. Asset items constituting claims carrying the explicit guarantees of Zone A central governments and central banks.
5. Asset items constituting claims on Zone B central governments and central banks, denominated and funded in the national currencies of the borrowers.

6. Asset items constituting claims carrying the explicit guarantees of Zone B central governments and central banks, denominated and funded in the national currency common to the guarantor and the borrower.

7. Asset items secured, to the satisfaction of the competent authorities, by collateral in the form of Zone A central government or central bank securities, or securities issued by the European Communities, or by cash deposits placed with the lending institution or by certificates of deposit or similar instruments issued by and lodged with the latter.

B. *20 per cent weighting*

1. Asset items constituting claims on the European Investment Bank (EIB).

2. Asset items constituting claims on multilateral development banks.

3. Asset items constituting claims carrying the explicit guarantee of the EIB.

4. Asset items constituting claims carrying the explicit guarantees of multilateral development banks.

5. Asset items constituting claims on Zone A regional governments or local authorities, subject to Article 7.

6. Asset items constituting claims carrying the explicit guarantee of Zone A regional governments or local authorities, subject to Article 7.

7. Asset items constituting claims on Zone A credit institutions but not constituting such institutions' own funds as defined in Directive 89/299/EEC (EC, 1989c).

8. Asset items constituting claims, with a maturity of one year or less, on Zone B credit institutions, other than securities issued by such institutions which are recognized as components of their own funds.

9. Asset items carrying the explicit guarantees of Zone A credit institutions.

10. Asset items constituting claims with a maturity of one year or less, carrying the explicit guarantees of Zone B credit institutions.

11. Asset items secured, to the satisfaction of the competent authorities, by collateral in the form of securities issued by the EIB or by multilateral development banks.

12. Cash items in the process of collection.

C. *50 per cent weighting*

1. Loans fully and completely secured, to the satisfaction of the competent authorities, by mortgages on residential property which is, or will be, occupied or let by the borrower.

2. Prepayments and accrued income: these assets shall be subject to the weighting corresponding to the counterparty where a credit institution is able to determine it in accordance with Directive 86/635/EEC (EC, 1986a). Otherwise, where it is unable to determine the counterparty, it shall apply a flat-rate weighting of 50 per cent.

D. *100 per cent weighting*

1. Asset items constituting claims on Zone B central governments and central banks except where denominated and funded in the national currency of the borrower.
2. Asset items constituting claims on Zone B regional governments or local authorities.
3. Asset items constituting claims with a maturity of more than one year on Zone B credit institutions.
4. Asset items constituting claims on the Zone A or Zone B non-bank sectors.
5. Tangible assets within the meaning of assets as listed in Article 4(10) of Directive 86/635/EEC (EC, 1986a).
6. Holdings of shares, participations and other components of the own funds of other credit institutions which are not deducted from the own funds of the lending institutions.
7. All other assets except where deducted from own funds.

118. The following conversion factors are to be applied to off-balance-sheet items:

A. *Full risk, subject to a conversion factor of 100 per cent*

1. Guarantees having the character of credit substitutes.
2. Acceptances.
3. Endorsements on bills not bearing the name of another credit institution.
4. Transactions with recourse.
5. Irrevocable standby letters of credit having the character of credit substitutes.
6. Asset sale and repurchase agreements as defined in Articles 12(1) and (2) of Directive 86/635/EEC, if these agreements are treated as off-balance-sheet items pending application of Directive 86/635/EEC (EC, 1986a).
7. Assets purchased under outright forward purchase agreements.
8. Forward forward deposits.
9. The unpaid portion of partly paid shares and securities.
10. Other items also carrying full risk.

B. *Medium risk, subject to a conversion factor of 50 per cent*

1. Documentary credits issued and confirmed (*see* also medium/low risk below).
2. Warranties and indemnities (including tender, performance, customs and tax bonds) and guarantees not having the character of credit substitutes.
3. Asset sale and repurchase agreements as defined in Article 12(3) and (5) of Directive 86/635/EEC (EC, 1986a).
4. Irrevocable standby letters of credit not having the character of credit substitutes.
5. Undrawn credit facilities (agreements to lend, purchase securities, provide guarantees or acceptance facilities) with an original maturity of more than one year.
6. Note issuance facilities (NIFs) and revolving underwriting facilities (RUFs).
7. Other items also carrying medium risk.

C. *Medium/low risk, subject to a conversion factor of 20 per cent*

1. Documentary credits in which underlying shipment acts as collateral, and other self-liquidating transactions.
2. Other items also carrying medium/low risk.

D. *Low risk, subject to a conversion factor of 0 per cent*

1. Undrawn credit facilities (agreements to lend, purchase securities, provide guarantees or acceptance facilities) with an original maturity of up to and including one year or which may be cancelled unconditionally at any time without notice.
2. Other items also carrying low risk.

119. Under the *current exposure* approach, the following conversion factors are to be used in the calculation of potential future credit exposures:

Residual maturity	Interest rate contracts (%)	Foreign exchange contracts (%)
One year or less	0.0	1
More than one year.	0.5	5

If the *original exposure* approach is used, the following conversion factors should be applied to calculate the deemed credit risk equivalents:

Original maturity[1]	Interest rate contracts (%)	Foreign exchange contracts (%)
One year or less	0.5	2
More than one year but not exceeding two years	1.0	5
Additional allowance for each additional year	1.0	3

Note: 1. In the case of interest rate contracts, credit institutions may, subject to the consent of their supervisory authorities, choose either original or residual maturity.

120. Credit institutions were granted a maximum period of five years, starting from 1 January 1993, within which to bring existing exposures into line with the prescribed limits, although loans of longer maturity with contractually binding terms for the lending institution are allowed to run until maturity.
121. Insurance companies, commodities traders, pension fund managers and others, however, are not covered by the legislation.
122. Note that EU credit institutions enjoyed a competitive advantage *vis-à-vis* EU investment firms to the extent that some 'investment' services were covered by the single passport available under the Second Banking Co-ordination Directive. Such credit institutions did not need further authorization under the Investment Services Directive to engage in cross-border investment activities unless their planned activities extended beyond those covered by the Second Banking Co-ordination Directive.
123. Many member states, including Germany, failed to meet this deadline.
124. 'Locals' are firms dealing on financial futures or options exchanges either solely on an own-account basis or dealing for other members of the exchanges in question and guaranteed by a clearing member of such an exchange. 'Order-takers', as the name implies, are firms acting merely as order-takers from clients, without holding their clients' money or securities.
125. Exempted firms comprise those which provide investment services exclusively for other group companies, pension fund managers, UCITs (Undertakings for Collective Investment in Transferable securities), commodities traders, central banks of member states, insurance companies and firms which provide investment services in a manner incidental to their main professional activities. 'Locals' and 'order-takers' – *see* note 124

– which do not benefit from the single passport or other opportunities (such as access to other member states' clearing and settlement systems and regulated markets) offered by the Investment Services Directive are also exempted from these provisions.

126. Both 'locals' and 'order-takers' are exempt. Moreover, at national discretion, the 'trading book' of either a credit institution or an investment firm may be made subject to the provisions of the Solvency Ratio Directive instead of the CAD, but only if: (1) the trading book business of such an institution does not normally exceed 5 per cent of its total business; (2) its total trading book position does not normally exceed ECU 15 million; and (3) its trading book business *never* exceeds 6 per cent of its total business and its total trading book position never exceeds ECU 20 million.

127. Note that the loan books of credit institutions are also subject to the limits and restrictions imposed under the Large Exposures Directive – *see* the text. The CAD's treatment of exposures relating to the trading book replaces the provisions of the Large Exposures Directive hitherto applied for such purposes.

128. The 'trading book' of an institution is defined in Article 2(6) of the CAD and comprises:

   1. Proprietary positions in financial instruments held for resale and/or with a view to benefiting from short-term variations in price or interest rates.
   2. Positions in financial instruments arising from matched principal broking.
   3. Positions taken in order to hedge other elements of the trading book.
   4. Exposures arising from unsettled transactions in debt securities and equities, from securities paid for but not yet received ('free deliveries'), and from over-the-counter derivatives such as swaps and options.
   5. Exposures arising from repurchase agreements and securities lending which are based on securities included in the trading book.
   6. Exposures due to reverse repurchase agreements and securities borrowing transactions, provided the regulatory authorities approve.
   7. Exposures arising from services provided by the firm, in the form of fees, commission, interest, dividends and margins on exchange-traded products which relate directly to items in the trading book.

To avoid their unjustified inclusion in the trading book, which could lead to application of lighter capital requirements, the CAD requires, however, that their inclusion be based on 'objective procedures', the terms and implementation of which should be reviewed by the regulatory authorities. Moreover, exposures of type (6) are only eligible for inclusion in the trading book if: (1) the exposures are marked to market on a daily basis; (2) the collateral is adjusted in a manner acceptable to the regulatory authorities to take account of material changes in the value of the underlying securities; (3) the agreement or transaction provides automatic 'set-off' in the event of default by the counterparty; and (4) such agreements and transactions are confined to their 'accepted and appropriate use' and additional transactions, especially those not of a short-term nature, are excluded. (Conditions (1) to (3) may be waived if the agreement or transaction in question is an inter-professional one.)

129. As noted in Hall, 1995c, national discretion manifests itself in the following areas: in the choice of risk assessment methodologies available; in the choice of capital definition allowed; in the permission given, under certain circumstances, to reduce minimum capital charges below the usual minima; in the myriad ways of treating options available; in the option given to apply the Solvency Ratio Directive instead of the CAD to firms with 'negligible' trading books; and in the right given to waive consolidated supervision for *investment* firms which satisfy certain criteria.

130. Other Directives, such as the Money Laundering Directive and the Winding-Up Directive, are not considered.

131. During a five-year transitional phase this figure may be reduced, at national discretion, to ECU 15,000.

132. In fact, the Bank did try to co-ordinate a rescue – eight banks with direct interests in the outcome of the affair were asked to consider providing a £100 million standby facility – but, in the face of opposition from some of the parties invited to participate in the rescue, the Bank accepted that closure should ensue. The banks, for once, had failed to fall into line.

133. Although the Bank maintained that all of the finance arms were throughout 'trading in compliance with regulatory requirements', this did not provide much of a saving grace at the end of the day.

134. In the case of B&C, the Bank acted as lead regulator to the SIB, the SA, other self-regulating organizations, the US Federal Reserve Board and Japan's Ministry of Finance. While little criticism of this arrangement has emerged – the SIB's decision to remove BCMB's name from the approved list, for example, was taken with the Bank's full knowledge – one can but wonder if institutional rather than functional regulation would be a better way of dealing with the myriad public interest considerations which arise in connection with the regulation and supervision of highly diversified financial conglomerates.

135. In BCMB's case, nearly half of its deposits came from the deposit of clients' funds arising elsewhere in the B&C group, the remainder comprising wholesale deposits. This suggests that BCMB's deposit base

was not adequately diversified, something which the Bank is supposed to ensure under its liquidity adequacy assessment regime (*see* Chapter 17).

136. The Bank had earlier responded to the two Treasury and Civil Service Committee Reports (HMSO 1991, 1992a) on the BCCI affair. The first response, which emerged on 30 May 1992, related to the Committee's recommendations concerning the tightening up of the arrangements governing the operations of local authorities in the wholesale money markets (some stood to lose a considerable amount of money as a result of deposits made with BCCI). In its response, the Bank accepted that the London Code (*see* Chapter 5) should be revised to make it crystal clear that local authorities, like other principals in the market, are entirely responsible for their own actions and cannot rely on any advice received from brokers or other third parties. It rejected, however, the recommendation that the tape-recording of all telephone calls by money brokers and dealers be made compulsory, preferring to give a strong recommendation of such practice in the London Code.

    The Bank's response to the Second Committee Report, which emerged on 8 July 1992, is consistent with its response to the Bingham Report and so is not duplicated here.

137. Talks between the Bank, the Cabinet Office, the Home Office and the Treasury led to the establishment of a new inter-agency group with a view to providing an effective, co-ordinated response to complex fraud covering both the exchange of information between interested parties and agreement on which body should lead an investigation when malfeasance is suspected. Measures were also taken to enforce information exchanges with overseas supervisors, a move especially welcomed by those US authorities frustrated in their dealings with the Bank over BCCI.

138. In its earlier response to the Treasury and Civil Service Committee (*see* note 136 above), the Bank suggested that the power might also be employed when substantial reorganization has been undertaken by an existing banking group or when the shape of the group's business has changed over a period of years, even though the formal ownership links between the group companies might not have done.

139. Some also suggested that the Banking Act 1987 should be amended to empower the Bank to pass information to foreign investigatory bodies in order to facilitate international co-operation.

140. That is, before receipt of the Section 41 report from the auditors detailing evidence of massive and pervasive fraud.

141. This section rests heavily on Hall, 1996c.

142. Solo consolidation may be permitted by the Bank in the following circumstances (see Singapore Ministry of Finance 1995, para. 13.5 and HMSO, 1995c, Volume III, Appendix 4, para.6):

- where the subsidiary in question is at least 75 per cent owned by the parent bank;
- where the subsidiary in question is effectively managed by the parent;
- where the subsidiary in question is either funded wholly by the parent or has risk exposure only to the parent;
- where there are no potential obstacles (e.g. exchange controls, or potential legal, regulatory or fiscal obstacles) to the transfer of surplus capital to the parent;
- where there is sufficient capital in the parent bank's balance sheet to fund its investments in those subsidiaries which are to be solo consolidated (i.e. when, if the investments were to be deducted from the parent bank's capital base, the parent bank would be left with positive net worth).

143. Exposures to solo-consolidated subsidiaries are excluded from the scope of the large exposures reporting requirements imposed on authorized institutions under Section 38 of the Banking Act 1987.

144. Under the 'connected lending limit', the aggregate exposure of a solo-consolidated group to group entities which have not been solo consolidated should not exceed 25 per cent of the former's capital base. However, if the solo-consolidated group is, in effect, the treasury for the entire group, it is possible to obtain a 'Treasury Concession' from the Bank which would allow the solo-consolidated group to lend funds in excess of 25 per cent of the capital base to unconsolidated entities. These 'Concessions', however, have to be specifically allocated to the entities within the group to which such lending is to be made. In the case of the Barings Group, the Connected Lending Limit, as at 25 November 1994, stood at £77 million (i.e. 25 per cent of £309.6 million) (Singapore Ministry of Finance, 1995, para.13.10). This amount could thus be made available to any related entities, whether or not they had been allocated limits under the terms of the Treasury Concessions. In addition, Treasury Concessions amounting to £364 million were available at this date (Singapore Ministry of Finance, 1995, para.13.10), although no Treasury Concession had been specifically allocated in respect of loans to BFS. Accordingly, the solo-consolidated group's exposure to BFS should never have exceeded 25 per cent of its capital base. Baring Securities (London) Limited (BSLL), however, was allocated a limit of £85 million under the Treasury Concession; and, because it was not solo consolidated, it could borrow from external sources to the extent it required additional funds without triggering the large exposures reporting requirements. BFS took advantage of this by booking all *proprietary* exchange-traded derivatives and other

house businesses into BSLL from the beginning of 1994 (Singapore Ministry of Finance, 1995, para.13.12).

145. As reported in HMSO (1995a), Section 6, BSL's loan exposure to BFS stood at £142 million at the end of 1994, rising to £337 million by 24 February 1995. (At the latter date, group loans to BFS amounted to some £742 million, £105 million coming from BSLL and £300 million from Baring Securities Japan (BSJ), the latter funded mainly by unsecured borrowings from Japanese banks.) These exposures were supposed to represent the margin funding requirements for Barings' clients positions on SIMEX – BSL would initially put up the money to meet the margin calls and would subsequently reclaim the sums from its clients – but, in practice, reflected the exposures run by Mr Leeson's (concealed) proprietary speculative trading.

146. Basically, this includes OECD central governments plus Saudi Arabia.

147. These exemptions are similar to those applied by the Bank pre-implementation of the Large Exposures Directive (*see* Chapter 5) when, although no statutory limit applied, there was a presumption that exposures did not exceed 25 per cent of the (adjusted) capital base, other than in exceptional circumstances.

148. In the event, Barings apparently assumed the concession released it from the obligation to pre-notify such exposures and that it also applied to its exposure to SIMEX – with the result that, by February 1995, Barings' exposures to the OSE and SIMEX stood at 73 per cent and 40 per cent of group capital, respectively.

149. In the event it was withdrawn, but Barings was given further time to reduce its exposures.

150. Its reticence in providing the Singapore Inspectors with the material requested in respect of their inquiry into the collapse of BFS – *see* Singapore Ministry of Finance, 1995, Appendix 1E, pp. 162–6 – strongly suggests that the Bank is still too secretive in its dealings with outside authorities, a situation reminiscent of the rebuff initially experienced by the Manhattan District Attorney in his attempts to unravel events at BCCI.

151. The Board asked the Bank to report to it by 31 December 1995 on the progress made towards implementation of its recommendations (HMSO, 1995a, para.14.62), which had been accepted in their entirety by the Bank. A further report to the Board was proposed at the completion of the work undertaken by a consultancy team from Arthur Andersen, who were commissioned in October 1995 to conduct a review of the operation of the Bank's supervision and to make recommendations for the establishment of a 'quality assurance' function. Work on this began on 1 November 1995 and was scheduled for completion in July 1996 – *see* the text.

152. Thirty-five additional analysts were recruited between the summer of 1996 and March 1997, and around 40 further graduates were being sought in the autumn of 1997. Such recruitment was intended to increase staffing within S&S to around 485. (In the event, staffing levels only reached 434 by the end of February 1998, partly due to recruitment problems arising from a general pick-up in the recruitment market, and partly because of the adjustments necessitated by the FSAu's plans for banking supervision.)

153. Staff were henceforth to be required to work for at least four years in supervision before they could move to a job in another part of the Bank. This compared with the previous term of around two and a half years. (The transfer of supervisory staff to the FSAu in the spring of 1998, however, rendered this concern redundant.)

154. Previously, about three Bank staff were seconded at any one time to commercial banks, where they spent an average of about three months. The intention was that eventually the number of staff on secondment at any one time would rise to about five and that their period of secondment would be extended to up to one year. Outside institutions were also encouraged to second staff to the Bank.

Bibliography: Part I

Arthur Andersen (1996), *Findings and Recommendations of the Review of Supervision and Surveillance* (Arthur Andersen Review), London, July.

Bank of England (1978), 'The Secondary Banking Crisis and the Bank of England's Support Operations', *Bank of England Quarterly Bulletin (BEQB)*, London, June.

Bank of England (1981), 'Foreign Currency Exposure', *BEQB*, London, June.

Bank of England (1984), *Bank of England, Report and Accounts*, London, June.

Bank of England (1985), *Bank of England, Report and Accounts*, London, June.

Bank of England (1986a), *Consolidated Supervision of Institutions Authorised Under the Banking Act 1979* (BSD/1986/3), London, March.

Bank of England (1986b), 'Accounting and Other Records and Internal Control Systems, and the Reporting Accountants' Reports Thereon', consultative paper, London, November.

Bank of England (1987a), *Guidance Note on Reporting Accountants' Reports on Bank of England Returns used for Prudential Purposes* (BSD/1987/3), London, October.

Bank of England (1987b), *The Bank of England's Relationship with Auditors and Reporting Accountants* (BSD/1987/4), London, December.

Bank of England (1987c), 'Agreed Proposals of the United States Federal Banking Supervisory Authorities and the Bank of England on Primary Capital and Capital Adequacy Assessment' (the 'accord'), *BEQB*, London, February.

Bank of England (1988a), *The Regulation of the Wholesale Markets in Sterling, Foreign Exchange and Bullion*, Wholesale Markets Supervision Division 'Grey Paper', London, April.

Bank of England (1988b), *Banking Act Report for 1987/88*, London, June.

Bank of England (1989a), *Amendment to BSD/1986/3* (BSD/1989/2), London, March.

Bank of England (1989b), *Capital Adequacy Reform* (Form BSD1), Banking Supervision Division, London.

Bank of England (1990), *Amendment to BSD/1986/3* (BSD/1990/4), London, December.

Bank of England (1996a), 'The Board of Banking Supervision's Report on Barings: The Post-Barings Recommendations – A Report', *Press Notice*, Supervision and Surveillance Division, London, 11 January.

Bank of England (1996b), 'The Bank's Review of Supervision: Major Changes Announced', *Press Notice*, Press Office, London, 24 July.

Bank of England (1996c), *The Bank's Review of Supervision*, London, July.

Bank of England (1997a), 'International Regulatory Structure: A UK Perspective', *Bank of England Quarterly Bulletin*, May, p. 215, London.

Bank of England (1997b), *Objectives, Standards and Processes of Supervision*, London, 19 February.

Bank of England (1997c), *Banks' Internal Controls and the Section 39 Process*, consultation paper, London, February.

Bank of England (1997d), *A Risk-Based Approach to Supervision*, consultation paper, London, March.

Bank of England (1997e), *A Risk-Based Approach to the Supervision of Non-EEA Banks*, consultation paper, London, July.

Bank of England (1998), 'The Bank of England Act', *BEQB*, May, pp. 93–9, London.

Barcroft, P. (1998), 'Derivatives and Market Risk Disclosure – Leaving no Stone Unturned?', *Butterworths Journal of International Banking and Financial Law*, Vol.13, No. 4, April, pp. 131–8.

Basle Committee (1992), *Minimum Standards for the Supervision of International Banking Groups and their Cross-Border Establishments*, Basle, July.

Basle Committee (1993a), *The Supervisory Recognition of Netting for Capital Adequacy Purposes: A Consultative Proposal*, Basle, April.

Basle Committee (1993b), *The Supervisory Treatment of Market Risks: A Consultative Proposal*, Basle, April.

Basle Committee (1993c), *Measurement of Banks' Exposure to Interest Rate Risk: A Consultative Proposal*, Basle, April.

Basle Committee (1994), *Risk Management Guidelines for Derivatives*, Basle, July.

Basle Committee (1995a), *Basle Capital Accord: Treatment of Potential Exposure for Off-Balance-Sheet Items*, Basle, April.

Basle Committee (1995b), *Proposal to Issue a Supplement to the Basle Capital Accord to Cover Market Risks: A Consultative Proposal*, Basle, April.

Basle Committee (1996a), *Report of the Working Group on Minimum Standards*, Basle, October.

Basle Committee (1996b), *Interpretation of the Capital Accord for the Multilateral Netting of Forward Value Foreign Exchange Transactions*, Basle, April.

Basle Committee (1996c), *Amendment to the Capital Accord to Incorporate Market Risks*, Basle, January.

Basle Committee (1996d), *Supervisory Framework for the Use of 'Backtesting'*
  in Conjunction with the Internal Models Approach to Market Risk Capital
  Requirements, Basle, January.

Basle Committee (1997a), *Principles for the Management of Interest Rate*
  Risk: A Consultative Proposal, Basle, January.

Basle Committee (1997b), *Core Principles for Effective Banking Supervision*,
  consultative paper, Basle, April.

BIS (1987), *Proposals for the International Convergence of Capital Measurement*
  and Capital Standards, December.

BIS (1990), *Report of the Committee on Interbank Netting Schemes* (Lamfalussy
  Report), Basle, November.

BIS (1996), 'Settlement Risk in Foreign Exchange Transactions', report prepared
  by the CPSS of the central banks of the G10 Countries (Allsopp Report), Basle,
  March.

Clarotti, P. (1997), 'EU Directives and their Impact on Netting', *Journal of*
  Financial Regulation and Compliance, Vol.5, No. 2, pp. 154–62.

Cooke, W. (1982), 'The Communities and the Banks in the 1980s: Supervisory
  Aspects – A Central Banker's View', speech given at a British Bankers
  Association Seminar, London, January.

Dale, R. (1994), 'Regulating Investment Business in the Single Market', *Bank*
  of England Quarterly Review Bulletin, November, pp. 333–40.

Dale, R. (1995), 'Derivatives: The New Regulatory Challenge', *Butterworths*
  Journal of International Banking and Financial Law, January, pp. 11–17.

Department of Trade and Industry (1991), *The Single Market: Financial*
  Services, London, March.

Dimson, E. and P. Marsh (1995), 'Capital Requirements for Securities Firms',
  Journal of Finance, Vol.50, No. 3, July, pp. 821–52.

EC (1977), *Co-ordination of Laws, Regulations and Administrative Provisions*
  Relating to the Taking-up and Pursuit of the Business of Credit Institutions
  (First Banking Co-ordination Directive) (77/780/EEC), Brussels, December.

EC (1983), *Consolidated Supervision Directive* (83/350/EEC), Brussels, June.

EC (1986a), *Bank Accounts Directive* (86/635/EEC), Brussels, December.

EC (1986b), *Recommendation on 'Large Exposures'* (87/62/EEC), Brussels,
  December.

EC (1986c), *Recommendation on 'Deposit Guarantee Schemes'* (87/63/EEC),
  Brussels, December.

EC (1989a), *Solvency Ratio Directive for Credit Institutions* (Solvency Ratio
  Directive) (89/647/EEC), Brussels, December.

EC (1989b), *Co-ordination of Laws, Regulations and Administrative Provisions*
  Relating to the Taking-up and Pursuit of the Business of Credit Institutions
  (Amending Directive 77/780/EEC) (Second Banking Co-ordination Directive)
  (89/646/EEC), Brussels, December.

EC (1989c), *Own Funds of Credit Institutions* (Own Funds Directive) (89/229/EEC), Brussels, April.

EC (1989d), *Bank Accounts Directive* (89/117/EEC), Brussels, February.

EC (1991a), *Draft Capital Adequacy Directive*, Brussels, April.

EC (1991b), *Proposal for a Large Exposures Directive*, Brussels, April.

EC (1991c), *Draft Investment Services Directive*, Brussels, May.

EC (1992a), *Supervision of Credit Institutions on a Consolidated Basis* (Second Consolidated Supervision Directive) (92/30/EEC), Brussels, April.

EC (1992b), *Monitoring and Control of Large Exposures of Credit Institutions* (Large Exposures Directive) (91/121/EEC), Brussels, December.

EC (1993a), *Investment Services in the Securities Field* (Investment Services Directive) (93/22/EEC), Brussels, May.

EC (1993b), *Capital Adequacy of Investment Firms and Credit Institutions* (Capital Adequacy Directive) (93/6/EEC), Brussels, March.

EC (1994), *Deposit Guarantee Schemes* (Deposit Guarantee Directive) (94/19/EEC), Brussels, May.

EC (1995), *Post BCCI Directive* (95/26/EEC), Brussels, June.

EC (1996), *Directive Amending Directive 89/647/EEC (Solvency Ratio Directive)* (Netting Directive) (96/10/EC), Brussels, March.

Goldstein, M. (1996), *The Case for an International Banking Standard*, Institute for International Affairs, Washington, August.

Group of Thirty (1982), 'How Bankers See the World Financial Market', New York.

Hall, M.J.B. (1983), *Monetary Policy since 1971: Conduct and Performance*, London: Macmillan

Hall, M.J.B. (1987a), *Financial Deregulation: A Comparative Study of Australia and the United Kingdom*, London: Macmillan.

Hall, M.J.B. (1987b), 'UK Banking Supervision and the Johnson Matthey Affair', Chapter 1 in C. Goodhart, D. Currie and D. Llewellyn (eds), *The Operation and Regulation of Financial Markets*, London: Macmillan.

Hall, M.J.B. (1987c), 'The Johnson Matthey Affair: Have the Lessons been Learnt?', *Journal of International Securities Markets*, Vol.1, Autumn, pp. 59–71.

Hall, M.J.B. (1987d), *The City Revolution: Causes and Consequences*, London: Macmillan.

Hall, M.J.B. (1989), 'The BIS Capital Adequacy "Rules": A Critique', *Banca Nazionale del Lavoro Quarterly Review*, June, pp. 207–27.

Hall, M.J.B. (1990), 'The Financial Services Act and its Consequences for Europe', in the special edition of *Wirtschaft und Recht* on 'Capital Market Law and its Reform', Vol.42, December, pp. 211–36.

Hall, M.J.B. (1991a), 'The BCCI Affair', *Banking World*, September, pp. 8–11.

Hall, M.J.B. (1991b), 'The BCCI Affair', *Banking World*, October, pp. 11–14.

Hall, M.J.B. (1991c), 'The BCCI Affair', *Banking World*, December, pp. 8–9.

Hall, M.J.B. (1992a), 'Implementation of the BIS "Rules" on Capital Adequacy Assessment: A Comparative Study of the Approaches Adopted in the UK, USA and Japan', *Banca Nazionale Del Lavoro Quarterly Review*, No. 180, March, pp. 35–57.

Hall, M.J.B. (1992b), 'Regulation in Crisis', *mimeo*, November (an edited version appears in the December 1992 and January 1993 issues of *Banking World*).

Hall, M.J.B. (1992c), 'The BCCI Affair', *Banking World*, February, pp. 10–11.

Hall, M.J.B. (1992d), 'The BCCI Affair', *Banking World*, July, pp. 15–21.

Hall, M.J.B. (1992e), 'Towards Better Banking Regulation and Supervision', consultancy report published by the International Federation of Commercial, Clerical, Professional and Technical Employees, Geneva.

Hall, M.J.B. (1993a), 'BCCI: The Lessons for Bank Supervisors – Part 1: Deficiencies in National Supervisory Practices and Supervisory Frameworks', *International Journal of Regulatory Law and Practice*, Vol.1, No. 2, February, pp. 298–313.

Hall, M.J.B. (1993b), *Banking Regulation and Supervision: A Comparative Study of the UK, USA and Japan*, Cheltenham: Edward Elgar.

Hall, M.J.B. (1994a), 'The Measurement and Assessment of Capital Adequacy for Banks: A Critique of the G10 Agreement', Chapter 11 in C.A. Stone and A. Zissu (eds), *Global Risk-Based Capital Regulations*, Vol.1 ('Capital Adequacy'), Burr Ridge, Illinois: Irwin Publishers, pp. 270–86.

Hall, M.J.B. (1994b), 'The PIA: Stop-Gap or Lasting Solution?', *Journal of Financial Regulation and Compliance*, Vol.2, No. 4, pp. 286–313.

Hall, M.J.B. (1994c), 'BCCI and the Lessons for Bank Supervisors', Chapter 6 in *Banks, Fraud and Crime*, Proceedings of the 11th Annual Banking Law Seminar organized by the Chartered Institute of Bankers and the Centre for Commercial Law Studies, Queen Mary and Westfield College, University of London, Lloyd's of London Press Ltd., January.

Hall, M.J.B. (1995a), 'The Measurement and Assessment of Market Risk: A Comparison of the European and Basle Committee Approaches', *Banca Nazionale del Lavoro Quarterly Review*, Vol.XLVIII, No. 194, September, pp. 283–330.

Hall, M.J.B. (1995b), 'The Investment Services and Capital Adequacy Directive: Further Steps Towards Completion of the European Single Market in Financial Services', *Journal of Financial Regulation and Compliance*, Vol.3, No. 4, pp. 358–82.

Hall, M.J.B. (1995c), 'The Capital Adequacy Directive: An Assessment', *Journal of International Banking Law*, Vol.10, Issue 3, March, pp. 78–87.

Hall, M.J.B. (1995d), 'A Review of the Board of Banking Supervision's Inquiry into the Collapse of Barings: Part 1', *Butterworths Journal of International Banking and Financial Law*, Vol.10, No. 9, October, pp. 421–5.

Hall, M.J.B. (1995e), 'A Review of the Board of Banking Supervision's Inquiry into the Collapse of Barings: Part 2', *Butterworths Journal of International Banking and Financial Law*, Vol.10, No. 10, November, pp. 470–4.

Hall, M.J.B. (1995f), 'A Review of the Singapore Inspectors' Report on Baring Futures (Singapore) Pte Ltd', *Butterworths Journal of International Banking and Financial Law*, Vol.10, No. 11, pp. 525–9.

Hall, M.J.B. (1996a), 'The Revised Supervisory Treatment of Netting and Potential Exposure for Off-Balance-Sheet Items under the Basle Capital Accord', *Journal of International Banking Law*, Vol.11, No. 3, March, pp. 93–102.

Hall, M.J.B. (1996b), 'The Amendment to the Capital Accord to Incorporate Market Risk', *Banca Nazionale del Lavoro Quarterly Review*, Vol.XLIX, No. 197, June, pp. 271–7.

Hall, M.J.B. (1996c), 'The Collapse of Barings: The Lessons to be Learnt', *Journal of Financial Regulation and Compliance*, Vol.4, No. 3, pp. 255–77.

Hall, M.J.B. (1996d), 'Barings: The Bank of England's First Report to the Board of Banking Supervision', *Butterworths Journal of International Banking and Financial Law*, Vol.11, No. 3, March, pp. 128–30.

Hall, M.J.B. (1996e), 'UK Banking Supervision After the Arthur Andersen Review', *Butterworths Journal of International Banking and Financial Law*, Vol.11, No. 11, December, pp. 525–9.

Hall, M.J.B. (1997a), 'The Treatment of Multilateral Netting of Forward Value Foreign Exchange Transactions under the Basle Capital Accord', *Journal of International Banking Law*, Vol.12, No. 8, pp. 333–9.

Hall, M.J.B. (1997b), 'All Change at the Bank', *Butterworths Journal of International Banking and Financial Law*, Vol.12, No. 7, July, pp. 295–302.

Hall, M.J.B. (1997c), 'Banking Regulation in the European Union: Some Issues and Concerns', *The International Executive*, (special issue entitled 'Moving Towards Borderless Financial Markets'), Vol.39, No. 5 pp. 675–705.

Hall, M.J.B. (1998), 'BCCI and the Lessons for Bank Supervisors', Chapter 6 in J.J. Norton (ed.), *Banks, Fraud and Crime*, 2nd edition, London: Lloyd's of London Press Ltd (forthcoming).

Heimann, J. and Lord Alexander of Weedon (1997), 'Global Institutions, National Supervision and Systemic Risk', *Financial Stability Review*, Issue 3, Autumn, pp. 82–91.

Henriksen, O. (1983), 'How the EEC Influences Banking in Europe', *The Banker*, March.

HM Treasury (1998a), *Financial Services and Markets Bill: A Consultation Document*, London, 30 July.

HM Treasury (1998b), *Debt Management Report 1998–99*, London, March.

HMSO (1982), *HongKong and Shanghai Banking Corporation, Standard Chartered Bank Ltd and The Royal Bank of Scotland Group Ltd: Monopolies and Mergers Commission Report on the Proposed Mergers*, Cmnd 8476, London, January.

HMSO (1985a), *Report of the Committee set up to Consider the System of Banking Supervision*, Cmnd 9550, London, June.

HMSO (1985b), *White Paper on Banking Supervision*, Cmnd 9695, London, December.

HMSO (1987), *Banking Act 1987*, Chapter 22, London.

HMSO (1991), *Banking Supervision and BCCI: The Role of Local Authorities and Money Brokers*, Second Report of the Treasury and Civil Service Committee, HC26, London, December.

HMSO (1992a), *Banking Supervision and BCCI: International and National Regulation*, Fourth Report of the Treasury and Civil Service Committee, London, March.

HMSO (1992b), *Inquiry into the Supervision of the Bank of Credit and Commerce International* (the Bingham Report), House of Commons Paper 198, London, 22 October.

HMSO (1995a), *Report of the Board of Banking Supervision Inquiry into the Circumstances of the Collapse of Barings*, House of Commons Paper 673, London, 18 July.

HMSO (1995b), *Board of Banking Supervision: The Report on the Collapse of Barings, Minutes of Evidence*, Treasury and Civil Service Committee, House of Commons Paper 746-i, London, 19 July.

HMSO (1995c), 'The Regulation of Financial Services in the UK, Volume I, Report together with the Proceedings of the Committee', *Sixth Report of the Treasury and Civil Service Committee for the 1994–95 Session*, House of Commons Paper 332-I, London, 23 October.

House of Commons (1996), *First Report of the Treasury Committee for the Session 1996–97*, Paper 65-I, London, December.

ICAEW (1998), 'Auditing Guideline – Banks in the United Kingdom', Exposure Draft, London, February.

IIF (1997), *Report of the Task Force on Conglomerate Supervision*, Washington, London, May.

Kerry, John and Hank Brown (1992), 'BCCI Affair', a report to the Senate Committee on Foreign Relations, Washington, 30 September.

Kupiec, P.H. and J.M. O'Brien (1996), 'Bank Capital Regulation for Market Risks', *Financial Markets Group*, Special Paper No. 90, London: London School of Economics.

Price Waterhouse (1991), *Banking Capital Adequacy and Capital Convergence*, London, July.

Reid, M. (1982), *The Secondary Banking Crisis 1973–75*, London: Macmillan.

Revell, J. (1975), 'Solvency and Regulation of Banks', *Bangor Occasional Papers in Economics*, No. 5, Bangor: University of Wales Press.

SIB (1988), *The Financial Regulation of Overseas Institutions with UK Branches*, London, March.

Singapore Ministry of Finance (1995), *Baring Futures (Singapore) Pte Ltd.: Investigation Pursuant to Section 231 of the Companies Act (Chapter 50) – The Report of the Inspectors Appointed by the Minister for Finance*, Singapore, 17 October.

Taylor, M. (1997), '"Strengthening, but not Ensuring, the Protection of Depositors": The Bank of England on the Objectives of Supervision', *Butterworths Journal of International Banking and Financial Law*, April, pp. 151–4.

Tugendhat, C. (1985), 'Opening up Europe's Financial Sector to Intra-community Competition', *The Banker*, January.

Vlaar, P.J. (19,26), 'Methods to Determine Capital Requirements for Options', *Banca Nazionale del Lavoro Quarterly Review*, No. 198, September, pp. 351–73.

PART II

The structure of UK banking supervision

13. An overview of the Bank's supervisory approach[1]

Despite the existence of a statutory framework in the shape of the Banking Act 1987 (the provisions of which were discussed in Part I), the Bank continues to rely heavily on its informal authority in discharging its supervisory obligations (Bank of England, 1987a, pp. 380–85).[2] The objective of supervision explicit in the 1987 Act and its predecessor is the protection of depositors' interests, the Bank's wider concern with the soundness and stability of the overall banking system (and, consequently, financial markets) deriving from its role as central bank. It is from this latter role that the Bank's informal authority is derived, thereby complementing the statutory powers provided in the Act.

The Bank, rightly, prides itself on the flexibility of its supervisory approach and the degree of consultation which takes place before supervisory initiatives are implemented. The framing of the Banking Act assists the Bank in this strategy by deliberately being vague about the standards banks are required to observe. Thus the assessment of capital and liquidity adequacy and the limiting of exchange rate and other risks, perhaps the key elements of banking supervision, can be undertaken in an equitable and flexible fashion, making due allowance for differences in business mix and managerial competence. This approach also serves to further the cause of the economy and the banking system as a whole by limiting the competitive distortions introduced and the damage done to the innovative capacity of the industry. Accordingly, the Bank will continue to eschew the inspection-based approach adopted by some of its foreign counterparts (although, as noted in Part I, the number of informal visits being made to institutions in the UK is on a dramatic incline and, post-BCCI and Barings, on-site inspection is set to assume greater significance), preferring to rely upon periodic management interviews as the core of its supervisory approach.

At these interviews, the results of the Bank's analysis of the wealth of data gathered from the prudential returns will be fully discussed, as will the bank's future business plans and profitability forecasts and the reporting accountants' (and possibly auditors') reports. The last mentioned cover the bank's accounting procedures, the keeping of other records, its internal control systems, and other issues on which the Bank has called for a report or a report has been produced at the accountants' own initiative. Making full use of quantitative analytical techniques where relevant,[3] subjective evaluations as to the adequacy of prudential arrangements on a variety of fronts are eventually produced. Where deficiencies have been identified, advice is then given to each bank (for the prudential regulation and supervision of discount houses, GEMMs, stock exchange money brokers and gilt-edged inter-dealer brokers, *see* Hall, 1993, Appendices 1–3) as to how, and over what time span, remedial action should be taken. Close monitoring would then ensue to ensure compliance with the Bank's requests.

Since the publication of the Arthur Andersen Review, in the wake of the collapse of Barings, the Bank has become more 'risk-focused' in its supervision (*see* Chapter 12). Building on the 'RATE' model developed by Arthur Andersen, the Bank now undertakes risk assessment of UK-incorporated[4] institutions using nine evaluation factors, six quantitative – Capital, Assets, Market Risk, Earnings, Liabilities and Business ('CAMELB') – and three qualitative – Controls, Organization and Management ('COM') (Bank of England, 1997a). (Numerical ratings for both the quantitative and qualitative elements of assessment are eventually likely to materialize but they will not be disclosed to the market place.) The purpose of the increased focus on risk is to provide for more consistent and better identification of risks in institutions and their wider groups. RATE also seeks to ensure that supervisory action is focused on the main risks and uses the most appropriate tools to deal with those risks.

The approach, which is designed to underpin the flexibility and the application of judgement by individual supervisors, introduces the concept of a 'supervisory period', which is the length of time between formal risk assessments on a particular bank. This period will usually be one year, but may vary – from six months to over two years – according to the risk profile of the bank concerned. In each supervisory period, the Bank will perform a risk assessment, take appropriate supervisory action, apply the tools of supervision and undertake a formal evaluation. The objective of the risk assessment – which will also cover control functions, such as internal audit and risk management functions, and other areas of support, including information technology and human resource departments – will be to identify the business or inherent risks of a bank and to assess the adequacy and effectiveness of its controls, organization and management in a systematic manner.

Where the Bank identifies significant concerns, either from the risk assessment or at any time during the supervisory period, it will seek appropriate remedial action. In addition, after each assessment, the Bank will feed back its views on the bank's profile to the bank's board of directors. The Bank will also outline any remedial action it is seeking or intends to take, and a supervisory programme, setting out the tools of supervision it intends to use (e.g. reporting accountants' reports on internal controls, Traded Markets Team and Review Team visits, etc.) and the likely timing of their application. The tools will be targeted at areas considered to be of higher risk or will be used to follow up issues identified during the risk assessment. The results coming from use of the tools will be examined as they become available, which may require the Bank to assess the risk profile of the bank or take appropriate supervisory action.

During the course of the supervisory period, the Bank will constantly evaluate the information it receives. In addition, at the end of the period, the Bank will undertake a formal evaluation to ensure that it has completed its original work plan, to check that it has acted appropriately on the results of the application of the supervisory tools, and generally to assess how effectively it has supervised the bank in question. The conclusions from the evaluation will be a key input into the next risk assessment.

The RATE and SCALE frameworks were tested on a number of banks during the latter half of 1997. Feedback will result in a revised paper on risk-based supervision being issued by the FSAu in mid 1998. All banks will be subject to a full risk assessment by the FSAu by the end of 1999.

Apart from relying upon the work of auditors and reporting accountants, whose supervisory role has been extended considerably in recent years (*see* Chapter 14), and the management interviews (with all that these entail), the Bank is able to draw upon other weaponry in its fight to enhance the effectiveness of banking supervision. It can call upon the combined wisdom and experience of the Board of Banking Supervision to assist it in its deliberations. It can further draw upon the expertise of practitioners and secure acceptance of supervisory initiatives through the medium of consultations. And it can aid management decision-making through the dissemination of information relevant to the supervisory process. Beyond this it can, hopefully, rely upon the deterrent effects of the criminal sanctions built into the 1987 Act, the extended powers given to it under the same Act, the expertise of its own staff in identifying problems at an early stage through continuous monitoring, and the co-operation provided by other supervisory bodies.

At the end of the day, however, the Bank cannot guarantee – nor should it seek to do so (*see* Bank of England, 1997c)[5] – the soundness of every bank that it supervises. Rather, it seeks to ensure that banks do not become insolvent *unnecessarily* – some commercial judgement has to remain with the banks – and that, in those unfortunate cases where insolvency does occur, depositors receive adequate compensation and the system is insulated from the damage wrought by the ensuing contagion. In this way the Bank, as supervisor and central bank, seeks to protect depositors' interests and the wider interests[6] of the banking system and the economy at one and the same time.

Following the government's decision in 1986 to make the Bank, rather than the SIB or an SRO, responsible for the supervision of certain wholesale markets (bullion, foreign exchange and money markets),[7] the Bank was reorganized. A new division was established to cover this area – the Wholesale Markets Supervision Division (WMSD). This complemented the existing Banking

Exhibit 2.1   S&S organogram (as at 1 March 1997)

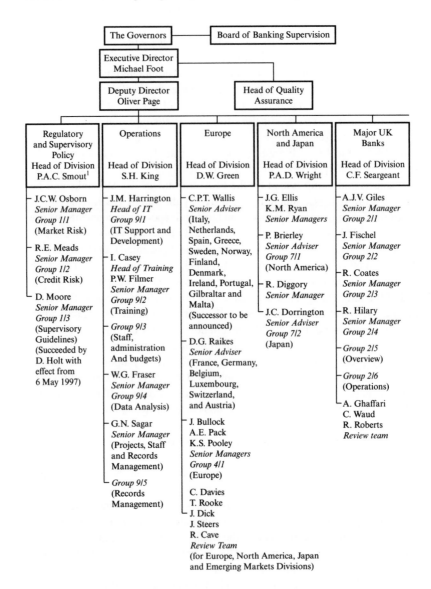

Notes:
1. Reports jointly to the Deputy Director, Financial Structure.
2. Also Secretary, Deposit Protection Board.

Source: Bank of England, 1997d, p. 46.

Stephen Drayson (Deputy Head of Quality Assurance)

Capital and Wholesale Markets	UK Banks and Enforcement	Emerging Markets (North)	Emerging Markets (South)	
Head of Division C.E. Briault	Head of Division W.D.R. Swanney	Head of Division C.M. Miles	Head of Division D.J. Reid	

- D.J. Strachan
  Senior Manager Group 8/1
  (UK Investment Banks)
- A.G. Jennings
  S.J. Bereza
  Senior Managers Group 8/2
  (Traded Markets Team)
- D. Sunderland
  Senior Manager Groups 8/3 and 8/4
  (Discount Houses and Gilts)
- A.J. Murfin
  Senior Manager Groups 8/6
  (S43 Grey Paper and Code)
- J. Patterson
  Senior Manager Group 8/6
  (FX Clearing houses)

- J.E. Moorhouse
  Senior Manager Group 3/1
  (To be succeeded by C.P.T. Wallis with effect from 16 June 1997)
- D.A. Reeves
  Senior Manager Group 3/2
- I.M. Cobbold [2]
  Senior Manager Group 3/3
- P.J. Marr
  Senior Manager Group 3/4
  (Enforcement)
- A. Wallace
  S. Elsom
  M. Pollard
  Review Team

- E. Young
  Senior Manager Group 6/1
  (Central and Eastern Europe)
- J. Milne
  Senior Manager Group 6/2
  (Gulf)
- G.R. Dargie
  Senior Manager Group 6/3
  (East Asia I – China, Taiwan, Hong Kong, and Singapore)
- P. Phelan
  Senior Manager Group 6/4
  (East Asia II – Korea, Thailand, Malaysia, Philippines and Indonesia)
- M. Stephenson
  Senior Economist Group 6/5
  (Emerging Markets Policy)

- A. Bulley
  Senior Manager Group 5/1
  (Latin America)
  (To be succeeded by J.E. Moorhouse w.e.f. 16 June 1997)
- D.M. Sutherland
  Senior Manager Group 5/2
  (Africa and Israel)
  (w.e.f. 15 April 1997)
- M. Ainley
  Senior Manager Group 5/3
  (West Asia)
- C. Walsh
  Senior Manager Group 5/4
  (South Asia and Australia)
- R.D. Chalmers
  Senior Manager
- T. Smith
  Senior Adviser Group 5/5
  (Offshore Centres)
- R. MacDonald
  D. Ware
  Senior Managers Group 5/6
  (Technical Assistance)

Change Management

- A.S. Watson
  Senior Manager

Supervision Division (BSD). This structure survived intact until July 1994, when the Bank introduced a new management structure which divided its activities into two wings: financial stability and monetary stability (Bank of England, 1995a, pp. 41–2). Within the financial stability wing, supervision was aligned with S&S. The financial stability wing subsequently underwent structural change during 1995/96 when the Division within S&S that dealt specifically with banking supervisory policy issues merged with those working on broader regulatory policy subjects outside S&S, to form the Regulatory and Supervisory Policy Division. At the same time, the Wholesale Markets Supervision Division (WMSD) was required to report to the Deputy Director for S&S, thereby bringing all supervisory operations together in one part of the wing (Bank of England, 1996a, p. 42). Finally, on 1 September, 1996 S&S was restructured to accommodate the recommendations of the Arthur Andersen Review (*see* Chapter 12). The new organization is presented in Exhibit 2.1.

14. The role of auditors and reporting accountants in the supervisory process[8]

DEVELOPMENTS SINCE ENACTMENT OF THE BANKING ACT 1987

As noted in Chapter 6, under the Banking Act of 1987, each authorized institution was required to commission an independent firm (preferably UK-based) of accountants to produce two separate reports, both of which were to be made available to the Bank. These comprised an annual report on the bank's internal control systems and accounting and other records and, as and when requested by the Bank, a report on the statistical returns made to the Bank on prudential matters (*see* BSD/1987/2; Bank of England, 1987b). Accountants were also able to disclose information, through the medium of *ad hoc* reports, to the Bank without contravening a duty of confidentiality to their clients. UK-incorporated authorized institutions were required to notify the Bank of any change in their auditors, and auditors had to notify the Bank if they resigned, qualified the accounts or did not seek reappointment. As for dialogue between auditors and the Bank, direct contact normally took place at trilateral meetings, which had to be held once a year, at which the client bank was also present. In exceptional circumstances, however, such as when fraud was suspected or the bank was thought to be in imminent danger of collapse, auditors had the *right* (not a duty) to consult with supervisors without informing their clients. In such instances, they were immune from legal action by their clients provided the disclosures were made in good faith and the information was relevant to the supervisory process.

The first major change to these arrangements came in March 1994 when, following a review of the way it utilizes reporting accountants' reports commissioned under Section 39 of the Banking Act, the Bank issued a new notice (BSD/1994/2; Bank of England, 1994b) providing revised guidance to reporting accountants on the format of such reports. This replaced BSD/1987/2. And, in the same month, in response to the auditors' new *statutory* duty (as from 1 May 1994) to report relevant information to the Bank (this followed concerns raised by the collapse of BCCI – *see* Chapter 11), the Auditing Practices Board (APB) published a 'Statement of Auditing Standards 620' and a Practice Note ('Direct Reports to the Bank') establishing standards and giving guidance to the accountancy profession on the situation (e.g. when they have doubts about whether a bank should remain authorized) in which auditors and reporting accountants should report matters to the regulators.

Later that year (December), the Cadbury Committee issued guidance to directors of listed companies on, *inter alia*, stating their compliance with the Code of Best Practice in respect of 'Internal Control and Financial Reporting'. The APB duly responded in March 1995, giving guidance to auditors on reporting on internal control systems in the light of the Cadbury Committee's guidance. The APB was keen to point out that a number of important issues have to be resolved before auditors can report on directors' statements of the effectiveness of internal financial controls.

The next development occurred in April 1996, when the Bank reissued in revised form its three Notices on reporting accountants: 'The Bank of England's Relationship with Auditors and Reporting Accountants' (S&S/1996/5; Bank of England, 1996b); 'Guidance Note on Reporting Accountants' Reports on Accounting and Other Records and Internal Control Systems' (S&S/1996/6; Bank of England, 1996c); and 'Guidance Note on Reporting Accountants' Reports on Bank of England's Returns used for Prudential Purposes' (S&S/1996/7; Bank of England, 1996d). The main changes made, which took account of the recommendations made by the Board of Banking Supervision inquiry into the collapse of Barings (*see* Chapter 12), are that reporting accountants may now be commissioned to form an opinion on the systems of controls over the accuracy of the information contained in an institution's records and its transfer to prudential returns; that the Bank may use Section 39 reviews more flexibly (i.e. via *ad hoc* reports), to cover group operations (especially non-banking) other than those carried out by the institution itself; and that reporting accountants will be required to state the extent of the work performed for each Section 39 review. The Bank's use of the *ad hoc* reports referred to above is likely to occur when there has been a significant change in business of a bank/group or when evidence of a weakness in the bank/group has been identified.

Then, in July 1996, the scope of auditors' and reporting accountants' statutory duty to report to regulators was widened on implementation of the Post-BCCI Directive' (EC, 1995). Henceforth, their statutory tasks in relation to financial undertakings and closely linked undertakings extended to reporting material breaches of relevant laws and certain other concerns to the relevant supervisor.

Finally, in February 1997, the Bank published a consultation paper (Bank of England, 1997e) outlining its view on how it could improve its ability to monitor the effectiveness of banks' internal controls. It looked particularly at the Section 39 regime, as requested by Arthur Andersen in its post-Barings Review (*see* Chapter 12), and considered, *inter alia*, the following proposals:

(1) that an institution's board of directors be required to provide an annual statement to the Bank on the adequacy of the systems in place to monitor and control the institution's material risks; (2) that the institution's reporting accountants and auditors be required formally to confirm that nothing has come to their attention to give them cause to believe that a breach in the minimum criteria for authorization has occurred; (3) that bilateral meetings be held routinely between the Bank and reporting accountants; and (4) that the Section 39 process be changed in a variety of ways (e.g. that a bank's auditors should not operate as reporting accountants for the purposes of a Section 39 report).

Following consultation with interested parties the Bank, in July 1997, published, by way of a letter, its planned changes to the Section 39 process in respect of internal controls reviews. With effect from 1 May 1998, reporting accountants (which may still be the auditors to an institution) will be required to make a statement that nothing has come to their attention to cause them to believe that a breach of the Schedule 3 criteria for authorization has occurred. The rotation of lead audit partners every seven years (the previous proposal was five years) will also be enforced,[9] and bilateral meetings between the Bank and reporting accountants/auditors will be formally instigated. The feedback system is also to be changed by assessing individual partners (and supervisors), and Bank analysts are to be seconded to reporting accountants to undertake Section 39 work. The Bank, together with other UK financial services regulators, is still working on a cohesive FSAu approach towards the responsibilities of directors and senior managements. Until this emerges, the Bank's proposals for corporate governance guidance (a subject advanced since Cadbury by the Hampel Report (Committee on Corporate Governance, 1998)) and directors' attestations remain on hold.

15. Relationships between the Bank and other supervisory bodies

Close liaison between supervisors is maintained both within the Bank and between the Bank and non-bank supervisors, both domestic and international. Within the Bank itself, close working relationships were formed between the BSD, WMSD and those responsible within the Bank for supervising (on a voluntary basis) GEMMs.[10] Given that most of the GEMMs were owned by banks or represented part of banking groups, as were many of the market-makers and brokers (as well as some discount houses) supervised by the WMSD, the need for such close co-operation was self-evident. And since the internal restructuring of the Bank (carried out since 1994 – *see* Chapter 13), this degree of co-operation has continued within S&S.

As for relationships with external supervisors, the Bank, under the lead regulator approach adumbrated in the Financial Services Act 1986, is required to liaise closely with the SIB and the relevant SROs in its supervision of banks' investment business. As explained in Part I, the formal division of supervisory responsibilities is carried out according to the Memoranda of Understanding agreed in March 1988 with the Financial Services Act regulators.[11] Under these agreements, the Bank assumed the role of lead regulator for *all* UK-incorporated banks engaged in investment business. This involves it in the monitoring of capital adequacy on behalf of the SIB/SRO according to an agreed set of rules (*see* pp. 92–4). Only in the case of banks whose non-investment business is negligible, business being almost exclusively securities trading or investment-related, does the SIB/SRO become the monitoring supervisor of capital adequacy. Rather, the main function of the SIB/SRO in most cases is to monitor compliance with 'conduct of business' rules.

At the international level, supervisory co-operation is effected through the maintenance of close contacts with a large variety of supervisory bodies. The list embraces: the national supervisors of the G10 countries who make up the *Basle Committee of Supervisors*, where responsibilities for supervising international banks are split according to the Basle *Concordat*, as subsequently revised, and EC Directives, where relevant (*see* Chapters 3 and 9); the various EC bodies involved in banking regulation and supervision, such as, the *Banking Advisory Committee*, the *Groupe de Contact*, the European Monetary Institute Banking Supervisory Sub-Committee and the Commission itself; the *Committee* on *Financial Markets* of the OECD; non-European supervisory groups such as the *Offshore Group of Supervisors* and the *Commission of Latin American and the Caribbean Supervisory and Inspection Organizations*; and, finally, national supervisors of banking, securities and financial markets with whom discussions take place on a bilateral basis during the normal course of supervision or consultation. (Memoranda of Understanding govern co-operation with banking supervisors in the EEA.)

Through this vast network of contacts the Bank seeks to promote closer supervisory co-operation, to influence supervisory developments and to enhance the effectiveness of its own supervisory effort through obtaining clearer pictures of the nature of the business operations engaged in by the institutions it supervises and of the methods and operations of its international counterparts.

16. Authorization procedures under the Banking Act 1987

As required under Section 16 of the Banking Act 1987, the Bank published, in May 1988, the 'statements of principles' it uses in interpreting the authorization criteria set out in Schedule 3 of the Act and the grounds for revocation (or restriction) specified in Section 11. A summary of this document, as revised in May 1993 to take account of the latest EC Directives and in the light of BCCI experience (it will be revised again by the FSAu in mid 1998 to accommodate more recent developments) follows. (For a list of those institutions authorized by the Bank as at end-February 1998 *see* Exhibit 2.2.)

Exhibit 2.2   List of institutions authorized as at 28 February 1998

This list is made available pursuant to Section 17(2) of the Banking Act 1987 as amended by the Banking Co-ordination (Second Council Directive) Regulations. The inclusion of an institution does not mean that the Bank in any way guarantees its obligations. The list includes institutions authorized by the Bank under the Banking Act 1987 and European authorized institutions (EAIs).

EAIs are institutions which are recognised under the Banking Co-ordination (Second Council Directive) Regulations 1992. The EAIs included in the list are those in respect of which the Bank has received a notification from the relevant supervisory authority in the home state – i.e. the country in the EEA in which they are incorporated or formed – entitling them to establish a branch or provide services on a cross-border basis in the UK. EAIs are authorized by the relevant home state supervisory authority. They are not authorized by the Bank.

1.   Institutions authorized by the Bank to accept deposits in the UK

(i)   UK-incorporated institutions authorized by the Bank[1]

The following UK-incorporated institutions are authorized by the Bank under the Banking Act 1987 to accept deposits in the UK. Qualifying deposits in sterling, ECU or other EEA currencies made with these institutions in the UK or other EEA countries are covered by the UK Deposit Protection Scheme.[2]

AABC International Bank plc
AMC Bank Ltd
AY Bank Ltd
Abbey National plc
Abbey National Treasury Services plc
Adam & Company plc
Afghan National Credit & Finance Ltd
Airdrie Savings Bank
Alliance & Leicester plc
Alliance & Leicester Group Treasury plc
Alliance Trust (Finance) Ltd
Allied Bank Philippines (UK) plc
Allied Irish Bank (GB)/First Trust Bank – (AIB Group (UK) plc)
Alpha Bank London Ltd
Anglo-Romanian Bank Ltd
Henry Ansbacher & Co. Ltd
Arbuthnot Latham & Co. Ltd
Assemblies of God Property Trust
Associates Capital Corporation Ltd
Avco Trust plc

Bank Leumi (UK) plc
Bank of America International Ltd
Bank of China International (UK) Ltd
Bank of Cyprus (London) Ltd
Bank of Montreal Europe Ltd
Bank of Scotland
Bank of Scotland Treasury Services plc
Bank of Tokyo – Mitsubishi (UK) Ltd
Bank of Wales plc
Bankers Trust International plc
Bankgesellschaft Berlin (UK) plc
Banque Nationale de Paris plc
The Baptist Union Corporation Ltd
Barclays Bank plc
Barclays Bank Trust Company Ltd
Barclays de Zoete Wedd Ltd
Barclays Private Bank Ltd
Baring Brothers Ltd
Beneficial Bank plc
Bristol & West plc
British Arab Commercial Bank Ltd

Exhibit 2.2 (continued)

The British Bank of the Middle East
The British Linen Bank Ltd
Brown, Shipley & Co Ltd

CIBC Wood Gundy plc
Cafcash Ltd
Capital Bank plc
Cater Allen Ltd
Chartered Trust plc
Charterhouse Bank Ltd
Chase Manhattan International Ltd
Cheltenham & Gloucester plc
Citibank International plc
Clive Discount Company Ltd
Close Brothers Ltd
Clydesdale Bank plc
Consolidated Credits Bank Ltd
The Co-operative Bank plc
Coutts & Co
Crédit Agricole Lazard Financial Products Bank
Credit Suisse Financial Products
Crown Agents Financial Services Ltd

Daiwa Europe Bank plc
Dalbeattie Finance Co. Ltd
Dao Heng Bank (London) plc
Dexia Municipal Bank plc
Direct Line Financial Services Ltd
The Dorset, Somerset & Wilts Investment Society Ltd
Dryfield Trust plc
Dunbar Bank plc
Duncan Lawrie Ltd

EFG Private Bank Ltd
Eccles Savings and Loans Ltd

FIBI Bank (UK) plc
Fairmount Capital Management Ltd
Financial & General Bank plc
First National Bank plc
First National Commercial Bank plc
Robert Fleming & Co Ltd

Ford Credit Europe plc
Forward Trust Group Ltd
Frizzell Bank Ltd

Gartmore Money Management Ltd
GE Capital Bank Ltd
Gerrard & King Ltd
Girobank plc
Goldman Sachs International Bank
Granville Bank Ltd
Gresham Trust plc
Guinness Mahon & Co. Ltd

HFC Bank pic
HSBC Equator Bank plc
HSBC Investment Bank plc
Habibsons Bank Ltd
Halifax plc
Hambros Bank Ltd
Hampshire Trust plc
The Hardware Federation Finance Co. Ltd
Harrods Bank Ltd
Harton Securities Ltd
Havana International Bank Ltd
The Heritable and General Investment Bank Ltd
Hill Samuel Bank Ltd
C. Hoare & Co.
Julian Hodge Bank Ltd
Humberclyde Finance Group Ltd

3i plc
3i Group plc
IBJ International plc
Investec Bank (UK) Ltd
Iran Overseas Investment Bank Ltd
Italian International Bank plc

Jordan International Bank plc
Leopold Joseph & Sons Ltd

KDB Bank (UK) Ltd
KEXIM Bank (UK) Ltd
Kleinwort Benson Ltd
Kleinwort Benson Investment Management Ltd
Korea Long Term Credit Bank International Ltd

Exhibit 2.2   (continued)

Lazard Brothers & Co. Ltd
Legal & General Bank Ltd
Lloyds Bank plc
Lloyds Bank (BLSA) Ltd
Lloyds Bowmaker Ltd
Lloyds Private Banking Ltd
Lombard Bank Ltd
Lombard & Ulster Ltd
Lombard North Central plc
London Scottish Bank plc
London Trust Bank plc

MBNA International Bank Ltd
W. M. Mann & Co. (Investments) Ltd
Marks and Spencer Financial Services Ltd
Matheson Bank Ltd
Matlock Bank Ltd
Meghraj Bank Ltd
Merrill Lynch International Bank Ltd
The Methodist Chapel Aid Association Ltd
Midland Bank plc
Midland Bank Trust Company Ltd
Minster Trust Ltd
Samuel Montagu & Co. Ltd
Morgan Grenfell & Co. Ltd
Moscow Narodny Bank Ltd
Mutual Trust & Savings Ltd

NIIB Group Ltd
National Bank of Egypt International Ltd
National Bank of Kuwait (International) plc
National Westminster Bank plc
NationsBank Europe Ltd
The Nikko Bank (UK) plc
Noble Grossart Ltd
Nomura Bank International plc
Northern Bank Ltd
Northern Bank Executor & Trustee Company Ltd
Northern Rock plc

PaineWebber International Bank Ltd
Philippine National Bank (Europe) plc

Pointon York Ltd
Prudential-Bache International Bank Ltd
Prudential Banking plc

RBS Trust Bank Ltd
R. Raphael & Sons plc
Rathbone Bros & Co. Ltd
Rea Brothers Ltd
Reliance Bank Ltd
Riggs Bank Europe Ltd
Riyad Bank Europe Ltd
N.M. Rothschild & Sons Ltd
Royal Bank of Canada Europe Ltd
The Royal Bank of Scotland plc
RoyScot Trust plc
Ruffler Bank plc

SBI European Bank plc
Sabanci Bank plc
Sainsbury's Bank plc
Sanwa International plc
Saudi American Bank (UK) Ltd
Saudi International Bank
   (Al-Bank Al-Saudi Al-Alami Ltd)
Schroder Leasing Ltd
J. Henry Schroder & Co Ltd
Scotiabank Europe plc
Scottish Widows Bank plc
Seccombe Marshall & Campion plc
Singer & Friedlander Ltd
Smith & Williamson Investment Management Ltd
Southsea Mortgage & Investment Co. Ltd
Standard Bank London Ltd
Standard Chartered Bank
Standard Life Bank Ltd
Sun Banking Corporation Ltd

TSB Bank plc
TSB Bank Scotland plc
Tesco Personal Finance Ltd
Tokai Bank Europe plc
Toronto Dominion Bank Europe Ltd
Turkish Bank (UK) Ltd

Exhibit 2.2   (continued)

UCB Bank plc
Ulster Bank Ltd
Union Discount Company Ltd
The United Bank of Kuwait plc
United Dominions Trust Ltd
United Trust Bank Ltd
Unity Trust Bank plc

Weatherbys & Co. Ltd
Wesleyan Savings Bank Ltd
West Merchant Bank Ltd
Whiteaway Laidlaw Bank Ltd
Wintrust Securities Ltd
Woolwich plc

Yamaichi Bank (UK) plc
Yorkshire Bank plc

(ii)   Institutions incorporated outside the EEA authorized by the Bank
The following institutions incorporated outside the EEA are authorized by the
Bank under the Banking Act 1987 to accept deposits in sterling, ECU or other
EEA currencies. Deposits made with the UK offices of these institutions are
covered by the UK Deposit Protection Scheme (cover is limited to 90 per cent
of a depositor's total qualifying deposits subject to a maximum payment to any
one depositor of £18,000 or ECU 20,000 if greater).

ABSA Bank Ltd
Allied Bank of Pakistan Ltd
American Express Bank Ltd
Arab African International Bank
Arab Bank plc
Arab Banking Corporation BSC
Arab National Bank
The Asahi Bank, Ltd
The Ashikaga Bank Ltd
Australia & New Zealand Banking Group Ltd

BSI-Banca della Svizzera Italiana
Banca Serfin SA
Banco de la Nación Argentina
Banco do Brasil SA
Banco do Estado de São Paulo SA

Banco Mercantil de São Paulo SA – Finasa
Banco Nacional de Mexico SA
Banco Real SA
Bancomer SA
Bangkok Bank Public Company Ltd
Bank Julius Baer & Co. Ltd
BankBoston, NA
Bank Bumiputra Malaysia Berhad
PT Bank Ekspor Impor Indonesia (Persero)
Bank Handlowy w Warszawie SA
Bank Hapoalim BM
Bank Mellat
Bank Melli Iran
PT Bank Negara Indonesia (Persero) Tbk
Bank of America NT & SA
Bank of Baroda
Bank of Ceylon
Bank of China
Bank of Cyprus Ltd
The Bank of East Asia Ltd
The Bank of Fukuoka Ltd
Bank of India
Bank of Montreal
The Bank of New York
The Bank of Nova Scotia
The Bank of Tokyo – Mitsubishi, Ltd
The Bank of Yokohama, Ltd
Bank Saderat Iran
Bank Sepah-Iran
Bank Tejarat
Bankers Trust Company
Beirut Riyad Bank SAL

Canadian Imperial Bank of Commerce
Canara Bank
Capital One Bank
Chang Hwa Commercial Bank Ltd
The Chase Manhattan Bank
The Chiba Bank Ltd
Cho Hung Bank
The Chuo Trust & Banking Co., Ltd
Citibank NA

Exhibit 2.2   (continued)

Commercial Bank of Korea Ltd
Commonwealth Bank of Australia
CoreStates Bank NA
Credit Suisse First Boston
The Cyprus Popular Bank Ltd

The Dai-lchi Kangyo Bank, Ltd
The Daiwa Bank Ltd
The Development Bank of Singapore Ltd
Discount Bank and Trust Company

Emirates Bank International PJSC

First Bank of Nigeria plc
First Commercial Bank
The First National Bank of Chicago
First Union National Bank
The Fuji Bank Ltd

Ghana Commercial Bank
Gulf International Bank BSC

Habib Bank AG Zurich
Habib Bank Ltd
Hanil Bank
The Hiroshima Bank, Ltd
The Hokuriku Bank Ltd
The Hongkong and Shanghai Banking Corporation Ltd
Housing & Commercial Bank, Korea

The Industrial Bank of Japan, Ltd

The Joyo Bank Ltd

KorAm Bank
The Korea Development Bank
Korea Exchange Bank
Korea First Bank

The Long-Term Credit Bank of Japan, Ltd

Macquarie Bank Ltd
Malayan Banking Berhad
MashreqBank PSC
Mellon Bank, NA

The Mitsubishi Trust and Banking Corporation
The Mitsui Trust & Banking Co. Ltd
Morgan Guaranty Trust Company of New York

Nacional Financiera SNC
National Australia Bank Ltd
National Bank of Abu Dhabi
National Bank of Canada
The National Bank of Dubai Public Joint Stock Company
National Bank of Pakistan
NationsBank, NA
NationsBank of Texas, NA
Nedcor Bank Ltd
The Norinchukin Bank
The Northern Trust Company

Oversea-Chinese Banking Corporation Ltd
Overseas Trust Bank Ltd
Overseas Union Bank Ltd

People's Bank
Philippine National Bank

Qatar National Bank SAQ

Rafidain Bank (provisional liquidator appointed)
Republic National Bank of New York
Riggs Bank NA
Riyad Bank
Royal Bank of Canada

The Sakura Bank, Ltd
The Sanwa Bank, Ltd
Saudi American Bank
The Saudi British Bank
SEOULBANK
Shanghai Commercial Bank Ltd
Shinhan Bank
The Siam Commercial Bank Public Company Ltd
Sonali Bank
State Bank of India
State Street Bank and Trust Company
The Sumitomo Bank, Ltd
The Sumitomo Trust & Banking Co. Ltd
Swiss Bank Corporation
Syndicate Bank

Exhibit 2.2   (continued)

TC Ziraat Bankasi
The Thai Farmers Bank Public Company Ltd
The Tokai Bank, Ltd
The Toronto-Dominion Bank
The Toyo Trust & Banking Company, Ltd
Turkiye Is Bankasi AS

Uco Bank
Union Bancaire Privée, CBI-TBD
Union Bank of Nigeria plc
Union Bank of Switzerland
United Bank Ltd
United Mizrahi Bank Ltd
United Overseas Bank Ltd

Wachovia Bank
Westpac Banking Corporation

The Yasuda Trust & Banking Co., Ltd

Zambia National Commercial Bank Ltd
Zivostenská Banka AS

2.   EAIs entitled to establish UK branches

(i)   EAIs which are entitled to accept deposits through a branch in the UK
The following institutions have exercised their entitlement to provide one or more
of the services listed in Schedule I of the Banking Co-ordination (Second
Council Directive) Regulations 1992, including deposit-taking. EAIs may
appear under both Sections 2 and 3 of this list. This occurs when institutions
notify the Bank under 2BCD of their intention to provide services both through
a branch and on a cross-border basis. Qualifying deposits made with UK offices
of these institutions are covered by the Deposit Protection Scheme established
in the institution's home state.[3] Such institutions have the right to join the UK
Scheme to supplement the cover available from their home state Scheme if that
is less generous than the UK Scheme. Those institutions that have joined the
UK Scheme are marked with an asterisk.

Name of institution	**Country of home state supervisory authority**
ABN AMRO Bank NV	Netherlands
Allied Irish Banks plc	Republic of Ireland

Alpha Credit Bank AE	Greece
Anglo Irish Bank Corporation plc	Republic of Ireland
BfG Bank AG	Germany
BHF BANK AG	Germany
Banca Cassa di Risparmio di Torino SpA	Italy
Banca Commerciale Italiana	Italy
Banca di Roma SpA	Italy
Banca March SA	Spain
Banca Monte dei Paschi di Siena SpA	Italy
Banca Nazionale dell'Agricoltura SpA	Italy
Banca Nazionale del Lavoro SpA	Italy
Banca Popolare di Milano	Italy
Banca Popolare di Novara	Italy
Banco Ambrosiano Veneto SpA	Italy
Banco Bilbao-Vizcaya	Spain
Banco Central Hispanoamericano SA	Spain
Banco de Sabadell	Spain
Banco di Napoli SpA	Italy
Banco di Sicilia SpA	Italy
Banco Español de Crédito SA	Spain
Banco Espirito Santo e Comercial de Lisboa	Portugal
Banco Exterior de España SA	Spain
Banco Nacional Ultramarino SA	Portugal
Banco Portugês do Atlântico	Portugal
Banco Santander	Spain
Banco Santander de Negocios SA	Spain
Banco Totta & Açores SA	Portugal
Bank Austria AG	Austria
Bank Brussels Lambert	Belgium
The Bank of Ireland*	Republic of Ireland
Bankgesellschaft Berlin AG	Germany
Banque AIG	France
Banque Arabe et Internationale d'Investissement	France
Banque Banorabe	France
Banque CPR	France
Banque Française de l'Orient	France
Banque Internationale à Luxembourg SA	Luxembourg
Banque Nationale de Paris	France
Banque Paribas	France
Bayerische Hypotheken-und Wechsel-Bank AG	Germany
Bayerische Landesbank Girozentrale	Germany
Bayerische Vereinsbank AG	Germany
Belgolaise SA	Belgium

Exhibit 2.2   (continued)

Berliner Bank AG	Germany
Byblos Bank Belgium SA	Belgium
CARIPLO – Cassa di Risparmio delle Provincie Lombarde SpA	Italy
CETELEM	France
Caisse Nationale de Crédit Agricole	France
Cariverona Banca SpA	Italy
Christiania Bank og Kreditkasse	Norway
Commerzbank AG	Germany
Compagnie Financière de CIC et de l'Union Européenne	France
Confederacion Espanola de Cajas de Ahorros	Spain
Crédit Agricole Indosuez	France
Crédit Commercial de France	France
Crédit du Nord	France
Crédit Lyonnais	France
Creditanstalt-Aktiengesellschaft	Austria
Credito Italiano	Italy
De Nationale Investeringsbank NV	Netherlands
Den Danske Bank Aktieselskab	Denmark
Den norske Bank ASA	Norway
Deutsche Bank AG	Germany
Deutsche Bau- und Bodenbank AG	Germany
Deutsche Genossenschaftsbank	Germany
Dresdner Bank AG	Germany
Equity Bank Ltd	Republic of Ireland
Ergobank SA	Greece
Erste Bank der oesterreichischen Sparkassen AG	Austria
FIMAT International Banque	France
First National Building Society	Republic of Ireland
Generale Bank	Belgium
Hamburgische Landesbank Girozentrale	Germany
ICC Bank plc	Republic of Ireland
ING Bank NV	Netherlands
Industrial Bank of Korea Europe SA	Luxembourg
Ionian and Popular Bank of Greece SA	Greece

Irish Nationwide Building Sociey	Republic of Ireland
Irish Permanent plc*	Republic of Ireland
Istituto Bancario San Paolo di Torino SpA	Italy
Jyske Bank	Denmark
Kas-Associatie NV	Netherlands
Kredietbank NV	Belgium
Landesbank Berlin Girozentrale	Germany
Landesbank Hessen-Thüringen Girozentrale	Germany
Lehman Brothers Bankhaus AG	Germany
MeesPierson NV	Netherlands
Merita Bank Ltd	Finland
Natexis Banque	France
National Bank of Greece SA	Greece
Norddeutsche Landesbank Girozentrale	Germany
Postipankki Ltd	Finland
Rabobank International (Coöperatieve Centrale Raiffeisen-Boerenleenbank BA)	Netherlands
Raiffeisen Zentralbank Osterreich AG	Austria
Skandinaviska Enskilda Banken AB (publ)	Sweden
Société Générale	France
Südwestdeutsche Landesbank Girozentrale	Germany
Svenska Handelsbanken AB (publ)	Sweden
SwedBank (FöreningsSparbanken AB (publ))	Sweden
Triodosbank NV	Netherlands
Ulster Bank Markets Ltd	Republic of Ireland
Unibank A/S	Denmark
Westdeutsche Landesbank Girozentrale	Germany

(iii) EAIs which are not entitled to accept deposits through a branch in the UK

The following institutions have exercised their entitlement to provide one or more of the services listed in Schedule I of the Banking Co-ordination (Second Council Directive) Regulations 1992, *excluding* deposit-taking

Name of Institution	**Country of home state supervisory authority**
Bank Labouchere NV	Netherlands
Bikuben GiroBank A/S	Denmark
Carr Futures SNC	France

Exhibit 2.2   (continued)

International Finance Futures SNC	France
LGT Bank in Liechtenstein (Deutschland) GmbH	Germany
Schröder Münchmeyer Hengst & Co.	Germany
Société de Transaction et d'Arbitrage sur Futurs Financiers	France
Sparebanken Nor (trading as UBN Securities)	Norway
Transoptions Finance	France
Westdeutsche ImmobilienBank	Germany

3.   EAIs entitled to provide services on a cross-border basis in the UK

(i)   EAIs which are entitled to accept deposits in the UK on a cross-border basis

The following institutions have exercised their entitlement to provide on a cross-border basis one or more of the services listed in Schedule I of the Banking Co-ordination (Second Council Directive) Regulations 1992, *including* deposit-taking. Qualifying deposits with these institutions are covered by the Deposit Protection Scheme in the institution's home state.

Name of institution	Country of home state supervisory authority
ABN AMRO Lease Holding NV	Netherlands
ACCBank plc	Republic of Ireland
Achmea Hypotheekbank NV	Netherlands
BACOB Bank Luxembourg SA	Luxembourg
BG Bank International SA	Luxembourg
BNP Finance	France
BW Bank Ireland plc	Republic of Ireland
Banca Toscana SpA	Italy
Banco Borges & Irmão SA	Portugal
Banco Chemical (Portugal) SA	Portugal
Banco ESSI, SA	Portugal
Banco Português de Investimento, SA	Portugal
Bank Austria AG	Austria
NV Bank Nederlandse Gemeenten	Netherlands
Bankgesellschaft-Berlin (Ireland) plc	Republic of Ireland
Bankinter SA	Spain

Banque Arabe et Internationale d'Investissement	France
Banque Cogeba-Gonet SA	Luxembourg
Banque de Bretagne	France
Banque de la Cité	France
Banque et Caisse d'Epargne de l'Etat	Luxembourg
Banque Générale du Luxembourg SA	Luxembourg
Banque Indosuez Luxembourg	France
Banque Nationale de Paris	France
Banque Nationale de Paris Guyane	France
Banque Nationale de Paris Intercontinentale	Luxembourg
Banque Paribas Luxembourg	France
Banque pour l'Expansion Industrielle	France
Banque Scalbert DupontBear Sterns Bank plc	Republic of Ireland
Bikuben GiroBank A/S	Denmark
Caja de Ahorros de Galicia	Spain
Cedel Bank SA	Luxembourg
Chang Hwa Commercial Bank (Europe) NV	Netherlands
Chiao Tung Bank Europe NV	Netherlands
Citibank Belgium SA	Belgium
Commerzbank Europe (Ireland)	Ireland
Compagnie Financière de CIC et de L'Union Européenne	France
Corporación Bancaria de España, SA	Spain
Cortal Bank	Luxembourg
Crédit Agricole Indosuez	Luxembourg
Crédit Communal de Belgique SA	Belgium
Crédit Suisse (Luxembourg) SA	Luxembourg
Crédit Universel	France
Crédito Predial Portugues SA	Portugal
Den Danske Bank International SA	Luxembourg
Den Københavnske Bank A/S	Denmark
Den norske Bank ASA	Norway
DePfa-Bank Europe pic	Republic of Ireland
Deutsche Ausgleichsbank	Germany
Deutsche Bank AG	Germany
Deutsche Bank/DB Ireland plc	Republic of Ireland
Deutsche Bank Luxembourg SA	Luxembourg
Deutsche Bau- und Bodenbank AG	Germany
Deutsche Handelsbank AG	Germany
Deutsche Hypothekenbank AG	Germany
Deutsche Siedlungs- und Landesrentenbank	Germany

Exhibit 2.2   (continued)

Dornbirner Sparkasse	Austria
Dresdner Bank Luxembourg SA	Luxembourg
Eurohypo European Mortgage Bank Ireland plc	Republic of Ireland
Finansbank (Holland) NV	Netherlands
Fokus Bank ASA	Norway
Helaba Dublin Landesbank Hessen-Thüringen International	Republic of Ireland
Helaba Luxembourg Landesbank Hessen-Thüringen International SA	Luxembourg
ING Bank NV	Netherlands
The Investment Bank of Ireland Ltd	Republic of Ireland
Irish Intercontinental Bank Ltd	Republic of Ireland
Irish Nationwide Building Society	Republic of Ireland
Irish Permanent plc	Republic of Ireland
Kredietbank SA Luxembourgeoise	Luxembourg
Landeskreditbank Baden-Württemberg	Germany
Merrill Lynch Capital Markets Bank Ltd	Republic of Ireland
Nordbanken AB (publ)	Sweden
Rabobank Ireland Ltd	Republic of Ireland
Rheinhyp Bank Europe plc	Republic of Ireland
Robeco Bank (Luxembourg) SA	Luxembourg
SGZ-Bank Ireland plc	Republic of Ireland
SNVB Financements	France
Smurfit Paribas Bank Ltd	Republic of Ireland
Société Européenne de Banque	Luxembourg
Société Nancienne Varin-Bernier	France
State Street Banque SA	France
Westdeutsche Landesbank Girozentrale	Germany

(ii)   EAIs which are not entitled to accept deposits in the UK on a cross-border basis

The following institutions have exercised their entitlement to provide one or more of the services listed in Schedule I of the Banking Co-ordination (Second Council Directive) Regulations 1992, *excluding* deposit-taking.

Name of Institution	Country of home state supervisory authority
Anglo Irish Bank Corporation plc	Republic of Ireland
Banco de Fomento e Exterior SA	Portugal
Banco Finantia, SA	Portugal
Bank of America SA	Spain
Banque de Gestion Edmond de Rothschild Luxembourg	Luxembourg
Bayerische Handelsbank AG	Germany
Berlin-Hannoversche Hypothekenbank AG	Germany
Caja Bilbao Bizkaia Kutxa	Spain
Crédit Européen SA	Luxembourg
Credito Italiano	Italy
Delahaye Générale Options SA	France
Deutsche Genossenschafts-Hypothekenbank AG	Germany
Deutsche Hypothekenbank Frankfurt AG	Germany
Deutsche Schiffsbank AG	Germany
EBS Building Society	Republic of Ireland
Europäische Hypothekenbank SA	Luxembourg
FGH Bank NV	Netherlands
Frankfurter Hypothekenbank Centralboden AG	Germany
Garras Bank-Naspa Dublin	Republic of Ireland
Hypothekenbank in Hamburg AG	Germany
IKB Deutsche Industriebank AG	Germany
Incentive Credit AB	Sweden
Investmentbank Austria AG	Austria
Irish Nationwide Building Society	Republic of Ireland
LGT Bank in Liechtenstein (Deutschland) GmbH	Germany
Nedship Bank (Nederlandse Scheepshypotheekbank NV)	Netherlands
Realkredit Danmark A/S	Denmark
Republic National Bank of New York (Luxembourg) SA	Luxembourg
Rheinboden Hypothekenbank AG	Germany
Rheinische Hypothekenbank AG	Germany
S-E-Banken Luxembourg SA	Luxembourg

Exhibit 2.2   (continued)

Saltzburger Landeshypothekenbank AG	Austria
Société de Caution Mutuelle des Professions Immobilières et Foncières	France
Sparebanken Nor	Norway
Telia Finans AB	Sweden
Westfälische Hypothekenbank AG	Germany
Württembergische Hypothekenbank AG	Germany

Notes:
1. Including partnerships formed under the law of any part of the UK.
2. Cover is limited to 90 per cent of a depositor's total qualifying deposits subject to a maximum payment to any one depositor of £18,000 (or ECU 20,000 if greater).
3. The level and/or scope of cover provided by the home state Scheme for deposits with UK offices may not be greater than is available under the UK Scheme.

Source: Bank of England, 1998a, Appendix 4.

MINIMUM CRITERIA FOR AUTHORIZATION

The minimum criteria that an institution has to fulfil before authorization may be granted by the Bank are set out in Schedule 3 of the Act. They include the following:

1. A requirement for a bank to conduct its business in a 'prudent manner' (para.4(1)). This involves, *inter alia*, an institution satisfying the Bank that it has adequate capital (paras 4(2) and 4(3)), liquidity (paras 4(4) and 4(5)) and provisions (para.4(6)); that it maintains adequate accounting and other records, and adequate systems of control of its business and records (paras 4(7) and 4(8)); that it generally behaves in a prudent manner (para.4(9)); and that it is effectively directed by at least two individuals (para.2).
2. A requirement relating to the composition of the board of directors (para.3).
3. A requirement for the business to be carried out with 'integrity and skill' (para.5).
4. A requirement for a bank to have minimum net assets of £1 million at the time of authorization (para.6).
5. A requirement for directors, controllers and managers to be 'fit and proper' persons.

THE BANK'S INTERPRETATION OF THESE REQUIREMENTS

The approaches taken by the Bank to the assessment of capital and liquidity adequacy and to the adequacy of provisions are examined in detail in later sections and so need not detain us here. The other requirements, however, merit further consideration.

Prudent Conduct

The Bank's detailed interpretation of the paragraph 4(7) requirement to maintain adequate records and controls systems is set out in BSD/1987/2 (Bank of England, 1987b), issued in September 1987, as subsequently revised by BSD/1994/2 (Bank of England, 1994b) and S&S1996/6 (Bank of England, 1996c) (see Chapter 14). In short, the Bank requires that the nature and scope of the records and systems maintained are commensurate with its needs and particular circumstances, and are sufficient to ensure protection of the interests of depositors and potential depositors. In assessing whether or not this is the case, the Bank pays regard to the institution's size, the nature of its business, the manner in which the business is structured, organized and managed, and to the nature, volume and complexity of its transactions. The requirement applies to all aspects of an institution's business, both on- and off-balance-sheet, and whether undertaken as a principal or an agent.

Further requirements on this front are imposed according to paragraph 4(8). This requires that the records and systems must be such as to allow for the fulfilment of the various other elements of the 'prudent conduct' criterion and for the identification of threats to depositors' interests. They should also be sufficient to enable the institution to comply with the notification requirements of the Act (e.g. as set out in Sections 36 and 38) and with requirements relating to the provision of information and documents according to Sections 39 and 41. This means that the requirement may not be fulfilled if delays occur in the provision of information or if inaccurate information is provided.

Finally, paragraph 4(8) also requires the Bank to 'have regard to the functions and responsibilities' of directors in assessing the adequacy of records and systems. This is interpreted by the Bank as referring to the role of non-executive directors on audit committees which was the subject of a Bank consultative paper in January 1987. (For further details *see* below.)

Other considerations relevant to the prudent conduct requirement are set out in paragraph 4(9). These include: management arrangements; strategy and objectives; planning arrangements; policies on accounting, lending and other exposures, and bad debt and tax provisions; policies and practices on the taking and valuation of security, on the monitoring of arrears, on following up debtors in arrears and interest rate matching; and recruitment arrangements and training.

The final Schedule 3 requirement for prudence (though not formally part of the prudent conduct criterion) is that the business of a bank be effectively directed by at least two individuals – the so-called 'four eyes' requirement. In the case of a body corporate, the Bank normally expects that the individuals concerned will be either executive directors or persons granted executive powers by, and reporting immediately to, the board; and in the case of a partnership, the Bank will look for at least two general or active partners.

According to its interpretation of paragraph 2, the Bank also requires that at least two independent minds be applied to both the formulation and implementation of policy. The Bank thus seeks to ensure that each of the parties has the necessary qualities to contribute on all aspects of the business and does so in practice. Evidence of domination by some particular individual will raise doubts about the fulfilment of the criterion.

Composition of Board of Directors

Paragraph 3 provides that all UK-incorporated institutions include within their directorates such numbers (if any) of non-executive directors as the Bank considers appropriate, having regard to the circumstances of the institution and the nature and scale of its operations.

Because of the importance attributed by the Bank to the independent perspective provided by non-executive directors, particularly in the performance of audit committee functions, the Bank is committed to the principle that all UK-incorporated institutions and UK-based banking groups should have an audit committee and that, unless there are sound reasons to the contrary, all authorized institutions should appoint at least one non-executive director to undertake some audit committee functions. This requirement may be waived by the Bank in instances where small authorized institutions experience difficulties in appointing a sufficient number of suitable non-executive directors or where an institution's holding company has an audit committee of non-executive directors which undertakes the functions of an audit committee in respect of the institution itself.

Carrying on the Business with Integrity and Skill

Under the 'integrity' element of this criterion, an institution is required to observe high ethical standards in the conduct of its business. Criminal offences or other breaches of statute will obviously call the fulfilment of this criterion into question. Of particular relevance are contraventions of any provision made by, or under enactments designed to protect, the general public against financial loss due to dishonesty, incompetence or malpractice. Failure to comply with recognized ethical standards of conduct – such as those embodied in the London Code of Conduct for wholesale markets, the Code of Banking Practice and the

Takeover Code – might also call into question fulfilment of the criterion, depending on the nature of the breach of the Code.

The 'skill' element of the criterion requires that banks conduct their business with the skills appropriate to allow them to discharge their duties as banks. Of particular relevance are the skills appropriate to accounting, risk analysis, establishing and operating systems of internal controls, ensuring compliance with legal and supervisory requirements, and the provision of financial services. The level of skills required will depend on the nature and scale of the particular institution's activities.

Minimum Net Asset Requirement

Paragraph 6 provides that, at the time of authorization, a UK-incorporated credit institution must have net assets of at least ECU 5 million (or an equivalent amount in foreign currency or mix of sterling and foreign currency) (£1 million for non UK-incorporated institutions). This requirement does not apply after authorization, although institutions must continue to meet the capital adequacy requirement specified by the Bank (*see* Chapter 17).

The 'Fit and Proper' Requirement

Paragraph 1 provides that every person who is, or is to be, a director, controller or manager of an authorized institution must be a 'fit and proper' person. In considering whether a person fulfils this criterion, the Bank has regard to a number of general considerations, while also taking account of the circumstances of the particular position held and the institution concerned.

In deciding whether a person who is, or is to be, a director, chief executive, managing director or manager (as defined in Section 105 of the Act) fulfils the criterion, relevant considerations include whether the person has sufficient skill, knowledge and soundness of judgement to undertake and fulfil his or her duties and responsibilities properly. A person's prior experience, career track record, formal qualifications and training will be examined to ascertain this. The standards required in these respects will vary considerably, depending upon the precise position concerned. The diligence with which duties are, or are likely to be, performed is also considered by the Bank.

The probity requirement is much the same whatever position is involved. Only those of the highest integrity will be regarded as suitable for running a deposit-taking business. Accordingly, the Bank will consider whether the person has a criminal record – convictions for fraud or other dishonesty are particularly relevant – and whether the person has contravened any provision of banking, insurance, investment or other legislation designed to protect the general public against financial loss due to dishonesty, incompetence or malpractice. In addition, the Bank considers whether the person has been involved in any business practices which, in the eyes of the Bank, are improper or reflect discredit on the chosen business methods. In this connection, compliance with various non-statutory codes, such as the London Code of Conduct and the Takeover Code, in so far as they are relevant, are taken into account.

Following authorization, the Bank will have regard to the performance of the person in the exercise of their duties. Imprudence or actions which threaten the interest of depositors or potential depositors will reflect adversely on the competence and soundness of judgement of those responsible. Similarly, the failure of an institution to conduct business with integrity or professional skill will reflect adversely on the probity and/or competence and/or soundness of judgement of those responsible. While individual 'lapses' (unless particularly serious) might not lead the Bank to conclude that the criterion is not being fulfilled, a number of lapses is likely to call into question its fulfilment as the Bank takes a cumulative approach in assessing the significance of such actions.

The application of the 'fit and proper' criterion to shareholder controllers and indirect controllers (as defined in Section 105 of the Act) has to take into account the wide variety of positions that they may hold in relation to an authorized institution. The general presumption is that the greater the influence on the authorized institution, the higher the threshold will be for the controller to fulfil the criterion.

In considering the application of the criterion to *shareholder controllers* or persons proposing to become such controllers, the Bank has regard to two main considerations. First, it considers what influence the person has, or is likely to have, on the conduct of the affairs of the institution. In general, the closer the control the person has over the business, the more rigorous the Bank's requirement. Thus for those exercising close control, the Bank will expect the same range of qualities and experience – that is, probity, soundness of judgement, relevant knowledge and skills – that it expects of executive directors. For those not seeking to influence the directors and management, however, the requirement will be less onerous. In assessing how demanding this requirement should be, the Bank will also take into account the possibility of conflicts of interest arising from the influence of the shareholders, particularly those which could arise from too close an association with a non-financial company.

The second consideration is whether the financial position, reputation or conduct of the shareholder controller or prospective shareholder controller has damaged, or is likely to damage, the authorized institution through 'contagion' which undermines confidence in it. For example, publicity about illegal or unofficial conduct by the holding company or another member of the group may damage confidence in the authorized institution. In general, the higher the shareholding, the greater the risk of contagion if the shareholder encounters financial difficulties.

In determining its requirements for the fitness and probity of *indirect controllers*, the Bank will also take into account the precise position held. For those who direct or instruct shareholder controllers, the minimum standards likely to be asked are those of the person indirectly controlled. The highest standards will be asked of those who are indirect controllers by virtue of directing or instructing the board of an institution; they will be required to have the probity and relevant knowledge, experience, skills and diligence for running an authorized institution. The qualities required would be those which are also appropriate for the board of directors of an authorized institution.

FURTHER CONSIDERATIONS RELEVANT TO THE GRANT OF AUTHORIZATION

Once the Bank has examined all the information and documents requested from an applicant institution, and is satisfied that the statutory minimum criteria for authorization have been met, yet further considerations will be taken into account. Of paramount importance are the interests of depositors and potential depositors, and authorization will not be granted if, for whatever reason, the Bank considers that these are threatened. The Bank also pays particular attention to the likelihood of it receiving adequate flows of information to allow for effective monitoring of the fulfilment of the criteria and identification and assessment of any threats to depositors' interests. In assessing this issue, the Bank requires to be satisfied that the institution and the group to which it may belong will be subject to consolidated supervision in accordance with the Basle *Concordat*, as revised in 1992 (*see* Chapter 3).

A final consideration relates to the previous track record of the applicant institution. The Bank's experience since the Banking Act 1979 has been that applicants not supported by an established deposit-taking institution have found it difficult to satisfy the Bank that they are able to carry on a deposit-taking business in a prudent manner – unless they had already been successfully conducting a similar business for some time but financed from sources not involving the acceptance of deposits.

Overseas Institutions

For those institutions whose principal place of business is outside the UK, the Bank, under the terms of Section 9(3), may regard itself as satisfied that the criteria relating to fit and proper persons, prudent conduct, and integrity and professional skill are fulfilled if:

1. The banking supervisory authority in the country or territory where most of the business is conducted informs the Bank that it is satisfied with respect to the prudent management and overall financial soundness of the institution.

2. The Bank is satisfied as to the nature and scope of the supervision exercised
   by that authority.

The requirement relating to the composition of the board of directors does not
apply to such institutions, unless they are incorporated in the UK, but the 'four
eyes' and minimum net assets criteria do; the Bank has to form its own views
on the fulfilment or otherwise of these.

Although the Bank does place some reliance on the assurances received
from overseas supervisors, it nevertheless examines in detail the planned
business of the applicant's UK branch, its business plan, its liquidity policies,
its internal controls, its accounting and other records, and staffing and
management arrangements. Authorization will not be granted if the
applicant/overseas supervisor fails to allay, either through implementing an
advised course of remedial action or providing suitable assurances, any doubts
that the Bank may have about the fulfilment of the statutory criteria.

Once authorization has been secured, supervision becomes a joint responsibility
of the 'host' (i.e. the Bank) and home supervisor, the allocation of responsibilities
being determined according to the principles enshrined in the Basle *Concordat*,
as revised in 1983 and 1992 (*see* Chapter 3).

GROUNDS FOR THE REVOCATION OF AUTHORIZATION

The grounds on which the Bank may revoke or restrict an authorization are set
out in Section 11 of the Act, although, generally, whether such a ground exists
depends on the Bank's evaluation of the prevailing situation. For this reason,
it is important to understand how the Bank interprets the statutory grounds.

In general, the Bank's powers become exercisable when there is a perceived
threat to the interests of depositors or potential depositors. Because the immediacy
and severity of such threats are likely to vary from case to case the Bank is, as
a general rule (but *see* below for circumstances necessitating mandatory
revocation), given the discretion to decide whether to revoke authorization,
impose restrictions or take some other course of action.

The Bank would be unlikely to revoke or restrict authorization in situations
where it anticipated that the institution itself, or its shareholders (e.g. through
the injection of new capital or the appointment of new directors), would take
speedy and adequate action to protect the interests of (potential) depositors.
However, revocation *would* generally result where there was no reasonable
prospect of speedy and comprehensive remedial action, even though the threat
to depositors might not be immediate. Depending on the financial position of
the institution, the Bank, where in the interests of depositors, actual and

potential, will fully explore the prospects of remedial action in such circumstances before reaching a decision on the appropriate course of action. Such decisions, themselves, will usually involve the Bank in a delicate balancing act, the difficulty lying in the derivation of the appropriate weights to be ascribed to the interests of existing and potential depositors.

Restriction rather than revocation is likely to result in cases where the Bank considers that the imposition of conditions is necessary to underpin the institution's efforts to improve matters, and that there is a reasonable prospect that all the relevant criteria for authorization will be fulfilled, again within a reasonable period. Usually, such a restricted authorization would be without time limit, although the presumption is that the restrictions would be lifted by the Bank once the remedial action was taken. On occasion, however, restrictions may be imposed for a limited term, subject to a maximum of three years. Generally, such a course of action would be taken in order to facilitate an orderly repayment of deposits by avoiding liquidity pressures which might otherwise arise from a sudden loss of authorization. A restricted authorization may also be used as a holding measure to protect depositors and potential depositors while the Bank seeks further information.

Section 11(1)(a)

This provides that the Bank's powers become exercisable if it appears to the Bank that any of the criteria in Schedule 3 are not or have not been fulfilled, or may not be or may not have been fulfilled. The Bank would consider that a criterion 'may not be ... fulfilled' in circumstances where it needs further information to form a firm view but has not been able to obtain that information in a reasonable time. This provision thus enables the Bank to protect depositors pending clarification of whether or not there is a significant threat to depositors.

Section 11(1)(b)

This provides that the Bank's powers become exercisable if the institution fails to comply with any requirement imposed by the Act, by secondary legislation under the Act, or by the Bank using its powers under the Act.

Section 11(1)(d)

Under this part of the Act, the Bank's powers become exercisable if false, misleading or inaccurate information is provided to the Bank by, or on behalf of, the institution or, at the application for authorization stage, by a person who is, or is to be, a director, controller or manager of the institution. Minor inaccuracies, alone, however, are not likely to induce the Bank to exercise its powers.

Section 11(1)(e)

This part of the Act ensures that, in *all* circumstances and not just those covered by Schedule 3 (e.g. it embraces situations such as a natural catastrophe or the imposition by a government of a debt moratorium), the Bank is empowered to protect depositors, actual and potential, through restriction or revocation of authorization.

Section 11(2)

This subsection of the Act enables the Bank, in certain circumstances, to revoke the authorization of an institution if it has failed to make use of it. (Authorization is intended to enable a person to accept deposits (as defined in Section 5) in the UK in the course of carrying on a deposit-taking business (as defined in Section 6).)

Section 11: Subsections l(c), (3), (4), (6), (7), (8) and (9)

These subsections of the Act set out the circumstances in which the Bank's powers become exercisable because of certain specified events occurring. These include withdrawal of authorization (in respect of an overseas institution) by the banking supervisory authority of the country or territory in which the institution has its principal place of business; revocation of authorization under the Financial Services Act 1986 or a licence under the Consumer Credit Act 1974; and certain events connected with insolvency, receivership and the like, such as the making of a winding-up order or the passing of a resolution for voluntary winding up. (Section 11(lA) sets out additional grounds on which the Bank's powers to revoke or restrict authorization become exercisable.)

Mandatory, rather than discretionary, revocation is also covered by these subsections of the Act. The two circumstances necessitating mandatory revocation are: (1) where an institution has its principal place of business in another member state of the EU and the banking supervisory authority there withdraws the institution's authorization; and (2) where a winding-up order has been made against the institution in the UK, or a resolution for its voluntary winding up in the UK has been passed, or where analogous proceedings have occurred in other jurisdictions.

APPEALS PROCEDURES

The rights of appeal available under the Banking Act 1987 were clarified with the introduction of *the Banking Appeal Tribunal Regulations 1987* (1987, No. 1299) which came into force on 1 October 1987. These made provisions with respect to appeals under Part I of the Act against decisions of the Bank to refuse to grant authorization; to revoke authorization; to impose restrictions or give directions, or as to the restrictions imposed or directions given; or that a person should not become, or should cease to be, a director, controller or manager of an authorized institution. Provision is made as to the time and manner in which appeals are to be brought, the evidence and procedure at the hearing, the procedure after the hearing, and the payment of costs of appeals and miscellaneous matters connected with them.

It is interesting to note that Mount Banking became only the first institution to appeal, albeit unsuccessfully, against the Bank's decisions (in this case, to petition for a provisional liquidation in October 1992) under the Regulations in November 1993. (For a full discussion of the Bank's 'enforcement' activities, *see* HMSO, 1995, Appendix 7.) Moreover, the Bank's unhappy experience in supervising BCCI (*see* Chapter 11), in respect of which it was accused by both the Treasury and Civil Service Committee and Lord Justice Bingham of being inhibited from taking tough action – a charge the Bank still denies today – suggests there remains a case for redrafting the procedures, if only to allow the Bank to operate in a less inhibited fashion.

CONCLUDING COMMENTS ON AUTHORIZATION

The material presented in this chapter has set out the minimum criteria for authorization in Schedule 3 to the Banking Act 1987 and the grounds for revocation and restriction set out in Section 11 of that Act. Further, it has indicated how the Bank interprets the minimum authorization criteria and grounds for revocation/restriction, highlighting the principles underlying the exercise of its corresponding powers. (For a review of the actual use made by the Bank of these powers *see* Bank of England, 1992a, Table XIII, p. 24.) These principles, however, are not 'cast in stone'. Fortuitously, for historians and prospective authorized institutions alike, any material changes have to be recorded by the Bank (under Section 16(2) of the Act) in its annual report. In addition, as noted earlier, the FSAu is to issue a revised version of the statements of principles to accommodate developments since BCCI.

17. The assessment of capital adequacy

The Bank's general approach to the assessment of the capital adequacy of banks was first outlined in a paper entitled the 'The Measurement of Capital', which was issued in September 1980.[12] This paper was subsequently amended by BSD/1986/4 (Bank of England, 1986a) and the definition of capital updated by BSD/1986/2 (Bank of England, 1986b) and, more recently, by notices – that is, BSD/1988/3 (Bank of England, 1988a), BSD/1990/2 (Bank of England, 1990a), BSD/1990/3 (Bank of England, 1990b) and BSD/1992/1 (Bank of England, 1992b) – putting the Basle convergence agreement (*see* Chapter 7) and the EC Directives on own funds and solvency ratios (*see* Chapter 9) into effect.[13]

For capital to be sufficient for the purposes of satisfying the minimum statutory criteria for authorization (i.e. Schedule 3, paras (4) and 4(3)) it must be of an amount which is commensurate with the nature and scale of the institution's operations; and of an amount and nature sufficient to safeguard the interests of its depositors and potential depositors, having regard to the nature and scale of the institution's operations, to the risks inherent in those operations and (where the institution is a body corporate) in the operations of any other body corporate in the same group[14] so far as they are capable of affecting the institution, and to any other factors which appear to be relevant to the Bank.

Before explaining how the Bank, in practice, seeks to ensure that the capital held by authorized institutions is 'adequate' in this sense, it is first necessary to focus on the Bank's definition of capital used for this purpose.

DEFINING CAPITAL: THE EVOLUTION OF THE CURRENT APPROACH

The Bank's early approach to defining capital for this purpose was to include net assets – that is, paid-up capital and reserves for a body corporate – plus allowable subordinated loan stock, as defined in BSD/1986/2. Acceptable subordinated loan stock came in two forms: term subordinated debt and perpetual debt.[15] To rank as *primary capital* (see Exhibit 2.3), the definition of capital favoured at the time by UK and US regulators as it was supposed to comprise only the highest quality components (i.e. those which are able to absorb current losses and allow an institution to continue on a 'going concern' basis), the subordinated loan stock had to be in the form of perpetual debt which satisfied fairly exacting conditions.[16] Moreover, a limit was placed on the amount of 'qualifying' perpetual debt which could be counted as primary capital.[17]

Exhibit 2.3   The definition of 'primary capital' prior to the UK/US accord

---

Primary capital is composed of the following elements:

1. Partly or fully paid-up share capital.
2. Share premium.
3. General reserves.[1]
4. The balance on the profit and loss account.
5. Minority interests in consolidated subsidiaries.
6. General bad debt provisions, less any associated deferred tax asset.
7. Allowable perpetual debt.[2]

Notes:
1. This includes any hidden (i.e. undisclosed 'inner') reserves.
2. 'Qualifying' perpetual debt (*see* note 2 to Exhibit 2.4) may count as primary capital up to a maximum of one-third of total primary capital (i.e. half of the capital base less all loan capital (including perpetual debt)).

Although term subordinated debt did not rank as primary capital, it had long been included, subject to limits and restrictions, in what the Bank termed the 'capital base' (*see* Exhibit 2.4). This definition of capital played an important part in the Bank's quantitative assessment of capital adequacy which is discussed below.

Exhibit 2.4   Definitions of the 'capital base' and 'adjusted capital base' used by the Bank in assessing the capital adequacy of authorized institutions

---

1.   Definition of the 'capital base'
The capital base comprises:

- paid-up share capital;[1]
- share premium;
- allowable loan capital;[2]
- general bad debt provisions, less any associated deferred tax asset;
- general reserves[3] plus the balance on the profit and loss account;
- minority interests.[4]

Exhibit 2.4   (continued)

2.   Definition of the 'adjusted capital base' used in calculating the gearing ratio

The adjusted capital base (ACBg) is derived by subtracting from the capital base[5] the value of:

- premises;
- plus equipment and other fixed assets;
- plus goodwill and other intangible assets;
- plus investments in subsidiaries and associated companies and trade investments (including loans of a capital nature).

3.   Definition of the 'adjusted capital base' used in calculating the RAR

The adjusted capital base (ACBr) is derived by subtracting from the capital base[5] the value of:

- equipment and other fixed assets (bar premises);
- plus goodwill and other intangible assets;
- plus investments in subsidiaries and associated companies and trade investments (including loans of a capital nature). (i.e. ACBr = ACBg plus value of premises).

Notes:
1. Amounts partly or fully paid up on issued share (ordinary and non-redeemable preference) capital.
2. This consists of two components: term subordinated debt and perpetual debt. The sum of these will only be included in the capital base up to a maximum of 50 per cent of the total capital base (including subordinated debt). Any subordinated debt which does not qualify for inclusion in the capital base will be treated as long-term funding.

    Term subordinated debt (plus any perpetual debt not counted as primary capital – *see* Exhibit 2.3) may be included, up to a maximum of one-third of the total capital base (net of outstanding goodwill and other intangible assets), provided that: it is fully subordinated to depositors and other creditors; it has an initial term to maturity of at least five years; it does not suffer from restrictive covenants which might trigger early repayment; it is subject to straight-line amortization during the last five years of its life; and no early repayment is made without the Bank's consent.

    Perpetual debt may be included up to a maximum of half of the capital base less *all* loan capital (and net of outstanding goodwill and other intangible assets) provided that: the claims of the lender on the borrowing bank are fully subordinated to those of all unsubordinated creditors; the debt agreement does not include any clauses which might trigger repayment of the debt; no repayment of the debt is made without the prior consent of the bank; the debt agreement provides the bank with an option to defer interest payments in certain circumstances (e.g. when a dividend payment has not been paid or declared in a preceding period); and the documents governing the issue of the debt provide for the debt and unpaid interest to be able to absorb losses, while leaving the bank able to continue trading (e.g. as could be achieved by providing for automatic conversion of the perpetual debt and unpaid interest into share capital should reserves become negative and where a capital reconstruction has not been undertaken).

3. Including any 'inner' reserves.
4. When included in accounts as a result of the consolidation of subsidiary companies not wholly-owned.
5. As defined in 1 above.

Sources: Bank of England, 1980, 1986a, 1986b.

The current stance of official thinking on the appropriate statistical definition of capital reflects recent developments in international supervisory co-operation. In particular, both the UK/US accord (although it was never implemented) and the BIS proposals on the measurement of capital and assessment of capital adequacy (*see* Chapter 7) have played an important part in shaping current policy.

Had the agreed proposals of the UK/US accord of January 1987 been implemented, the Bank would have been obliged to amend its definition of primary capital slightly (*see* Exhibit 1.4). Most noticeably, this would have meant the phasing out of hidden reserves. The limits and restrictions placed on perpetual debt, however, were much the same as before. As a result, the previous approach adopted towards defining capital would have been left more or less intact. (For a critique of the accord, *see* Baestaens, 1987, and Hall, 1989.)

Of more far-reaching importance, the BIS proposals, which superseded the accord and were confirmed in July 1988, fundamentally changed the terminology used in defining capital. In came the terms *Tier 1* (*core*) and *Tier 2* (*supplementary*) capital, and out went the terms primary and secondary capital. Under the proposals (*see* Exhibit 1.8), the capital base is defined to comprise both Tier 1 and Tier 2 components. The former group consists solely of ordinary paid-up share capital and disclosed reserves, and is included without limit. The latter group, however, comprising undisclosed reserves, asset revaluation reserves, general provisions, hybrid capital instruments and subordinated term debt, can only constitute, in aggregate, a maximum of 100 per cent of Tier 1 capital. This means that at least 50 per cent of the capital base must comprise Tier 1 (core) capital. Additionally, the inclusion of subordinated term debt within the capital base is subject to a maximum of 50 per cent of Tier 1 capital, that is, 25 per cent of the capital base. A further limit also applies to the inclusion of general provisions (*see* item B of Exhibit 1.8), and asset revaluation reserves in the form of latent gains on unrealized securities are subject to a discount of 55 per cent.

Although signatories to the document were obliged to implement its proposals by the end of 1992 at the latest, transitional arrangements were agreed (*see* Exhibit 1.13). As far as the definition of the capital base was concerned, this involved the gradual phasing out of supplementary elements from core capital and the gradual introduction of limits on the amount of general provisions (expressed as a percentage of *risk assets* – *see* below) that could be included as Tier 2 capital.[18] At the discretion of national supervisors, introduction of the limit on term subordinated debt as an element of supplementary capital and the deduction of goodwill from Tier 1 capital could be left until the end of 1992.

What, then, did these new arrangements mean for authorized institutions in the UK? It was made clear that the Bank would move swiftly to implement the new proposals – by the middle of 1989 at the latest – and would not seek to avail itself of the full period of grace. Moreover, it was announced in January 1988 that general provisions which reflected lower valuations of assets – notably against less developed country (LDC) debt – would, after some future date, not count at all as Tier 2 capital. (This policy would be reviewed should further discussions in Basle result in a clearer definition being drawn between provisions and reserves. In the meantime, the Bank would allow qualifying general provisions to be included in Tier 2 capital up to a level of 1.5 per cent of weighted risk assets up to the end of 1992 and 1.25 per cent thereafter.) This, of course, would be a major change for UK institutions which, up until then, had been allowed to include such provisions, where unearmarked, without limit, in both the definition of the capital base and primary capital.

Further changes on the previous position would result from the following (*see* Bank of England, 1988a):

1. The change in the limit imposed on subordinated debt from $33\frac{1}{3}$ per cent to 25 per cent of the capital base.
2. The stipulation that core capital represents at least 50 per cent of the capital base.
3. The change in the limit imposed on perpetual debt from 50 per cent of the capital base less all loan capital to 50 per cent of the capital base.
4. Cessation of the practice of deducting trade investments from the capital base.

In practice, the relief provided through channels 3 and 4 is unlikely to have done much to offset the 'squeeze' exerted through the first two channels[19] and by the change in policy on general provisions.[20] The net result is thus likely to have been that, on a *ceteris paribus* assumption, authorized institutions would have found themselves recording a lower capital base figure than they did under the Bank's previous approach.[21] This did not, of course, necessarily imply an increase in capital *requirements*, as the new capital adequacy assessment regime (discussed below) had also to be taken into account.

The next changes to the Bank's approach to defining capital (*see* Exhibit 2.5) came with the issue of the Bank's notices (BSD/1990/2 and BSD/1992/1) giving effect to the EC's Directive on own funds (*see* Chapter 9). Neither involved any immediate change in policy to that adopted under BSD/1988/3 except that, under the latter, no further scrip issues capitalizing property revaluation reserves would be eligible for inclusion in Tier 1 capital. Accordingly, the Bank determined to continue with its existing policy of allowing the inclusion in Tier 1 capital of the current year's retained earnings (net of foreseeable charges and distributions) where they had been published in the form of an interim statement, including retained earnings of authorized subsidiaries within banking groups which published interims even if not separately disclosed, but to require verification by external auditors from 1 January 1993 (BSD/1992/5; Bank of England, 1992c). Interim profits verified by internal audit will only be eligible for inclusion in Tier 2 capital. As for its treatment of revaluation reserves, and subject to the caveat above, the Bank determined to continue with its existing policy of including revaluation reserves relating to tangible fixed assets within Tier 2 capital and other revaluation reserves, including those relating to fixed asset investments, within Tier 1 capital until the end of 1992. From 1 January 1993, however, the latter would only be eligible for inclusion in Tier 2 capital.

Exhibit 2.5   The Bank's approach to defining capital under the Own Funds Directive

---

1.   Tier 1: core capital

(a)   Permanent shareholders' equity:

- allotted, called up and fully paid share capital/common stock (net of any own shares held, at book value);
- perpetual non-cumulative preferred shares,[1] including such shares redeemable at the option of the issuer and with the Bank's prior consent, and such shares convertible into ordinary shares.

(b)   Disclosed reserves in the form of general and other reserves created by appropriations of retained earnings, share premiums and other surplus.[2]

(c)   Published interim retained profits.[3]

(d)   Minority interests arising on consolidation from interests in permanent shareholders' equity.

Exhibit 2.5 (continued)

2. Tier 2: supplementary capital

less

(e) goodwill and other intangible assets[4]

and

(f) current year's unpublished losses.
(a) Undisclosed reserves and unpublished current year's retained profits.[5]
(b) Reserves arising from the revaluation of tangible fixed assets and, from 1 January 1993, of fixed asset investments.
(c) General provisions:

- provisions held against possible or latent loss but where these losses have not as yet been identified will be included, subject to a limit (*see* 4(c));
- provisions earmarked or held specifically against lower valuations of particular claims or classes of claims will *not* be included in capital;
- this treatment of general provisions will remain in force pending further agreement in Basle on a more precise definition of unencumbered provisions.

(d) Hybrid capital instruments:

- perpetual cumulative preferred shares, including such shares redeemable at the option of the issuer and with the prior consent of the Bank, and such shares convertible into ordinary shares;
- perpetual subordinated debt which meets the conditions for primary perpetual subordinated debt set out in BSD/1986/2,[6] including such debt which is convertible into equity.

(e) Subordinated term debt:

- dated preferred shares (irrespective of original maturity);
- convertible subordinated bonds not included in the second part of point (d);
- subordinated term loan capital with a minimum original term to maturity of over five years and otherwise meeting the conditions set out in BSD/1986/2, subject to a straight-line amortization during the

last five years leaving no more than 20 per cent of the original
amount issued outstanding in the final year before redemption.

(f)   Minority interests arising on consolidation from interests in Tier 2 capital
      items.

3.   Deductions from total capital (total of Tier 1 and Tier 2)

(a)   Investments in unconsolidated subsidiaries and associates.
(b)   Connected lending of a capital nature.
(c)   All holdings of other banks' and building societies' capital instruments.
      However, the existing concessions (as set out in BSD/1986/2) that apply
      to primary and secondary market-makers in such instruments will remain
      in place but will be subject to amendment after 1 January 1993.

4.   Limits and restrictions

(a)   The total Tier 2 supplementary elements (2(a)–(f)) should not exceed a
      maximum of 100 per cent of Tier 1 elements.
(b)   Subordinated term debt (item 2(e)) should not exceed a maximum of 50
      per cent of Tier 1 elements.
(c)   General provisions (item 2(c)) should not exceed 1.5 per cent of weighted
      risk assets up to the end of 1992 and 1.25 per cent of weighted risk assets
      from 1 January 1993.

Notes:
1. Sometimes referred to as 'preferred stock'.
2. Including capital gifts and capital redemption reserves.
3. These must be verified by external auditors with effect from 1 January 1993.
4. Mortgage servicing rights will continue to be regarded as intangible assets, unless it can be
   demonstrated that there is an active and liquid market in which they can be reliably traded. At
   present, this condition is only met in respect of mortgage servicing rights traded in the US market.
5. Unpublished current year's retained profits must be verified by internal audit from 1 January
   1993.
6. Bank of England, 1986b.

Source: Bank of England, 1990a, pp. 4–5.

In respect of the definition of Tier 2 capital, the only Article of significance
is that dealing with *unpublished profits*. Article 3(1) states that they will only
be eligible for inclusion if they have been verified by internal audit (eventually,
external audit may be required). Again, the Bank's response was to continue with
prevailing policy, (which placed unpublished current year profits in Tier 2

capital) but, from 1 January 1993, to make eligibility for inclusion dependent on verification by internal audit.

The final item of note, at least from a UK perspective (other elements of capital set out in Article 2(1), covering such items as funds for general banking risks and permitted value adjustments, are not relevant in the UK), concerns the deductions to be made from total capital. For, under Articles 2(12) and 2(13), full deduction of the following is required: (1) holdings of another credit or financial institution's capital instruments which constitute more than 10 per cent of the equity of the institution in which the investment is made; and (2) such holdings which constitute less than 10 per cent of the equity of the institution in which the investment is made but which, in aggregate, exceed 10 per cent of the own funds of the reporting institution (the excess amount must be deducted).

The Bank's response was, once again, to continue with its existing policy, which entailed full deduction (in line with Article 2(12); however, this may be waived if such holdings are temporary, resulting from a financial rescue of an institution) from total capital of all holdings of another credit institution's capital, subject to the market-making concessions granted (as set out in Bank of England, 1986a), but to agree to limit such concessions from 1 January 1993 in line with the requirements of Articles 2(12) and 2(13).

The final major[22] changes to the Bank's approach to defining capital (*see* Exhibit 2.6) were made when the Bank moved to accommodate the EC's CAD (see Chapter 9). Under its policy notice S&S/1995/2 (Bank of England, 1995b) of April 1995, the risks arising from banks' lending activities (covered by the 'banking book') will continue to be covered by capital of the form permitted under the Own Funds Directive (*see* Exhibit 2.5). Banks, however, will be allowed to adopt an alternative measure of capital, so-called 'Tier 3' capital – *see* Exhibit 2.6 – to satisfy the market risk capital requirements (other than counterparty and settlement risk requirements) arising from the CAD, although this will be subject to strict limits and restrictions and to a 'lock-in' rule. The new measure of capital may comprise 'qualifying' short-term subordinated debt plus daily (net) marked-to-market profits arising from trading activities, net of any foreseeable charges or dividends, subject to the Bank being satisfied that they have been calculated in an appropriate fashion.

Exhibit 2.6   The Bank's approach to defining capital under the CAD

Banks may use three types of own funds to meet their capital requirements, as set out below. Tiers 1 and 2 may be used to support any activities. Tier 3 may only be used to support trading book activities and foreign currency risk, and may not be applied to those trading book capital requirements arising out of counterparty and settlement risk. (The latter restriction may, with the Bank's prior consent, be waived, but only at a consolidated level. This concession is designed to accommodate the Own Funds regimes of other supervisors.)

1. Tier 1: core capital

(a) Permanent shareholders' equity:

- allotted, called up and fully paid share capital/common stock (net of any own shares held, at book value);
- perpetual, non-cumulative preferred shares (sometimes referred to as 'preferred stock'), including such shares redeemable at the option of the issuer and with the Bank's prior consent, and such shares convertible into ordinary shares.

(b) Disclosed reserves in the form of general and other reserves created by appropriations of retained earnings, share premiums, capital gifts, capital redemption reserves and other surplus.

(c) Interim retained profits which have been verified by external auditors (in accordance with the terms of BSD/1992/5; Bank of England, 1992c).

(d) Minority interests arising on consolidation from interests in permanent shareholders equity.

Less

(e) Goodwill and other intangible assets (including mortgage servicing rights, unless it can be demonstrated, to the Bank's satisfaction, that there is an active and liquid market in which they can be traded).

(f) Current year's cumulative unpublished net *losses* on the banking and trading books.

(g) Fully paid shareholders' equity issued after 1 January 1992 by the capitalization of property revaluation reserves.

2. Tier 2: supplementary capital

(a) Reserves arising from the revaluation of tangible fixed assets and fixed asset investments.

(b) General provisions:

- provisions held against possible or latent loss, but where these losses have not as yet been identified, will be included to the extent that they do not exceed 1.25 per cent of the sum of risk-weighted assets in the banking book and notional-risk weighted assets in the trading book;
- provisions earmarked, or held specifically, against lower valuations of particular claims or classes of claims *will not* be included in capital.

Exhibit 2.6   (continued)

(c)   Hybrid capital instruments:

- perpetual, cumulative preferred shares, including shares redeemable at the option of the issuer and with the prior consent of the Bank, and such shares convertible into ordinary shares;
- perpetual subordinated debt, including such debt which is convertible into equity. Where such debt was issued prior to May 1994, it should meet the conditions for primary perpetual subordinated debt set out in BSD/1986/2 (Bank of England, 1986b). Where it was issued after May 1994, it should meet the conditions for hybrid capital instruments set out in BSD/1994/3 (Bank of England, 1994c).

(d)   Subordinated term debt:

- dated preferred shares (irrespective of original maturity);
- subordinated term loan capital with a minimum original maturity of at least five years plus one day. Where such debt was issued prior to May 1994, it should meet the conditions set out in BSD/1986/2, subject to a straight-line amortization during the last five years leaving no more than 20 per cent of the original amount issued outstanding in the final year before redemption. Where such debt was issued after May 1994, it should meet the conditions for subordinated term debt set out in BSD/1994/3.

(e)   Minority interests arising upon consolidation from interests in Tier 2 capital items.

(f)   Fully paid shareholders' equity issued after 1 January 1992 by the capitalization of property revaluation reserves.

3.   Deductions from Tiers 1 and 2 capital

(a)   Investments in unconsolidated subsidiaries and associations.

(b)   Connected lending of a capital nature.

(c)   All holdings of capital instruments issued by other banks, building societies and those investment firms that are subject to the CAD or an analogous regime. As currently, concessions to this deduction may be granted to banks making markets in such instruments under limits agreed with the Bank.

(d)   Qualifying holdings in financial and non-financial companies (*see* Consolidated Supervision of Credit Institutions, BSD/1993/1) (Bank of England, 1993a).

(e)   Others to be agreed on a case-by-case basis.

4. Tier 3: trading book ancillary capital

(a) Short-term subordinated debt subject to the following restrictions (and otherwise meeting the conditions for term subordinated debt set out in BSD/1994/3):

- Minimum original maturity of two years.
- The terms of the debt must provide that if the bank's allowable capital falls below its target capital requirement *then the Bank must be notified* and the Bank may require that interest and principal payments be deferred on Tier 3 debt. (Where Tier 3 capital is issued by a company within the consolidated group but it is not subject to a lock-in clause that refers to 'target capital', the Bank should be consulted prior to its inclusion in the consolidated capital base.)
- The Bank would not normally expect to give consent to any repayment within two years from the date of issuance or drawdown. Repayment will only be granted when the Bank is satisfied that the institution's capital will be adequate after repayment and is likely to remain so.
- The contribution that this subordinated debt can make to the capital base does *not* have to be amortized over its life.

(b) Daily net trading book profits, net of any foreseeable charges or dividends, subject to the Bank being satisfied that they have been calculated using appropriate techniques.

5. Limits on the use of different forms of capital

At both a solo (solo-consolidated) and a consolidated level, an institution must satisfy the following limits:

- *limit regarding Tier 2 subordinated term debt.* Total Tier 2 subordinated term debt cannot exceed 50 per cent of total Tier 1.
- *limit on capital used to meet banking book capital requirements.* Tier 2 capital used to meet the banking book capital requirements cannot exceed 100 per cent of the Tier 1 capital used to meet those requirements.
- *limit on capital used to meet the trading book capital requirements.* Tier 2 capital and Tier 3 subordinated debt used to meet the trading book capital requirements must not – in total – exceed 200 per cent of the Tier 1 capital used to meet those requirements.

In addition, at the consolidated level (or the solo level when a bank is not part of a consolidated group), the following *overall limit* applies:

Exhibit 2.6   (continued)

> • Tier 2 and Tier 3 capital cannot – in total – normally exceed 100 per
>   cent of the bank's Tier 1 capital. This limit cannot be exceeded
>   without the Bank's express permission, which will normally only be
>   granted where a bank's trading book accounts for most of its business.

Where a bank has any subordinated debt surplus to the ratios described above,
this debt will be disregarded in the calculation of a bank's own funds and
treated as part of the long-term funding of the bank.

Source: Bank of England, 1995b, Chapter 9, pp. 2–5.

To qualify for inclusion in Tier 3 capital, the short-term subordinated debt
must satisfy the following conditions: (1) it meets the conditions set out in
BSD/1994/3 (Bank of England, 1994c), paras 4–8 and 10–11; (2) no early
repayment can be made without the prior consent of the Bank;[23] (3) the
minimum original maturity of the debt does not exceed two years and one day;
and (4) the terms of the debt provide that the Bank has to be notified if the bank's
allowable capital falls below its 'target' (*see* below) capital requirement.[24]
Unlike its counterpart in Tier 2 capital, however, it does not have to be amortized
for supervisory purposes once it nears maturity.

While the Bank is thus willing to sanction a new form of capital for supervisory
purposes it will, nevertheless, limit its ability to be used to meet trading book
requirements. The limits will be of the following form: (1) overall limits will
apply, at the solo (or solo-consolidated) and consolidated levels, to the combined
aggregate of Tier 2 and Tier 3 capital – the proposed limits are 200 per cent and
100 per cent of Tier 1 capital respectively;[25] and (2) a limit will apply to the
combined aggregate of Tier 2 and Tier 3 capital which can be used to meet trading
book capital requirements, subject simultaneously to satisfying (1) above – the
proposed limit is 200 per cent of the trading book Tier 1 capital used to meet
these requirements.[26] (For a critique of the Bank's approach to defining capital
for capital adequacy assessment purposes, *see* Hall, 1989, 1995.)

THE BANK'S CAPITAL REQUIREMENTS: THE
EVOLUTION OF THE CURRENT APPROACH

Moving away from the definition of capital,[27] the next step is to explore the nature
of the capital requirements imposed on authorized institutions.

In assessing capital adequacy, the Bank seeks to take account of *all* the possible risks of loss to which an institution may be exposed. These risks include the following:

1. The risk of counterparty default, whether arising from on-balance-sheet or off-balance-sheet operations (*credit risk*).
2. Risks arising from open foreign exchange positions (*foreign exchange risk*).
3. Risks arising from open interest rate positions or unhedged investment positions (*interest rate risk and position risk*).
4. Risks arising from management negligence or incompetence (*operational risk*).
5. Risks arising from the concentration of business (e.g. geographically, sectorally or on an individual counterparty basis) (*concentration risk*).
6. The risks arising from subsidiaries, associates and other connected companies which might expose the institution to direct financial costs or general loss of confidence by association (*contagion risk*).

Because of this, the Bank has to take into account both an institution's on-balance-sheet and off-balance-sheet activities, and the nature of its relationships with group and other connected companies.

The Pre-CAD Approach

Each of the risks outlined above was analysed on the basis of regular standardized returns – using Form BSD1 (*see* Hall, 1993, Chapter 15, pp. 102–21) submitted to the Bank. Additionally, individual institutions could provide internal management information on an *ad hoc* basis. Some of the risks were subject to formal measurement: credit risk according to a model outlined in the Bank's 'Measurement of Capital' paper of September 1980 (Bank of England, 1980), as amended by subsequent Bank notices; and foreign exchange risk according to the Bank's papers on 'Foreign Currency Exposure' (Bank of England, 1981) and 'Foreign Currency Options' (Bank of England, 1984a). Risk analysis was undertaken on a consolidated basis, so as to capture exposures arising in subsidiaries and other connected companies, and on an unconsolidated basis, in order to assess whether there was an appropriate distribution of capital within a group. Finally, special reporting arrangements for large exposures were deployed to facilitate monitoring of concentration risk.

The overriding objective of the Bank in assessing risk is the provision of a subjective evaluation which takes full account of all the risks to which the institution is exposed and the ability of its management to handle those risks.

The latter requires the Bank to assess the expertise, experience and track record of an institution's management, its internal control and accounting systems, its future business plans, its size and position in the chosen markets, and other factors, such as future business prospects, which the Bank may deem relevant.

The results of this exhaustive analysis were encapsulated in the form of a minimum capital ratio – the so-called 'trigger' RAR.[28] This ratio related an institution's capital base to the measures of credit risk and foreign exchange risk discussed above. More formally, an RAR was derived by expressing an institution's *adjusted capital base* – *see* Exhibit 2.5 – as a percentage of its TOWRA. The denominator, in turn, was derived by summing the products of the nominal values of each distinct balance-sheet component and their corresponding *risk weights*, according to a classification system established by the Bank (*see* Exhibit 2.7), and adding this figure to the sum of the weighted loan requirements arising from off-balance-sheet activities (*see* below).[29]

Exhibit 2.7   Risk weights applied to on-balance-sheet assets by the Bank pre-CAD

A

0 per cent

1. Cash and claims collateralized by cash deposits placed with the lending institution (or certificates of deposit (CDs) and similar instruments issued by, and lodged with, the reporting institution) and meeting the conditions set out in the Bank's reporting requirements for 0 per cent.
2. Gold and other bullion held in own vaults or on an allocated basis.
3. Claims[1] on Zone A central governments and central banks, including claims on the European Communities.
4. Claims[1] guaranteed by Zone A central governments and central banks.[2]
5. Claims[1] on Zone B central governments and central banks denominated in local currency and funded in that currency.
6. Claims[1] guaranteed by Zone B central governments or central banks, where denominated in local currency and funded in that currency.
7. Certificates of tax deposit.
8. Items in suspense.[3]

B

10 per cent

1. Holdings of fixed interest securities issued (or guaranteed) by Zone A central governments with a residual maturity of one year or less, and floating rate

and index-linked securities of any maturity issued or guaranteed by Zone A central governments.

2. Claims collateralized by Zone A central government fixed interest securities with a maturity of one year or less, and similar floating rate securities of any maturity.

3. Holdings of securities issued by Zone B central governments with a residual maturity of one year or less and dominated in local currency and funded by liabilities in the same currency.

4. Loans to discount houses, GEMMs, institutions with a money-market dealing relationship with the Bank and those stock exchange money brokers which operate in the gilt-edged market, where the loans are secured on gilts, UK Treasury bills, eligible local authority and eligible bank bills, or London CDs.

C
20 per cent

1. Holdings of fixed interest securities issued (or guaranteed) by Zone A central governments with a residual maturity of over one year.

2. Claims collateralized by Zone A central government fixed interest securities with a residual maturity of one year.

3. Holdings of Zone B central government securities with a maturity of over one year denominated in local currency and funded by liabilities in the same currency.

4. Claims on multilateral development banks and claims guaranteed by, or collateralized by, the securities issued by these institutions.

5. Claims on credit institutions incorporated in Zone A and claims guaranteed (or accepted or endorsed) by Zone A-incorporated credit institutions.

6. On-balance-sheet claims in gold and other bullion on the non-bank market-making members of the London Bullion Market Association.[4]

7. Claims on credit institutions incorporated in Zone B with a residual maturity of one year or less and claims of the same maturity guaranteed by Zone B credit institutions.

8. Claims secured by cash deposited with, and held by, an agent bank acting for a syndicate of which the reporting institution is a member.

9. Claims on Zone A public sector entities and claims guaranteed by such entities. In the UK, these comprise local authorities and certain non-commercial public bodies.

10. Claims on discount houses and claims which are guaranteed (or accepted) by discount houses which are unsecured, or secured on assets other than specified in B4 above.

11. Cash items in the process of collection.

Exhibit 2.7   (continued)

D

50 per cent

1. Loans to individuals fully secured by a first priority charge on residential property that is (or is to be) occupied by the borrower or is rented.
2. Loans to housing associations registered with the Housing Corporation, Scottish Homes and Tai Cymru that are fully secured by a *first priority* charge on the residential property which is under development and fully secured by a charge on the housing association's residential property that is being let, and where the project attracts HAG (Housing Authority Grant). If HAG is not available, such loans must be fully secured by a *first priority* charge on residential property that is being let.
3. Mortgage sub-participations, where the risk to the sub-participating bank is fully and specifically secured against residential mortgage loans which would themselves qualify for the 50 per cent weight.
4. Holdings of securities issued by special-purpose mortgage finance vehicles where the risk to the security holders is fully and specifically secured against residential mortgage loans which would themselves qualify for the 50 per cent weight or by assets which qualify for a weight of less than 50 per cent,[4] as long as the mortgage loans are fully performing on origination of the vehicle.

E

100 per cent

1. Claims on the non-bank private sector.
2. Claims on credit institutions incorporated in Zone B with a residual maturity of over one year.
3. Claims on Zone B central governments and central banks (unless denominated in the national currency and funded in that currency).
4. Claims guaranteed by Zone B central governments or central banks which are not denominated and funded in the national currency common to the guarantor and borrower.
5. Claims on commercial companies owned by the public sector.
6. Claims on Zone B public sector entities.
7. Premises, plant, equipment and other fixed assets.
8. Real estate, trade investments[5] and other assets not otherwise specified.
9. Aggregate net short open foreign exchange position.[6]
10. Gross deferred tax assets.

Notes:
1. Other than securities issued by these bodies.

2. Including lending under Export Credit Guarantee Department (ECGD) bank guarantee and equivalent schemes in other Zone A countries, but excluding lending against the security of ECGD insurance cover.
3. Where such items do not represent a credit risk but rather position risk, as detailed in the guidance notes to Form BSD1.
4. Until 1 January 1993, from which time such claims will be weighted at 100 per cent.
5. Excluding: (1) holdings of capital instruments issued by credit institutions which will be deducted from total capital; and (2) holdings of capital instruments of other financial institutions which must be deducted according to Articles 2(12) and (13) of the Own Funds Directive.
6. This is a proxy weight for a bank's foreign exchange risk, and will remain in effect until an international framework for capturing foreign exchange risk is agreed. Includes the net short open position in gold, silver, platinum and palladium.

Source: Bank of England, 1990b, pp. 7–9.

The Bank's derivation of risk weights was, necessarily, somewhat arbitrary, but the intention was to relate such balance-sheet items to their perceived susceptibility to three[30] specific types of risk: *credit, investment* and *forced-sale risk*.[31] Inevitably, concern with credit risk predominated. Commercial advances were used as a benchmark and given a weighting of unity. The risk weights initially varied from 0 to 2, with the *aggregate foreign currency position* (as defined in the Bank's 1981 paper on 'Foreign Currency Exposure') being given a weight of unity, but the chosen range was only from 0 to 100 per cent (*see* Exhibit 2.7).

In considering the appropriate level for this trigger ratio, the Bank took into account, as far as possible, all the other risks to which an institution was exposed, its capacity to manage those risks, and its profitability and general prospects. Individual trigger ratios were set for each institution after discussions with senior management. In this manner, capital adequacy assessment was extremely flexible, with the ability to accommodate differences in characteristics between institutions. While no norms were established, the trigger ratios set for a group of similar institutions were likely to lie within a fairly narrow range, so that peer group assessment imposed a measure of standardization on the assessment process. In general, the Bank expected each institution to conduct its business so as to maintain its RAR at a margin above the trigger level, which was set substantially higher than the minimum RAR figure of 8 per cent agreed on by the Basle Committee. This higher ratio was known as the 'target' RAR.

Off-Balance-Sheet Business[32]

In the discussion of the derivation of trigger and target RARs, little has, so far, been said about the treatment of *off-balance-sheet* activities, other than to note that they were somehow taken into account. The first move by the Bank objectively to assess the inherent risks of off-balance-sheet business (other than business which gave rise to contingent liabilities, which was 'captured' from 1980) was taken in April 1985 when NIFs and RUFs were brought within the risk-weighting system. Whether or not they had been drawn down, the Bank required, pending a review of the risks involved, that they be treated as contingent liabilities for the purpose of calculating RARs, bearing a risk weight of a half.

Following the Bank review (which resulted in the issue of a Bank consultative paper in March 1986; Bank of England, 1986c), involving industry participation, and after consultations with Federal bank supervisors in the US, a more generalized risk-weighting system for off-balance-sheet items duly materialized under the accord in January 1987. This, however, was never implemented, the BIS initiative emerging before the agreed proposals could be put into effect. Given that the BIS proposals were based on the accord, however, it is worthwhile exploring the latter further before focusing on the former.

Under the accord, the notional principal amounts of certain[33] off-balance-sheet activities were first to be converted into on-balance-sheet loan equivalents (the *deemed credit risk equivalents*) by multiplying by the appropriate conversion factors, which varied from 10 per cent to 100 per cent (*see* Chapter 7, Exhibit 1.6). The loan equivalents were then to be slotted into the basic weighting framework (*see* Chapter 7, Exhibit 1.5), usually according to the nature of the counterparty ('obligor') involved but, occasionally, according to the remaining maturity of the obligation or to the nature of the qualifying collateral or guarantees.

This suggested approach was carried a stage further in May 1987 with the release of a document, as part of the accord, on the proposed treatment of interest rate- and foreign exchange rate-related instruments. The instruments covered in this document were single currency swaps, forward rate agreements, interest rate options purchased by a bank, cross-currency swaps, forward foreign currency contracts and foreign currency options purchased by a bank.

As before, a two-stage process was to have been deployed to transform the notional principal amounts of off-balance-sheet items into risk-weighted amounts. The notional principal amounts were to be first converted into balance-sheet equivalent credit exposures and then assigned one of the five risk weights specified in Exhibit 1.5 in the manner described above. The first stage of the process, however, differed from that described earlier.

For interest rate- and foreign exchange rate-related instruments, the equivalent credit exposure was to be measured as the sum of two components:

1. The current exposure faced by the institution, which equals the mark-to-market value (i.e. the amount the bank would have to pay to replace the net payment stream specified by the contract if the counterparty were to default) of all its contracts with a positive value.
2. An estimate of the potential future credit exposure faced over the life of the instrument owing to fluctuations in interest rates or exchange rates.

The second component was to have been calculated by multiplying the notional principal amounts by the appropriate conversion factors (for justification of the numbers, *see* Bank of England, 1987c) – *see* Exhibit 2.8. (For illustrative purposes, the Bank's worked examples are reproduced as Exhibit 2.9.)

Under the agreed BIS proposals, as modified by the Bank's notice (BSD/1990/3; Bank of England, 1990b) implementing the EC's Solvency Ratio Directive, the same methodology was applied,[34] although the precise schema of conversion factors used in the translation of off-balance-sheet exposures to on-balance-sheet credit risk equivalents was different (*see* Exhibits 2.10 and 2.11).

Exhibit 2.8   *Potential credit exposure: proposed conversion factors[1] for interest rate and foreign exchange rate contracts (percentage of notional principal amount)*

Remaining maturity	Interest rate[2] contracts (%)	Exchange rate[3] contracts (%)
Less than one year:		
Less than three days	0	0
Three days to one month	0	1 to 2
One month to three months	0	2 to 4
Three months to one year	0	4 to 8
One year or longer	(1/2 to 1) per complete year	(5 to 10) + (1 to 2) per complete year

Notes:
1. The authorities will carefully review these proposed credit conversion factors in light of public comments on the implications for pricing and competition.
2. Interest rate contracts include single-currency interest rate swaps, FRAs, interest rate options purchased (except for those purchased on exchanges) and similar instruments. However, no potential credit exposure will be calculated for single-currency floating/floating interest rate swaps; the credit exposure on these contracts would be evaluated solely on the basis of their mark-to-market value.
3. Exchange rate contracts include cross-country interest rate swaps, forward foreign exchange options purchased (except those purchased on exchanges) and similar instruments.

Source: Bank of England, 1987c.

As far as the Bank was concerned, the changes necessitated by the adoption of the Solvency Ratio Directive (all measures bar implementation of the minimum capital standard requirement had to be put into effect by 1 January 1991) related to its treatment of the following items:

1. On-balance-sheet claims in gold and silver bullion on the non-bank market-making members of the London Bullion Market Association.

Exhibit 2.9 *Calculation of credit equivalent amounts: interest rate- and foreign exchange rate-related transactions*

Type of contract (remaining maturity)	1 Notional principal (dollars) ×	2 Potential exposure conversion factor[1] =	3 Potential exposure (dollars) +	4 Current exposure (dollars)[2] =	5 Credit equivalent (dollars)
1. 120-day forward foreign exchange	5,000,000	0.04	200,000	100,000	300,000
2. 120-day forward foreign exchange	6,000,000	0.04	240,000	−120,000	120,000
3. three-year single-currency fixed/floating interest rate swap	10,000,000	0.015	150,000	500,000	650,000
4. three-year single-currency fixed/floating interest rate swap	10,000,000	0.015	150,000	−600,000	0
5. seven-year cross-currency floating/floating interest rate swap	20,000,000	0.12	2,400,000	−1,300,000	1,100,000
Total	51,000,000				2,170,000

Notes:
1. For illustrative purposes only, these examples use credit conversion factors at the lower end of the ranges.
2. These numbers are purely illustrative.

Source: Bank of England, 1987c.

2. Mortgage-backed securities.
3. Claims on regional governments and local authorities of another member state.
4. Claims secured by cash deposited with, and held by, an agent bank acting for a syndicate of which the reporting institution is a member.
5. Multilateral Development Banks.
6. Loans secured by residential property.
7. Deferred tax assets.
8. Guarantees received from a banking subsidiary.
9. Commodity-related transactions and equity options.

While the Bank contended that none of the policy changes which took effect from 1 January 1990 were substantive, the new policy adopted in respect of the treatment of mortgage-backed securities is worthy of a second mention. This is because the Directive, by not specifically covering mortgage-backed securities, forced the Bank to ascribe a 100 per cent risk weighting to them (albeit only from 1 January 1993), which was double the weighting previously used.[35] Unless the Directive was amended by the Comitology procedure, it was feared that such action might retard the growth of the market in such instruments in the UK (and, indeed, in the EC), a development likely to be viewed in an unfavourable light by the UK authorities. In the event, the Bank issued an amendment (BSD/1992/6; Bank of England, 1992d) to its 1990 notice implementing the Solvency Ratio Directive in December 1992, clarifying the treatment of holdings of mortgage-backed securities. In particular, it established the conditions which would allow mortgage-backed securities to qualify for the 50 per cent weight.[36]

Exhibit 2.10   Credit conversion factors for off-balance-sheet risk applied by the Bank[1]

Instrument	Credit conversion factor (%)
A.	Direct credit substitutes, including general guarantees of indebtedness, standby letters of credit serving as financial guarantees, acceptances and endorsements (including *per aval* endorsements).	100
B.	Sale and repurchase agreements and asset sales with recourse where the credit risk remains with the bank.[2]	100
C.	Forward asset purchases, forward forward deposits placed and the unpaid part of partly paid shares and securities,[2] and any other commitments with a certain drawdown.	100

D.	Transaction-related contingent items not having the character of direct credit substitutes (e.g. performance bonds, bid bonds, warranties and standby letters of credit related to particular transactions).	50
E.	Short-term self-liquidating trade-related contingent items (such as documentary credits collateralized by the underlying shipments).	20
F.	NIFs and RUFs.[3]	50
G.	Other commitments (e.g. formal standby facilities and credit lines) with an original[4] maturity of over one year.	50
H.	Similar commitments with an original[4] maturity of up to one year, or which can be unconditionally cancelled at any time.	0
I.	Endorsements of bills (including *per aval* endorsements) which have previously been accepted by a bank.	0

Multi-option facilities and other composite products should be disaggregated into their component parts, for example, into a credit commitment or NIF, and each component part converted according to the above classification. However, components carrying the lowest credit conversion factors should be disregarded to the extent necessary to ensure that the total value of all the components does not exceed the value of the facility.

Notes:
1. Credit conversion factors should be multiplied by the weights applicable to the category of the counterparty for an on-balance-sheet transaction to derive the 'weighted loan equivalents'.
2. These items are to be weighted according to the category of the issuer of the security (or the borrower in the underlying loan agreement) and not according to the counterparty with whom the transaction has been entered into. Reverse repos (i.e. purchase and resale agreements where the bank is the receiver of the asset) are treated as collateralized loans, with the risk being measured as an exposure to the counterparty. Where the security temporarily acquired attracts a preferential risk weighting, this is recognized as collateral and the risk weighting of the loan accordingly reduced (e.g. a Zone A government security).
3. To be applicable to the total amount of the institution's underwriting obligations of any maturity. Where the facility has been drawn down by the borrower and the notes are held by anyone other than the reporting institution, its underwriting obligations must continue to be reported as the full nominal amount. (Own holdings of notes underwritten are, however, deducted from the overall value of the commitment, because they are weighted as an on-balance-sheet item.)
4. Banks may report on the basis of residual maturity until the end of 1992 to assist data collection.

Source: Bank of England, 1990b, p. 10.

Exhibit 2.11　The Bank's treatment of interest rate- and foreign exchange rate-related instruments

---

Banks are exposed to the potential cost of replacing the cash flow arising from these instruments. This cost depends on the maturity of the contract and on the volatility of the underlying interest or exchange rates. Higher conversion factors are applied to those contracts which are based on exchange rate risk, reflecting the greater volatility of exchange rates. For interest rate- and exchange rate-related contracts, a 50 per cent weight is applied to counterparties which would otherwise attract a 100 per cent weight.

A.　*Exchange rate contracts include:*[1]
1. Cross-currency swaps.
2. Cross-currency interest rate swaps.
3. Outright forward foreign exchange contracts.
4. Currency futures.[2]
5. Currency options purchased.[2]

B.　*Interest rate contracts include:*
1. Single-currency interest rate swaps.
2. Basis swaps.
3. FRAs, forward forward deposits accepted and products with similar characteristics.
4. Interest rate futures.[2]
5. Interest rate options purchased.[2]

Replacement cost method
In order to calculate the credit equivalent amount of these instruments, a bank should add together:

1. The total replacement cost (obtained by 'marking to market') of all its contracts with a positive value.
2. An amount for potential future credit exposure which reflects the residual maturity of the contracts, calculated as a percentage of notional principal amount according to the following matrix:

Residual maturity	Interest rate contracts (%)	Exchange rate contracts (%)
One year or less	nil	1.0
Over one year	0.5	5.0

Exhibit 2.11 (continued)

No potential exposure should be calculated for single-currency interest rate basis swaps; the credit exposure on these contracts should be evaluated solely on the basis of mark-to-market value.

In the case of interest rate or cross-currency swaps arranged at off-market prices, the Bank requires special treatment for contracts which have been created in order to disguise a credit exposure to the counterparty.

Original exposure method
To obtain the credit equivalent amount using the original exposure method, the notional principal amount should be multiplied by the following conversion factors to obtain the future credit exposure:

Original maturity	Interest rate contracts (%)	Exchange rate contracts (%)
One year or less	0.5	2.0
Over one year, not exceeding two years	1.0	5.0
For each additional year	1.0	3.0

Notes:
1. Exchange rate contracts with an original maturity of 14 calendar days or less are excluded. Foreign currencies are to include gold, silver, platinum and palladium.
2. Instruments traded on exchanges may be excluded where they are subject to daily margining requirements.

Source: Bank of England, 1990b, pp. 11–12.

CAPITAL ADEQUACY ASSESSMENT UNDER THE CAD[37]

The Trading Book

Under the new arrangements introduced in January 1996 (*see* Bank of England, 1995b, 1995c),[38] which necessitated use of a new prudential return – CAD1 (*see* Exhibit 2.12) – to complement a revised BSD1 (i.e. BSD2 – not reproduced here) now applicable only to the banking book, banks are required to allocate positions and exposures to the trading book and the banking book, as explained in Chapter 9. Given the significance of this division for the determination of a bank's overall capital adequacy requirement – *see* below – it is obviously very important to understand how the Bank expects banks to handle this task.

Exhibit 2.12   Prudential return form (CAD1)

Form CAD1

Private and confidential

Capital Adequacy Return (Trading Book)

as at_____

Reporting institution _____
                    (Unconsolidated/Solo consolidated/Consolidated - delete as appropriate)

I confirm that I have read the relevant reporting instructions issued by the Bank, including paragraphs relating to accurate returns, and this return has been completed in accordance with them.

_____
Signature of director or senior manager of the reporting institution

In the event of a query, the Bank of England may contact (block letters please)

_____   Tel No_____   Ext_____

Notes on completion

If you have any difficulty in completing this return, please telephone your Supervision and Surveillance analyst for guidance.

1   Complete the return quarterly on an unconsolidated/solo consolidated basis as at end of March, June, September and December, or at dates which coincide with the financial year end if agreed with Supervision and Surveillance.

2   Complete the return half-yearly on a consolidated basis as at end of June and December, or at dates which coincide with the financial year end if agreed with Supervision and Surveillance.

3   Enter amounts to the nearest thousands omitting £000s. Calculated amounts should be rounded to the nearest thousands, or two decimal places as appropriate.

4   For definitions of items, refer to the "Guidance Notes and Definitions".

5   Submit within 10 working days for unconsolidated/solo consolidated returns and 20 working days for consolidated returns to:

        Monetary and Financial Statistics Division
        Domestic Banking Statistics (HO-5)
        Bank of England
        Threadneedle Street
        London EC2R 8 AH

6   Returns may also be delivered to the Reception Desk at the Threadneedle Street entrance of the Bank of England between 9.00am and 5.00pm, Monday to Friday. Envelopes should be clearly addressed as above.

Bank of England use only

Logged in	Data entered	Amendment Book	Amendment Input

September 1995
(3631)

NON-MARKET RISK IN THE TRADING BOOK

			Amount £000s		Weighted amount £000s		Capital Requirement £000s
COUNTERPARTY RISK ARISING FROM:							
10	Free Deliveries						☐
10.1			☐	0%	☐	8%	☐
10.2			☐	10%	☐	8%	☐
10.3			☐	20%	☐	8%	☐
10.4			☐	100%	☐	8%	☐
20	Margins						☐
20.1			☐	0%	☐	8%	☐
20.2			☐	10%	☐	8%	☐
20.3			☐	20%	☐	8%	☐
20.4			☐	100%	☐	8%	☐
30	Fees						☐
30.1			☐	0%	☐	8%	☐
30.2			☐	10%	☐	8%	☐
30.3			☐	20%	☐	8%	☐
30.4			☐	100%	☐	8%	☐
40	Other counterparty risk in the trading book						☐
40.1			☐	0%	☐	8%	☐
40.2			☐	10%	☐	8%	☐
40.3			☐	20%	☐	8%	☐
40.4			☐	100%	☐	8%	☐
50	Unsettled transactions (from Appendix 1)						☐
60	OTC Derivatives (from Appendix 2)				☐	8%	☐
70	Forward transactions (from Appendix 4)				☐	8%	☐
80	Repos (from Appendix 4)				☐	8%	☐
90	Reverse Repos (from Appendix 4)				☐	8%	☐
100	TOTAL COUNTERPARTY RISK IN THE TRADING BOOK						☐

LARGE EXPOSURES IN THE TRADING BOOK

		Specific Risk Charge (£000s)		Capital Requirement (£000s)
110	Adjusted Capital Base (including Tier Three capital)			[Amount £000s]
120	Excesses that have existed for 10 days or less...	[ ]	200%	[ ]
130	Excesses that have existed for more than 10 days...	[ ]		[ ]
130.1	>25% and ≤40% of adjusted capital base..	[ ]	200%	
130.2	>40% and ≤60% of adjusted capital base..	[ ]	300%	
130.3	>60% and ≤80% of adjusted capital base..	[ ]	400%	
130.4	>80% and ≤100% of adjusted capital base..	[ ]	500%	
130.5	>100% and ≤250% of adjusted capital base..	[ ]	600%	
130.6	>250%..	[ ]	900%	
140	CAPITAL REQUIREMENT FOR LARGE EXPOSURES...	[ ]		[ ]

MARKET RISKS IN THE TRADING BOOK

Capital
Requirement
(£000s)

FOREIGN EXCHANGE RISK

150   For basic approach (from Appendix 5).. [ ]

160   For backtesting approach (from Appendix 5) .... [ ]

170   Additional Capital Charge for Options... [ ]

170.1 Using Carve Out... [ ]
170.2 Using Models Approach .... [ ]

180   TOTAL FOREIGN EXCHANGE RISK .... [ ]

INTEREST RATE POSITION RISK	Amount (£000s)	Specific Risk Weights	Capital Requirement (£000s)
190 Specific Risk			[ ]
190.1	[ ]	0.00%	[ ]
190.2	[ ]	0.25%	[ ]
190.3	[ ]	1.00%	[ ]
190.4	[ ]	1.60%	[ ]
190.5	[ ]	8.00%	[ ]

200   General Market Risk (from Appendix 6).. [ ]

210   Additional Capital Charge for Options... [ ]

210.1 Using Carve Out... [ ]
210.2 Using Models Approach .... [ ]

215   Embedded Interest Rate Risk in Equity Derivatives... [ ]

220   TOTAL INTEREST RATE POSITION RISK .... [ ]

EQUITY RATE POSITION RISK

Capital
Requirement
(£000s)

230   Specific Risk (from Appendix 7) .... [ ]
240   General Market Risk (from Appendix 7)... [ ]

250   Additional Capital Charge for Options... [ ]

250.1 Using Carve Out... [ ]
250.2 Using Models Approach .... [ ]

260   Alternative method for equity position risk .... [ ]

270   TOTAL EQUITY POSITION RISK.. [ ]

EXPOSURES COLLATERALISED/GUARANTEED/NETTED

This return records the adjustments made by the reporting institution to the Capital Adequacy Return (Trading Book) [CAD1] in respect of exposures collateralised, guaranteed, or netted where the collateral/guarantee has been used to reduce the risk weight coefficient of the asset, eg show the amounts in column 3 transferred from item 40.4 (100% weight) to item 40.1 (0% weight).

ITEM NUMBERS [CAD1 - Capital Adequacy Return (Trading Book)]   £000s

1	2	3	4	5
From	To	Amount Collateralised	Amount Guaranteed	Amount Netted

APPENDIX 1: COUNTERPARTY RISK ON UNSETTLED TRANSACTIONS

Standard Method (Capital Charge based on potential loss)

	Unsettled Transactions	Potential Loss		Capital Charge
10	0 - 4 days		0%	
20	5 - 15 days		8%	
30	16 - 30 days		50%	
40	31 - 45 days		75%	
50	46 or more days		100%	
60	Total			

Alternative Method (Capital Charge based on agreed settlement price)

	Unsettled Transactions	Agreed Settlement price		Capital Charge
70	0 - 4 days		0%	
80	5 - 15 days		0.5%	
90	16 - 30 days		4%	
100	31 - 45 days		9%	
	46 or more days	Use Standard Method		
110	Total			
120	Total unsettled transactions			

APPENDIX 2: COUNTERPARTY EXPOSURE ON OTC DERIVATIVE CONTRACTS (TRADING BOOK)

REPLACEMENT COST METHOD (£000s)

	OTC CONTRACTS Counterparty Risk Weight All maturities	Replacement cost	Potential Future Exposure	Credit Equivalent Amount	Weight	Weighted Amount
10	0%				0%	
20	10%				10%	
30	20%				20%	
40	50%				50%	
50	Unanalysed				50%	
60	TOTAL					

APPENDIX 3: SUPPLEMENTARY INFORMATION ON DERIVATIVE CONTRACTS (TRADING BOOK)
REPLACEMENT COST METHOD (£000s)

INTEREST RATE CONTRACTS	Notional Principal Amounts By Residual Maturity				Replacement Cost By Residual Maturity			
	≤1 Year	1-5 Years	over 5 Years	Total	≤1 Year	1-5 Years	over 5 Years	Total
10 0%								
20 10%								
30 20%								
40 50%								
50 Exchange-traded								
of which								
60 OTC Options								
70 Exchange Traded Options								

FOREIGN EXCHANGE CONTRACTS	Notional Principal Amounts By Residual Maturity				Replacement Cost By Residual Maturity			
	≤1 Year	1-5 Years	over 5 Years	Total	≤1 Year	1-5 Years	over 5 Years	Total
80 0%								
90 10%								
100 20%								
110 50%								
120 Exchange-traded								
of which								
130 OTC Options								
140 Exchange Traded Options								

EQUITY CONTRACTS	Notional Principal Amounts By Residual Maturity				Replacement Cost By Residual Maturity			
	≤1 Year	1-5 Years	over 5 Years	Total	≤1 Year	1-5 Years	over 5 Years	Total
150 0%								
160 10%								
170 20%								
180 50%								
190 Exchange-traded								
of which								
200 OTC Options								
210 Exchange Traded Options								

APPENDIX 3: SUPPLEMENTARY INFORMATION ON DERIVATIVE CONTRACTS (TRADING BOOK)
REPLACEMENT COST METHOD (£000s)

COMMODITY CONTRACTS

	Notional Principal Amounts By Residual Maturity				Replacement Cost By Residual Maturity			
	≤1 Year	1-5 Years	over 5 Years	Total	≤1 Year	1-5 Years	over 5 Years	Total
220 0%								
230 10%								
240 20%								
250 50%								
260 Exchange-traded								
of which								
270 OTC Options								
280 Exchange Traded Options								

PRECIOUS METALS

	Notional Principal Amounts By Residual Maturity				Replacement Cost By Residual Maturity			
	≤1 Year	1-5 Years	over 5 Years	Total	≤1 Year	1-5 Years	over 5 Years	Total
290 0%								
300 10%								
310 20%								
320 50%								
330 Exchange-traded								
of which								
340 OTC Options								
350 Exchange Traded Options								

TOTAL CONTRACTS

	Notional Principal Amounts By Residual Maturity				Replacement Cost By Residual Maturity			
	≤1 Year	1-5 Years	over 5 Years	Total	≤1 Year	1-5 Years	over 5 Years	Total
360 0%								
370 10%								
380 20%								
390 50%								
400 Exchange-traded								
of which								
410 OTC Options								
420 Exchange Traded Options								

APPENDIX 4: COUNTERPARTY EXPOSURE FOR REPOS AND REVERSE REPOS (AND SIMILAR TRANSACTIONS)

FORWARD TRANSACTIONS

	1 Replacement Cost	2 Potential Future Credit Exposure	3 Amount at Risk (1 + 2)	4 Weight	5 Weighted Amount (3 * 4)
10				0%	
20				10%	
30				20%	
40				50%	
50	TOTAL				

REPOS

	1 Market value of securities sold or lent	2 Market value of collateral taken	3 Amount at Risk (1 - 2)	4 Weight	5 Weighted Amount (3 * 4)
60				0%	
70				10%	
80				20%	
90				50%	
100	TOTAL				

REVERSE REPOS

	1 Market value of collateral given	2 Market value of securities bought or borrowed	3 Amount at Risk (1 - 2)	4 Weight	5 Weighted Amount (3 * 4)
110				0%	
120				10%	
130				20%	
140				50%	
150	TOTAL				

APPENDIX 5: CAPITAL REQUIREMENT FOR FOREIGN EXCHANGE RISK

		Column 1 Net Overall Long (Short) Position	Column 2 Positions to be treated under basic method	Column 3 Positions being treated under backtesting approach
BASE CURRENCY		(1 = 2 + 3)		
Other Currencies				
Belgium/Luxembourg Francs	BE BELG			
Canadian Dollars	CA CANA			
Danish Kroner	DK DENM			
European Currency Units	EU ECUS			
French Francs	FR FRAN			
Deutschmarks	DE RGER			
Irish Pounds	IE EIRE			
Italian Lire	IT ITAL			
Japanese Yen	JP JAPA			
Netherlands Guilders	NL NETH			
Spanish Pesetas	ES SPAI			
Swedish Kroner	SE SWED			
Swiss Francs	CH SWIT			
Sterling	UK UKIN			
US Dollars	US USA			
....				
....				
....				
Other Aggregate Net Long Positions	OTHL			
Other Aggregate Net Short Positions	OTHS			
TOTAL		ZERO		
Higher of aggregate net short/long open positions				
Gold and precious metals				
GOLD	GO GOLD			
....				
....				
SUM OF GROSS POSITION				
CAPITAL REQUIREMENT				

APPENDIX 6: CAPITAL REQUIREMENT INTEREST RATE GENERAL MARKET RISK

	1 Zone One Net Long Position	2 Zone One Net Short Position	3 Zone Two Net Long Position	4 Zone Two Net Short Position	5 Zone Three Net Long Position	6 Zone Three Net Short Position	7 Maturity based approach (Method one)	8 Duration based Approach (Method two)	9 Simplified Method	10 Total General Market Interest Rate Risk (7 + 8 + 9)
Australia	AU AUSL									
Austria	AT AUSR									
Belgium	BE BELG									
Brazil	BR BRAZ									
Canada	CA CANA									
Denmark	DK DENM									
ECU	EU ECUS									
Finland	FI FINL									
France	FR FRAN									
Germany	DE RGER									
Greece	GR GREE									
Ireland	IE EIRE									
Italy	IT ITAL									
Japan	JP JAPA									
Malaysia	MY MALA									
Mexico	MX MEXI									
Netherlands	NL NETH									
Norway	NO NORW									
Portugal	PT PORT									
Singapore	SG SING									
South Africa	RA SAFR									
Spain	ES SAPI									
Sweden	SE SWED									
Switzerland	CH SWIT									
Turkey	TR TURK									
UK	UK UKIN									
Sterling Index Linked Gilts										
USA	US USA									
Other Material Countries										
Non Material Countries										
TOTAL										

280

APPENDIX 7: CAPITAL REQUIREMENT FOR EQUITY POSITION RISK

	Gross Positions for Specific Risk				Positions for General Market Risk			
	1 Positions attracting 8% specific risk	2 Positions attracting 2% specific risk	3 Positions attracting 4% specific risk	4 Total Gross Equity Positions for specific risk (1 + 2 + 3)	5 Excess amount of concentrated positions (Gross)	6 Positions qualifying for Inter-market offsets	7 Other Positions	8 Total Equity Positions for General Market Risk (5 + 6 + 7)

Qualifying Countries eligible for offsetting markets adjustment

Australia	AU	AUSL
Belgium	BE	BELG
Canada	CA	CANA
France	FR	FRAN
Germany	DE	RGER
Japan	JP	JAPA
Netherlands	NL	NETH
Spain	ES	SPAI
Sweden	SE	SWED
Switzerland	CH	SWIT
United Kingdom	UK	UKIN
United States	US	USA
Other		

Other qualifying countries

Denmark	DK	DENM
Finland	FI	FINL
Greece	GR	GREE
Ireland	IE	EIRE
Italy	IT	ITAL
Luxembourg	LU	LUXE
Portugal	PT	PORT
Other		

Non qualifying countries

Countries not specified above (not offsetting)

TOTAL

The treatment of instruments

Consistent with Article 2.5 of the CAD, the Bank will usually only allow certain instruments – the so-called 'financial instruments' – to be included in the trading book. Such instruments embrace: transferable securities; units in collective investment undertakings; money-market instruments (excluding deposits and loans); financial futures contracts (including equivalent cash-settled instruments); forward interest rate agreements; interest rate, currency and equity swaps; and options on the above instruments. In limited circumstances, however, certain other ('non-financial') instruments may be included in the trading book, namely those used to hedge, wholly or partially, a trading book position which is subject to the prescribed procedures (*see* Bank of England, 1994e, Chapter 1, paras 12–13) for marking to market on a daily basis. If such instruments are included in the trading book, they will attract both counterparty risk requirements and general market risk requirements on their mark-to-market valuation but *not* specific risk requirements.

Transfers between the trading book and the banking book are also possible, although they must be accompanied by documentation which is in a prescribed format (see Bank of England, 1994e, Chapter 1, para. 17) and capable of audit verification. An example of an eligible transfer out of the trading book and into the banking book would be the use of an instrument, which would normally qualify in its own right for inclusion in the trading book, to hedge an exposure held outside the trading book. For the period of the hedge, such an instrument would not form part of the trading book, and hence would not generate trading book capital requirements. It may, however, attract counterparty or other capital requirements generated by application of the Solvency Ratio Directive. Additionally, general market risk arising in the trading book which has been designated as a hedge for the banking book may be excluded from trading book capital requirements, without reference to particular financial instruments, provided that the transfer of risk is fully documented, and that the transfer procedures are subject to audit verification and to Bank approval.

Further, positions in instruments issued by credit institutions and investment firms are subject to special treatment. For example, short positions in so-called 'fund-raising financial instruments' (e.g. certificates of deposit and commercial paper) may be included in the trading book if the instrument complies with the trading book definition[39] and other CAD requirements. The treatment of such instruments, however, must be applied continuously. Such instruments, moreover, will only attract capital requirements for general market risk. Positions in so-called 'capital-raising instruments' are likewise subject to a separate regime[40] to avoid the problems associated with 'double-gearing'. Accordingly, where such positions are generated via holdings of, or exposures to, broad-based equity indices or other products, the physical long positions will be deducted from a bank's capital base, but only after the recognition of any hedging benefits against other market exposures as might be generated by index arbitrage positions. In other words, such holdings can be used to reduce risk elsewhere but will, nevertheless, be treated as a deduction from capital. If no, or only partial, hedging benefits arise, then that position, without an offsetting exposure, will be deducted from a bank's capital base without generating any market-related capital requirements, so that the total capital charge on the position can never exceed the 100 per cent deduction from capital.

The treatment of positions

Consistent with Article 2(6) of the CAD, positions (in eligible instruments) may be considered as being held for a trading intent, and thus eligible for inclusion in the trading book, if the following conditions are satisfied: (1) the positions are marked to market, in prescribed fashion, on a daily basis as part of the internal risk management process; (2) the position-takers have autonomy in entering into transactions within predetermined limits; or (3) the positions satisfy any other criteria which the bank applies to the composition of its trading book on a consistent basis. Each bank will also be asked to agree a policy statement with the Bank about which activities are normally considered trading activities, and thus constitute part of the trading book, and those which are not. Finally, for a repurchase, or equivalent, transaction to be considered as part of the trading book, the securities being repurchased, lent, or contributing collateral for such a transaction, must be in the trading book.

Exemptions from trading book requirements

As catered for in the CAD under its *de minimis* rules (Article 4, paras 6 and 7), the Bank will exempt from the CAD's risk-based capital requirements – other than the charge to cover foreign exchange risk – those banks with 'minimal' trading books. The definition of 'minimal' adopted is exactly the same as that proposed in the CAD, with the criteria being applied on a solo or consolidated basis to the combination of on- and off-balance-sheet positions.[41] Any bank which breaches any of the criteria must automatically comply, in full, with the CAD's risk-based requirements unless the Bank deems such breaches to be 'short term'.

Treatment of banks with 'small' trading books

For those banks which are subject to the *de minimis* exemption but which breach the 5 per cent trading book benchmark, an alternative to full compliance with the CAD's risk-based capital regime is offered. This involves compliance with special capital requirements set for interest rate position risk and equity position risk (see Bank of England, 1994e, Chapter 1, paras 8–32) which, although tougher than their counterparts under the CAD, allow for a reduction in systems costs.

Market Risk Requirements

Position risk

Equities   The Bank has proposed that banks be given a choice in how to calculate their equity position risk capital requirements. They can either adopt the methodology outlined in the CAD – *see* Exhibit 2.13 – which the Bank describes as the 'basic method', or, alternatively, employ a methodology (*see* Bank of England, 1994e, Chapter 10, annexe 1, for further details) virtually identical to that proposed by the SFA for the investment firms which it regulates.

Exhibit 2.13   Capital requirements imposed under the CAD to deal with position risk

Under the CAD, a different set of rules applies to each of equities, traded debt instruments, derivatives, and the underwriting of equities and debt securities when calculating position (i.e. market) risk requirements. Before looking at each set in turn, it is worth noting at this point, however, that both 'long' (i.e. net asset) positions and 'short' (i.e. net liability) positions are taken into account in the calculations, and that firms have to adopt a 'mark-to-market' approach to valuing such positions in their trading books. Moreover, the so-called 'building-block approach' to assessing position risk is adopted in the CAD, requiring that total position risk be broken down into 'specific risk' and 'general risk' components. The specific risk attaching to an instrument is the risk of a price change due to factors relating specifically to the issuer (or, in the case of a derivative, factors relating to the underlying instrument); in contrast, general risk is the risk of a price change due, in the case of equities or their derivatives, to market movements unrelated to any specific equity or, in the case of debt instruments or their derivatives, to interest rate fluctuations.

The treatment of equities

The *specific risk capital requirement* is calculated as 4 per cent of the firm's 'overall gross position' in equities, where the 'overall gross position' is defined as the sum of the net positions (long or short) in all equities. The 4 per cent figure may, however, at national discretion, be reduced to 2 per cent for 'diversified' or 'highly liquid'[1] portfolios, but the reduction will *not* apply to equities of an issuer any of whose traded debt instruments attract a specific risk weighting of 8 per cent. (As the 8 per cent weighting applies to all debt instruments except 'central government items' and 'qualifying items' *see* below – the reduction will therefore only apply to the equities of the issuers of the debt falling within the latter category.)

The *general risk capital requirement* is to be calculated as 8 per cent of the firm's 'overall net position' in equities where the 'overall net position' is derived by offsetting the sum of the firm's long positions against the total of its short positions.

The *total position risk capital requirement* is then derived by adding together the specific risk capital requirement and the general risk capital requirement.

The treatment of traded debt instruments

The *specific risk capital requirement* is to be derived by summing all the 'weighted positions' (short or long) for the different instruments, where the 'weighted position' of a given instrument is the 'net position' (i.e. the difference between the firm's long and short positions, converted daily at spot rates into the firm's reporting currency) multiplied by the relevant risk weighting – *see* below.[2]

The *risk weightings* are designed to reflect the level of specific risk perceived to be attracted to traded debt instruments by virtue of the nature of the issuer:

- central government-issued debt instruments attract a risk weighting of 0 per cent;
- 'Qualifying items'[3] attract concessionary weights depending on their residual maturity
  - up to 6 months   0.25 per cent
  - over 6 months and up to   1.00 per cent
    24 months
  - over 24 months   1.6 per cent;
- all other items attract a risk weight of 8 per cent.

The *general risk capital requirement* may be derived in one of two ways. Under the so-called 'maturity-based' approach it is to be calculated as:

10 per cent of the sum of the 'matched-weighted positions' in all maturity bands

plus 40 per cent of the matched weighted position in Zone 1 (residual maturity of up to one year)

plus 30 per cent of the matched weighted position in Zone 2 (residual maturity of between one and four years)

plus 30 per cent of the matched weighted position in Zone 3 (residual maturities of over four years)

plus 40 per cent of the matched weighted position between Zones 1 and 2

plus 40 per cent of the matched weighted position between Zones 2 and 3

plus 150 per cent of the matched weighted position between Zones 1 and 3

plus 100 per cent of the residual unmatched weighted positions between zones

Exhibit 2.13   (continued)

where:

1. The 'matched weighted position' in a given *maturity band* (*see* Table 1) is the amount of the firm's total risk-weighted long positions matched by its risk-weighted short positions in that particular time band.[4] The residual long or short position is referred to as the '*unmatched* weighted position' for that band.
2. The 'matched weighted position' in a particular *zone* (*see* Table 1) is the amount of the firm's total of unmatched weighted long positions for all bands in that zone matched by the total of its unmatched weighted short positions for those bands. The residual, or difference between the two sums, is called the '*unmatched* weighted position' for that zone.
3. The 'matched weighted position between Zones 1 and 2' is the amount of the unmatched weighted long (short) position in Zone 1 which is matched by the unmatched weighted short (long) position in Zone 2. The 'matched weighted position between Zones 2 and 3' is the residual of the above calculation that is matched by the unmatched weighted position in Zone 3.[5]
4. The 'matched weighted position between Zones 1 and 3' is the amount of the residual unmatched weighted position in Zone 1 matched by the residual of Zone 3's matching with Zone 2.

(For an illustrative example of these calculations *see* Price Waterhouse, 1993, Annexe III.)

As can be seen, the general risk capital requirements for traded debt instruments are thus determined by the residual maturities (for fixed rate instruments) of the instruments and their coupons, with allowance being made for offsetting positions within the same maturity band, within the same zone (groups of maturity bands) and across zones. The capital charges, or 'disallowances', prescribed reflect the residual general risks that remain after netting, for, even if the weighted longs fully offset the weighted shorts within a given maturity band, there would still be some general risk as each band includes positions whose maturities are not identical as well as different instruments with the same maturity. Generally, the closer the residual maturity of the positions held by a firm, the greater the allowances given.

The alternative approach which may be adopted in respect of the calculation of the general risk capital requirement, with the consent of national supervisors, is the 'duration-based' approach. Under this approach, instead of allocating positions to maturity bands the 'modified duration'[6] of each instrument is calculated and the weights applied are based on assumed changes in interest-rates (for further details *see* Annexe 1 of the CAD).

Finally, as before, the *total position risk requirement* is derived by summing the specific and general risk requirements.

Table 1   *Risk weight framework employed under the maturity-based approach to calculating the general market risk requirement applicable to traded debt instruments*

Zone	Maturity band		Weighting (%)	Assumed interest rate change (%)
	Coupon of 3% or more	Coupon of less than 3%		
1	0 ≤ 1 month	0 ≤ 1 month	0.00	–
	> 1 ≤ 3 months	> 1 ≤ 3 months	0.20	1.00
	> 3 ≤ 6 months	> 3 ≤ 6 months	0.40	1.00
	> 6 ≤ 12 months	> 6 ≤ 12 months	0.70	1.00
2	> 1 ≤ 2 years	> 1.0 ≤ 1.9 years	1.25	0.90
	> 2 ≤ 3 years	> 1.9 ≤ 2.8 years	1.75	0.80
	> 3 ≤ 4 years	> 2.8 ≤ 3.6 years	2.25	0.75
3	> 4 ≤ 5 years	> 3.6 ≤ 4.3 years	2.75	0.75
	> 5 ≤ 7 years	> 4.3 ≤ 5.7 years	3.25	0.70
	> 7 ≤ 10 years	> 5.7 ≤ 7.3 years	3.75	0.65
	> 10 ≤ 15 years	> 7.3 ≤ 9.3 years	4.50	0.60
	> 15 ≤ 20 years	> 9.3 ≤ 10.6 years	5.25	0.60
	> 20 years	> 10.6 ≤ 12.0 years	6.00	0.60
		> 12.0 ≤ 20.0 years	8.00	0.60
		> 20 years	12.50	0.60

The treatment of derivative instruments

To incorporate these instruments into the 'building-block' approach, they are generally broken down into long and short positions in the respective underlying debt or equity instruments. For example, an interest rate swap where the institution receives fixed interest and pays floating would be split into a long position in a fixed rate debt instrument and a short position in a floating rate instrument maturing at the next interest rate reset date.

For contracts exposed to *interest rate risk* (e.g. interest rate futures, swaps and forward interest rate agreements), the long and short positions derived are treated as notional holdings in central government securities and thus attract a nil *specific risk* weighting. For the *general risk* requirement, the positions are to be slotted into their respective maturity or duration time zones, in the same manner as ordinary securities. Alternatively, at national discretion, institutions which mark to market their interest rate products and employ discounted cash

Exhibit 2.13   (continued)

flow techniques to measure and monitor interest rate sensitivity may use such models to calculate their positions as long as the results obtained are in line with the interest rate sensitivity of the underlying cash flows.

For all *exchange-traded instruments*, the capital charge may, at national discretion, be set equal to the margin required by the exchange.

Equity index derivatives (including stock index futures and options) may be treated as positions in the underlying equities, and firms may offset them against positions in those equities if 'close correlation' exists between the derivatives and the underlying equities.

Finally, exchange-traced *futures* covering what regulators decide are 'broadly diversified indices' attract a general risk capital requirement of 8 per cent and a specific risk requirement of zero.

The treatment of underwriting exposures

The CAD requires institutions progressively to increase their capital cover the longer the underwriting exposures on debt and equity instruments last, with the maximum capital requirement being reached five working days after the institution's initial commitment. In calculating its capital requirement, an institution may disregard underwriting positions which are subscribed or sub-underwritten by 'third parties'.

The procedure for calculating the '*reduced underwriting position*', to which the specific and general risk requirements are applied (treating the position as a position in the debt or equity in question), is as follows:

1. Calculate the institution's 'net' position in the instrument, arising from its underwriting obligation, by disregarding that part of the issue subscribed or sub-underwritten and deducting short positions in the same instruments.
2. Apply a sliding scale of percentage factors to the net underwriting positions to derive the 'reduced underwriting position'. The scale is:

   - working day 0 (i.e. the working day on which the institution becomes unconditionally committed to accepting a known quantity of securities at an agreed price)   0;
   - working day 1   10%;
   - working days 2 to 3   25%;
   - working day 4   50%;
   - working day 5   75%;
   - after working day 5   100%.

Notwithstanding that an institution's underwriting exposure is treated as being nil on 'day 0', the CAD imposes an additional obligation on regulators to ensure that a firm holds 'sufficient capital' against the risk of loss which exists between the time of the initial commitment and 'working day 1'. No guidance is given, however, as to what constitutes 'sufficient capital'.

Notes:
1. This is defined in the CAD.
2. Holdings of debt instruments issued by the firms themselves are disregarded.
3. Comprising: those qualifying for a 20 per cent weighting under the Solvency Ratio Directive; those issued by investment firms (plus debt issued by comparable non-EU firms subject to prudential rules as stringent as those in the CAD); and debt which is (a) listed on a regulated market within the EU (or on a non-EU stock exchange which is 'recognized' by the firm's member state); (b) of acceptable liquidity; and (c) a debt the solvency of whose issuer is considered such that the risk of default is no greater than that for an instrument bearing a 20 per cent risk weighting under the Solvency Ratio Directive (member states have some flexibility, however, in interpreting this criterion).
4. The risk weights (*see* Table 1) depend on the residual maturity of the security – the longer it is, the greater the risk weight – for fixed rate instruments, and on the basis of the period until the interest rate is next set for variable rate instruments. Debt instruments are also distinguished according to whether they have a coupon of less than 3 per cent or 3 per cent or more – the former tend to attract a slightly higher risk weighting.
5. The firm may, alternatively, carry out the matching between Zones 2 and 3 and offset the residual unmatched position against that of Zone 1.
6. Duration is a concept designed to measure the price sensitivity of debt securities to changes in interest rates. In mathematical terms, it is derived as follows:

$$D = \frac{\sum_{t=1}^{m} \left(\frac{tC_t}{(1+r)^t} \right)}{\sum_{t=1}^{m} \left(\frac{C_t}{(1+r)^t} \right)}$$

where r = yield to maturity (% p. a.), expressed as a decimal;
           C_t = cash payment in time t;
and m = time to maturity in years.

The 'modified duration' of a debt instrument can then be defined as $\dfrac{D}{(1+r)}$.

Source: EC, 1993.

As outlined in Exhibit 2.13, under the basic method, *specific risk* capital requirements are derived by applying a set of risk weights to the 'overall gross position' for each country.[42] The risk weights vary from 0 to 8 per cent: the zero figure applies to equity indices; a 2 per cent risk weight to stocks represented in a 'recognized'[43] equity index or part of a 'diversified'[44] country portfolio,[45] provided they are also deemed 'highly liquid';[46] a 4 per cent risk weight to stocks, or portfolio of stocks, listed in certain 'qualifying'[47] countries; and an 8 per cent risk weight to all other equities. *General risk* capital charges are, in turn, generated under the basic method by multiplying the 'overall net position' in equities for each country by 8 per cent.[48] The overall equity position risk capital charge is then determined by a simple addition of the specific and general position risk requirements.

Traded debt instruments   As explained in Exhibit 2.13, the *specific risk* capital charge arising from holdings of debt instruments is derived, according to the CAD, by summing all the 'weighted positions' arising from the different instruments. Because the risk weight framework proposed for adoption by the Bank, which is to be used in the generation of these 'weighted positions', is virtually identical to that outlined in the CAD (*see* Bank of England, 1994e, Chapter 9, pp. 3–5 for full details), further discussion on this point is unnecessary.

Calculation of *general position risk* charges on debt holdings is also to be undertaken in line with the CAD's proposals, involving the adoption of either the 'maturity-based approach' or the 'duration-based approach'. The Bank's treatment of the former approach is virtually identical to the CAD's treatment, in that the sum of the matched weighted positions (including the residual unmatched weighted positions) has to be multiplied by their relevant 'disallowances' (*see* Exhibit 2.13).[49] Similarly, the general position risk capital requirement under the duration-based approach is to be derived by applying a (different) set of 'disallowances' to a series of matched and residual unmatched duration weighted positions.[50]

The *total position risk* capital requirement is then derived, as before, by summing the specific and general risk requirements.

Derivatives   For *equity-based* derivative positions (i.e. positions in equity futures, forwards, options and swaps based on individual equities, portfolios of equities or equity indices), the positions are generally to be notionally converted into long and short positions in the underlying instruments to allow for their incorporation within the building-block approach. The resultant positions may then be netted against offsetting positions in the underlying instruments or against other notional positions generated by other derivatives.

For equity *swaps*, a bank must treat the equity exposure separately from the interest rate exposure. If the Bank is satisfied that sufficient controls are in place, and gives express written agreement, such embedded interest rate exposures may be included in the interest rate position risk treatments as a low coupon and thus become a component of the general market risk.

For derivative positions in *forwards*, *futures* and *options*, the embedded interest rate exposures will attract capital requirements[51] prior to being netted, in addition to any specific and general market risk requirements on the individual net positions, unless the Bank agrees, in writing, that they may be included as a component of the general market risk.

For *options* or *warrants* (plus any related hedging positions) on equities with a residual maturity of up to six months,[52] a special approach has to be adopted (*see* Bank of England, 1994e, Chapter 10, para. 22) unless a bank is using an option model 'recognized' by the Bank (*see* below).

Finally, for exchange-traded *futures* contracts, the Bank sets capital requirements as a multiple of the clearing house margin. For futures on 'recognized' stock indices,[53] however, the position should be included in the general risk calculation as a single position, based upon the sum of the current market values of the underlying instruments. The specific risk requirement would then be 0 per cent, with the current market value of the underlying instrument being used in determining the overall net position for use in the generation of the general market risk requirement, in the usual fashion.

Debt-based derivative positions are also subject to special treatment. As far as *specific risk* is concerned, a capital charge of 0 per cent will apply where the underlying exposure is an interest rate exposure (e.g. a swap based upon interbank rates); otherwise the underlying debt instrument will generate a positive capital charge, in the usual fashion. For options, the specific risk will be based upon the delta of the position and the underlying instrument or security where the capital requirements are generated through the application of approved models (see below). For those banks not using approved models, the market risk requirements on debt-based options (or warrants) with a residual maturity of less than six months[54] have to be calculated in accordance with a separate, prescribed regime (*see* Bank of England, 1994e, Chapter 9, para. 29).

As for equity-based futures contracts, market risk requirements on exchange-traded *futures* contracts on interest rates and debt futures may also be based on the clearing house margin, if the Bank finally agrees to adopt such a policy.

Finally, for those banks not using approved models,[55] *general* (i.e. interest rate) *risk* requirements arising from debt-based derivative positions have to be calculated in accordance with prescribed procedures which involve splitting each position into two legs (for full details *see* Bank of England, 1994e, Chapter 9, paras 25–8).

Underwriting exposures The Bank's proposed treatment of position risk deriving from underwriting exposures, while consistent with the CAD – *see* Exhibit 2.13 – is distinctive in a number of respects.[56] First, in the derivation of net positions (or commitments), the following have to be deducted from the gross position: underwriting or sub-underwriting commitments obtained from others; purchases and sales of the securities; and allocations granted or received with respect to the underwriting commitments. Second, the 'scaling factors' (equal to 100 per cent minus the corresponding 'reduction factors' referred to in the CAD) applied to the bond and equity positions to derive the 'reduced underwriting positions' are differentiated according to whether the underwriting position is in respect of a debt or equity, and whether the focus of attention is on specific or general market risk – *see* Exhibit 2.14.[57] The two differences evident on comparison with the CAD's scale of percentage factors are, first, that the requirement to cover the risks arising from the time of the initial commitment to 'working day 1' is accommodated in the first time band and, second, that the scaling factors applying beyond 'working day 0'[58] in the CAD are *not* to be applied in the UK in the calculation of the general market risk requirement on bond-type underwritings. Rather, in the latter case, a 100 per cent scaling factor is to be employed irrespective of the time band concerned. In other words, for bond-type underwritings the specific risk requirement only enjoys the application of reduction factors.

Exhibit 2.14   Scaling factors to be applied to net underwriting positions to derive the 'reduced underwriting positions' under the Bank's proposals

Time band	Bond-type issues		Equity-type issues	
	Specific risk (%)	General market risk (%)	Specific risk	General market risk (%)
Up to and including working day 0	0	100	10	10
Working day 1	10	100	10	10
Working day 2	25	100	25	25
Working day 3	25	100	25	25
Working day 4	50	100	50	50
Working day 5	75	100	75	75
After working day 5	100	100	100	100

Source: Bank of England, 1995b, Chapter 7, p. 15.

Settlement risk

The Bank is proposing to allow UK-incorporated banks to calculate capital requirements to cover settlement risk arising on trading book transactions remaining unsettled five business days after their due date in precisely the same way as agreed under the CAD (see Exhibit 2.15). As a result, no further discussion is necessary at this point.

Exhibit 2.15   Capital requirements imposed under the CAD to deal with settlement risk

Settlement (or delivery) risk arises because movements in the market prices of securities may involve a loss to institutions if transactions entered into are not settled on the agreed dates.

Under the CAD, institutions are allowed to calculate the capital requirements[1] imposed to cover this risk in one of two ways:

1. By applying, in the instances where the institution is exposed to loss, to the *price difference* (i.e. the difference between the agreed settlement price and the current market price) a percentage factor which increases with the delay in settlement (*see* Column A of Table 1).
2. By applying a different set of factors (*see* Column B of Table 1) to the *agreed settlement price* when the delay in settlement does not exceed 45 days.

Option (2), however, can only be adopted with the permission of regulators. If it is adopted, it must be used for calculating the institution's settlement on *all* of its transactions.

Table 1   Weighting factors employed in the calculation of capital requirements to cover settlement risk

Delay in settlement: number of working days after due settlement date	Column A (%)	Column B (%)
5–15	8	0.5
16–30	50	4.0
31–45	75	9.0
46 or more	100	–

Note: 1. These requirements do not cover repos (sale and repurchase agreements), reverse repos, or securities lending or borrowing, which are dealt with under the treatment of 'counterparty risk' – *see* Exhibit 2.16.

Source: EC, 1993.

Counterparty risk

As noted earlier, positions and exposures not within the trading book are governed by the counterparty risk requirements arising from the application of the Solvency Ratio Directive (*see* Bank of England, 1990b). The treatment of the banking book will thus remain unchanged. Some exposures within the trading book, however, will also attract counterparty risk requirements (in addition to other market risk requirements). These embrace exposures arising from trades in over-the-counter derivatives, settlement exposures, margins and fees, and certain other positions in tradable securities.

The main difference between the counterparty risk requirements imposed on the two books (for full details *see* Bank of England, 1994e, Chapter 5) is that a reduction in the risk weightings applies to exposures on some investment firms[59] while the counterparty exposure is in the trading book, as well as to claims on recognized clearing houses and exchanges.[60]

The treatment of 'free deliveries' and over-the-counter derivatives is identical to that outlined in the CAD – *see* Exhibit 2.16 – except that, in the latter case, the Bank insists that all banks adopt the 'current exposure' (rather than the 'original exposure') method when computing their trading book counterparty risk requirements in respect of interest rate- and foreign exchange rate-related instruments.

Exhibit 2.16   Capital requirements imposed under the CAD to deal with counterparty risk

---

Counterparty risk is the risk that the other party to a transaction defaults before completion, exposing an institution to a loss up to the total value of the transaction.

Under the CAD, the capital requirement to cover such risk on 'free deliveries' (i.e. where payments do not match deliveries) is set at 8 per cent of the value of the securities or cash owed to the institution multiplied by the Solvency Ratio Directive risk weighting applicable to the counterparty. The reduced risk weightings applicable, under certain circumstances, to EU and OECD banks under the Solvency Ratio Directive are extended under the CAD to other categories of counterparty namely: (1) investment firms subject to the CAD; (2) similar firms subject to comparable supervision in non-EU countries; and (3) recognized clearing houses and exchanges.

For *repurchase (repos) and reverse repurchase agreements and securities lending and borrowing* based on securities included in the trading book, the capital requirement is 8 per cent of any 'unfavourable difference' between the market value of the securities concerned and the loan or collateral, multiplied by the Solvency Ratio Directive risk weighting applicable to the counterparty.

For all *over-the-counter* derivatives, the counterparty risk requirement is to be calculated in accordance with the Solvency Ratio Directive. Thus assuming the 'current exposure' method is used, the charge must be equal to the replacement cost of the contract multiplied by a counterparty weighting, plus an 'add-on' in respect of potential future credit exposure.[1]

Note: 1. If the 'original exposure' method is adopted instead, which is permitted if national regulators agree, a simpler two-stage transformation is required which avoids the need to mark the contracts to market.

Source: EC, 1993.

Finally, in respect of the treatment of repos and reverse repos and similar transactions (i.e. stock lending and borrowing),[61] which are treated differently to collateralized loans under the CAD, the Bank will usually impose no counterparty risk capital requirements if the transactions are fully collateralized and satisfactorily documented and the collateral is adjusted daily. However, where the collateral is not adjusted daily or when the volume of such business is deemed to create 'significant' risks for a bank, the Bank may apply capital requirements commensurate with the potential risks arising from changes in the value of either securities or collateral.[62]

In determining the adequacy of collateral for counterparty risk exposures arising from repos and stock lending, both the current value of the securities and collateral, and the risk associated with unexpected changes in the value of either, have to be taken into account. If a bank can call for adjustments to the collateral daily, the capital requirement will usually be based on whether the current value of the collateral covers the exposure, rather than on the risk that it may no longer do so in the future. Where there is an 'unfavourable difference' between the market value of the securities sold or lent and the market value of collateral taken, the counterparty risk requirement is to be computed as 8 per cent of the unfavourable difference multiplied by the Solvency Ratio Directive counterparty risk weight, as suggested in the CAD. However, if the Bank deems that there is a significant risk that the current value of the collateral may not cover the exposure in the future, or if the collateral is not adjusted daily, it may apply an additional requirement in the form of a 'risk cushion' based on the matrix of 'add-ons' used to calculate the potential future exposure on derivatives contracts.[63] In such circumstances, the counterparty risk requirement would be computed as: [the market value of securities sold or lent × (100% + risk cushion factor) *minus* the market value of collateral taken × (100% − risk cushion factor)] × Solvency Ratio Directive counterparty risk weight × 8%.[64] A similar approach is adopted in respect of reverse repos and stock borrowing (see Bank of England, 1994e, Chapter 6, paras 18–29 for further details).

Large exposures risk

UK-incorporated banks have to comply with both the Large Exposures Directive (*see* Bank of England, 1993c) and the CAD's provisions for dealing with large exposures in the trading book, on both a consolidated and unconsolidated (solo) level. Accommodation of the latter will mean that policy will have to be adjusted to account for the so-called 'soft limits' introduced under the CAD – *see* Exhibit 2.17. Under this regime, large exposures attributable to positions held in the trading book are allowed to exceed the 25 per cent of the (amended)[65] capital base limit established in the Large Exposures Directive although, if they do so, they will attract incremental capital requirements.

Exhibit 2.17   Capital requirements imposed under the CAD to deal with large exposures risk arising from intermediaries' trading book business

---

Under the CAD, institutions are required to monitor and control their 'large' market risk exposures to individual counterparties and groups of connected counterparties. The basis for measuring these (overall)[1] exposures and the limits to be imposed upon them derive mainly from the Large Exposures Directive that is, no exposure should exceed 25 per cent of own funds,[2] and the sum of all such large exposures (i.e. those whose value is greater than, or equal to, 10 per cent of own funds) should not exceed 800 per cent of own funds.

However, at national discretion, institutions may be allowed to exceed the 25 per cent limit, but only if:

1. Such 'excesses' relate only to the trading book.
2. An additional capital charge is taken to cover such trading book excesses. This charge is calculated by selecting the individual exposures which attract the highest specific risk capital requirements and applying designated capital requirements. For exposures no more than ten days old, a 200 per cent factor must be applied to the specific risk requirement. For those over ten days old, the following factors must be applied to the specific risk requirements:

Size of the excesses (as % of own funds)	Factors (%)
Up to 40	200
40–60	300
60–80	400
80–100	500
100–250	600
Over 250	900

3. For those counterparty exposures where the excess is no more than ten days old, the total trading book exposure to that counterparty does not exceed 500 per cent of own funds.
4. Excesses more than ten days old do not, in aggregate, exceed 600 per cent of own funds.
5. Institutions running such excesses report to the regulatory authorities, on a three-monthly basis, all excesses that have arisen in the preceding three months.

Notes:
1. For each individual counterparty or group of connected counterparties, the 'overall exposure' is defined as the sum of the firm's trading book and non-trading book large exposures. Trading book exposures to individual counterparties are made up of:

   - net long positions in all financial instruments issued by the counterparty concerned;
   - net underwriting exposures as adjusted by the specified scale factors (*see* the text);
   - positions in repos (and reverse repos) and securities lending (and borrowing) and derivative instruments and exposures to settlement risk. (These exposures are to be calculated as described in the text but without application of the weightings for counterparty risk.)
2. Certain large exposure exemptions which may be granted to credit institutions under the Large Exposures Directive are extended to exposures on investment firms and recognized clearing houses and exchanges. In particular, national regulators may exempt firms' exposures to other investment firms with maturities of one year or less and may also allow firms' exposures to other firms with maturities of greater than one year to be weighted and reported at lower amounts.

Source: EC, 1993.

In general, the Bank restricts the availability of soft limits to excesses caused by positions in traded securities (including underwriting exposures). Counterparty exposures in the trading book will normally be subject to the 25 per cent overall 'hard limit', although in cases where a soft limit is permitted (i.e. where the exposures relate to short-term exposures in the trading book of a subsidiary), the soft limit will only be allowed on consolidation.[66]

As far as underwriting exposures are concerned, positions in securities that are acquired as part of an underwriting process, and which are part of the trading book,[67] will contribute to the large exposure for the issues commencing on 'working day 0'. The exposure is to be based upon the 'net underwriting position', which may be further reduced to form the 'net position exposure' by the application of discount factors (these are the 'reduction factors' referred to earlier – *see* p. 288), which range from 100 per cent on working day 0 to 0 per cent after working day 5. The net exposure is then aggregated with any other securities exposures for the same issue generated in the trading book. Although the trigger point for incremental capital and related calculations apply to these securities from working day 0, the bank must have systems in place which enable it to monitor the gross exposure from the time the initial commitment was actually acquired.

Foreign exchange risk

Under the Bank's new approach[68] to measuring and controlling foreign exchange risk, two techniques will be available to banks for determining their corresponding capital requirements. These two approaches, which may be used independently or jointly, are referred to as the 'standard' (or 'basic') method and the 'backtesting' method. Under the standard method, which allows for the recognition of binding intergovernmental agreements to set particular exchange rates within narrow bands,[69] the capital requirement will be 8 per cent of the overall net foreign exchange position (as opposed to the 8 per cent of the *excess* of the overall net foreign exchange position above 2 per cent of own funds proposed under the CAD – *see* Exhibit 2.18). Under the backtesting method, which can only be used with the Bank's agreement and which is based on the use of historic data, a portfolio of currency positions, involving all or some of the net open positions, is assessed against a database of past exchange rates. The database has to contain the ten-day holding period returns, calculated daily, for the previous three and five years. The capital requirement is based upon the 'loss' indicated by a 99 or 95 per cent confidence interval for the past three or five years, respectively (*see* p. 300 and Bank of England, 1994e, Chapter 8, para. 6, for further details). If this method is adopted, it can be used to calculate the capital requirements for either all of a bank's foreign exchange positions (as a portfolio) or the net open position in designated currencies (as a portfolio), although the latter cannot be changed without the prior agreement of the Bank.

Exhibit 2.18   Capital requirements imposed under the CAD to deal with foreign exchange risk

---

Under the CAD, capital is required to cover any excess in a firm's 'overall net foreign exchange position' above 2 per cent of its own funds. The capital requirement is 8 per cent of the excess, and applies to virtually all foreign exchange exposures, not just those arising from the trading book.

The firm's 'overall net foreign exchange position' is the higher of: (1) the total of the net short positions; and (2) the total of the net long positions, in all currencies other than the firm's reporting currency, converted at spot rates into the reporting currency.

For each currency, the *net open position* comprises:

- the net spot position (i.e. the net asset position in the currency in question);

- the net forward position (i.e. all amounts to be received less all amounts to be paid under forward exchange transactions, including currency futures and the principal on currency swaps not included in the spot position);
- irrevocable guarantees that are certain to be called;
- net future income/expenses not yet accrued but already fully hedged (including, with the consent of regulators, net future income/expenses not yet entered into accounting records but already fully hedged by forward foreign exchange transactions);
- the net delta equivalent[1] of the firm's foreign currency options;
- the market value of non-foreign currency options.

In calculating the net open position, firms may exclude, with regulatory consent, non-trading or structural positions taken to hedge foreign exchange movements adversely affecting its capital ratio, as well as such positions relating to items deducted in the calculation of own funds. A firm may also, again with regulatory consent, apply discounting techniques to arrive at its net open currency position.

For the time being, considerable discretion is also given member states to set alternative procedures for the calculation of the overall capital requirement against foreign exchange risk, provided they notify the Council and Commission of the methods allowed. For example:

1. Lower capital requirements may be set in respect of positions in currencies which are '*closely correlated*' (i.e. those for which historical evidence indicates a very low likelihood – *see* Annexe III, para.6 of the CAD – of significant rate variations). If this discretion is adopted, the capital requirements are:

   - for matched positions in closely correlated currencies, 4 per cent of their value;
   - for unmatched positions in closely correlated currencies and for all positions in other currencies, 8 per cent of the higher of: (a) the sum of the net short positions; and (b) the sum of the net long positions, in those currencies.

   Positions to which the 4 per cent capital requirement applies are excluded in performing the calculation.

2. Regulators are permitted to allow firms to employ *other methods* of calculating capital requirements to cover foreign exchange risk, provided that the resulting capital requirement is sufficient to exceed each of the following:

Exhibit 2.18 (continued)

- any losses which have occurred in the firm's current positions in at least 95 per cent of the rolling ten working day periods over the preceding five years (or in at least 99 per cent of such periods over the preceding three years);
- based on an analysis of such ten-day periods over the preceding five years, the likely loss over the following such ten-day period 95 per cent or more of the time (99 per cent where the analysis covers the preceding three years only);
- 2 per cent of the firm's (overall) net open foreign exchange position (as calculated above).

3. The CAD also provides that where currency fluctuations are limited by legally binding *intergovernmental agreements*, regulators may permit firms to exclude their positions in those currencies when calculating capital for foreign exchange risk under the above rules. Nevertheless, capital must still be provided to cover the foreign exchange risk on such currencies, albeit at reduced levels:

- matched positions in such currencies attract a capital requirement of at least half of the permissible fluctuations under the intergovernmental agreement. For currencies participating in the second stage of European Monetary Union, regulators may reduce the capital requirements to 1.6 per cent of the value of the matched positions;
- unmatched positions are treated in exactly the same way as other currencies.

Note: 1. Where the delta is the expected change in price as a proportion of a small change in the price of the underlying instrument.

Source: EC, 1993.

Finally, a new treatment of (carved out) foreign currency *option* positions (and related hedges) is proposed for those banks which do not use their own 'recognized' models (for further details *see* Bank of England, 1994e, Chapter 8, para.4).

SUPERVISORY RECOGNITION OF IN-HOUSE MODELS

As permitted under the CAD, the Bank is proposing to 'recognize' the use of certain in-house models in the calculation of market risk capital requirements.

For a given quantity of position or foreign exchange risk, the models will generally generate lower capital requirements than would result from the application of the standard techniques outlined in the CAD, and so are likely to prove popular with banks. Models eligible for recognition comprise interest rate sensitivity models, options pricing models and models ('simulation models') used to generate capital charges to cover foreign exchange risk.

Interest rate sensitivity models, for interest rate and/or equity derivatives, involve the conversion of individual deals into cash flows, which are then subject to predetermined changes in yield to calculate net sensitivities. These are then used within the derivative-based ladder approach measuring interest rate position risk to generate the appropriate capital charges (for further details see Bank of England, 1994e, Chapter 12, paras 29–33). The models, however, must generate positions which have the same sensitivity to defined interest rate changes as the underlying net cash flows.

The *options pricing models* which the Bank is proposing to recognize comprise three broad groupings: 'buffers', 'scenarios' and 'simulations'. The buffer approach (*see* Annexe 1 to the CAD) generates capital requirements for each of the major classes of option risk (delta, gamma, vega, etc.), whereas the scenario matrix approach involves a revaluation of an option for a series of given changes in parameters. The simulation approach – see below – in contrast, is relevant only to foreign exchange options (for further details see Bank of England, 1994e, Chapter 12, paras 36–49).

Finally, with the agreement of the Bank, *simulation* (i.e. 'backtesting') *models* may be used to calculate capital charges to cover either all of an institution's foreign exchange positions (as a portfolio) or the net open position in designated currencies (as a portfolio). Subject to review by the Bank, foreign exchange options may be allowed to be included in the model, as also noted above.[70]

Before recognizing any of these models, the Bank will review not only the model algorithms (including its underlying assumptions) but also its operating environment. This will involve looking at, *inter alia*, the following: systems and control; risk management; reporting procedures and limits; staffing issues; the setting of capital requirements; and reconciliation and valuation procedures. Where banks use multiple models for a given product, the one in which the Bank will be most interested is that used for risk management purposes and/or for determining profit and loss.

Supervisory recognition of *value-at-risk (VAR) models* reflects a concern for the compliance costs[71] associated with the implementation of the CAD, as it allows those banks given permission by the Bank to go down this route to avoid the need for daily computation of CAD requirements other than on the (two) benchmark dates specified each year. For, under the 'benchmarking' procedures set out in Bank of England (1995c), a bank will be obliged to compare, at a date randomly chosen by the supervisor, a scaled-up version of its own VAR model calculation with the CAD requirement. The capital requirement will then be the higher of the CAD capital requirement resulting from the latest benchmark test (scaled by any increase in the bank's current VAR capital requirement compared with the benchmark date) and the VAR capital requirement. Subject to satisfying certain conditions, a bank may then use its VAR model for monitoring compliance with the CAD requirements until the next benchmarking date (roughly six months later). Permission to use VAR models for supervisory purposes, however, will only be granted if a range of stringent conditions are satisfied (*see* Chapter 7). Full flexibility in the use of VAR models, as allowed under the Basle Committee's 'rules' (see Chapter 7), will not materialise until 'CAD II' comes on stream (*see* Chapter 9) (the Bank is currently working towards an implementation deadline of end-September 1998 for both the EU and Basle market risk amendments so as to limit the costs of systems changes borne by the banks).

THE CALCULATION OF CAPITAL ADEQUACY

Finally, to comply with the CAD's provisions, all EU banks must observe a minimum capital requirement which is the higher of: (1) the minimum initial capital requirement (ECU 5 million for most) specified in the Second Banking Co-ordinating Directive; and (2) the sum of the minimum risk-based capital requirements deriving from the application of the CAD. As explained above, the latter figure is derived, in turn, by adding the minimum capital requirement deriving from the application of the Solvency Ratio Directive to a bank's banking book to the minimum market risk requirements deriving from the application of the CAD to a bank's trading book, with 'add-ons' to account for overall foreign exchange risk and risks arising from business outside the scope of the CAD and the Solvency Ratio Directive.

Accommodation of the above by UK-incorporated banks will involve the banks in calculating the RARs on a new common basis (*see* Exhibit 2.19). These ratios, which will be subject to the current 8 per cent minimum, will be published and used for comparative purposes.

UK banks will also be required to calculate their capital positions for supervisory purposes in a way which incorporates separate 'trigger' and 'target' ratios for their banking and trading books – *see* below.[72] The minimum capital requirement on the trading book will be notional risk-weighted assets multiplied by the trading book trigger. Eligible capital (comprising Tier 1, Tier 2 and Tier 3 components, subject to prescribed limits and restrictions) will then be expressed as a percentage of the sum of the minimum banking and trading book nominal capital charges to arrive at its 'capital adequacy' position.[73] A bank which is at its trigger – which will, in turn, be below its target ratio to allow room for manoeuvre – and which will thus be deemed to be holding adequate capital for supervisory purposes, will be recording a ratio of 100 per cent.

Exhibit 2.19   The new RAR methodology to be employed by UK-incorporated banks under the CAD

$$RAR(\%) = \left[\frac{(Adjusted)^1 \, eligible \, capital}{Banking \, book \, risk\text{-}weighted \, assets^3 \, + \atop Notional \, trading \, book \, risk\text{-}weighted \, assets^4} \right] \times 100$$

Notes:
1. That is, after carrying out the deductions from Tier 1 and Tier 2 capital outlined in Exhibit 2.6.
2. Eligible capital equals Tier 1 capital plus eligible Tier 2 and Tier 3 capital, subject to the prescribed limits and restrictions outlined in Exhibit 2.6.
3. This is represented by the 'TOWRA' expression in note 29.
4. Calculated by summing the capital charges required under the CAD to deal with position risk in debt, equities and foreign exchange, large exposures risk, and trading book counterparty and settlement risk, and multiplying the resultant figure by 12.5 (i.e. the reciprocal of the minimum RAR).

As was previously the case, triggers on banking books will vary according to the individual characteristics, including management, of banks. Trading book triggers, which are likely to vary from close to 8 per cent to up to 12 per cent in most cases, will likewise depend on how well diversified the banks' trading books are and on the Bank's view of the quality of their internal risk management systems.

Apart from setting trigger ratios, the Bank will also set *target* ratios for the banking and trading books of each bank. The target capital requirement for the banking book will thus be equal to risk-weighted assets on the banking book multiplied by the banking book target ratio; while the target capital requirement for the trading book will be equal to notional risk-weighted assets on the trading book multiplied by the trading book target ratio. A bank meeting both target capital requirements will be deemed to have met its (overall) target capital requirement. If capital falls below the target level, the Bank must be informed immediately, and it may prevent the payment of interest and/or principal on outstanding subordinated debt.

18. The assessment of liquidity adequacy[74]

The Bank's current approach to the assessment of the liquidity adequacy of authorized institutions is still based on the principles established in its July 1982 paper on 'The Measurement of Liquidity', although separate treatment has been accorded large UK retail banks since January 1996.[75]

In assessing liquidity adequacy, the main objective[76] of the Bank is to ensure that each bank is capable of meeting its commitments, on both sides of the balance sheet, as they fall due. In normal circumstances, a bank's ability to do this will depend, in particular, on its ability to renew or replace its deposits and other funding, on the extent to which the profile of future cash flows from maturing assets matches that of its maturing liabilities, and on the amount of high-quality liquid assets that it has readily available. Accordingly, to achieve its objective, the Bank will seek to ensure that management adopts a prudent[77] mix of liquidity forms – cash, readily liquifiable assets, asset maturity monies, a diversified (in terms of both maturities and range of counterparties) deposit base and other borrowing sources – appropriate to the business undertaken; that appropriate maturity-matching policies are adopted; and that satisfactory monitoring and control systems are in place to allow management to assess whether or not such policies are being pursued on a continuous basis. As with the assessment of capital adequacy, the success of the assessment process thus relies heavily on the assessment of the quality of management at the interview stage. Each institution is assessed in the light of its own particular circumstances, including any potential liquidity problems which could arise in group or other connected companies.

THE APPROACH ADOPTED IN RESPECT OF LARGE UK RETAIL BANKS

Although most banks in the UK are supervised on the basis of the 'maturity mismatch' approach, whereby assets and liabilities are allocated on a maturity ladder and limits are set on the size of the mismatch in various time bands (*see* below), this approach was deemed less suitable for very large banks whose balance sheets are characterized by a highly diversified retail deposit base. For these banks, holding an adequate *stock* of liquid assets was deemed more important (Bank of England, 1996a, p. 28), and they were asked to complete a different return – SLR1 (*see* Exhibit 2.20) – from other banks.

Exhibit 2.20   SLR1 form

Form SLR1

Private and confidential

Stock Liquidity Return

as at _____

Reporting institution _____

_____
Name (block letters please) and signature of authorised official of reporting institution

In the event of a query, the Bank of England may contact (block letters please)

_____ Tel No_____

Notes on completion

If you have any difficulty in completing this return, please telephone your usual supervisory contact.

1   For definitions refer to SLR1 Guidance Notes.

2   Enter amounts to nearest thousands omitting £000s.

3   Unless otherwise agreed, form should be completed as at the **SECOND WEDNESDAY OF THE MONTH** and for any exception within the month.

4   Return within **SIX WORKING DAYS** of reporting date, addressed to:

   OPERATIONS MANAGER
   MAJOR UK BANKS' DIVISION (HO-2)
   BANK OF ENGLAND
   THREADNEEDLE STREET
   LONDON
   EC2R 8AH

Bank of England use only

Logged in	Date entered	Amendments Input	Type E/O

(3/97)

1   STERLING STOCK:

1.1   Cash..

1.2   Operational balances with Bank of England..............................

1.3   Treasury bills..

1.4   Gilts..

1.5   Eligible bank bills...

1.6   Eligible local authority bills...

1.7   Certificates of tax deposit...

1.8   Secured money with discount houses..

1.0   **TOTAL** ....   (A)

(Item 1 should be equal or greater than item 2.2)

2.1   **WHOLESALE STERLING NET OUTFLOW LIMIT**...................................

5 WORKING DAYS as agreed with Bank of England

2.2   **STERLING STOCK FLOOR**...

5 WORKING DAYS as agreed with Bank of England

3.0   **WHOLESALE STERLING NET OUTFLOW**...   (B)

5 WORKING DAYS

4.0   **STERLING CERTIFICATES OF DEPOSIT HELD**

4.1   **TOTAL**...

4.2   Liquidity conversion factor ....**X**   0.85

4.3   Total discounted certificates of deposit..................................**=**

(Equal to item 4.1 times item 4.2)

4.4   Allowable certificates of deposit..   (C)

(Item 4.4 should not be greater than 50% of item 3.0)

4.5   Remaining certificates of deposit...

(Item 4.4 plus item 4.5 should equal item 4.3)

5.0   **STERLING RETAIL DEPOSITS:**

5.1   Sterling retail deposits falling due in next 5 working days ....

5.2   Liquidity conversion factor ....**X**   0.05

5.3   Sterling retail deposits to be covered...**=**   (D)

(Equal to item 5.1 times item 5.2)

6.0   **STERLING LIQUIDITY RATIO (LQR)**...   **%**

$$LQR = \left(\frac{A}{(B-C)+D} \right) \times 100\%$$

The Bank's objective in developing the new system for sterling stock liquidity was to establish a framework that directly addresses the liquidity needs of the major UK retail banks and to introduce a common minimum standard. The system is designed to ensure that at all times a bank maintains a stock of highly liquid assets which it can mobilize quickly and discreetly to replace funding that has been withdrawn because of a perceived problem in the institution. The aim is to provide a breathing space during which the institution can try to arrange more permanent funding solutions.

The Bank decided that, in order to provide adequate time to investigate various forms of remedial action, a bank should, as a minimum, be able to meet its obligations without any renewal of maturing wholesale funding (on a net basis) for a period of five working days, after allowing for the loss of a proportion of its retail deposit base. To prevent stock holdings from becoming excessively volatile, institutions are also expected to hold sufficient sterling stock to meet a minimum 'floor' requirement with the Bank.

An institution will thus be expected to hold a stock of sterling liquid assets sufficient to cover the higher of:

1. Its wholesale sterling net outflow 'floor' over five working days, as agreed with the Bank. Unless otherwise agreed, the floor will normally be set at 50 per cent of the institution's internal wholesale sterling net outflow limit over five working days, as agreed with the Bank; or
2. 100 per cent of the actual sterling net outflow over five working days, plus 5 per cent of sterling retail deposits falling due in the same period.

The stock of sterling liquidity comprises assets which carry a low credit risk, are traded in sizeable amounts in deep and liquid markets, and which the Bank is prepared, by convention, to lend against in the course of its money-market operations. These comprise:

- cash and operational balances with the Bank;
- UK Treasury bills and gilts;
- UK bank bills eligible for rediscount at the Bank;
- UK local authority bills eligible for rediscount at the Bank;
- secured overnight and callable deposits with money-market dealing counterparties of the Bank which are authorized under the Banking Act 1987;
- secured overnight and callable deposits (including secured callable fixtures) with stock exchange money brokers and GEMMs, including money-market dealing counterparties of the Bank which are not authorised institutions under the Banking Act.

When considering the adequacy of a bank's stock of liquid assets, the Bank will also consider the diversification of the assets held and the bank's ability to mobilize them quickly and discreetly. The Bank has taken the view that CDs do not meet the requirements for inclusion in the sterling liquidity stock because of the absence of any lender-of-last-resort facility and the consequent risk that this may make the CD market unpredictable in the event of a problem in a major bank. However, it recognizes that CDs do have a role to play in liquidity management; so although CDs cannot be included in the sterling liquidity stock, institutions are permitted to offset their holdings of CDs against a maximum of 50 per cent of the wholesale sterling actual net outflow over five working days. For this purpose, CDs will be subject to a 15 per cent discount to reflect the cost of a forced sale in a troubled market.

THE APPROACH ADOPTED IN RESPECT OF OTHER AUTHORIZED INSTITUTIONS

The *liquidity measure* adopted by the Bank and used as a first step in the overall (qualitative) assessment of liquidity adequacy is based upon cash flow analysis and the use of a 'maturity ladder'. The Bank describes the measure as 'a series of accumulating net mismatch positions in successive time bands' (*see* Exhibit 2.21, Annexe 2). Agreed guidelines for this measure are established, on an individual basis, with each bank, and subsequently monitored by the Bank. Additionally, a separate assessment is made by the Bank of the overall level of maturity transformation undertaken.

Exhibit 2.21   Procedures adopted in the assessment of liquidity adequacy for banks other than large UK retail banks

---

Annexe 1: discounts applying to marketable assets
UK central government debt, local authority paper and eligible bank bills (and comparable assets from other Zone A countries):
    The following benchmark discounts will apply to assets' market values:

- central government and central government-guaranteed marketable securities with 12 or fewer months' residual maturity, including Treasury bills; and, in addition, eligible local authority paper and eligible bank bills   0%
- other central government, central government-guaranteed and local authority marketable debt with five or fewer years residual maturity or at variable rates   5%

- other central government, central government-guaranteed and local
  authority marketable debt with over five years' residual maturity   10%

Other securities denominated in freely tradable currencies (usually Zone A):
The following benchmark discounts will apply to assets' market values:

- Non-government debt securities which are classified as 'qualifying'
  by the Bank (S&S) in its implementation of the CAD, and which
  have six or fewer months' residual maturity   5%
- Non-government debt securities which are classified as 'qualifying'
  by the Bank (S&S) in its implementation of the CAD, and which
  have five or fewer years' residual maturity   10%
- Non-government debt securities which are classified as
  'qualifying' by the Bank (S&S) in its implementation of the CAD,
  and which have more than five years' residual maturity   15%
- Equities which (in the Bank's (S&S) implementation of the CAD)
  qualify for a specific risk weight no higher than 4 per cent   20%

Zone B central government debt:
Where it is actively traded, a benchmark discount of 40 per cent will apply to
market values. Note, however, that where debt is denominated in local currency,
it will only usually be deemed to be available to provide liquidity in that
currency.

Annexe 2   The system of measurement

		Sight– 8 days	8 days– 1 month	1–3 months	3–6 months	6–12 months
	Liabilities					
	Deposits					
	Commitments					
Less	Assets					
	Marketable					
	Non-marketable					
	Standby facilities					
	available					
=	Net position					
±	Carried forward					
=	Net cumulative position					

Sources: Bank of England, 1982, p. 402, as modified by S&S/1996/1 (Bank of England, 1996i).

Returning to the construction of the liquidity measure, it can be seen from Exhibit 2.21 (Annexe 2) that the maturity ladder stretches through to one year, with particular attention being paid to the period up to one month. Assets and liabilities are slotted into the maturity ladder and the net mismatch positions in each period are then accumulated. Sterling and currency mismatches are usually considered separately (*see* Hall, 1988, pp. 135–42).

The insertion of balance-sheet items into the maturity ladder has to be undertaken according to a pre-specified system. *Marketable assets* are placed at the start of the ladder, irrespective of their maturity dates, although account is taken of their differing degrees of marketability and susceptibility to price volatility by providing for the application of varying discounts – the more marketable and the less susceptible to price volatility the asset, the *lower* the discount (*see* Annexe 1 to Exhibit 2.21) – against the (normally market) value of the assets. Other assets are dealt with by reference to maturity.

Following the Bank's amendment to its 1982 Policy Notice in January 1996 (*see* S&S/1996/1; Bank of England, 1996i), the range of marketable securities which can be regarded as sight assets for the purposes of calculating liquidity mismatches was extended and a new set of 'discounts', covering both sterling and foreign currency denominated assets was introduced (*see* Annexe 1 to Exhibit 2.21). The new set of discounts now distinguishes between 'Zone A' and 'Zone B' country assets, in line with the distinction drawn in the risk weighting of balance-sheet assets within the assessment of capital adequacy – *see* Chapter 17 – and the scale of the discount factors now ranges from 0 per cent to 40 per cent, compared with the original range of 0 per cent to 10 per cent. Marketable assets, however, may now only be placed at the start of the maturity ladder if settlement procedures permit receipt of cash within eight days. Marketable assets not covered in the Annexe are subject to treatment, on a common basis, agreed with the individual banks.

The treatment of loans only nominally repayable on demand (e.g. overdrafts) has to be agreed individually with the Bank, and assets of a doubtful value are excluded or otherwise treated on a case-by-case basis. Finally, lending commitments are taken into account through their inclusion as liabilities in the appropriate time band or as otherwise agreed.

On the *liabilities* side, deposits are included according to their earliest maturity, although account is taken of the stability and diversification of the deposit base in establishing guidelines. Contractual standby facilities negotiated with other banks are treated as sight assets, with due note being taken of their remaining term and likelihood of renewal. And lastly, non-deposit liabilities maturing within one year are included, but contingent liabilities, unless they are thought likely to materialize, are not.

Exhibit 2.22   LR form

Form LR

Private and confidential

Liquidity Return

Reporting institution _____

D	D	M	M	Y	Y	Y	Y

Reporting date (eg 31 May 1998 = 31051998)_____

Unconsolidated	Solo consolidated

Unconsolidated / Solo consolidated (tick as appropriate) _____

Please tick if this return is completed in Euros (Item A) _____

I confirm that I have read the relevant reporting instructions issued by the Financial Services Authority (FSA), including paragraphs relating to accurate returns, and this return has been completed in accordance with them.

_____

Signature of director or senior manager of the reporting institution

In the event of a query, the FSA may contact (block letters please)

_____   Tel No_____   Ext _____

Notes on completion

1. If you have any difficulty in completing this return, please telephone your FSA supervisor, or 0171-601 5858.

2. Complete the return quarterly on an unconsolidated / solo consolidated basis.

3. Monthly BT reporters should complete Form LR as at the end of February, May, August and November.
   Quarterly BT reporters should complete Form LR as at the end March, June, September and December.

4. Enter amounts to the nearest thousand omitting £000s/€000s.
   Calculated amounts should be rounded to the nearest thousand, or two decimal places as appropriate.

5. For definitions of items, refer to the "Form LR: Guidance Notes and Reporting Instructions".

6. To assist with the scanning process, please enter all data neatly within the relevant boxes and do not enter the % symbol in any boxes on this return.

7. Submit the form within **10 working days** of the reporting date or **12 working days** for those institutions reporting electronically, clearly addressed to:

   Financial Services Authority
   c/o Monetary and Financial Statistics Division
   Domestic Banking Statistics (HO-5)
   Bank of England
   Threadneedle Street
   London EC2R 8 AH

   Returns may also be delivered to the Works Gate at the Lothbury entrance of the Bank of England between 9.00am and 5.00pm, Monday to Friday. Envelopes should be clearly addressed as above.

Bank of England use only

Logged in	Data entered	Amendment Book	Amendment Input

PART 1

Marketable Assets

Mark to market value

Item no		1
A1A	Cash held and Gold	
	Debt instruments issued in Zone A countries	
A2A	Central government/central government guaranteed, including Treasury bills, eligible Local Authority paper and eligible bank bills with a residual maturity of 1 year or less..	
A2B	Central government/central government guaranteed and Local Authority marketable debt of 1 to 5 years......	
A2C	Central government/central government guaranteed and Local Authority marketable debt of over 5 years	
A2D	Non-government of 6 months or less.........................	
A2E	Non-government of 6 months to 5 years.......................	
A2F	Non-government of over 5 years	
	Debt instruments issued in Zone B countries	
A3A	Central government/central government guaranteed with a residual maturity of 1 year or less..............	
A3B	Central government/central government guaranteed of 1 to 5 years...........................	
A3C	Central government/central government guaranteed of over 5 years..........................	
A3D	Eligible non-government of 6 months or less................	
A3E	Eligible non-government of 6 months to 5 years.............	
A3F	Eligible non-government of over 5 years	
A4A	*Brady bonds*...	
A5A	*Highly liquid equities / equity indices*	
A6A	**Total discounted amount**	

Zone B currencies	Discount where denominated in zone A currency (%)	Discount where denominated in zone B currency (%)	Discounted to		
Mark to market value			8 days and under	Over 8 days to 1 month	
2			3	4	Item no
....					A1A
	0	20			A2A
	5	25			A2B
	10	30			A2C
	5	25			A2D
	10	30			A2E
	15	35			A2F
	20	20			A3A
	30	30			A3B
	40	40			A3C
	30	30			A3D
	40	40			A3E
	50	50			A3F
	40	40			A4A
	20	40			A5A
....					A6A

PART 2

Contractual basis: residual maturity

Item no		Cashflow basis			
		1	2	3	4
	Inflows	Overdue	Demand (incl. next day)	8 days and under (excl. next day)	Over 8 days to 1 month
B	Please tick if reported on a Cashflow basis (blank represents Maturity basis)				
	Retail				
B1A	Mortgages				
B1B	Personal loans				
B1C	Overdrafts				
B1D	Credit card inflows				
B1E	Repayment of advances				
B1F	Other retail inflows				
	Wholesale				
B2A	Non-marketable securities and debt instruments and marketable assets maturing within 1 month				
B2B	Intragroup / connected				
B2C	Interbank (excluding any intragroup)				
B2D	Corporate (non interbank, non intragroup)				
B2E	Government / Public sector				
B2F	Repos / reverse repos				
B2G	Trade related letters of credit				
B3A	Swaps and FRAs				
B3B	Forward foreign exchange				
B3C	Forward sales and purchases				
B3D	Other off balance sheet				
B4A	Fees and other income				
B4B	Other funding sources				
B5A	**Total inflows**				

Assets: Maturity analysis

5	6	7		8	9	10	11	Item no
Over 1 month to 3 months	Over 3 months to 6 months	Total (Cashflow basis)		Over 6 months to 1 year	Over 1 year to 3 years	Over 3 years to 5 years	Total (Maturity basis)	
								B
								B1A
								B1B
								B1C
								B1D
								B1E
								B1F
								B2A
								B2B
								B2C
								B2D
								B2E
								B2F
								B2G
								B3A
								B3B
								B3C
								B3D
								B4A
								B4B
								B5A

PART 2 (continued)

Contractual basis: residual maturity

Item no	Outflows	Cashflow basis			
		1 Overdue	2 Demand (incl. next day)	3 8 days and under (excl. next day)	4 Over 8 day to 1 month
C	Please tick if reported on a Cashflow basis (blank represents Maturity basis)				
	Retail				
C1A	Time deposits..				
C1B	No notice / current accounts.....................................				
C1C	Additional advances committed..................................				
	Wholesale				
C2A	Non-marketable securities and debt instruments and marketable assets maturing within 1 month.................				
C2B	Additional advances committed..................................				
C2C	Intragroup / Connected..				
C2D	Interbank (excluding any intragroup)..........................				
C2E	Corportate (non-interbank and non-intragroup).............				
C2F	Government / Public sector.......................................				
C2G	Repos / Reverse Repos				
C2H	Trade related letters of credit..................................				
C3A	Swaps and FRAs...				
C3B	Forward foreign exchange..				
C3C	Forward sales and purchases...................................				
C3D	Other off balance sheet...				
C4A	Dividends, tax, other costs and outflows...................				
C5A	**Total outflows**				
	Memo Items				
D1A	Options inflows..				
D1B	Option outflows				
D1C	Undrawn committed facilities granted to the bank........				
D1D	Undrawn committed facilities granted by the bank				
D1E	Commitments to lend under credit card and other revolving credit type facilities				
D1F	Total deposits..				
D2A	Undrawn treasury concessions granted by the bank......				
D2B	Amount of total cash inflows in arrears......................				

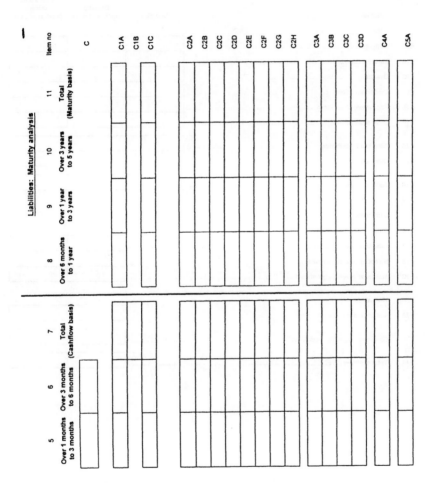

Liabilities: Maturity analysis

PART 3

"Behavioural" adjustments to standard cashflow basis

Item no	Inflows	1 Overdue	2 Demand (incl. next day)	3 8 days and under (excl. next day)
	Retail			
E1A	Mortgages			
E1B	Personal loans			
E1C	Overdrafts			
E1D	Credit card inflows			
E1E	Repayment of advances			
E1F	Other retail inflows			
E2A	Fees and other income			
E2B	Other inflows			
E3A	Total inflows			

Outflows

Retail

Item no		Overdue	Demand
F1A	Time deposits		
F1B	No notice / current accounts		
F1C	Additional advances committed		
	Wholesale		
F2A	Additional advances committed		
F3A	Dividends, tax, other costs & outflows		
F4A	Total outflows		

t 4	5	6	7	8	9	Item no
Over 8 days to 1 month	Over 1 month to 3 months	Over 3 months to 6 months	Over 6 months to 1 year	Over 1 year	Total (Columns 1 to 8)	
						E1A
						E1B
						E1C
						E1D
						E1E
						E1F
						E2A
						E2B
						E3A
						F1A
						F1B
						F1C
						F2A
						F3A
						F4A

PART 4

Calculation of liquidity mismatches

Item no	Contractual Basis	Overdue (excluded) 1	Demand (incl. next day) 2	8 days and under 3	1 month and under 4	Item no
	Inflows					
G1A	Cumulative discounted marketable assets...	■■■■				G1A
G1B	Plus total cumulative standard inflows......................................					G1B
G1C	Plus Y% * committed lines granted to the bank	■■■■	■■■■	■■■■	■■■■	G1C
G1D	Y% = (nnnn format)	■■■■	■■■■	■■■■	■■■■	G1D
G1E	**Equals total inflows (A)**...					G1E
	Outflows					
G2A	Total cumulative standard outflows.......................................	■■■■				G2A
G2B	Plus undrawn commitments to lend granted by the bank...................					G2B
G2C	Z% = (nnnn format)	■■■■	■■■■	■■■■	■■■■	G2C
G2D	Plus undrawn credit card and other revolving commitments to lend.....					G2D
G2E	W% = (nnnn format)	■■■■	■■■■	■■■■	■■■■	G2E
G2F	**Equals total outflows (B)**					G2F
	Mismatch					
G3A	Net mismatch: standard basis (A - B)...................................					G3A
G4A	Total deposits (X)..					G4A
G5A	**Mismatch as a percentage of deposits [(A - B) / X] (nnnn format)...**					G5A

	Behaviourally Adjusted Basis					
	Inflows					
G6A	Cumulative discounted marketable assets................................	■■■■				G6A
G6B	Plus total cumulative behaviourally adjusted inflows......................					G6B
G6C	Plus Y% * committed lines granted to the bank					G6C
G6D	Y% = (nnnn format)					G6D
G6E	**Equals total inflows (C)**...					G6E
	Outflows					
G7A	Total cumulative behaviourally adjusted outflows......................					G7A
G7B	Plus undrawn commitments to lend granted by the bank..................					G7B
G7C	Z% = (nnnn format)					G7C
G7D	Plus undrawn credit card and other revolving commitments to lend.....					G7D
G7E	W% = (nnnn format)					G7E
G7F	**Equals total outflows (D)**					G7F
	Mismatch					
G8A	Net mismatch: behaviourally adjusted basis (C - D)...................					G8A
G8B	Total deposits (X)...					G8B
G8C	**Mismatch as a percentage of deposits [(C - D) / X] (nnnn format)...**					G8C

In order to assist with the scanning process please enter percentages in nnnn format (eg -5.25% as -525 and -10% as -1000) and do <u>not</u> enter the % symbol in any of the boxes of this form

PART 4 (continued)

Exceptions to guidelines

Net cumulative mismatch as a percentage of total deposits

	1	2	3	
Item no	Date (ddmm format)	Sight to eight days (nnnn format)	Sight to one month (nnnn format)	Item no
H1A				H1A
H1B				H1B
H1C				H1C
H1D				H1D
H1E				H1E
H1F				H1F
H1G				H1G
H1H				H1H
H1J				H1J
H1K				H1K
H1L				H1L
H1M				H1M
H1N				H1N
H1P				H1P
H1Q				H1Q
H1R				H1R
H1S				H1S
H1T				H1T
H1U				H1U
H1V				H1V

In order to assist with the scanning process please enter percentages in nnnn format (eg -5.25% as -525 and -10% as -1000) and do <u>not</u> enter the % symbol in any of the boxes of this form

PART 5: Deposit Concentration

Part A: Large Deposits

Item no	Customer (a)	Maturity date (b) (ddmmyy format blank = undated, V = various)	Currency (c) (using international country codes blank = sterling, V = various)
	1	2	3
J1A			
J1B			
J1C			
J1D			
J1E			
J1F			
J1G			
J1H			
J1J			
J1K			
J1L			
J1M			
J1N			
J1P			
J1Q			
J1R			
J1S			
J1T			
J1U			
J1V			

	4	5	6	7	8	Item no
	Amount (d)	Maximum amount in reporting period (e)	Client money (C) (f) (please tick)	Mandated accounts (M) (g) (please tick)	Customers connected to reporting bank (CC) (please tick)	
						J1A
						J1B
						J1C
						J1D
						J1E
						J1F
						J1G
						J1H
						J1J
						J1K
						J1L
						J1M
						J1N
						J1P
						J1Q
						J1R
						J1S
						J1T
						J1U
						J1V

PART 5 (continued)

Part B: Client money and mandated accounts held

Item no		1	2	3	Item no
			Amount	Maximum amount in reporting period	
K1A	Client Money (f)..				K1A
K1B	Mandated accounts (g)...................................				K1B

Notes for completing Part 5

a) Principal customer in the case of closely related depositors/lenders.

b) Where an individual deposit comprises 25% or more of the total for a particular depositor / group of depositors and has a different maturity from the remainder, it should be reported separately and bracketed. Otherwise where deposits have been received with a variety of maturity dates, reporting institutions need not supply a full list of dates but may write the letter V in the first section of column 2. Where the deposit is undated, this column should be left blank.

c) Enter the currency and not the amount. The codes used for each currency should be consistent with the international codes used for the Bank of England returns. Where an individual deposit comprises 25% or more of the total for a particular depositor/group of depositors and has a different currency from the remainder, it should be reported separately and bracketed. Otherwise, where deposits are received in a variety of currencies, reporting institutions need not supply details of each currency amount but may write the letter V in the first section of column 3. Where the deposit is in sterling, this column should be left blank.

d) Enter the sterling (or euro amount, if appropriate) or the sterling equivalent (or euro equivalent) if the deposit/loan is in currency other than sterling (or euro).

e) Only complete this column for deposits still outstanding at the reporting date.

f) Funds subject to the FSA's (previously SIB's) client money regulations.

g) Funds held in accounts operated by a Financial Services Act authorised firm under a mandate signed by the account holder.

This assessment regime remained in force until 1997. However, in September of that year, as envisaged in the Bank's paper of June 1997 (Bank of England, 1997f), the method for measuring liquidity mismatch was revised to gain a more comprehensive and accurate picture of a bank's liquidity mismatch position. Under the new approach, which was confirmed in February 1998, inflows and outflows of cash, such as interest payments and receipts, other income and expenses, and off-balance-sheet cash flows, are captured within a cash flow analysis for the period from sight to one month (the original suggestion was for sight to one year). For the period beyond one year, items continue to be reported in the form of a maturity analysis of assets and liabilities, although in a much abbreviated form. An integrated liquidity reporting form – *see* Exhibit 2.22 – replaced the forms previously used (i.e. the 'Q6', 'S5', 'L1' and 'D1') in spring 1998; and the liquidity position of a bank is now assessed in all currencies combined, although the Bank may require additional detail on individual currencies, including sterling, where these are material (i.e. constituting more than 20 per cent of the bank's business) or where there may be a material risk that cannot readily, quickly and easily be converted into other currencies. The discounting of marketable assets to sight continues with broadly the same range of discounts applying to the mark-to-market values of assets, the main change relating to some debt items issued by 'Zone B' entities (i.e. Zone B investment grade government debt now attracts discounts of 20, 30 or 40 per cent, while investment grade non-government debt attracts discounts of 30, 40 or 50 per cent).

THE TREATMENT OF OVERSEAS BANKS AND UK BANKS' OVERSEAS OPERATIONS

In determining the approach to be taken towards the overseas operations of UK-incorporated banks and the UK operations of banks incorporated overseas, the Bank, of course, has to take due account of the relevant principles enshrined within the Basle *Concordat* (*see* Chapter 3) (as affected by relevant EC Directives). The original document proposed that the supervision of liquidity should be the primary responsibility of the host supervisory authorities since foreign establishments generally have to conform to local liquidity management practices and must comply with local regulations. The revised *Concordat* (June 1983) reaffirmed this principle but stressed more heavily than the original the need for consultation between host and parent supervisors. It also clarified the treatment of joint ventures by advising that, unlike the case for branches and subsidiaries, primary supervisory responsibility should lie with the authorities in the country of incorporation and not with the host authorities.

Bearing in mind these principles, the Bank noted in its 1982 paper that parental responsibilities for the liquidity of affiliates (i.e. subsidiaries and participations) of UK-incorporated banks operating mainly in the UK might require the Bank to seek additional information from individual banks to allow monitoring to be conducted on a consolidated basis. In the case of the foreign operations of such affiliates (or, indeed, branches), a consolidated approach was thought likely to prove less helpful, although the Bank indicated that it might wish to examine the internal arrangements of the parent bank for the monitoring and control of its worldwide liquidity needs. Finally, the Bank indicated its desire to monitor more closely than hitherto the liquidity position, especially in sterling, of the UK branches of foreign banks, taking due note of the relationship between the branch and its head office and of its exposure to country risk (Bank of England 1984b, p. 238).

More recently, the Bank has clarified its treatment of EEA institutions (Bank of England, 1997d). Under the Second Banking Co-ordination Directive, the supervision of liquidity remains a responsibility shared by the home and host supervisor. Where a bank manages its liquidity on a global basis (and is monitored as such by its home supervisor), the Bank's policy is to look to head office to ensure that the UK branch has appropriate liquidity. Once the Bank is able to agree with the home supervisor that supervisory monitoring by the Bank of the branch's liquidity would not be of value, it seeks to agree to a 'global liquidity arrangement' with the home supervisor. This allows the Bank to discharge its host responsibilities under the Directive without imposing quantitative local liquidity requirements on the branch.

19. The treatment of foreign currency operations

THE OLD APPROACH

Until recently, foreign exchange position risk was assessed by the Bank on the basis of the formal measurement system set out in its papers on 'Foreign Currency Exposure' (Bank of England, 1981) and 'Foreign Currency Options' (Bank of England, 1984a).

Although the Bank accepted that primary responsibility for the control of exposures arising from foreign currency operations should rest with the banks' own management, it nevertheless agreed dealing position guidelines with each bank, on an individual basis, and sought to ensure that banks' internal controls were adequate to allow for effective and continuous monitoring of exposures against the 'guidelines'.

In assessing a bank's exposure, with a view to relating it to other risks incurred and to its capital base, the Bank was concerned with all exposures arising from any uncovered foreign currency position (including, since April 1984, those incurred through the writing of options business)[78] in any currency. Net positions in single currencies, including sterling, were considered alongside the aggregate net position in all currencies.

Accepting the market distinction drawn between structural (i.e. those creating exposures of a longer-term nature) and dealing positions (i.e. those creating exposures as a result of normal, day-to-day operations), the Bank excluded agreed structural positions from consideration in formulating dealing guidelines.[79] Additionally, an institution's expertise in foreign exchange operations and its particular circumstances was taken fully into account during the discussions aimed at agreeing such guidelines.

Generally speaking, UK-incorporated banks experienced in foreign exchange operations could expect to agree the following guidelines: (1) a limit on the net 'open' (i.e. the difference between assets and liabilities) dealing position in any one currency of 10 per cent of the adjusted capital base;[80] and (2) a limit on the net 'short' open dealing (spot and forward) positions (i.e. the net foreign currency *liability* positions) of all currencies taken together of 15 per cent of the adjusted capital base.

The arrangements described above applied to the operation of all UK banks' branches at home and abroad. Their subsidiaries were monitored separately, however, although such monitoring could be used to provide a consolidated assessment of banks' foreign currency exposures for capital adequacy purposes.

In monitoring the foreign currency operations of the UK branches of *foreign banks*, the Bank took account of a branch's own internal controls, those exercised by its head office and the monitoring arrangements of its home supervisory authority. Where it considered these to be satisfactory, the Bank did not apply separate guidelines; but where they were not deemed satisfactory, the Bank agreed appropriate absolute levels of exposure to serve as guidelines.

Finally, monthly returns (*see* Hall, 1993, pp. 145–8) were required of all banks, domestic and foreign, which had to provide, in contracted currency amounts, information on the following:

1. The net spot long or short position in each currency at the close of business on the reporting day.
2. The net forward long or short position in each currency at the close of business on the reporting day.
3. All the occasions during the reporting period on which the agreed guidelines were exceeded.

THE NEW APPROACH

The assessment regime outlined above survived intact until the CAD's market risk proposals, which embraced foreign exchange risk, were implemented at the beginning of 1996 (see Chapter 17). The Bank's April 1981 and April 1984 papers, covering the treatment of foreign currency exposures (Bank of England, 1981) and foreign currency options (Bank of England, 1984a) respectively, however, were not formally withdrawn until September 1997, following the introduction of a new risk-based regime (*see* Bank of England, 1997g). Under this regime, institutions were required to continue operating within their original, individually set, 'guidelines', and to continue submitting the 'S3' return (*see* Exhibit 2.23) until such time as they could demonstrate to the Bank that they met the new requirements and that their internal controls were adequate. At this point, reporting via the S3 would cease and institutions would, henceforth, set their own internal limits for foreign exchange in a manner appropriate to their business. The role of the Bank/FSAu is to seek to ensure the adequacy of internal systems and controls.

Exhibit 2.23   *The S3 return*

Private and Confidential   **Form S3**

Foreign Currency Exposure

as at _____

Reporting Institution _____

_____

Name (block letters please) and signature of authorised official at reporting institution

In the event of a query, the Bank of England may contact (block letters please)

_____ Tel No _____ Ext _____

Notes on completion

If you have any difficulty in completing this form, please telephone 0171-601 4218/4544/5574. Telephone enquiries relating to general reporting difficulties should be made to the Monetary and Financial Statistics Division's 'Help Desk' on 0171-601 5360.

1   Complete form monthly as at the last day of the calendar month.

2   For definition of items refer to the blue *Banking statistics definitions folder*.

3   Enter amounts in sterling to nearest thousand, omitting £000s.

4   Ensure that the items in the shaded areas agree with the related items on Form BS column 2 (other currencies).

5   Return form within **TEN WORKING DAYS** of reporting date clearly addressed to:

     Monetary and Financial Statistics Division
     Domestic Banking Statistics
     Bank of England
     Threadneedle Street
     London EC2R 8AH

6   Forms may also be delivered to the Works gate at the Lothbury entrance of the Bank of England between 9.00 am and 5.00 pm, Monday to Friday. Envelopes should be clearly addressed as above.

Bank of England use only		
Logged in	Data entered	Amendments input

December 1992

(5016)

SECTION 1 - FOREIGN CURRENCY EXPOSURE OF REPORTING INSTITUTION

Analysis by currency		Operations transacted by the United Kingdom offices					
		Gross spot claims	Gross spot liabilities including internal accounts	Net spot claims (liabilities), including internal accounts (= col 1 minus col 2)	Net forward purchases (sales)	Known net future income (expense) not included already in column 3 (d)	Net purchases (sales) of currency and gold futures contracts
		1	2	3	4	5	6
US dollars	US USA						
Belgian francs	BE BELG						
Canadian dollars	CA CANA						
Danish kroner	DK DENM						
Deutschemarks	DE RGER						
French francs	FR FRAN						
Irish pounds	IE EIRE						
Italian lire	IT ITAL						
Japanese yen	JP JAPA						
Netherlands guilders	NL NETH						
Saudi riyals	SA SAUA						
Spanish pesetas	ES SPAI						
Swedish kroner	SE SWED						
Swiss francs	CH SWIT						
Gold (a)	GO GOLD						
European Currency Units	EU ECUS						
Special Drawing Rights	SS SDRS						
(b)							
Foreign currencies not separately specified above (c)	long / short	}					
Translation/revaluation adjustment (d)							
TOTAL							

(BS col 2 item 21)　　(BS col 2 item 6)

SECTION 2 - NET POSITION OF EACH OVERSEAS BRANCH OR DEALING CENTRE OF REPORTING INSTITUTION

Analysis by currency		Location of branch or dealing centre				
US dollars	US USA					
Belgian francs	BE BELG					
Canadian dollars	CA CANA					
Danish kroner	DK DENM					
Deutschemarks	DE RGER					
French francs	FR FRAN					
Irish pounds	IE EIRE					
Italian lire	IT ITAL					
Japanese yen	JP JAPA					
Netherlands guilders	NL NETH					
Saudi riyals	SA SAUA					
Spanish pesetas	ES SPAI					
Swedish kroner	SE SWED					
Swiss francs	CH SWIT					
Gold (a)	GO GOLD					
European Currency Units	EU ECUS					
Special Drawing Rights	SS SDRS					
(b)						
Foreign currencies not separately specified above (c)						

(a) Includes bullion and coin

(b) Enter here details for other individual foreign currencies with net spot claims or liabilities (including, for UK registered banks, the balances of overseas branches and dealing centres) equivalent to £1 million or more. Institutions asked to report positions in silver should do so here

£000s

Adjustment for profit and loss and specific provision account (d)	Adjusted options position	Net long (short) position of overseas branches listed in section 2	Disaggregation of net positions in CCUs	Net overall long (short) position (= cols 3+4+5+6+ 7+7A+8+8A)	Adjustment for structural assets (liabilities) (d)	Net dealing long (short) position (= col 9 minus col 10)	
7	7A	8	8A	9	10	11	
							US USA
							BE BELG
							CA CANA
							DK DENM
							DE RGER
							FR FRAN
							IE EIRE
							IT ITAL
							JP JAPA
							NL NETH
							SA SAUA
							ES SPAI
							SE SWED
							CH SWIT
							GO GOLD
							EU ECUS
							SS SDRS
		{	( )	} {		( )	long / short

Sterling balancing item (d)					
TOTAL	ZERO		ZERO		
Aggregate of net short open positions (d)	( )		( )		

£000s

					Total long (short) position of all branches and dealing centres

(c) Enter here details for currencies with a net spot claims on liabilities equivalent to less than £1 million. The subdivision into long and short positions is required only in columns 9 and 11 (see notes).

(d) See the notes regarding the completion of these boxes.

ANNEX A £000s

Analysis by currency		Net dealing long (short) spot & forward position	Potential purchases under option rights granted to others	Potential sales under option rights granted to others	Dealing exposure to depreciation	Dealing exposure to appreciation	Options held to purchase currencies	Options held to sell currencies
		11	12	13	14	15	16	17
US dollars	US USA							
Belgian francs	BE BELG							
Canadian dollars	CA CANA							
Danish kroner	DK DENM							
Deutschemarks	DE RGER							
French francs	FR FRAN							
Irish pounds	IE EIRE							
Italian lire	IT ITAL							
Japanese yen	JP JAPA							
Netherlands guilders	NL NETH							
Saudi riyals	SA SAUA							
Spanish pesetas	ES SPAI							
Swedish kroner	SE SWED							
Swiss francs	CH SWIT							
Gold (a)	GO GOLD							
European Currency Units	EU ECUS							
Special Drawing Rights	SS SDRS							
(b)								
Foreign currencies not separately specified above (c)	long							
	short	( )	( )	( )	( )	( )	( )	( )
UK								
TOTAL		ZERO						
Aggregate of net short open positions		( )						

ANNEX B £000s

Analysis by currency		Gross value of potential purchases under option rights granted	Gross value of potential sales under option rights granted	Gross value of potential purchases under option rights held	Gross value of potential sales under option rights held	Adjusted options position
		12	13	14	15	16
US dollars	US USA					
Belgian francs	BE BELG					
Canadian dollars	CA CANA					
Danish kroner	DK DENM					
Deutschemarks	DE RGER					
French francs	FR FRAN					
Irish pounds	IE EIRE					
Italian lire	IT ITAL					
Japanese yen	JP JAPA					
Netherlands guilders	NL NETH					
Saudi riyals	SA SAUA					
Spanish pesetas	ES SPAI					
Swedish kroner	SE SWED					
Swiss francs	CH SWIT					
Gold (a)	GO GOLD					
European Currency Units	EU ECUS					
Special Drawing Rights	SS SDRS					
(b)						
Foreign currencies not separately specified above (c)	long					
	short	( )	( )	( )	( )	( )
UK						
TOTAL						ZERO

(a), (b), (c) - see footnotes to sections 1 and 2

SECTION 3 - EXCEPTION REPORT (e)

£000s

Analysis by currency	Net dealing long (short) positions (equivalent to column 11 in section 1)							
	Date:	Date:	Date:	Date:	Date:	Date:	Date:	
US dollars								US USA
Belgian francs								BE BELG
Canadian dollars								CA CANA
Danish kroner								DK DENM
Deutschemarks								DE RGER
French francs								FR FRAN
Irish pounds								IE EIRE
Italian lire								IT ITAL
Japanese yen								JP JAPA
Netherlands guilders								NL NETH
Saudi riyals								SA SAUA
Spanish pesetas								ES SPAI
Swedish kroner								SE SWED
Swiss francs								CH SWIT
Gold (a)								GO GOLD
Eurpoean Currency Units								EU ECUS
Special Drawing Rights								SS SDRS
(b)								
Foreign currencies not separately specified above (c) — long								long
— short								short
Sterling balancing item (d)								
TOTAL	ZERO	ZERO	ZERO	ZERO	ZERO	ZERO	ZERO	

Aggregate of net short open positions (d)	( )	( )	( )	( )	( )	( )	( )

(a). (b). (c). (d) - see footnotes to sections 1 and 2

(e) A column should be completed for any date since the previous end-month reporting date on which banks have exceeded the guidelines agreed with Banking Supervision Division, Bank of England.

333

20. The treatment of large exposures

THE EVOLUTION OF THE CURRENT APPROACH

The Bank's Original Approach

As noted in Chapter 6, the Banking Act 1987 (Section 38(1)) required all UK-incorporated banks and UK banking groups to notify the Bank of any exposure – defined as the sum of all claims plus undrawn facilities, contingent liabilities, other counterparty risks and equity holdings (*see* BSD/1987/1; Bank of England, 1987d) – to a single non-bank party or group of 'closely related' non-bank parties which exceeds 10 per cent of the bank's adjusted capital base as defined for the purposes of calculating a bank's RAR (*see* Exhibit 2.5 as amended by BSD/1990/1; Bank of England, 1990c). Additionally, the institutions were required to give the Bank prior notice of proposed transactions which would raise exposure to over 25 per cent of the (adjusted) capital base. The requirements, which took effect from 1 April 1988, were consistent with the EC's proposals (*see* Chapter 9), although the Bank was eventually obliged to apply a formal limit to 25 per cent of the adjusted capital base and to amend the definition of an 'exposure' (*see* below).

The Bank's view, as set out in BSD/1987/1, was that exposure should not normally exceed 10 per cent of the capital base – those that did would receive thorough examination and required justification; and, apart from the most exceptional circumstances, no exposure should exceed 25 per cent of the capital base. The main exceptions to the 25 per cent rule were as follows:

1. Exposures to other banks with a maturity of up to one year.[81]
2. Exposures to overseas central governments.[82]
3. Exposures of up to one year to group financial companies.
4. Exposures secured by cash or an ECGD guarantee or British government stocks.
5. Underwriting exposures incurred by 'experts' (*see* BSD/1987/1.1; Bank of England, 1988c).
6. In the case of bank subsidiaries, exposures guaranteed by the parent bank.[83]

Limits on such exposures were agreed, beyond which normal pre-notification requirements applied. Sectoral exposures were not assessed under this policy, although banks were required to report such exposures (e.g. in respect of property and manufacturing, and of individual countries) and heavy concentrations of risk would be discussed at the management interview. The eschewal of exposure limits was in keeping with the Bank's desire to preserve as much flexibility as possible within the supervisory process.

The presumption was that a bank with a number of exposures[84] in excess of 10 per cent of the capital base, or any in excess of 25 per cent or which had particular concentrations of risk, would be required to hold additional capital – the amount being dependent on the standing of the borrower, the nature of the bank's relationship with the borrower, the nature and extent of security taken against the exposure, the bank's expertise in the particular type of lending, and the number of such exposures, their individual size and nature.

Although, formally, the large exposures notification requirements only applied to UK-incorporated banks, the principles adopted by the Bank were applied as far as possible to the UK branches of overseas banks. Thus while acknowledging that the assessment of large exposures is the prime responsibility of the home supervisor, the Bank sought to examine and discuss with the management of each bank its large exposures (measured in relation to branch capital and not that of the bank as a whole), reserving the right to discuss the size of such branch exposures with the home supervisory authority. Additionally, such branches were required to report their 20 largest exposures.

For banks which were subsidiaries of overseas banks, the Bank agreed with the parent bank supervisor what exposures were appropriate, taking into account the degree and extent of the consolidated supervision of the banking group exercised by the latter authority. Overseas subsidiaries of UK banks were expected to conform to the local regulatory requirements, although the Bank, as a part of its consolidated supervision of banking groups, sought to identify subsidiaries other than UK banks within the group which undertook significant exposures.

Modifications Required to Accommodate the Large Exposures Directive

In October 1993, the Bank issued a notice (BSD/1993/2; Bank of England, 1993c) concerning the implementation of the EC's Large Exposures Directive on the monitoring and control of credit institutions' large exposures, adopted in December 1992 (EC, 1992a). This notice replaced the three earlier notices on the subject.

Although the terms of the Large Exposures Directive were broadly in line with the Bank's existing large exposures policy, implementation necessitated two major changes. First, compliance with the Directive required the introduction of explicit *limits* on the size of exposure that could be undertaken by UK-incorporated authorized institutions at the consolidated level:

- in aggregate, exposures which individually exceed 10 per cent of the capital base should not exceed 800 per cent of the capital base;
- no exposure to an individual counterparty should exceed 25 per cent of the capital base;
- the total of exposures to unconsolidated connected counterparties should not exceed 25 per cent of the capital base.

Certain types of exposure were, however, exempted from the limits. These embraced: (1) exposures to banks and building societies of under one year in maturity (the Bank sets a limit of 20 per cent of the capital base and requires that each bank provides it with a list of limits individually set for counterparties); (2) exposures to Zone A central governments and central banks;[85] and (3) exposures secured by cash or Zone A government securities, or covered by a parental guarantee. The Bank's pre- and post-notification requirements, however, continued to apply to these exposures. Under the Bank's new policy, the limits operated in parallel with the notification requirements of the Banking Act.

Second, the definition of an exposure was extended to include exposures on interest rate- and foreign exchange rate-related contracts.

Although the Directive only applied formally at a consolidated level, the Bank placed the same limits and requirements on authorized institutions at an unconsolidated level.

Changes Necessitated by the Capital Adequacy Directive

Apart from the Large Exposures Directive, the EC's CAD (EC, 1993) also meant modification of the Bank's large exposures policy regime (the Large Exposures Directive's requirements apply to both the banking and trading books, while the treatment of large exposures under the CAD applies to the trading book).[86]

Exhibit 2.24 The treatment of large exposures under the CAD: calculation of the incremental capital requirements for excess exposures extant for more than 10 days

Excess exposure over 25% of the amended capital base	Factors to be applied to specific risk weightings (%)
Up to 40% of the amended capital base	200
From 40% to 60%	300
From 60% to 80%	400
From 80% to 100%	500
From 100% to 250%	600
Over 250%	900

Exhibit 2.25   Revised large exposures return

Form LE2

Private and confidential

ANALYSIS OF LARGE EXPOSURES
To be completed by UK incorporated banks only

as at _____

Reporting institution _____
(Unconsolidated/Solo consolidated/Consolidated - delete as appropriate)

Capital base for the period of this report:_____ Date agreed: _____

Currency of completion: _____

I certify that the information in this return submitted to the Financial Services Authority for the quarter ending on this reporting date conforms with the Financial Services Authority notices (BSD/1993/2 and S&S/1995/2 as amended by S&S/1995/4) setting out its policy on large exposures and reporting instructions for the completion of this return.

I undertake if there are further material facts relating to the company's large exposures which, in my judgement, should be disclosed, I will send a letter under sealed cover setting these out to the appropriate Head of Department, Complex Group Division / Banks and Building Societies Division, Financial Services Authority.

I am aware that section 38 of the Banking Act 1987, which relates to the reporting of large exposures on an unconsolidated basis, provides that an institution which fails to make a report as required by that Section may be guilty of an offence and shall be liable on summary conviction to a fine.

Signature of authorised signatory: _____ Date: _____

Name: _____ Position held: _____

In the event of a query, the Financial Services Authority may, in the first instance, contact:

_____ Tel No: _____ Ext: _____

Notes on completion

1   Complete the return quarterly on an unconsolidated/solo-consolidated basis and consolidated basis as at end of March, June, September and December, or at dates which coincide with the financial year end if agreed with Supervision and Surveillance.

2   The form must be returned within 10 working days of the reporting date when completed on an unconsolidated/solo-consolidated basis and within 20 days of the reporting date when completed on a consolidated basis. Please address the form to your normal supervisory contact in:

Financial Services

c/o Supervision and Surveillance
Bank of England
Threadneedle Street
London EC2R 8 AH

3   For definitions of items, refer to the reporting instructions.

4   If you have any difficulty in completing this form, please telephone your Supervision and Surveillance analyst for guidance.

Bank of England use only			
Logged in	Data entered	Amendment Book	Amendment Input

June 1998

PART 1

LARGEST EXPOSURES TO INDIVIDUAL NON-BANK COUNTERPARTIES AND GROUPS OF CLOSELY RELATED

Counterparty (i)	Gross exposure (ii) (2)		Net exposure (ii) (3)	
(1)	(a) At reporting date	(b) Maximum during period	(a) At reporting date	(b) Maximum during period

(i)   Principal counterparty(ies) in the case of groups of closely related non-bank counterparties.

(ii)   Any exposure denominated other than in £ (either partially or wholly) should be marked with a *.

£000s (unless
otherwise agreed)

NON-BANK COUNTERPARTIES

Specific bad debt provisions made at reporting date against the exposure in column 2(a) or 3(a) (4)	Eligible collateral held (5)		Covered by guarantees (6)		Amount included in clustering ratio calculation (7)
	(a) Cash	(b) Zone A Government securities	(a) Parent bank	(b) Third party	

PART 2 (i)

LARGEST EXPOSURES TO INDIVIDUAL NON-BANK COUNTERPARTIES AND GROUPS OF CLOSELY RELATED

Counterparty (i) (1)	Gross exposure (ii)(iii) (2)		Net exposure (ii)(iii) (3)		Specific bad debt provisions made at reporting date against the exposure in column 2(a) or 3(a) (4)
	(a) At reporting date	(b) Maximum during period	(a) At reporting date	(b) Maximum during period	

(i)   Principal counterparty(ies) in the case of groups of closely related non-bank counterparties.

(ii)   Any exposure denominated other than in £ (either partially or wholly) should be marked with a *.

£000s (unless
otherwise agreed)

NON-BANK COUNTERPARTIES CONNECTED TO THE REPORTING BANK

Eligible collateral held (5)		Covered by guarantees (6)		Amount exempt under a connected exposure concession (7)	Amount included in clustering ratio calculation (8)
(a) Cash	(b) Zone A Government securities	(a) Parent bank	(b) Third party		

(iii) The total exposure to the counterparty(ies) listed in column 1 should be reported but exposures up to and including 1 year (original) maturity to group financial companies should also be separately identified in brackets.

PART 2 (ii)

LARGEST EXPOSURES TO BANKS, BUILDING SOCIETIES, RECOGNISED INVESTMENT FIRMS, GILT-EDGED
RECOGNISED CLEARING HOUSES AND RECOGNISED EXCHANGES CONNECTED TO THE REPORTING BANK

Counterparty (1)	Gross exposure (i) (2)		Net exposure (i) (3)		Specific bad debt provisions made at reporting date against the exposure in column 2(a) or 3(a) (4)
	(a) At reporting date	(b) Maximum during period	(a) At reporting date	(b) Maximum during period	

(i)   Any exposure denominated other than in £ (either partially or wholly) should be marked with a *.

£000s (unless
otherwise agreed)

MARKET MAKERS, STOCK EXCHANGE MONEY BROKERS,

Eligible collateral held (5)		Covered by guarantees (6)		Amount exempt under a connected exposure concession (7)	Amount included in clustering ratio calculation (8)
(a) Cash	(b) Zone A Government securities	(a) Parent bank	(b) Third party		

PART 3 (i)

LARGEST EXPOSURES TO BANKS, BUILDING SOCIETIES, RECOGNISED INVESTMENT FIRMS, GILT-EDGED
RECOGNISED CLEARING HOUSES AND RECOGNISED EXCHANGES WITH A MATURITY OF 1 YEAR OR LESS

Counterparty	Gross exposure (i)		Net exposure (i)		Specific bad debt provisions made at reporting date against the exposure in column 2(a) or 3(a)
	(2)		(3)		
	(a) At reporting date	(b) Maximum during period	(a) At reporting date	(b) Maximum during period	
(1)					(4)

(i)   Any exposure denominated other than in £ (either partially or wholly) should be marked with a *.

£000s (unless
otherwise agreed)

MARKET MAKERS, STOCK EXCHANGE MONEY BROKERS,

Exposure to counterparties closely related to counterparty in column 1 (ii) (5)	Eligible collateral held (6)		Covered by guarantees (7)	
	(a) Cash	(b) Zone A Government securities	(a) Parent bank	(b) Third party

(ii) Other than banks, building societies, recognised investment firms, gilt-edged market makers, stock exchange money brokers, recognised clearing houses and recognised exchanges.

PART 3 (ii)

LARGEST EXPOSURES TO BANKS, BUILDING SOCIETIES, RECOGNISED INVESTMENT FIRMS, GILT-EDGED RECOGNISED CLEARING HOUSES AND RECOGNISED EXCHANGES WITH A MATURITY OF OVER 1 YEAR

Counterparty (1)	Gross exposure (i) (2)		Net exposure (i) (3)		Specific bad debt provisions made at reporting date against the exposure in column 2(a) or 3(a) (4)
	(a) At reporting date	(b) Maximum during period	(a) At reporting date	(b) Maximum during period	

(i)   Any exposure denominated other than in £ (either partially or wholly) should be marked with a *.

£000s (unless
otherwise agreed)

MARKET MAKERS, STOCK EXCHANGE MONEY BROKERS,

Exposure to counterparties closely related to counterparty in column 1 (ii) (5)	Eligible collateral held (6)		Covered by guarantees (7)		Amount exempt under a 1-3 year derivative concession (8)	Amount included in clustering ratio calculation (9)
	(a) Cash	(b) Zone A Government securities	(a) Parent bank	(b) Third party		

(ii) Other than banks, building societies, recognised investment firms, gilt-edged market makers, stock exchange money brokers, recognised clearing houses and recognised exchanges.

PART 4

LARGEST EXPOSURES TO CENTRAL GOVERNMENTS AND CENTRAL BANKS

Counterparty (1)	Gross exposure (i) (2)		Net exposure (i) (3)	
	(a) At reporting date	(b) Maximum during period	(a) At reporting date	(b) Maximum during period
ZONE A				
ZONE B				

(i)   Any exposure denominated other than in £ (either partially or wholly) should be marked with a *.

£000s (unless
otherwise agreed)

Specific bad debt provisions made at reporting date against the exposure in column 2(a) or 3(a) (4)	Eligible collateral held (5)		Covered by guarantees (6)		Amount included in clustering ratio calculation (7)
	(a) Cash	(b) Zone A Government securities	(a) Parent bank	(b) Third party	
					TOTAL OF PARTS 1-4

PART 5

EXPOSURES SUBJECT TO SOFT LIMITS

Adjusted capital base: _____

ISSUER	EXCESS OVER ADJUSTED CAPITAL BASE	CAPITAL CHARGE (i)

(i) To be carried to items 120 and 130 of the Form CAD1

In particular, as noted in Chapter 17, the 'hard' limits of the Large Exposures Directive can be breached under the CAD where the exposures are due to securities held in the trading book (including underwriting exposures).[87] In such circumstances, however, an additional capital requirement is incurred and separate limits apply, as shown below.

Determination of the incremental capital requirement, which can be met using any Tier 3 capital eligible for inclusion in the capital base and available to support the trading book (*see* Chapter 17), arising from breaches of the 25 per cent of the amended capital base limit due to long securities positions in the trading book, involve the following:

1. Netting any short securities positions against long securities positions, with the short items being netted against the highest long specific risk-weighted items.
2. Ranking the remaining net long securities positions in order, according to specific risk-weighting factors (i.e. lowest weighted items first, highest weighted items last).
3. Taking the lowest weighted items first, applying these exposures to the difference between the non-securities exposure to the counterparty and 25 per cent of the amended capital base (i.e. the 'headroom' up to 25 per cent of the amended capital base is employed to cover the lowest weighted exposures).
4. Applying the following incremental capital requirements for the remaining net long securities exposures:

    - if the excess exposure has been extant for ten days or less, the specific risk weightings for exposures ranked in excess of 25 per cent of the amended capital base have to be multiplied by 200 per cent;
    - if the excess exposure has been extant for more than ten days, the specific risk weightings for exposures ranked in excess of 25 per cent of the amended capital base have to be multiplied by the factors shown in Exhibit 2.24. (For an illustrative example of such calculations, *see* Bank of England, 1995b, Chapter 3, pp. 17–18.)

With regard to the new ('soft') limits applicable, where the trading book excess exposure has been extant for ten days or less, the trading book exposure to the counterparty must not exceed 500 per cent of the amended capital base. And any trading book exposures which have persisted for more than ten days must not, in aggregate, exceed 600 per cent of the bank's amended capital base.

Finally, with respect to reporting arrangements, a revised large exposures return, the 'LE2' (*see* Exhibit 2.25), was introduced in 1996, initially on an optional basis.

21. The assessment of the adequacy of provisions

A requirement to have adequate provisions is part of the 'prudent conduct' criterion which institutions have to satisfy in order to secure authorization. This mirrors the Companies Act 1985 requirement that provisions should be made for depreciation or diminution in the value of an institution's assets, for liabilities which will, or are expected to, fail to be discharged and for any losses which it will, or it expects to, incur. Thus provisions need to be made for, *inter alia*, bad and doubtful debts, expected losses on contingents and tax liabilities. The Bank expects liabilities and losses to be recognized in accordance with accepted accounting standards, as embodied in the *Statements of Standard Accounting Practice*.

In assessing the adequacy of an institution's provisions, the Bank has regard to

> its provisioning policy, including the methods and systems for monitoring the recoverability of loans (for example, the monitoring of the financial health of counterparties, their future prospects, the prospects of the markets and geographical areas in which they operate, arrears patterns and credit scoring techniques), the frequency with which provisions are reviewed, the policy and practices for the taking and valuation of security and the extent to which valuation exceeds the balance-sheet value of the secured loans. (Bank of England, 1988d, p. 7)

COUNTRY DEBT: THE PROVISIONING MATRIX

Although the overall evaluation of the adequacy of provisions is, necessarily, subjective, clear objective indicators do have a role to play in the assessment process in some cases. One such case is provisions against country debt.

The Bank considers that a reasonable assessment of the recoverability of country debt, and of an adequate level of provisions against such debt, can be made by reference to various objective criteria relating to the particular country's debt service performance, its economic situation and other factors. The Bank's views were first set out in a paper issued in August 1987,[88] within which a framework for provisioning (incorporating these objective criteria within a 'matrix') was established. The matrix was designed to assist banks in making a more objective assessment of significant economic and financial developments in 'problem' countries,[89] and became a focus of attention in discussions between banks, their auditors, the Inland Revenue and the Bank itself.

As Exhibit 2.26 demonstrates, the current matrix (it was revised in January 1990 and again in February 1993 – effective from 30 June 1993)[90] identifies a range of factors which influence the likelihood of partial or total failure to repay. A country (usually covering all claims) is scored against a total of 12 different criteria, weighted according to their relative seriousness, and divided into three main categories: 'A' factors, evidencing a borrower's inability or unwillingness to meet its debt service obligations, whether at the due date or thereafter; 'B' factors, evidencing a borrower's current debt service problems; and 'C' factors, providing evidence of the likelihood of repayment difficulties either persisting or arising in the future. The scores for each item are summed to provide an overall country score which is then translated into a recommended minimum provisioning level by applying the following: recommended minimum provisioning level = matrix score – 25. The recommended minimum provisioning levels range from 5 to 95 per cent.

Although the Bank seeks only to ensure that all significant country exposures attract at least the minimum level of provisions implied by the matrix scores, many UK-incorporated banks during 1987/88 set aside provisions at the top of the range (appropriate provisioning ranges were established in the original matrix) indicated by the matrix.[91] While this, no doubt, reflected a more realistic appraisal by the banks of the plight of LDCs and their ability to repay loans, it was also undoubtedly influenced by Citicorp's move to increase its loan loss reserves sharply in May 1987 to gain a short-term competitive advantage over less highly capitalized banks. UK-incorporated banks (albeit temporarily) were subsequently discouraged by the Bank from adopting a similar competitive provisioning strategy, although provisioning levels have increased substantially in recent years (*see* note 88).

More recently, the Bank (Bank of England, 1998a, p. 8) has indicated that the matrix is to be withdrawn as a supervisory tool in favour of a new requirement for a provisioning policy statement. This decision was made in the light of the limited usefulness of the scoring mechanism in assessing appropriate levels of provision for exposures to South East Asian countries at the end of 1997, and because of its increasing incompatibility with risk-based supervision. Once a bank provides the FSAu with its provisioning policy statement, the matrix will cease to apply.

The structure of UK banking supervision

Exhibit 2.26   Country debt provisioning matrix

Category	'A' factors		'B' factors		
Column	1	2	3	4	5
Definition	Rescheduled at any time in the last five years, or in the process of rescheduling, or in refusing to co-operate in the rescheduling process, or has significant transfer problems and/or a limit on debt servicing without agreement from creditors	Second or more rescheduling during the last five years of principal amounts rescheduled since Jan. 1983, or no money to clear arrears, or capitalization of interest arrears, or rescheduling of principal arrears, or is refusing to co-operate in the rescheduling process, or has significant transfer problems and/or a limit on debt servicing without agreement from creditors	Significant arrears of interest or principal to International Financial Institutions	Arrears of interest or principal on original or rescheduled loans from other external creditors excluding agreed arrears	Debt/ Gross domestic product ratio
Score range	≤ 6 mnths = 20 ≤ 12 mnths = 18 ≤ 18 mnths = 16 ≤ 24 mnths = 14 ≤ 30 mnths = 12 ≤ 36 mnths = 10 ≤ 42 mnths = 8 ≤ 48 mnths = 6 ≤ 54 mnths = 4 ≤ 60 mnths = 2	≤ 6 mnths = 20 ≤ 12 mnths = 18 ≤ 18 mnths = 16 ≤ 24 mnths = 14 ≤ 30 mnths = 12 ≤ 36 mnths = 10 ≤ 42 mnths = 8 ≤ 48 mnths = 6 ≤ 54 mnths = 4 ≤ 60 mnths = 2	10	≤ 6 mnths = 10 ≤ 12 mnths = 15 > 12 mnths = 20	≥ 30% = 2 ≥ 50% = 4 ≥ 70% = 6 ≥ 90% = 8 ≥ 110% = 10
Country	2–20	2–20	10	10, 15 or 20	2–10

Source: Bank of England, 1993d.

		'C' factors						
6	7	8	9	10	11	12		
Debts/ exports ratio	Scheduled debt service/ exports ratio	Scheduled interest service/ exports ratio	Visible import cover	Not meeting IMF targets/ unwilling to go to IMF	Secondary market price	Other factors	Total score (max.150)	Recommended minimum provisioning level
≥ 165% = 2	≥ 10% = 2	≥ 12% = 2	≤ 40 = 2	5	≤ 95% = 2	−5 to 5		5–95%
≥ 275% = 4	≥ 30% = 4	≥ 20% = 4	≤ 30 = 4		≤ 85% = 4			
≥ 385% = 6	≥ 42% = 6	≥ 28% = 6	≤ 20 = 6		≤ 75% = 6			
≥ 495% = 8	≥ 54% = 8	≥ 36% = 8	≤ 10 = 8		≤ 65% = 8			
≥ 605% = 10	≥ 66% = 10	≥ 44% = 10	≤ 5 = 10		≤ 55% = 10			
					≤ 45% = 12			
					≤ 35% = 14			
					≤ 25% = 16			
					≤ 15% = 18			
					≤ 5% = 20			
2–10	2–10	2–10	2–10	5	2–20	5 to 5	Total	

22. The assessment of country risk

An insight into the approach taken by the Bank to the assessment of country risk – that is, 'a situation in which a borrower is either unable or unwilling to meet his obligations to foreign creditors because of conditions affecting the availability of foreign exchange in the country in which he is situated' – is provided in an article entitled 'Supervisory Aspects of Country Risk' (Bank of England, 1984b). (For a discussion of the rating agencies' approach, *see* Bank of England/SIB, 1996a, pp. 31–7.) While stressing that it is the responsibility of the bank's management, first and foremost, to measure, assess and control country risks, the Bank will seek to ensure that suitable risk assessment systems are in place and that adequate resources are devoted to the task; that adequate systems for weighting the risks and controlling exposures through the setting of limits are in place; and that these limits are appropriate and are observed. The monitoring of statistical returns and the regular discussion of country exposures at management interviews play an important part in allowing the Bank to form a judgement on each bank's assessment and control procedures.

In looking at a bank's country exposure, the Bank is also concerned to judge how such exposures affect its assessment of the overall financial position of the bank. This means that exposures have to be considered in relation to the adequacy of a bank's capital and provisions (and liquidity for a UK branch of a foreign bank). Generally speaking, the larger a bank's exposure to problem debtors and the smaller its provisions, the higher the required RAR. And for the UK branch of a foreign bank close attention will be paid to the concentration of lending to its country of origin and its dependence on the wholesale market for the funding of this lending.

23. Ownership rules

Following the removal, in November 1986,[92] of the 'O'Brien rules', which restricted shareholding links between recognized brokers in foreign exchange and currency deposits and banks or other principals in the market to under 10 per cent,[93] the only formal ownership rules remaining relate to the Bank's powers, acquired under the Banking Act 1987, to influence the ownership and control of UK-incorporated banks, and to the various powers possessed by HM Treasury, the Office of Fair Trading and the Monopolies and Mergers Commission (*see* below). Informally, however, guidelines, practices and 'understandings' between the Bank and relevant government departments (e.g. the DTI in respect of links with insurance companies) governing the permissible degree of interlocking ownership with non-bank financial institutions do exist. These serve to limit the risks associated with connected lending and cross-contamination.

As noted in Chapter 16, under the Banking Act 1987 the Bank has certain powers, and considerable discretion within those powers, to determine who may or may not control a bank registered in the UK. In determining the suitability of prospective shareholder controllers,[94] the key consideration is the likely or actual impact on the interests of depositors and potential depositors of that person holding a position as controller. A prospective controller must therefore satisfy the Bank in its interpretation of the 'fit and proper' criterion, which, *inter alia*, involves consideration of the likely degree of influence the person will bring to bear on the conduct of the institution's affairs and whether the financial position, reputation or conduct of the person is likely to damage the institution through 'contagion'.

In the former consideration, the Bank expects of those likely to exercise close control due standards of 'probity', 'soundness of judgement' and the 'relevant knowledge and skills' appropriate for the running of an authorized institution; in other words, the same range of qualities and experience expected of executive directors. The greater the influence likely to be exerted, the higher the required standards, taking due account of the possible conflicts of interest that might arise (e.g. because of a close association with a non-financial company).

In the consideration of the likelihood of 'contagion', there is a presumption that the higher the shareholding the greater the risk of contagion, whether brought about through financial weakness or as a result of adverse publicity about other members of the group.

Assuming a prospective shareholder controller has satisfied the Bank that he or she is a 'fit and proper' person, there is only one remaining possible impediment to him/her becoming one[95] – the reciprocity clause inserted into the Banking Act 1987 to allow the Bank, on the direction of the Treasury, to block moves by those from a country which does not give reciprocal rights to UK residents and firms. Thus although it is unlikely that someone vetted by a major foreign supervisory body for the purposes of engaging in banking activities should fail to pass the Bank's 'fit and proper' test, some foreign stake-building can be blocked by the Bank through the invoking of this power. Whether or not the Treasury would automatically resort to such measures is, however, a different question.

Fortunately, some light was shed on the Bank's view of foreign ownership[96] of UK institutions at the time as a result of remarks made by the Governor in a speech presented at the President's Banquet of the Northern Ireland Chamber of Commerce on 13 October 1987 (reprinted in Bank of England, 1987e, pp. 525–6). In his talk the Governor, although confirming that the Bank does 'not look favourably on acquisitions of stakes designed to put banks "into play", solely with a view to making a quick investment gain' nor 'welcome bids whose purpose is to gain control so that the bank or the group of which it is a part may be sold or broken up' or which 'may be detrimental to depositors' interests', refuted suggestions that the Bank was anti-foreign ownership: 'As a general rule we would certainly not wish to stand in the way of overseas participation in a British bank or financial institution.'[97]

However, he went on to emphasize the great importance which the Bank attaches to a strong and continuing British presence in the UK banking system: 'It runs counter to common sense to argue that the openness of the London market must be carried to the point where control of the core of our financial system – the payments mechanism, the supply of credit – may pass into the hands of institutions whose business aims and national interest lie elsewhere'.

Reading between the lines, the Governor would appear to be saying that, in principle, the Bank is not opposed to foreign financial institutions building stakes[98] in UK banks and that this will be allowed provided that:

1. The shareholder controllers and indirect controllers satisfy its 'fit and proper' test.
2. The Bank is satisfied as to the nature and scope of the supervision exercised by the home authority and has received adequate assurances from the latter as to the institution's soundness.
3. Such moves are not designed to put the banks into play nor to lead to dismemberment of the bank or group.

4. Developments do not proceed to the point at which a strong and continuing British presence in the UK banking system is threatened.
5. UK institutions have, or are likely to have in the near future, reciprocal rights of action in the predator's home country.

As for stake-building by foreign non-financial companies, the Bank will take into account an additional range of factors, most notably the likely closeness of the ensuing relationship. Mirroring its approach to such stake-building activities by domestic industrial and commercial companies, the Bank is keen to avoid the creation of conflicts of interest and the risks and consequences of contagion that are inherent in such moves. For these reasons, it appears that the Bank might have difficulty in granting consent for the control of a UK bank to fall into the hands of an industrial or commercial company, irrespective of whether it is of foreign or domestic origin.[99] This is in stark contrast to the approach adopted in West Germany and elsewhere.

24. Deposit protection arrangements

A statutory Deposit Protection Scheme for bank depositors only came into existence in the UK in February 1982. It is administered by the Deposit Protection Board, which is chaired by the Governor of the Bank of England, and was set up in accordance with the requirements specified in the Banking Act 1979. Under the Scheme, depositors were originally protected to the tune of 75 per cent[100] of the first £10,000 of unsecured sterling deposits with an original maturity of up to five years held with either a recognized bank or a licensed deposit-taking institution. Following the amendments introduced under the Banking Act 1987, however, this cover was increased to 75 per cent of the first £20,000 of sterling deposits held with an authorized institution. Moreover, those foreign institutions previously granted exemption from the Scheme by the Treasury (*see* p. 39) had to participate so that appropriate deposits with all authorised institutions became protected. (The National Savings Bank, however, retained its exemption in the event of institutions becoming insolvent or subject to administration orders under the Insolvency Act 1986.) Finally, to accommodate the EC's Deposit Guarantee Schemes Directive (EC, 1994), the coverage was increased in July 1995 to 90 per cent of £20,000 (or ECU 20,000 if higher) and extended to cover deposits in ECUs and the currencies of all EEA states, as well as the EEA branches of UK-incorporated banks.[101]

The fund from which payments are made by the Deposit Protection Board[102] is financed by a levy, at the time of authorization, on all authorized institutions in proportion to their deposit bases. The levy on each institution is, however, subject to a minimum and maximum amount – currently £30,000 and £300,000 (to cover all contributions), respectively. Supplementary arrangements exist for raising such further contributions (i.e. to restore the fund at the end of the Deposit Protection Board's financial year) and special contributions (covering levies made at other times of the year to replenish resources)[103] as prove necessary, although net calls overall remain subject to the limit of 0.3 per cent of the sterling deposit base. The Deposit Protection Board may also borrow up to £125 million from other sources (i.e. the Bank). All corporate and personal depositors (except those associated with the institution) are covered by the Scheme, but interbank deposits are excluded (*see* note 101).

For a critique of these arrangements, *see* Hall, 1993, Chapter 24, pp. 206–8.

25. The supervision of banking groups/financial conglomerates

THE ISSUES

The emergence of large financial conglomerates offering a wide range of financial services (often including traditional banking services) across national frontiers poses a number of problems for financial supervisors. These might arise, for example, because of the complexity of the group's corporate structure, which may differ significantly from its management structure, because of the involvement of a number of regulators (domestic and foreign) in the supervisory process, or because of the inclusion of unregulated entities (financial or non-financial) in group structures.

The opacity of a group's structure may prevent the exercise of effective (consolidated) supervision. Differences between management and corporate structure may prevent appropriate oversight being exercised in respect of the management of regulated entities. The involvement of a multitude of regulators in the supervisory process raises problems of co-ordination and co-operation. And the group's inclusion of unregulated entities may increase the risk of contagion if such entities experience difficulties, thereby threatening both the group's future viability and the stability of the financial sector/system, not least because such entities are unlikely to be included in a prudential consolidation,[104] and may lead to a dilution in the quality of capital (*see* IOSCO, 1992, p. 6).

Whatever the source and nature of the problems, banking supervisors will want to ensure, *inter alia*, that they are in a position to appreciate fully the extent of the risks to which the banks in the group are exposed by virtue of the operation of the non-bank entities; that the capital held by the banks is commensurate with the risks involved; that the banks' controllers and shareholders are 'fit and proper' persons for those purposes; and that full co-operation between all supervisory parties is guaranteed and their activities effectively co-ordinated. Group-based risk assessment is thus essential to this exercise and, in the UK at least, prudential consolidation is complemented by capital adequacy assessment on a solo basis to ensure an appropriate distribution of capital within the group (*see* Chapter 17).[105]

THE IOSCO PRINCIPLES

Before looking at the Bank's approach to supervising banking groups, it is worth noting the work of IOSCO, which has drafted a set of principles (IOSCO, 1992) which it believes should govern the supervision of financial conglomerates and guide the development of regulatory practice and co-operation. The guiding principles established embrace the following:

1. *Group-based risk assessment.* 'Where a regulated firm, which is part of a financial conglomerate and subject to supervision on a solo basis, is vulnerable to the risk of contagion, supervision of the regulated firm should be complemented by group-based risk assessment.'
2. *Investments in other group companies.* 'Where a regulated firm has an investment in another group company or has provided regulatory capital to another group company, these amounts should be controlled by appropriate regulations.'
3. *Intra-group exposures.* 'Effective risk assessment of financial conglomerates requires careful monitoring of intra-group exposures, and where necessary limits on such exposures in the regulated entity.'
4. *Structure of financial conglomerates.* 'The corporate and managerial structure of the financial conglomerate should be fully understood by the regulator and should not create undue difficulties for effective regulation. Regulators should consider whether it is feasible and practical to acquire powers to prevent the manipulation of group structures which makes effective regulation difficult.'
5. *Relationships with shareholders.* 'Regulators should seek as far as possible to identify shareholders with a stake in a financial conglomerate which enables them to exert material influence on a regulated firm; the regulator should seek to ensure that these shareholders meet applicable fitness standards.'
6. *Management.* 'Regulators should ensure that managers who directly or indirectly exert control on a regulated entity are subject to appropriate regulatory standards; and should seek as far as possible to be able to impose sanctions on managers who have influenced the policy and decisions of a regulated entity in ways which are inconsistent with these regulatory standards.'
7. *Supervisory co-operation.* 'Wherever possible, regulators should seek to co-operate to improve the effectiveness of the supervision of financial conglomerates. In many cases where more than one regulator has responsibility for some part of the financial conglomerate, it may be desirable to identify one regulator who will have primary responsibility for group-based risk assessment. This regulator is likely to emerge as lead regulator when

serious concerns arise about a particular financial conglomerate. Each regulator will continue to be responsible for the solo entity in its jurisdiction and the lead regulator will have no authority to seek to take over or interfere with the exercise of that responsibility. The lead regulator's main role should be to ensure that relevant regulatory information about the conglomerate is shared promptly amongst all the regulators concerned to inform their actions.'

8. *External auditors*. 'Regulators should recognise the importance of the role of the external auditors of a regulated firm and the possible contribution they may be able to make to group-based risk assessment. Auditors should be encouraged, where they have serious concerns regarding the financial or operational condition of the regulated entity or the group, to ensure that such concerns are brought to the attention of the supervisor.'

On the subject of *group-based risk assessment*, there is still no consensus,[106] at least among non-banking supervisors,[107] as to what constitutes the ideal approach. At the very least, however, effective supervision will require the collection of relevant information about other group companies, which is likely to include data on capital, profitability and liquidity, and the risks arising from core activities and intra-group exposures. Those assessing capital adequacy on a consolidated basis will want to take account of the risks arising from unregulated group companies by, for example, deducting from the parent's capital its investment in such subsidiaries or affiliates.

As for the general approach to the treatment of *investments in other group companies*, there is a growing consensus that such investments (because they are effectively locked in), like the provision of regulatory capital[108] to group companies (because it allows for 'overgearing'), should be deducted in full from the parent's capital. This, indeed, is the traditional approach adopted by securities regulators, which provides for their full deduction as illiquid assets, and is also adumbrated by the Basle Committee in respect of investments in unconsolidated subsidiaries engaged in banking or other financial services. Whether or not this goes far enough, however, is a matter for debate. The IOSCO document suggests that deductions from the capital of the regulated (securities) firm to reflect any deficiencies in the net tangible assets of subsidiaries may also be in order.[109]

Concern with *intra-group exposures* arises because evidence suggests that they can exacerbate the problems encountered by a regulated firm when it is affected by the spread of contagion from other parts of the group.[110] This calls for, at a minimum, careful monitoring of the intra-group exposures affecting regulated firms and the level of such exposures existing more generally in the group. Reporting requirements and/or the setting of predetermined limits for such concerns may well prove necessary to offer further reassurance to supervisors.

The supervisory difficulties that can arise from opaque *financial structures* were only too well illustrated in the case of BCCI (*see* Chapter 11). Full awareness of the corporate and managerial structures of financial groups is essential if risk assessment is to be properly carried out, and full co-operation between interested supervisors is necessary if the group is to be adequately supervised. Ultimately, if supervisors wish to avoid all the problems which can arise, it may be necessary for them to possess an explicit power allowing them to require a corporate restructuring on pain of de-authorization (a feature of the 'Post-BCCI Directive' – *see* Chapter 10).

The need to ensure the 'fitness and properness' of dominant *shareholders* is self-evident: their self-interests may conflict with those of investors, depositors or policy-holders and they may be in a position to (adversely) influence group activities, including those of regulated firms. Ideally, regulatory requirements should be applied at both the authorization stage and beyond, with pre-notification requirements being employed to allow supervisors to vet and approve prospective dominant shareholders.

The case for assessing the 'fitness and properness' of *managers* who, directly or indirectly, exert control over a regulated entity is also self-evident and, as a result, is already undertaken by most financial supervisors in respect of the management of regulated entities. However, regulation of managers lying outside the regulated sector (perhaps at the holding company level) but who, nevertheless, may exercise direct or indirect control over the activities of regulated firms, is less systematic. Once again, if the objective is to avoid all possible problems arising from this source, the only solution may be for supervisors to be given powers allowing them to approve all managers in a financial conglomerate who are in a position to exert, either directly or indirectly, material influence on regulated firms.

Effective *supervisory co-operation* and *co-ordination* is also essential to the effective supervision of banking groups, as experience with the supervision of BCCI demonstrated all too clearly. This requires that there be adequate legal 'gateways' and procedures for the sharing of confidential information and the protection of the confidentiality of such information. And without mutual trust between supervisors, the system is unlikely to function as required. Beyond information-sharing, co-operation may prove most cost-effective when facilitated through the establishment of a lead regulator, who is likely to be charged with co-ordinating risk assessment and the supervisory response, if one is required.

Finally, the potential contribution which *external auditors* can make to the supervisory process should not be underestimated. While they should in no sense be used to displace supervision by the supervisors, they are uniquely placed to assist in the supervisory process by, for example, alerting supervisors to fraud or malpractice or, more contentiously, searching for fraud. Because steps in this direction increase auditors' exposure to litigation, appropriate legal safeguards may be necessary as a *quid pro quo* for ensuring the closer involvement of external auditors in the supervisory process (*see* Chapter 14).

Single-firm audits are, in principle, also desirable if the dangers associated with split jurisdictions are to be avoided, although there may be a case for the employment of local auditors, with specialist knowledge of parts of the group's activities, providing full co-operation can be guaranteed.

THE EU APPROACH

The Commission's approach is based on three guiding principles:

1. That, as far as possible, regulation should accommodate different market structures, varying from those subject to a high degree of functional separation and specialization to those operating along 'universal banking' lines.
2. That special rules for the consolidated supervision of banking groups should only be applied where regulatory problems cannot effectively be tackled through supervision on a solo basis.
3. That the rules devised, as far as possible, respect differences in the traditional regulatory approaches adopted to the different sub-sectors of the financial system (Fitchew, 1992).

Guided by this philosophy, the Commission has established a regulatory framework which can readily be assessed for adherence to the IOSCO principles (for further details, *see* Walker, 1996a).

Supervisory Co-operation

A set of EC Directives, covering banking, securities and insurance markets, require member states to remove any barriers arising from professional secrecy requirements to allow for the exchange of information both between supervisors in different sectors of the finance industry and in different member states. The legislation also allows the Commission, on behalf of the Community, to negotiate with supervisors in third countries. Further, under the (Second) Consolidated Supervision Directive (CSD) (EC, 1992b), EC banks, securities houses and insurance companies are required 'to provide one another with any information likely to simplify their task and to allow supervision of the activity and overall financial situation of the undertakings they supervise'.

Rules governing the determination of lead regulator for banking groups (and, via the CAD, for investment services groups which do not contain a bank) are also spelt out in this Directive. Usually, the lead regulator for internationally diversified financial groups will come from the country where the holding company is established but, if no banking or securities business is carried out in that country's territory, the designated supervisor will come from the country where the largest affiliate is located. (For further details, *see* Chapter 9.)

Relations with Shareholders and Management

All the Financial Directives, covering the three main sub-sectors of the finance industry, require the relevant supervisors to satisfy themselves that both major shareholders and managers of regulated entities are 'fit and proper' persons for the positions they hold. While some further refinement may be necessary, the Commission believes that these rules allow supervisors to refuse to issue licences to, and to withdraw licences from, regulated entities if they are uneasy about the controllers or managers of unregulated holding companies.

Group-Based Risk Assessment, Intra-group Exposures and Investments in other Group Companies

The combined effects of the CSD, the CAD and the Large Exposures Directive (*see* Chapter 9) mean that there are EC-wide rules governing group-based risk assessment for all groups containing one or more banks or non-bank investment firms. In addition to the solo supervision[111] of their individual banks and investment firms, group-based risk assessment according to the CSD means that financial[112] groups are subject to the requirements of the Solvency Ratio Directive, the Large Exposures Directive and the CAD (in respect of market risks) on a consolidated basis unless such consolidation would be 'inappropriate or misleading'. In the latter case, however, banking supervisors must be given access to any information they require from the holding company, even if it is in another member state. For mixed activity[113] groups, however, the CSD provides only that the supervisors of the banks in the group must be able to obtain relevant information from the non-bank holding company and to have that information verified by on-site inspection, if necessary using the good offices of a supervisor in another member state.

The Commission believes that these provisions, in aggregate, should allow EC banking supervisors to ensure that regulated entities within conglomerates have sufficient free regulatory capital to meet all the risks to which, directly or indirectly, they are exposed through group activities. They are also thought sufficient to prevent the circumvention of solo capital requirements through, for example, the use of borrowed funds to finance the parent's equity participation in the regulated subsidiaries.

As for the role played by the CAD in group-based risk assessment, it extends the principle of consolidated capital adequacy assessment in respect of market risks to financial groups in which there are no banks but where there are securities firms.[114] Additionally, it allows for greater flexibility in the rules relating to large exposures in respect of securities trading activities. Accordingly, the flat 25 per cent limit is dropped in favour of linking the size of the capital requirement to the length of time an exposure is run in excess of an initial ten-day 'window' (*see* Chapter 17).

Structure of Financial Conglomerates

As noted earlier, the Commission's philosophy is not to dictate the type of corporate structure that a group may adopt. Nevertheless, if the information-sharing 'rules' described above do not allow supervisors to gain a clear view of the group's activities, the Commission recognized that a further extension of supervisors' powers would be necessary. Accordingly, and in line with the Basle Committee's 'Statement of Minimum Standards' (see Chapter 3) and Lord Justice Bingham's recommendations (*see* Chapter 11), the Commission duly provided supervisors with the power to refuse or revoke authorization on the grounds that the opacity of the group's structure precludes effective group supervision in the 'Post-BCCI Directive' (*see* Chapter 11).

External Editors

Finally, in recognition of the potential contribution that external auditors can make to the supervisory process, the Commission placed auditors under a duty to inform the supervisory authorities of any breaches of relevant laws and certain other concerns under the 'Post-BCCI Directive'.

THE BANK'S APPROACH[115]

The Bank's supervision of banking groups is based principally on consolidated statistical returns, the annual report and accounts of group companies, and meetings (at least annually) with group management. In addition, however, the Bank is keen to ensure that effective co-ordination between the supervisors of different parts of financial conglomerates exists so that neither supervisory 'overlap' nor 'underlap' results; the Bank wants supervision to be effective but not unduly burdensome. To achieve the latter objective, the Bank adopted the 'lead regulator' principle adumbrated within the Financial Services Act 1986, whereby the Bank acts as lead regulator for all banking groups, responsible for promoting exchanges of information between supervisors, co-ordinating any necessary remedial action and chairing meetings (to be held at least once a year) of the 'colleges of supervisors' (*see* Chapter 15). (The arrangements have been tightened up since the Barings débâcle.) Moreover, at the international level, the Bank has participated in a number of bilateral and multilateral initiatives apart from those mandated by the Basle *Concordat* and EU Directives – to try to ensure effective supervisory co-operation – *see* below.

Consolidated Supervision

The Bank's policy statement on this subject is its March 1986 paper entitled 'Consolidated Supervision of Institutions Authorised Under the Banking Act 1979' (BSD/1986/3; Bank of England, 1986d), as amended by BSD/1989/2 (Bank of England, 1989b)[116] and, more recently, by BSD/1990/4 (Bank of England, 1990d).[117] The policy was agreed with HM Treasury and its implementation fulfils the UK's EC obligations under the (First) Consolidated Supervision Directive (Council Directive of 13 June 1983 on the supervision of credit institutions on a consolidated basis (83/350/EEC); EC, 1983). Implementation of the CSD, however, necessitated the issue of a new policy statement, which materialized in the shape of BSD/1993/1 (Bank of England, 1993a).[118]

Consolidated supervision, which complements supervision on an unconsolidated basis, is designed to provide a qualitative assessment of the overall strength of a banking group in order to evaluate the potential impact on a bank of the group's non-banking operations. It will usually, but not always, require the submission of consolidated financial statements. In deciding which parts of a group should be included in consolidated statistical reporting, the Bank will take account of the nature of the particular activities (activities which are usually expected to be included in consolidated returns are listed in the Annexe to BSD/1993/1); the position occupied by each company within the overall group structure; and the supervision exercised by other UK supervisory authorities.[119] The following factors, *inter alia*, are relevant to this consideration:

1. The managerial structure of the group.
2. The size of the company in relation to the bank.
3. The extent of any funding provided by the bank.
4. Potential calls on, or other adverse consequences for, the bank which may result from the company's activities.

As a general rule, all credit and financial companies (bar insurance companies – for a review of the approaches adopted in other European countries, *see* Bank of England/SIB, 1996c) owned by a bank, either directly or through intermediate holding companies, will be included in the consolidation, whereas non-financial companies will not. Sister companies owned by an ultimate non-bank parent and the ultimate parent itself will only be included if there are particular reasons for doing so. For those group companies which are not included in consolidated returns, the Bank may still ask for information if they are thought likely to have a potentially significant impact on the health of the bank(s) within the group.

Where consolidated returns – covering capital adequacy and large exposures to individual borrowers and countries[120] – are deemed necessary, the Bank requires full accounting consolidation for all majority[121] shareholdings in credit or financial institutions. Where the bank's risk cannot be assumed to be limited to its shareholding, full consolidation may also be justified; but, conversely, *pro rata* consolidation may be justified where there is good reason to believe that the responsibilities, and hence risks, can be limited to the extent of the shareholding.

Full consolidation of minority holdings may also be carried out if:

1. The management is provided by the bank concerned.
2. The name of the bank is used and/or the bank is strongly identified with the institutions.
3. There are no other substantial shareholders.
4. The associated company is substantially funded by the bank.

Consolidation of a minority holding will not normally be required unless the holding is a material one in a company of significance. The appropriate treatment of particular cases has to be agreed, individually, with the Bank.

Finally, holding companies are also normally included in the consolidated returns unless any of the following apply:

1. They are supervised by another UK supervisor (when consolidated supervision of the group as a whole, if undertaken at all, would normally fall to that supervisor).
2. They are industrial companies or their inclusion would otherwise be misleading.
3. They are themselves banks supervised by an overseas banking supervisory authority.

Where the holding company is included in the statistical returns, sister companies will also be included according to the same rules that apply to direct subsidiaries of the bank. Even if the holding company is not included in the statistical returns, sister companies may still be included in any of the following circumstances:

1. They are effectively managed by the bank or there is a definable financial sub-group in practice, if not in formal structure.
2. They are substantially funded by the bank.
3. They use the bank's name.

Banks are required to submit to the Bank a consolidated balance-sheet return and a consolidated supervisory return every six months. These returns must be submitted within two months of their respective reporting dates, although those whose business is mainly in the UK are expected to submit within one month of their reporting dates.

The final revisions to the Bank's approach to consolidated supervision were made in January 1996 to accommodate the implementation of the CAD (Bank of England, 1995c). Although consolidation for banks' banking books continued to be carried out on a 'line-by-line' (or accounting) basis across the group members being consolidated, *trading book* exposures (including counterparty exposures) and foreign exchange exposures became subject to an 'aggregation plus' method of consolidation unless an institution could satisfy the line supervisor that: (1) the parent bank calculates or monitors trading book positions in an integrated fashion across the entities using the line-by-line consolidation basis; (2) the banking subsidiary satisfies its local supervisory requirements on a solo basis; (3) the parent bank is able to carry out adequate line-by-line consolidation on a daily basis; and (4) capital resources are freely transferable between the banking subsidiary and the rest of the group. If the line supervisor is satisfied that all these conditions are met, line-by-line consolidation may be adopted instead of 'aggregation plus' consolidation.

As for *investment firms*, consolidation using 'aggregation plus' became the norm, although the Bank reserved the right to use line-by-line consolidation in instances where non-trading activity was large. Line-by-line consolidation of investment firms may also be adopted when an institution satisfies the line supervisor that a similar set of conditions – *see* above – to that specified for banks seeking to adopt line-by-line consolidation of trading book exposures is met.

Other financial companies (as defined in the Annexe to BSD/1993/1) are usually consolidated on a line-by-line basis.

Finally, the Bank decided that, in determining consolidated group capital requirements, recognition for offsetting exposures could only be given where consolidation is done on a line-by-line basis. (For further details on the Bank's approach to consolidation under the CAD, *see* Bank of England, 1995c, Chapter 10; and for a more detailed discussion of consolidation techniques, *see* Walker, 1996b.)

Supervisory Co-ordination and Co-operation with Other Domestic Supervisors[122]

An interdepartmental working group comprising personnel drawn from the Bank, HM Treasury, the DTI and the SIB, was established in 1986 to deliberate and make recommendations on the co-operative framework for supervising financial groups necessitated by the development of diversified and integrated financial conglomerates and the planned changes in the legislative framework governing the operation of financial intermediaries (as incorporated in the Financial Services Bill, the Building Societies Bill and the Banking Bill). The working group recommended that co-operation should be achieved through extrastatutory arrangements involving the nomination of one of the supervisors of a financial conglomerate as its 'lead regulator'. This recommendation was duly endorsed by the government and its adoption facilitated by the inclusion of provisions within the Financial Services Bill, the Building Societies Bill and the Banking Bill to allow for the exchange between supervisors of information obtained under the Banking, Companies, Insurance Companies, Building Societies and Financial Services Acts.

Under the approach adopted, the lead regulator appointed by the supervisors for each financial conglomerate is charged with responsibility for promoting exchanges of information and co-ordinating any necessary remedial action. The agreed solution promoted by the lead regulator must take account of the interests of all the regulators, who will continue to perform their statutory duties and responsibilities.

The Bank's chosen approach to supervising banking groups reflects its desire to maximize the potential economies of scope available to financial conglomerates and to accommodate structural change while ensuring prudent behaviour. Accordingly, neither the structure nor business mix of a banking group is mandated, and firewalls are not routinely applied to ensure physical separation of the different parts of the group. (They may, however, be used to isolate the bank from problems occurring elsewhere in the group in the case of smaller banks owned by much larger commercial or industrial groups. They also apply to GEMMs, stock exchange money brokers and gilt-edged market inter-dealer brokers (*see* Hall, 1993, Appendices 2 and 3).) Rather, emphasis is placed on functional regulation, regarded as the best means of ensuring competitive equity between competing institutions, and on establishing mechanisms that allow for effective co-operation between the relevant supervisory bodies and for the co-ordination of their activities.

Supervisory Co-ordination and Co-operation with Overseas Supervisors

Apart from the obligations assumed under the Basle *Concordat* (*see* Chapter 3) and EC Directives (*see* Chapter 9), and the Bank's response to criticisms of its supervision of Barings (*see* Chapter 12, Hall, 1996b and House of Commons, 1996), the Bank has also been involved in a number of other initiatives designed to improve international supervisory co-ordination and co-operation. Moreover, it has promoted the idea of lead regulation at the international level, with one (the 'lead') regulator being assigned for each internationally or functionally dispersed financial group with responsibility for coordinating the process of supervision between interested parties and assuming a primary role in the management of crisis situations.

As regards participation in multilateral initiatives, Bank staff acted as members of the informal 'Tripartite Group' of bank, securities and insurance supervisors established in July 1995 at the initiative of the Basle Committee. This Group produced a discussion document on issues relating to the supervision of financial conglomerates, examining, *inter alia*, the measurement of capital on a group-wide basis, group structures, the possible establishment of lead supervisors or 'convenors', and the contagion effects of intra-group exposures. The Group was reconstituted as the 'Joint Forum on Financial Conglomerates' in 1996, which comprises nine supervisors for each of the banking, securities and insurance sectors. Thirteen countries are represented in the Joint Forum, including the UK, and the EU Commission attends in an observer capacity to liaise with similar work undertaken in the EU. The Joint Forum took forward the work of the Tripartite Group, examining how criteria to identify a lead supervisor might be established, reviewing the means of facilitating information exchange between supervisors (both between and within sectors) and developing a set of principles to govern the future supervision of financial conglomerates.

Agreement that 'co-ordinators' should, in appropriate circumstances, be appointed to facilitate the exchange of information between supervisors involved in the supervision of financial conglomerates was formally reached in June 1997, and G7 finance ministers duly agreed, at their meeting in Denver the same month, to support changes in laws or regulations that would improve information exchange for supervisory purposes, while preserving the confidentiality of the information exchanged. This was followed, in February 1998, by the release of a set of seven consultation papers concerned with the supervision of financial conglomerates, covering such issues as how to measure capital adequacy for financial conglomerates and how to improve supervisory co-operation between supervisors. A definitive statement is likely to emerge once comments received during the consultation period have been digested. The Joint Forum is currently testing the principles established in these areas, including 'fit and proper' criteria.

In addition to participating in the work of the Tripartite Group/Joint Forum, the Bank contributed to the development of new guidelines on the responsibilities of home and host country supervisors dealing with the supervision of cross-border banking. (The paper, which was endorsed by the supervisors attending the

June 1996 ICBS, set out practical means to enhance the ability of supervisors to carry out effective consolidated supervision and to overcome impediments to information flows, and to enable this to happen while respecting legitimate customer confidentiality concerns.) It also contributed to the work of the Basle Committee in drafting a set of 'core principles' designed to ensure effective (consolidated) banking supervision (*see* Chapter 7).

26. Miscellaneous

Apart from the issues discussed in Part II of this book, the Bank has also been involved in other areas of activity as part of its on-going supervision of the banking sector. These additional activities are addressed below.

WIDER RISK FOCUS

In keeping with the development of risk-based supervision, the Bank has, in recent years, focused on risks other than those traditionally thought of as the prime concerns of supervisors. Thus attention has moved beyond an assessment of credit and market (including foreign exchange) risk, liquidity (including interest rate) risk and sovereign risk to embrace other risks, such as operational risk, legal risk and settlement risk.

Concern with *operational risk*, which covers the risks associated with fraud, computer breakdowns and loss of key personnel, has come to the fore because of worries about the possible extent of fraud within the City (worries not helped by the BCCI and Barings 'crises'), the increasing exposure faced by institutions because of the computerization of their operations (the 'year 2000' problem is a particular worry), and the increased willingness of staff, particularly teams of traders, to defect to the highest bidder. Unsurprisingly, internal controls, organization and management have become key elements of focus under the Bank's own risk-based assessment regime, alongside the more traditional areas of capital and liquidity adequacy, and so on.

A keener official interest in *legal risk* was taken following the local authority swaps débâcle whereby certain operations of local authorities, although entered into in good faith, were ultimately declared *ultra vires* by the Law lords. (Legal difficulties also posed difficulties for the stock lending market.) Accordingly, a committee, comprising leading City figures – from both foreign and domestic institutions – and members of the legal profession and Chaired by Lord Alexander, was established, at the initiative of the Bank, in April 1991 to identify areas of legal uncertainty which could harm London's standing as an international financial centre. (Many foreign banks and investors lost out in the local authority débâcle.) The committee – the 'Bank of England's Legal Risk Review Committee' – duly recommended in February 1992 that two standing bodies be established: a 'Financial Law Panel' and a 'Financial Law Liaison Group'. The former, comprising market and legal practitioners, would act as a problem-solving body. In co-operation with existing market bodies it would warn practitioners of potential problems, set out its views on good market practice and clarify how the law would apply in certain technical areas. It would also act as the focal point for the consideration of the potential impact of EU legislation. The latter body, comprising civil servants and market practitioners, would discuss problems identified by the Panel, decide whether government involvement was necessary and, if so, identify how the necessary changes in the law could be made. Both bodies would be resourced and funded by the City.

The final source of risk to attract keener attention from the Bank is *settlement risk*. The first major breakthrough came with the introduction, in April 1996, of RTGS systems for large value interbank payments whereby payments are debited and credited instantaneously on clearing accounts held at the Bank under the Clearing House Automated Payments System (CHAPS). Prior to this, a bank would credit a payment to its customer's account immediately upon being notified by the paying bank of the incoming payment for that customer, but it would not receive a balancing payment from the paying bank until the end of the trading day when the CHAPS member banks would settle up with each other. With the introduction of RTGS systems, something the Bank had pushed for back in 1992 and which it had worked on, in conjunction with the clearing banks ever since, the (huge) settlement risk arising from large interbank intra-day exposures was eradicated, thereby removing the systemic risk of contagion from an initial bank failure through the payments mechanism. (Limits on exposures incurred within the clearing system were previously employed as a way of reducing such settlement risk – *see* Bank of England, 1996j).

The next major development occurred with the introduction of the 'CREST' service for settling equities and corporate bonds in July 1996 (*see* Bank of England/SIB, 1996d). This service, which involves book-entry transfer of ownership and automated links with banks and brokers, and includes (albeit within customer limits) an assured payments mechanism, was developed by the Bank (*via* the 'Task Force on Securities Settlement') following the collapse, in March 1993, of the 'TAURUS' (Transer and Automated Registration of Uncertificated Stock) project initiated by the London Stock Exchange.

A system of 'assured payments' had also been secured in the gilt market with the introduction of the Central Gilts Office (CGO) in 1986 (*see* Hall, 1987a). This effectively eliminated the security risk inherent in the physical movement of bearer instruments around the City. Like CREST, however, it did not deliver the holy grail of DVP, and this led the Bank, in July 1996, to set up a working group to examine how to move the CGO onto a DVP basis, in which the transfer of the security would be synchronized with the transfer of the cash to pay for it. At the same time, the Bank announced that it was exploring the possibility of an eventual merger between a revamped CGO and CREST, so that DVP can be secured for all (exchange-traded) securities transactions. (A further link with CHAPS would secure full DVP for the City.) A revamped CGO system – 'CGO2' – duly emerged at the end of 1997 but, to the consternation of many market participants, contained modifications which appeared to take it further away from CREST, thereby fuelling the suspicion that the Bank was reluctant to cede control of gilts settlement via a full merger with CREST.

Finally, in respect of foreign exchange settlement risk (i.e. 'Herstatt' risk – *see* Chapter 3), the Bank fully endorsed the findings of the Allsopp Report (BIS, 1996) and supported the initiative of the G20 group of commercial banks (*see* Chapter 7) which are trying to develop a system of 'payment versus payment' on the foreign exchange market *via* link-ups between national RTGS systems. It remains to be seen if such a system can be delivered, as planned, by mid 1998.

DERIVATIVES

The Bank's growing interest in derivatives stems from the inexorable growth in importance of derivatives business for many banks, increased awareness (particularly following the Barings incident) of the risks associated with such business (*see* Board *et al.*, 1995), and the need to develop policy in respect of the assessment of credit derivatives for capital adequacy purposes.

Following publication of the Promisel Report (BIS, 1992), which examined, *inter alia*, the growth and implications of derivatives business, the Bank set up a working group, with the participation of the SFA, to examine derivatives business in the UK and to identify any supervisory and systemic issues arising. A report was subsequently produced (April 1993) which underlined the need for adequate supervisory and management understanding[123] (the report recommended that at least two members of the board, including the finance director, should be sufficiently knowledgeable to ensure effective control) of derivatives. Additionally, the Bank created a new specialist derivatives team, through outside recruitment and training and outward secondments of existing staff, in recognition of the fact that specialized supervisory skills would be necessary to ensure effective oversight of the banks' trading books (whether derivatives or on-balance-sheet instruments), as called for in the EC's CAD. Members of this specialist team – the 'Traded Markets Team' – spend much of their time visiting the trading operations of banks, assessing their trading strategies, and considering the control environment in which they operate and the monitoring and support functions available to both dealers and senior management. More recently, attention has been focused on reviewing the internal models used by banks to determine capital adequacy under the CAD (*see* Chapter 9). The Bank also participated in the derivatives market survey commissioned by the BIS on behalf of the G10 governors, the UK survey taking place in April 1995.

Apart from the above, the Bank also participated fully during 1994/95 in a number of other internationally co-ordinated initiatives designed to improve information about over-the-counter derivative markets, reflecting its desire for greater *disclosures*[124] in both published accounts and in supervisory returns. (The former desire led to the undertaking of parallel private sector initiatives, *see* for example, IIF (1994) and Group of Thirty (1993, 1994).) This followed earlier work of the G10 governors which culminated in the publication of the Fisher Report in September 1994 (BIS, 1994). As far as domestic policy was concerned, the call for greater disclosure[125] to supervisors manifested itself in additional reporting requirements being imposed on banks, to cover interest rate and equity position risk arising in their trading books as well as foreign exchange exposure, as required under the CAD. In addition, in order to accommodate the amendment to the Solvency Ratio Directive permitting the netting of counterparty risk on off-balance-sheet contracts, the Bank asked for data to be provided on both a gross and net basis (technically, the submission of net amounts would have been sufficient) so that supervisors could see the volume of derivatives business being undertaken and allow them to discuss with the banks the risk management and systems issues that may arise. In this way, the Bank took the opportunity to introduce many of the proposals put forward in a joint report by the Basle Committee and IOSCO (1995) for the introduction of a 'Common Minimum Framework' for the prudential reporting of derivatives.

The Bank's proposed treatment of *credit derivatives* for supervisory purposes was first outlined in a discussion paper published in November 1996 (Bank of England, 1996k). A relatively conservative approach to assessment for capital adequacy purposes was suggested. For example, for the time being (i.e. until credit and specific risk models have been developed further), only 'total return' swaps should be included in the trading book while all 'credit default' products should be included in the banking book, and relatively little recognition should be given to the hedging effects of credit derivatives. Following criticism from trade associations (i.e. the International Securities Dealers' Association and the British Bankers' Association) and individual institutions, however, the Bank fell into line behind the SFA in June 1997 and announced that it was now prepared to allow most credit default swaps to be included in the trading book alongside total return swaps, thereby generating lower capital charges for the institutions involved. Wider recognition of the hedging capabilities of credit derivatives still posed a problem, however, under European law, although the FSAu has indicated its willingness to allow for a partial cut in capital requirements on derivatives which do not exactly match the original loans.

MONEY LAUNDERING

The Bank's concern with money laundering in recent years has manifested itself in two ways. First, the Bank contributed to the work needed to ensure full UK implementation of the EC's Money Laundering Directive (EC, 1991), which was adopted by member states in June 1991. And, second, it has continued to monitor the adequacy of banks' relevant systems and controls against the minimum standards set out in the Joint Money Laundering Working Group's Guidance Notes (last revised in February 1995) designed to counter money laundering.

Implementation of the Money Laundering Directive in the UK was secured through amendments to the Criminal Justice Act 1993 and the introduction of Money Laundering Regulations ('the Regulations') in 1993, effective from January 1994. Under the former, the Criminal Justice Act was extended to cover the proceeds of all serious crime, in addition to drug- and terrorist-related activities. Under the latter: (1) it is a criminal offence for a bank, building society or other financial institution not to have in place procedures to combat money laundering; (2) Guidance Notes issued by a supervisory authority or trade association are recognized, so that a court may take account of such guidance in deciding whether a person or institution has complied with the requirements of the Regulations; and (3) supervisory authorities are themselves required to report to the National Criminal Intelligence Service any information they obtain which, in their opinion, indicates that any person has, or may have, engaged in money laundering. The Bank has established and implemented procedures to satisfy this last requirement.

SECURITIZATION

The Bank's approach to securitization, namely the process whereby institutions sell assets to independent special-purpose vehicles which finance the purchase through the issue of securities, has been important in supporting the development of the market in securitized assets in the UK. The Bank's initial concern was with the securitization of *mortgages*, uncertainties about which had stymied development of the market during the 1980s. Building on a consultative paper published in December 1987, the Bank produced, in February 1989 (Bank of England, 1989c), a definitive set of 'rules' concerning all forms of loan transfers, not just mortgages. The rules were designed to ensure that sellers wishing to reduce required levels of capital divested themselves fully of all risk on the assets (which might arise, for example, either because of a legal commitment or moral obligation on the originator to make good any loan losses), so that the securitized assets could be regarded as sold for prudential purposes. If the Bank is not satisfied that a 'clean transfer' has been made, a capital requirement will still be levied against the assets involved, even though they are no longer held on the balance sheet. Additionally, banks were forbidden from providing liquidity support to the investment vehicles in the event of the latter getting into financial difficulties. Finally, it is worth noting that the new rules operated alongside the Code of Practice drawn up by the Bank in respect of loan transfers.

The next major development occurred with the publication of an amendment to the 1989 paper in April 1992 (Bank of England, 1992f). The purpose of the amendment was threefold: (1) to make some amendments and refinements to existing policy in respect of changes in sub-participations and transfers of equipment and consumer finance loans; (2) to establish the criteria on which the Bank would allow securitized revolving credits (such as credit card receivables) to be regarded as sold for prudential purposes; and (3) to clarify the meaning of the 1989 notice in two places.

A further development occurred in 1992, when the Bank issued a notice (Bank of England, 1992d) amending its 1990 notice implementing the Solvency Ratio Directive. The purpose of the amendment was to clarify the treatment of holdings of mortgage-backed securities by establishing the conditions an issue has to meet in order to qualify for a 50 per cent risk weighting. (Adoption of the proposed 100 per cent risk weighting, as previously intended, would have retarded the development of the securitized mortgage market in the UK.)

The final development on the securitization front came with the Bank's decision to amend its treatment of *securitized revolving credits*. Following a consultation process begun in April 1995, the Bank, in April 1996 (Bank of England, 1996l), issued a policy notice which lifted the limit previously placed on the amount of outstanding revolving credits that a bank can securitize at any one time. (The concerns it was put in place to address are now met in other ways.) Additionally, the Bank promised to consult further on the setting of a minimum period for the scheduled amortization of schemes using the aggregated approach.

OTHER BANKING 'PROBLEMS'

Apart from routine supervision and the resolution of banking crises, such as BCCI and Barings, the Bank has also been involved over the years in a number of other bank investigations, not all of which have reflected well on the Bank. One particularly notorious case, the *Blue Arrow* 'Affair', embroiled the Bank because of County NatWest's actions in connection with a failed rights issue which Blue Arrow was using to finance the takeover of Manpower Services in 1987. A DTI inquiry which looked into the circumstances surrounding the failed takeover, which left County NatWest nursing sizeable losses on its own books following the worldwide stock market crash in the autumn of 1987, concluded, in July 1989, that directors of County NatWest, the advisers to Blue Arrow, and of Phillips and Drew, the stockbrokers to Blue Arrow, had deliberately set out to breach the disclosure requirement of the Companies Act 1985 in order to conceal the failure of the £837 million rights issue. Moreover, the DTI argued that NatWest directors had failed in their duty to ensure that its corporate finance arm – County NatWest – complied with the law. A number of executives and other employees were also singled out for censure in the report.

Publication of the damning report led to a number of resignations of senior financiers in the City. For example, Christopher Stainforth resigned as Corporate Finance Director at UBS Phillips and Drew, Lord Boardman resigned as Chairman of NatWest Bank (along with the three main board directors censured in the report), Sir Philip Wilkinson, author of the much-criticized internal report to the DTI, eventually resigned from the Bank's Board of Banking Supervision, and, following pressure from the Bank, Jonathan Cohen, Chief Executive at County NatWest at the time of the scandal, resigned as Vice-Chairman of Charterhouse Bank. Additionally, the SFO mounted a major fraud investigation which resulted, in February 1992, in the conviction of four individuals (three from County NatWest and one from UBS Phillips and Drew), although all the convictions were subsequently overturned on appeal. More worrying, from the Bank's perspective, was the launch by the DTI of a second inquiry, following a request from Lord Alexander, the Chairman of NatWest, in the light of allegations made during the Blue Arrow trial of 1991 of dishonesty on the part of senior NatWest executives. The findings of the second inquiry were duly released in January 1993. Although clearing NatWest of deliberately withholding information from the first DTI investigation, and NatWest and the Bank of conspiring to mislead DTI inspectors and to prevent the first inquiry from being launched, the report was highly critical of NatWest's internal report, which was submitted to the DTI during the first inquiry in 1988. Deficiencies in this report, which included a number of serious errors, were put down to the 'inefficiency and inexperience' of the report's author – Sir Philip Wilkinson – but not to his 'dishonesty'.

Although cleared of the more serious allegations made against it, the Bank did not emerge entirely 'smelling of roses'. The impression it created, for example, in 'coaching' NatWest in its response to DTI inspectors during the first inquiry, and in seeking to delay the first DTI inquiry pending the outcome of NatWest's own internal inquiry, was that the preservation of NatWest's good name, and the associated benefits for the stability of the UK banking sector, took precedence over the rooting out of any wrongdoing. Moreover, the Bank had to shoulder some responsibility for presiding over the shortcomings in NatWest's internal controls and for failing to detect anything untoward itself.

Another case which attracted unwelcome attention, as far as the Bank was concerned, was that of *Harrods Bank* for, notwithstanding a damning DTI report into the takeover of the House of Frazer by the Al Fayed brothers, owners of Harrods Stores, the Bank failed to remove any directors from the bank because of concerns about their 'fitness and properness' (see Hall, 1990). (Control of the bank was, however, eventually transferred from the House of Frazer to a company of independent trustees.)

More recently, the Bank has been forced to turn its attention again to the investment banking sector. The first problem to be dealt with concerned the activities of an options trader at *NatWest Markets*, the bank's investment banking arm (previously named County NatWest), who managed to hide £77 million of losses, run up over a period of two years, by 'mispricing' (interest rate) options. The problems associated with 'rogue traders' had surfaced yet again (the antics of Nick Leeson at Barings and of Mr Yasuo Hamanaka at Sumitomo were still fresh in people's minds) and the familiar sorry state of internal controls at a major bank was paraded for all to see. Five senior managers were subsequently suspended (in March 1997) for failure to exercise adequate supervision over the trader, the Chief Executive of NatWest Markets resigned, and certain bonuses were withdrawn from the departments involved. An independent investigation (conducted by C&L) was also launched, the results of which emerged in June 1997. Senior managers were cleared of collusion with the trader, although they were found guilty of failure to supervise him properly. Moreover, it emerged that a number of people, other than the trader at the centre of the scandal, had been directly involved in the mispricing of options contracts. The worry for the Bank was that, once again, NatWest's ability to manage and control its investment banking operations effectively had been called into question, a situation that seemed only to heighten speculation about the future of the bank's investment banking arm and, indeed, about the bank itself (Barclays conspicuously refused to deny suggestions that it wanted to merge with NatWest). In the event, NatWest sold off its US and Asian derivatives operations to Deutsche Morgan Grenfell and its pan-European equities business to Bankers Trust in December 1997 in the wake of an investment banking loss of £210 million during 1997. This followed the sale by Barclays of its European equities and corporate advisory businesses to Credit Suisse First Boston in November that year.

Finally, the Bank was called in (by the Swiss Banking Commission) to investigate yet another case of losses being incurred on derivatives trades, this time by the *Union Bank of Switzerland* (UBS). The losses, of £145 million, were only revealed after UBS announced its plans to merge with the Swiss Bank Corporation in December 1997. The Bank will clearly be hoping that no evidence of malpractice in UBS's derivatives department in London will be unearthed.

THE LONDON APPROACH

Another area of involvement for the Bank is in the 'London Approach', a voluntary, collective approach adopted by banks in the UK since the late 1980s when faced with a company in financial difficulty. The Approach, which has resulted in the survival, against the odds, of a large number of companies in recent years, is designed to ensure that decisions about whether to call in receivers, on the one hand, or to organize a 'workout', or company support operation, on the other, are orderly and well founded (Bank of England, 1993e). The role of the Bank is to act as an 'honest broker', an independent and neutral mediator whose aim is to ensure that all interested parties are allowed a say and that negotiations are brought to a satisfactory conclusion, that is, one which represents an acceptable compromise.

The main tenets of the London Approach are:

1. That banks remain for the time being supportive on hearing that a company to which they have an exposure is in financial difficulty. (In particular, this means that they keep their facilities in place and do not rush to appoint receivers.)
2. That decisions about a company's longer-term future are only made on the basis of reliable information, which is fully shared among all bank creditors.
3. That banks work together to reach a collective view on *whether* and *how* a company should be given a financial lifeline.

In order to command support within the London banking community, the London Approach must also seek to maximize value for financial creditors. While numerous difficulties are often encountered – for example, in achieving unanimous support for a large and diverse group of creditor banks, taking account of the interests of other 'stakeholders', such as bondholders, shareholders and non-bank creditors, and in minimizing costs at a time when a company's cash resources are often already in short supply – the Approach is generally seen as having been a resounding success. Evolution, however, is necessary (e.g. to accommodate cross-border failures) if such a broad measure of support is to be maintained in the future.

'VOLUNTARY' SELF-REGULATION

The final area worth mentioning, in so far as it serves to offer reassurance to depositors and investors over and above that derived from the prudential regulation and supervision of banks (and additional to the formal protection deriving from consumer protection legislation, such as the Consumer Credit Act 1974), is that which covers 'voluntary self-regulation' (Jamison, 1998). This form of regulation, which is distinct from that introduced under the Financial Services Act 1986 (*see* Chapter 8), affects the day-to-day operations of banks (and other financial institutions) by tying them down to voluntary codes of conduct, such as the Code of Banking Practice, last revised in July 1997, the Code of Mortgage Lending Practice issued by the Council of Mortgage Lenders in March 1997 (*see* Salt and Southern, 1997) and the Code of Practice on the Advertising of Interest Bearing Accounts, drawn up by the British Bankers' Association, the Building Societies' Association, and the Finance and Leasing Association. Compliance with the Codes is enforced through the various Ombudsman Schemes, the Council of Mortgage Lenders' Arbitration Scheme, and the Independent Review Body for the Banking and Mortgage Lending Codes (for further details, *see* Jamison, 1998).

Notes: Part II

1. It is assumed that the style and techniques of banking supervision developed by the Bank have remained largely intact on the transfer of responsibility for banking supervision from the Bank to the FSAu in the spring of 1998 (*see* Chapter 8). Indeed, the FSAu has publicly stated that it will 'continue to implement the changes designed to improve the overall effectiveness [of banking supervision], which were agreed in 1996 following the Arthur Andersen review' (FSAu, 1998, p. 14), and that the Board will remain in place as advisers to the FSAu Board. More explicitly, it indicated that its immediate priorities would embrace, *inter alia*, reviewing institutions' state of readiness for the year 2000 and for European and Monetary Union, and that work would be focused on the following:

   - credit and operational risk;
   - reporting lines within banking groups (the intention is to ensure that risk management and control functions are independent of the front office);
   - developing the risk-based approach to supervision of banks, building on the RATE/SCALE frameworks recently developed by the Bank;
   - implementing the changes to the Section 39 reporting accountants' process proposed in the February 1997 consultation paper, and issuing (for consultation) new guidelines for relationships with auditors and reporting accountants, and for further improvements to the Section 39 process;
   - updating the 'Statement of Principles', outlining how the FSAu will approach its responsibilities under the Banking Act 1987;
   - research into credit risk-modelling, developing policy responses to market developments such as credit derivatives and approving internal models in advance of the implementation of 'CAD II';
   - improving links with overseas supervisors (attempts will be made to transfer to the FSAu the supervisory Memorandum of Understanding to which the Bank is currently a party);

- developing an agreed approach to the 'lead supervisor' model in respect of the supervision of complex groups (FSAu, 1998 pp. 14–16).

An FSAu 'Guide to Banking Supervisory Policy' will also replaced the Bank's set of 'Policy Notices' in July 1998.

2. This, however, could change if the number of institutions willing to accept it were to diminish. Already, a problem has arisen as a result of the large number of overseas institutions operating in London which are unused to such a supervisory relationship and which are more concerned with the letter of the law and rule books than the gyrations of the Governor's eyebrows. A knock-on effect of this is that indigenous City institutions, traditionally more susceptible to such 'moral persuasion', have become less amenable to pressures, as exemplified in the recent British and Commonwealth affair (*see* Chapter 10). Nor is the lowering of the Bank's stock in the wake of the BCCI (*see* Chapter 11), Barings (*see* Chapter 12) and Harrods Bank (*see* Hall, 1990) affairs likely to do much to rescue the situation. And, finally, the codification of banking regulation and supervision under EU law (*see* Chapter 9) is likely to herald a new dawn for statutory supervision. Notwithstanding these developments, however, the Bank has sought to use its moral authority in recent years to slow the decline in mortgage lenders' margins (due to heavy 'discounting' and the payment of 'cashbacks') and the margins on commercial loans, and to get banks to try to ensure that their bonus payments do not engender excessive risk-taking (*see* Davies, 1997).

3. This is particularly useful to the Bank in its 'peer group assessment' exercise.

4. The assessment of non-EEA banks involves employment of a 'SCALE' framework to judge whether the banks meet the minimum criteria for authorization and satisfy UK standards of practice (Bank of England, 1997b).

5. 'Contestable market theory' developed by Baumol (1982) and others demonstrates that, even in instances of imperfect competition, optimal resource allocation requires that the barriers to entry and exit remain as low as possible.

6. The Bank will only consider activating its lender-of-last-resort facility if the following conditions are satisfied: (1) all options for a 'commercial' solution (e.g. support from major shareholders and/or creditors, bids from outsiders, assistance from a coherent group of other banks with a common interest in an orderly resolution) have been considered first; (2) any support provided is structured so that losses fall first on shareholders with benefits accruing first to the Bank, and will be on terms that are as

penal as possible without precipitating collapse; (3) the institution receiving the assistance is thought to be solvent at the time assistance is provided (i.e. liquidity rather than solvency support is to be provided); (4) arrangements are put in place to allow for a clear exit by the Bank (e.g. through imposed restructuring or a winding-down of operations under Bank management, as happened with JMB (*see* Chapter 5); and (5) the support operation can, if at all possible, be kept secret, with the facts being revealed to the market place once the danger has passed (as was the case with the support operation mounted in the aftermath of the closure of BCCI – *see* Chapter 11) (Bank of England, 1994a).

7. Such markets were excluded from the coverage of the Financial Services Act of 1986 in order to spare professional traders in the market the detailed regulations introduced by the SIB and SROs.

As supervisor of these markets, the Bank's first move was to propose, in December 1986, a London Code of Conduct under which the Bank would maintain a list of institutions authorized to operate in the markets and those authorized would agree to abide by both the spirit and the letter of the Code. Emphasized within the Code would be the need for integrity, fair dealing, confidentiality and sound practices, and authorized institutions would be committed to stamping out insider trading. The Code would carry no statutory force although the Bank, through continuous monitoring, would seek to ensure adherence to it.

Its proposals for a uniform system of non-statutory supervision for these markets were subsequently confirmed with the publication of a 'Grey Paper' on the subject in July 1987. Outlined within were the Code of Conduct and the authorization requirements: a 'fit and proper' test, based upon the adequacy of capital, managerial and operational resources, standards of business conduct and reputation and standing; a requirement that the company is regularly engaged in wholesale market operations; and agreement to abide by both the spirit and letter of the London Code of Conduct. (The London Code was revised in May 1992 to take account of both the recommendations made by the Treasury and Civil Service Committee in its report entitled *Banking Supervision and BCCI: The Role of Local Authorities and Money Brokers* (HMSO, 1991) and of recent changes in market practice. It was subsequently revised in July 1995 to meet the standards required under the Investment Services Directive and to accommodate changes in both market practice and the regulatory environment. Yet further revisions occurred in August 1995 and December 1995, the former designed to tighten the guidelines covering sales of 'over-the-counter' products, such as derivatives and leveraged financial instruments, to retail investors and the latter to create a 'Code of Best Practice' for participants in the gilt repo market.)

8. For a more detailed discussion of UK arrangements, *see* Hadjiemmanuil (1996). For a comparison with arrangements operating in other (mainly EU) countries, *see* Fédération des Experts Comptables Européens(1993).
9. The issues of whether or not statutory control over auditors (and reporting accountants) should be tightened and how their responsibilities and legal obligations should be extended are discussed in Hall, 1993, Chapter 24, pp. 179–86. Since then, however, a number of significant developments have taken place, which are documented below.

First, in November 1992, the APB – a self-regulatory standard-setting body established in 1991 to restore investor confidence – produced a document entitled the 'Future Development of Auditing' (the 'McFarlane Report'; APB, 1992). Interested parties were given until March 1993 to respond to the consultancy paper, which resulted in the publication of 'The Audit Agenda' in December 1994 (APB, 1994). Its main proposals were as follows:

- Audits at listed companies should be more extensive than those at owner-managed companies. The scope of the statutory audit should stay the same but the extended duties should be backed up by standards which have the power of law.
- The extended audit duties should be covered by contracts limiting liability.
- Auditors should be asked to make sure that the text sections of accounts, such as the chairman's report, match the accounts being audited.
- The audit should be signed personally by the audit partner rather than, as at present, carrying only the name of the firm from which the auditor comes.
- The audit partner should not have overall control of non-audit services for the company.
- Audit committees should have responsibility for appointing the auditors and setting their fees.
- The chairman of the audit committee should report on the auditor to the AGM – possibly in writing and orally.
- Separate reports should be made to the board and the audit committee by the auditor on standards of governance – and to the shareholders on whether the so-called 'Cadbury Code' was being followed properly.
- Auditors should comment on internal audit controls.
- The board should order periodic forensic audits in which teams of specialists look for fraud.

- The penalties for deceiving auditors should be toughened, with staff facing penalties as well.
- The professional bodies should teach auditors about fraud.
- The APB and the Accounting Standards Board should work on how to assure secondary and tertiary stakeholders in the company. While the prime duty is to shareholders, as confirmed by the 'Caparo' test case, other stakeholders should be able to rely on assurances given by auditors.

Opinion on the report was divided. Within the profession, there were those who thought that the APB had gone too far on certain fronts, while others deemed the report not radical enough. Outsiders were generally of the view that, while many of the suggestions were a step in the right direction, they would do little to close the so-called 'expectations gap', especially in respect of the detection of fraud, and failed to address the issue of independent regulation of the profession.

On the question of *regulation*, the DTI had commissioned an independent report from Professor Peter Moizer in 1993 to assess the effectiveness of the first two years of operation of the self-regulatory framework established in 1989. His draft report was sent to the DTI in December 1993, recommending that the three regulatory bodies in existence at the time – the Joint Monitoring Unit, the Chartered Association of Certified Accountants (CACA) and the Association of Authorized Public Accountants – be merged and subject to independent public scrutiny. Such a radical option, however, was ruled out by the government in 1994 in favour of trying to improve the existing monitoring system.

It soon became clear, however, that the profession did not back the government's opposition to independent regulation. In July 1995, for example, the ICAEW put forward proposals (in the so-called 'Swinson Report Mark II', which followed on from the earlier Swinson Report, produced in 1994, which looked into the future of regulation of the accountancy profession) for establishing an independent 'Public Oversight' body to regulate the regulators. Disciplining, monitoring and standard-setting, however, would remain 'in house' under a new 'Office of Professional Standards'. And in October 1995 the CACA went even further by recommending the establishment of a new supervisory body which would be financially independent of the profession. The new body would have lay and public interest representation on its board, and both the APB, which would become fully independent, and a reformed Joint Disciplinary Scheme would report to it. Finally, in April 1996, the six main professional groups within the accountancy profession announced a joint plan to set up an independent regulatory body – an 'oversight board' –

to regulate auditing standards, ethics and discipline. The working party, under the Chairmanship of Chris Swinson, recommended that the new body have about five members, who would all be nominated by a committee comprising representatives from City institutions. The accountancy profession would not be represented on the board although it might be invited to provide input to the board's deliberations. The new body would be free to publish regular reports on the profession and to make recommendations which, if they were not adopted, could be enforced through action by the DTI or the SIB. Formal proposals were sent to the DTI in February 1998.

As for developments on the detection of *fraud* (apart from post-BCCI developments, which are covered in the text), the APB published, for the first time, in January 1995, a 'checklist' which auditors could use to help them spot fraud. Under the 'Statement of Auditing Standards 110', auditors were urged to watch out for the following tell-tale signs:

- management dominated by one person or a small group of individuals;
- holiday entitlement not taken up;
- high turnover of important staff;
- excessive payments for services (e.g. to lawyers or consultants);
- excessive performance-based payments;
- incomplete files or altered accounts;
- evasive replies to auditor questions.

It was not until May 1996, however, that auditors, through the ICAEW, offered to give a wider range of assurances about companies, including whether *material* fraud might be present, but this was made conditional on the government agreeing to limit auditors' legal liability. (The ICAEW wanted the law of 'joint and several liability', under which accountants could be ordered to pay all the damages of an action regardless of the degree of negligence, to be replaced by a form of proportional liability law, and also wanted reform of Section 310 of the Companies Act which forbids auditors to limit their liability by contract.)

This conveniently leads into the final area of controversy surrounding the accountancy profession, namely, its quest for limited liability. KPMG, the UK's third largest accountancy firm, increased the pressure for reform when, in October 1995, it announced plans to convert its audit practice into a separate company – KPM Audit – with limited liability. The move to transform its audit business from a partnership into a separate body was a response to the mounting cost of litigation which, when added to the cost of insurance, amounted to about 8 per cent of turnover for KPMG.

Incorporation would not prevent litigation but it would ring-fence the personal assets of partners from any successful claim of negligence against their fellow partners. It would also involve replacing the legal principle of 'joint and several liability', which underpins partnerships, with corporate and individual liability. Individuals could still be forced to defend claims for negligent work, but partners on the audit side would have corporate liability as directors of an audit company. KPMG's action rekindled the debate about the benefits and costs of unlimited liability, putting pressure on the Government to accelerate the pace of reform (although, somewhat ironically, the Law Commission rejected wholesale reform of the principle of joint and several liability in February 1996) and on its competitors to follow suit.

10. In this last case, close liaison with the Bank's Gilt-Edged Division was also maintained.

11. Memoranda of Understanding were first agreed with the SIB, the TSA (which later became the SFA, with whom a new Memorandum was signed in April 1991) and IMRO in March 1988. These were subsequently reviewed following the implementation of the Investment Services Directive and in the wake of the collapse of Barings. Finally, with a view to ensuring an adequate information flow, Memoranda were also agreed with the LIFFE, the LCE (London Commodities Exchange) and the LME (London Metal Exchange) during 1996/97. Although the transfer of responsibility for banking supervision to FSAu in Spring 1998 – *see* Chapter 8 – will largely render these Memoranda redundant, those signed with HM Treasury and the FSAu in October 1997 will play an important part in ensuring that financial stability is maintained within the UK.

12. For a discussion of earlier developments, *see* Chapter 1.

13. Subsequent amendments, whether by way of BSD notices or S&S notices, are covered below.

14. Defined according to Section 106(1) as that body corporate, any other body corporate which is its holding company or subsidiary, and any other body corporate which is a subsidiary of that holding company.

15. Perpetual debt, in the form of perpetual floating rate notes, was only accepted as 'primary capital' – *see* Exhibit 2.3 – by the Bank in May 1985. Moreover, the term 'primary capital' was only adopted by the Bank in 1984. And, under the UK/US accord on capital adequacy agreed in January 1987, the definition was changed again.

16. The qualifying conditions, as applied prior to the accord, are explained in note (2) to Exhibit 2.4.

17. The position, prior to the accord, is explained in note (2) to Exhibit 2.3.

18. This assumed that no agreement was reached on a consistent basis for including unencumbered provisions or reserves in capital. In the event,

the Basle Committee agreed in November 1991 to implement an amendment to the 1988 agreement, along the lines suggested in its paper of February 1991 (BIS, 1991).

19. The perpetual floating rate note market, for example, had been in the doldrums for some time, and few banks, since the global stock market crash of October 1987, were likely to be running large open positions in equities providing the potential for paper profits. Some UK institutions, however, took advantage of the concession granted in the final version of the BIS paper which allowed banks to count perpetual preferred stock as core capital so long as there was no obligation to make up for interrupted dividend payments (i.e. they are non-cumulative, like common stock). The Bank's approval of the terms of such issues, however, is required if they are to be permitted to rank as Tier 1 capital.

20. Nor will authorized institutions in the UK benefit from the discretion given to supervisors to allow banks to count their holdings of other banks' capital instruments within their capital base on a gross basis. As before, the Bank will insist that banks deduct all such holdings from their own issues in calculating figures for their capital bases, although concessions (*see* Bank of England, 1986b, pp. 1–2) may be granted to primary and/or secondary market-makers in such instruments.

21. For further discussion of this issue, *see* Llewellyn, 1988, pp. 51–4.

22. The only amendment made prior to implementation of the CAD embraced revisions to the requirements for perpetual and dated subordinated loan capital to qualify for inclusion in Tier 2 capital (applicable only to subordinated loan capital issued after May 1994) (BSD/1994/3; Bank of England, 1994c). Since implementation of the CAD (*via* S&S/1995/2; Bank of England, 1995b) amendments have embraced: (1) clarification of the Bank's policy in respect of implementation of the CAD (S&S/1995/4; Bank of England, 1995c); (2) amendment to the policy implementing the Own Funds Directive to accommodate the Commission's decision to *exclude* internally audited interim profits from own funds (S&S/1995/5; Bank of England, 1995d); and (3) clarification of the conditions to be satisfied before perpetual non-cumulative preference share issues through a separate issuing entity can contribute towards Tier 1 capital (Bank of England, 1998b). The Bank is also considering – a draft Policy Notice on the subject was issued in December 1996 – exempting banks' holdings of the capital instruments of credit and financial institutions and non-financial companies from the requirement to deduct them from capital as long as they are held in the 'trading book' and they do not exceed the limits set out in the Own Funds Directive.

23. The Bank will permit the early repayment of this debt only when it is satisfied that the bank's capital will be adequate after repayment and is

likely to remain so. The Bank would not normally be expected to give consent to any repayment of perpetual subordinated debt within five years and one day from the date of the drawdown. Similarly, the Bank would not normally expect to give consent to any repayment of other subordinated debt within two years and one day from the date of issuance or drawdown.

24. The Bank may require that interest and principal payments be deferred on Tier 3 debt.

25. The latter limit cannot be exceeded without the Bank's express permission, and this will only be granted in cases where a bank's trading book forms the overwhelming majority of its business.

26. Note, the 50 per cent of Tier 1 capital limit currently imposed on the Tier 2 subordinated term debt will remain in operation, as will the current restriction limiting the amount of Tier 2 capital used to meet the banking book capital requirements to 100 per cent of the Tier 1 capital used to meet such requirements.

27. One aspect not touched upon in the text is the Bank's conceptual approach to this. Given the Bank's overriding concern with the protection of depositors and potential depositors, the emphasis given to the role of capital as a cushion for the absorption of any losses which might occur is not surprising. If the cushion provided is large enough, then an institution should be able to weather the storm and continue trading. In the light of this requirement, the Bank emphasizes the qualities of permanence and capacity to absorb losses. Accordingly, most types of capital recognized by the Bank are irredeemable as far as the holder is concerned, and only those distributable reserves which have a remote likelihood of being paid are eligible for inclusion in the capital base.

    Not all elements of capital recognized by the Bank have these two qualities. Some, nevertheless, can provide some protection to depositors. Term debt, for example, which is included in the capital base within the limits set out in BSD/1986/2 (Bank of England, 1986b), provides a measure of protection to depositors against loss in a liquidation if it is of the appropriate type (i.e. of an appropriate term, fully subordinated to the interests of depositors and highly unlikely to be repaid before maturity). The diminishing comfort afforded by the shortening in maturity is taken into account by a requirement that straight-line amortization be applied once the stock passes through the five years to maturity threshold.

28. An additional ratio which the Bank monitored in assessing capital adequacy was the *gearing ratio*, which expresses the adjusted capital base (*see* Exhibit 2.4, item 2) as a percentage of current, non-capital liabilities. (Justification for the adjustments required to the capital base are given in Bank of England, 1980, p. 327.) This ratio was taken to represent the

acceptability of an institution's capital to its depositors and other creditors and, accordingly, a priority was placed on constructing it on the basis of published information (although the inclusion of inner reserves and general bad debt provisions hinders meaningful comparisons between institutions).

29. In mathematical terms:

$$RAR(\%) = \frac{ACB}{TOWRA}$$

where *ACB* is the adjusted capital base

and

$$TOWRA = \sum_{i=1}^{s} \sum_{j=1}^{t} \left(A_{ij}W_j\right)$$

$$+ \sum_{i=1}^{u} \sum_{j=1}^{v} \sum_{k=1}^{w} \left(B_{ijk}X_kW_j\right)$$

$$+ \sum_{i=1}^{x} \sum_{j=1}^{y} \sum_{k=1}^{z} \left[\left(C_{ijk}X_k + M\right)W_j\right]^*$$

where

A_{ij} is the value of the ith asset with risk weight W_j;

B_{ijk} is the notional principal amount of off-balance-sheet activity i with risk weight W_j and conversion factor X_k;

C_{ijk} is the notional principal amount of the interest- or exchange-rate related activity i with risk weight W_j and conversion factor X_k;

s is the number of distinct asset components;

u is the number of distinct off-balance-sheet activities (excluding interest rate- and exchange rate-related activities);

x is the number of distinct interest- and exchange rate-related off-balance-sheet instruments

M is the mark-to-market value of the underlying contract where $x < u < s$; $v \leq t = 5$; $y \leq t = 5$; $w = 4$; and $z = 4$.

* 'Current exposure' assessment method employed.

30. The Bank believed in 1980 that to attempt to take account of additional forms of risk in the formulation of risk weights would only serve to complicate matters without necessarily enhancing the validity of the risk measure. The Basle Committee, meanwhile, was working on ways to

accommodate interest rate risk and position risk within its assessment framework.

31. Credit risk is defined as the risk that claims may not be redeemable on their due dates at book values; investment risk is the risk that the market values of marketable claims may fall below book values; and forced-sale risk is the risk that additional losses will actually be incurred because of the forced sale of assets at prices below book values.

32. For a more detailed analysis, *see* Lewis, 1988.

33. Conversion factors for interest rate swaps and other interest rate contracts and for foreign exchange rate contracts remained to be determined. (Discussion proposals were issued by the Bank in May 1987 for the treatment of these items.)

34. Although it should be noted (*see* Exhibit 2.11) that, in calculating the credit risk equivalents arising from interest- and exchange rate-related activities, a bank may, at the discretion of the Bank, be allowed to employ the so-called 'original exposure' assessment method rather than the 'current exposure' (alternatively termed the 'replacement cost') assessment method sponsored under the UK/US accord.

35. The 50 per cent weighting would thus, from 1 January 1993, only apply to fully secured, first mortgages on primary residences given to individuals or to housing associations registered with the Housing Corporation and to certain mortgage sub-participations (*see* category D claims, Exhibit 2.7).

36. Subsequent pre-CAD capital adequacy developments embraced revisions to the treatment of on-balance-sheet netting and cash collateralization, the treatment of off-balance-sheet netting, and the treatment of repos and reverse repos. The criteria defining the group of countries ('Zone A') whose central governments, local governments and banks carry lower risk weightings were also changed, and the risk weighting for the EIB was lowered.

Revision to the Bank's reporting rules in the area of *on-balance-sheet netting* and *cash collateralization* was implemented *via* BSD/1993/3 (Bank of England, 1993b). The on-balance-sheet netting rules gave guidance on the circumstances in which banks could report debit and credit balances with a single customer (or customers in the same company group) as a single net item. This reduced the amount of the reported asset against which capital had to be held. The revised cash collateralization rules, meanwhile, gave guidance on the occasions on which banks could weight assets at 0 per cent in recognition of the existence of cash security.

Although the Basle capital accord was amended in July 1994 to give wider recognition to bilateral netting arrangements in the calculation of a bank's counterparty exposures for certain *off-balance-sheet* items (*see* Chapter 7), the Bank was forced to delay its accommodation of the new rules because of a delay in amending the Solvency Ratio Directive. In December 1995, however, the Bank issued policy notice S&S/1995/3; (Bank of England, 1995e) on the netting of counterparty risk associated with sale and repo arrangements, and draft rules on over-the-counter (OTC) derivatives. The notice (which supplemented BSD/1990/3) set out the legal and systems requirements that authorized institutions are required to meet before the Bank is prepared to treat the counterparty credit risk arising from such transactions on a net basis for capital adequacy and large exposures reporting purposes. Following adoption of the Contracted Netting Directive in February 1996, the Bank issued a further notice (S&S/1996/3; Bank of England, 1996e) confirming the 'final' rules to take effect from 30 April. This Notice replaced S&S/1995/3. The new rules, however, still did not allow for the netting of 'add-ons', as allowed under Basle rules since end-1995 (*see* Chapter 7). (Although an EU Directive, proposed in April 1996, will eventually permit the partial netting of 'add-ons' for a potential future credit exposure, this was still not operational by mid-1998 (*see* Clarotti, 1997).)

In order to gain recognition of netting arrangements, banks are required to write to the Bank setting out the agreement, jurisdictions, counterparty types and product types involved, and to confirm that they have obtained legal opinions which satisfy the terms of the notice. They are also required to maintain detailed records of their due diligence so that compliance with the notice may subsequently be examined, either via supervisory visits or the Section 39 process, and to manage their resulting exposures on a net basis.

The revised treatment of *repos and reverse repos* (and stock borrowing and lending) was outlined in BSD/1994/4 (Bank of England, 1994d) (which supplemented BSD/1990/3). It gave banks the choice to use a new approach subject to meeting certain minimum requirements relating to documentation, daily marking to market of positions and regular recalculation of collateral. The new approach is likely to result in a reduction in the capital requirement for reverse repos but a small increase in the requirement for repos.

Changes to the criteria defining 'Zone A' status, were accommodated in S&S/1995/1 (Bank of England, 1995f) (which amended BSD/1990/3) and resulted in the addition of the Czech Republic to the Zone A grouping in December 1995 (confirmed in S&S/1996/2; Bank of England, 1996f).

And finally, the lowering of the *risk weighting* of the EIB, from 100 per cent to 20 per cent, was confirmed in S&S/1995/5 (Bank of England, 1995d).

37. This section rests heavily on Hall, 1997.

38. Capital adequacy developments since the implementation of the CAD relate to an extension made to the list of Multilateral Development Banks (which enjoy a reduced risk weighting of 20 per cent), the introduction of new arrangements for those banks employing the replacement cost method for calculating the credit exposure arising from off-balance-sheet contracts, a further enlargement of the Zone A group of countries, and an increase in the risk weighting (from 10 per cent to 20 per cent) given to (appropriately secured) loans to GEMMs and stock exchange money brokers (henceforth treated as investment firms).

The first-mentioned development involved the addition of the Inter-American Investment Corporation to the list of Multilateral Development Banks (S&S/1996/2; Bank of England, 1996f). The second development, which involved the introduction of an expanded 'matrix' (*see* Chapter 7) – to cover equities, precious metals other than gold, other commodities, and contracts of greater than five years' residual maturity – and the limiting of the 'original exposure method' to interest rates, foreign exchange and gold contracts in the banking book only, was effected through S&S/1996/4 (Bank of England, 1996g). The third-mentioned resulted in South Korea acquiring Zone A status (S&S/1996/10; Bank of England, 1996h). And the final change followed the introduction of money-market reforms in March 1997.

39. The 'trading book' of an institution is defined in Article 2(6) of the CAD and comprises:

1. Proprietary positions in financial instruments held for resale and/or with a view to benefiting from short-term variations in price or interest rates.
2. Positions in financial instruments arising from matched principal broking.
3. Positions taken in order to hedge other elements of the trading book.
4. Exposures arising from unsettled transactions in debt securities and equities, from securities paid for but not yet received ('free deliveries'), and from over-the-counter derivatives such as swaps and options.
5. Exposures arising from repurchase agreements and securities lending which are based on securities included in the trading book.
6. Exposures due to reverse repurchase agreements and securities borrowing transactions, provided the regulatory authorities approve.
7. Exposures arising from services provided by the firm, in the form of fees, commission, interest, dividends and margins on exchange-traded products which relate directly to items in the trading book.

To avoid their unjustified inclusion in the trading book, which could lead to application of lighter capital requirements, the CAD requires, however, that their inclusion be based on 'objective procedures', the terms and implementation of which should be reviewed by the regulatory authorities. Moreover, exposures of type (6) are only eligible for inclusion in the trading book if: (a) the exposures are marked to market on a daily basis; (b) the collateral is adjusted in a manner acceptable to the regulatory authorities to take account of material changes in the value of the underlying securities; (c) the agreement or transaction provides automatic 'set-off' in the event of default by the counterparty; and (d) such agreements and transactions are confined to their 'accepted and appropriate use' and additional transactions, especially those not of a short-term nature, are excluded. (Conditions (a) to (c) may be waived if the agreement or transaction in question is an inter-professional one.)

40. The treatment described below assumes the (limited) concessions granted to 'market-makers' – as provided for in the Own Funds Directive – are not applicable.

41. For the purposes of this requirement, debt instruments have to be valued at their market price or principal values, equities at their market prices, and derivatives according to the nominal or market values of the instruments underlying them. Long and short positions have to be summed regardless of sign.

42. If individual equities are listed in more than one country, a bank can allocate the position across one or more of the countries concerned.

43. *See* Bank of England, 1994e, Chapter 10, para.13, for further details.

44. *See* Bank of England, 1994e, Chapter 10, para.12.

45. Assuming the stocks are listed in a 'qualifying' country (*see* note 47).

46. Individual stocks, of either UK or non-UK incorporated companies, which are traded on the London Stock Exchange but are not a component of a recognized index may, nevertheless, be deemed 'highly liquid', and hence subject to the 2 per cent risk weight, if they satisfy certain conditions – *see* Bank of England, 1994e, Chapter 10, paras 14–15.

47. Comprising, at present, Belgium, Canada, Denmark, France, Germany, Greece, Ireland, Italy, Japan, Luxembourg, the Netherlands, Portugal, Spain, Sweden, Switzerland, the UK and the US.

48. Subject to satisfying certain criteria (*see* Bank of England, 1994e, Chapter 10, para.17), however, concessions are granted for inter-market offsets between country portfolios of 'recognized' indices.

49. The Bank's proposed use of a 'defined currency factor' to reflect differences in the volatility of interest rates between currencies was eventually dropped (Bank of England, 1995c), although in setting individual target and trigger capital ratios, the Bank will take account of the volatility of yield curves, alongside the liquidity of markets and the availability of hedging mechanisms.

50. More precisely, the capital charge is calculated as the sum of:

	2 per cent of the matched duration-weighted position for each zone
plus	40 per cent of the matched duration-weighted positions between Zones 1 and 2 and between Zones 2 and 3
plus	150 per cent of the matched duration-weighted positions between Zones 1 and 3
plus	100 per cent of the residual unmatched duration-weighted positions

| | where 'Zone 1' refers to modified durations of between 0 and 1 year, 'Zone 2' to modified durations of over 1 and up to 3.6 years, |
| and | 'Zone 3' to modified durations in excess of 3.6 years. |

51. The capital requirements, which have to be applied to the current market values of underlying equities, are as follows:

For exposures of up to 3 months	0.2%
For exposures of over 3 and up to 6 months	0.4%
For exposures of over 6 months and up to 12 months	0.7%
For exposures of over 1 year and up to 1.9 years	1.25%
For exposures of over 1.9 years and up to 2.8 years	1.75%
For exposures of over 2.8 years and up to 3.6 years	2.25%
For exposures of over 3.6 years and up to 5.7 years	3.75%
For exposures of over 5.7 years	6.0%

52. Advice from the Bank has to be sought for the treatment of those with a residual maturity of over six months.

53. For stock indices which are not recognized by the Bank, positions arising directly or via equity derivatives have to be broken down into their underlying instruments.

54. *See* note 52.

55. Even where a bank has express written approval for the use of non-interest rate derivative models, the embedded interest rate exposures may also be treated in accordance with this regime.

56. For the purposes of generating the capital requirements pre-'working day 5', rights issues and warrant issues are to be converted into the underlying instrument using the current market price of the underlying instrument.

57. Reductions in position risk capital requirements are not, however, available to banks which make purchases on the grey market, and which are neither underwriters nor members of the syndicate for underwriting or distributing the particular securities. Moreover, they only apply to new instruments and new tranches of existing instruments.

58. The Bank defines 'working day 0' as the working day on which the bank becomes unconditionally committed to accepting a known quantity of securities at a known price.

59. Namely those subject to the CAD or otherwise to a regulatory regime deemed as stringent as that applied under the CAD.

60. In each case the risk weight is 20 per cent (as opposed to the 100 per cent weight imposed on similar claims reported in the banking book) – treatment which is consistent with the CAD's provisions – *see* Exhibit 2.16.

61. The only issue overlooked is the treatment of 'deferred settlement' – for details *see* Bank of England, 1994e, Chapter 5, paras 62–4.

62. Currency mismatches between the securities lent and the collateral received will also incur higher capital requirements.

63. The risk cushion factors depend on the maturity of the securities sold or lent and of the collateral, as outlined below:

   - for interest rate products
     - residual maturity of less than one year, risk cushion = 0.25%
     - " one to five years, " = 0.50%
     - " over five years, " = 1.50%
   - for equities, the risk cushion = 6.00%.

   Where the collateral provided is denominated in a currency other than that of the securities being lent, the higher risk cushion factor is increased by 1 per cent.

64. If daily adjustment to capital is made, each risk cushion factor may be halved.

65. Any available Tier 3 capital eligible for inclusion in the capital base may be used to meet this requirement where the excesses result from long securities positions in the trading book.

66. Shorter-term (i.e. with a residual maturity of less than one year) trading book exposures with investment firms subject to the CAD or an analogous assessment regime are, however, exempt from both the individual 25 per cent and the aggregate 800 per cent of own funds limits. Moreover, other trading book counterparty exposures to such firms and exposures to banks and building societies in derivative products may be scaled down by the application of a 20 per cent weighting before inclusion in the measure of exposure if the residual maturity is between one and three years.

67. For those which are not part of the trading book, the measure of exposure has to be calculated in the same manner as for exposures arising from securities from the time of the initial commitment. In such cases, the amount will be based on the *gross* commitment adjusted for any net sales and sub-underwriting agreements.

68. It replaces the policies outlined in Bank of England, 1981 and 1984a.

69. Capital requirements for such currency pairs (presently covering only the Belgium–Luxembourg franc) will be set at 50 per cent of the maximum movement stipulated by the intergovernmental agreement on the matched net open positions of the individual currencies.

70. Losses due to changes in the underlying exchange rate and to changes in the volatility of the option would need to be captured by the model. If losses due to changes in volatility are not captured, additional capital requirements will apply, based on the buffer approach.

71. The Bank's revised proposals of December 1995 (Bank of England, 1995c) also sanctioned a new set of 'simplified methods' for calculating market risk-related capital charges. Although they may well deliver higher capital charges for certain portfolios compared with the 'standard' methods, they may allow for a reduction in compliance costs. They may also be of interest to those banks which are marginally above the prescribed cut-off point for CAD exemption. In most cases, however, they must be used to generate both equity *and* debt position risk capital charges.

72. Only one trigger will be set, however, where either the trading book business or the banking book business of a bank, on a solo or consolidated basis, does not normally exceed 10 per cent of its combined on- and off-balance-sheet positions.

73. In mathematical terms, a bank's capital adequacy position (%) equals

$$
\left(\frac{\text{Tier 1 capital } + \text{ eligible Tier 2 capital } + \text{ eligible Tier 3 capital}}{\chi\% \text{ of } [12.5 \times (A+B+C+D+E)] + y\% \text{ of } F} \right) \times 100
$$

where $\chi\%$ is the trading book trigger ratio;
A, B, C, D and E are the minimum nominal capital charges to cover foreign exchange position risk, equity position risk, debt position risk, large exposures risk, and trading book counterparty and settlement risk, respectively;
$y\%$ is the banking book trigger ratio;
F is the total of risk weighted assets ('TOWRA') on the banking book.

74. For a more detailed analysis, *see* Hall, 1988.

75. The Bank originally intended to complement this approach with a high-quality liquidity stock requirement (*see* Bank of England, 1988b), but following opposition from the UK banking industry – particularly the

foreign contingent – it dropped the idea in favour of strengthening assessment on the basis of the 1982 paper. Accordingly, from April 1990, the Bank sought to improve its assessment of each bank's liquidity by asking for a description of its liquidity policy, identification of particular strengths and weaknesses, and an analysis of its capacity to survive a crisis. The description was expected to include an assessment of the contribution that a stock of high-quality liquidity in conjunction with measures of maturity mismatch could make to securing the goals of liquidity adequacy assessment. In January 1996, however, a new regime for large UK retail banks was introduced based upon a stock requirement – *see* the text.

76. Emphasizing the Bank's concern with funding (i.e. liquidity) risk as opposed to interest rate risk – *see* Hall, 1988, pp. 56–60.

77. That is, 'one which offers security of access to liquidity without undue exposure to suddenly rising costs from liquefying assets or bidding for deposits' (Bank of England, 1982, p. 399).

78. Unless the Bank was satisfied that an individual bank's hedging techniques were sufficiently developed, a 'worst view' approach was taken to the calculation of (potential) exposures to be contained within the dealing guidelines. This approach took account of the potential effect of the exercise of option rights held by a bank's customers on its open position in individual currencies, including the possibility that a bank's position in a particular currency may be transformed from a long position to a short position, or *vice versa*. No account was taken of the likelihood of particular options being exercised, nor was any credit given for options purchased by the bank, on the grounds that, without a detailed analysis of periods and strike prices, there was no way of knowing whether the options held were effective in hedging options written.

Before the Bank would permit a bank to use for reporting purposes its own formula for measuring the extent of its exposure on currency options, it needed to be satisfied not only with the mathematical basis of the formula and procedures for monitoring its continuing validity, but also that the operating systems for conducting the business and controlling the options book (including limits) were adequate. Also, the operation of a bank's own formula was kept under review and the Bank expected to discuss options business with such banks on a frequent and regular basis. Where the Bank did permit the use of a particular formula for a bank, the exposure to foreign currency options was assessed along with that on the cash markets to determine the overall open position for the purpose of monitoring a bank's foreign exchange exposure against the agreed guidelines.

79. The risks associated with structural exposures were not, however, overlooked. They were captured within the Bank's assessment of capital adequacy as the 'aggregate foreign currency position' included in the RAR framework, and included both dealing and structural positions.
80. As defined for the purpose of computing a bank's RAR – *see* Exhibit 2.5.
81. Limits on interbank exposures (including exposures to Stock exchange money brokers and GEMMs) had to be agreed with the Bank at least once a year and large exposures had to be reported quarterly.
82. Exposures to central government (and public sector bodies whose liabilities are guaranteed by the central government – this excluded local authorities) were not covered by the scheme; instead they were handled under the Bank's assessment of country risk (*see* Chapter 22).
83. For banks which were subsidiaries of other UK banks, the Bank might have allowed exposures of over 100 per cent of the subsidiary's capital base where the exposure was to individual borrowers unconnected with the banks and certain conditions and terms specified by the Bank were met (e.g. that the exposure was less than 25 per cent of the parent's capital base and the parent agreed to take over the exposure if problems occurred). For exposures in excess of 10 per cent of the capital base, however, additional capital backing would generally be required of the parent, the amount being dependent upon the same range of factors which determined the amount of additional capital that non-bank subsidiaries had to hold in a similar position.
84. Most forms of exposure were measured by their face value in the books. This, however, was obviously not appropriate for underwriting commitments and interest rate- and exchange rate-related contracts, where the bank was, in practice, at risk for only a proportion of the nominal value of the commitment. Accordingly, exposures in the former cases were derived by calculating 'credit equivalent amounts' based on BSD/1987/1.1, while the Bank promised to consider how to incorporate interest rate- and exchange rate-related contracts within the scope of the large exposures policy. (It should also be noted that greater flexibility in respect of the treatment of 'expert' underwriters had operated since 1989, alleviating some of the constraints which would have been faced by banks heavily involved in securities trading; and that further modifications to the Bank's original policy on large exposures, as set out in BSD/1987/1, were introduced in February 1992 under BSD/1992/2 (Bank of England, 1992e). The latter changes involved treating banks' exposures to building societies in the same way as their exposures to banks, and a broadening of the range of collateral which could permit an exposure to exceed 25 per cent of the adjusted capital base.)

85. Exposures to Zone B central governments or central banks which are denominated and funded (if necessary) in the national currency of the borrower are also exempt, irrespective of their maturity.

86. BSD/1994/4 (Bank of England, 1994d), covering the treatment of repurchase agreements and stock lending and borrowing agreements, was also withdrawn with effect from 1 January 1996.

87. The exempt categories were also expanded under the Large Exposures Directive to embrace investment firms subject to the CAD or an analogous regime, recognized exchanges and clearing houses.

88. This followed the Bank's decision in April 1987 to require banks to attain an agreed level of specific provisions.

    Prior to that date, banks, subject to meeting the requirements of the Companies Acts (1981 and 1985), were largely left to their own devices in determining their *levels* of bad debt provisions. The decision inevitably reflected a compromise between adequately reflecting the risk of losses likely to arise (and hence satisfying auditors, regulators and the long-term interests of shareholders), recording profits that were thought politically acceptable to the incumbent administration (i.e. levels which were likely to dissuade the Treasury from mounting new revenue-raising exercises), and satisfying the short-run desires of shareholders, actual and prospective, by declaring 'appropriate' dividends.

    The major problem facing the supervisory authorities was how to reconcile their desire for higher bank capital ratios, at a time when the perceived risks of banking, especially on the international front, had risen appreciably, with the need to ensure adequate provisioning against bad and doubtful debts, especially those incurred against LDC countries. The *exclusion* of specific provisions from the capital base after 1980, despite their tax deductibility, favoured (subject to the room allowed for manoeuvre) general rather than specific provisions for all but the most highly capitalized banks. It was this bias (which will be substantially reduced under the BIS arrangements) which the April 1987 decision, in effect, sought to counter, to force specific reserve holdings up to more realistic levels.

    By the end of 1987, specific provisions provided against problem country debt by the five largest British banks approached 30 per cent of their total exposures to problem countries, as compared with 10 per cent at the end of 1986. This reflected, in part, publication of the Bank's matrix framework and the Bank's exhortations to raise reserve levels, but also Citicorp's decision in May 1987 to increase its loan loss reserves sharply. Current levels of provisioning for such purposes vary between UK clearing banks from around 50 per cent to 75 per cent of exposures.

89. Prior to publication of this matrix, the banks were left to determine such objective criteria, although the Bank did monitor the policy adopted by each bank and aided the development of appropriate measures through dissemination of additional information relevant to the assessment of the adequacy of provisions.

90. Changes introduced in January 1990 comprised:

1. *In respect of the factor analysis*: adding one new factor to penalize countries which are able to clear interest arrears only by capitalization or by advances of new money; extending the scoring ranges for a number of the factors, to score more heavily those countries with deep-seated payment difficulties; and refining some of the definitions.

2. *In respect of the country score*: introducing a smoothing technique, based on the use of a moving average score, in order to avoid sharp fluctuations in the country scores which might exaggerate an underlying change in the position of a debtor country.

3. *In respect of the minimum score*: removing the restriction under which the minimum country score (below which provisioning did not need to be considered) had to be attributable to actual events of default, in order to take account of the likelihood of future default in assessing the need for provision. However, a score just above the minimum which is attributable to economic factors rather than to a default, although it should prompt a bank to consider the need for provision, may not always lead to provision being required.

4. *In respect of the provisioning bands*: adjusting the bands which relate country scores to provisionary percentages.

5. *In respect of tax allowances*: announcing new rules for calculating the amount of debt eligible for tax relief (which will broadly follow the new matrix guidelines) and for the phasing in of relief where appropriate.

The changes introduced in February 1993 involved the following:

1. Abolition of the recommended provisioning bands (*see* Hall, 1993, p. 162) and their replacement with a recommended minimum provisioning level.

2. Raising the thresholds at which required provisions come into play from a score of 10 to one of 30.

3. Replacement of the five-quarter moving average system by the latest score in all situations.

4. Reduction in the number of columns in the matrix from 16 to 12, and an increase in the significance attached to 'C' factors (Bank of England, 1993d).

91. This initially posed a problem for the Bank in its treatment of deferred tax assets for capital adequacy assessment purposes. For those banks which did not have sufficient current or prior year taxable profits against which to offset tax losses resulting from the higher specific provisions, created deferred tax assets to recognize the carry forward of losses for tax purposes which are available to relieve future profits from tax.

92. They had last been invoked earlier in 1986 to prevent the merchant bank Morgan Grenfell from merging with the money-broking group, Exco International.

93. The new rule required recognized brokers 'not to undertake business in foreign exchange or currency deposits on behalf of principals where there is a shareholding link of 10 per cent or more'.

94. As defined in Section 105 of the Act. Before implementation of the EC's Second Banking Co-ordination Directive (*see* Chapter 9), this was defined as someone who owns or exercises control over the voting rights associated with over 15 per cent of the institution's equity. (For the treatment of prospective indirect controllers, *see* p. 238.) Similarly, no minority shareholder controller could become a majority shareholder (over 50 per cent), and no majority shareholder a principal shareholder (over 75 per cent) without acquiring the Bank's prior assent. (See Bank of England, 1989a, pp. 32–3). Compliance with the Directive, however, changed these notification requirements. Three separate prior notification levels now apply – at the 10, 20 and 33 per cent levels – and, additionally, credit institutions are obliged to notify the Bank of those controllers with a less than 10 per cent interest but who, nevertheless, are able to exercise significant influence over the institution. The directors, managers and controllers of 90 per cent owned finance subsidiaries of banks which are guaranteed by their parent are also subject to the 'fit and proper' tests.

95. If, however, the predator goes for full control, the Office of Fair Trading may be able to block the move on grounds of competition policy or the Monopolies and Mergers Commission on 'national interest' grounds, the criterion used to reject the HongKong and Shanghai Banking Corporation bid for the Royal Bank of Scotland in 1982.

96. A degree of uncertainty existed because of the Bank's earlier opposition to the proposed takeover by the HongKong and Shanghai Banking Corporation of the Royal Bank of Scotland and the official blessing later given to the tie-up between the former bank and Midland Bank. (The alliance between the two banks subsequently broke down, but the HongKong Bank then successfully launched a takeover bid for the Midland in 1992.)

97. The acquisition by the National Australia Bank of Northern Bank and Clydesdale Bank in July 1987 (it subsequently acquired the Yorkshire

Bank) can be cited as early evidence of this. Since then, Equiticorp, the New Zealand financial services company, has been allowed to take a 61 per cent stake in the merchant bank Guinness Mahon through the purchase of a similar stake in the Guinness Peat Group in October 1987; Morgan Grenfell was allowed to fall into the hands of Deutsche Bank; and, as noted earlier, Midland Bank has been swallowed up by the HongKong and Shanghai Banking Corporation (following Lloyds Bank's decision to abandon its hostile bid in the face of a referral to the Monopolies and Mergers Commission – Lloyds later merged with the Trustee Savings Bank). In addition, three discount houses are now under foreign ownership; Barings has been acquired by the Dutch financial services group ING (*see* Chapter 12); Swiss Bank Corporation has acquired S.G. Warburg (May 1995); and Kleinwort Benson has been acquired by Dresdner Bank (June 1995).

98. Only stake acquisitions of over 5 per cent have to be notified to the Bank under Section 37 of the Banking Act 1987.

99. For example, the ambitions of the advertising company Saatchi and Saatchi in respect of proposed links with Midland Bank were scornfully dashed by the Bank in September 1987.

100. The purpose of limiting cover to less than 100 per cent of the nominal value of deposits is to encourage prospective depositors to undertake some assessment of risk as well as prospective return before deciding on which institutions to entrust with their money.

101. Deposits with UK branches of banks incorporated in other EEA states are now primarily covered by their home scheme, although, as noted in Chapter 9, where the UK Scheme offers more favourable protection a bank is allowed to 'top up' into the UK Scheme. Deposits with UK offices of banks from outside the EEA continue to be protected by the UK Scheme unless the Deposit Protection Board is satisfied that they are at least as well protected under the arrangements operating in the bank's home country. It is also worth noting that, under the revised rules (which are implemented under the 'Credit Institutions (Protection of Depositors) Regulations 1994'), the categories of depositor and deposit not protected under the Scheme were extended to include deposits by credit institutions, other financial institutions and insurance undertakings, as well as those which form part of a bank's own funds or which the Deposit Protection Board deems were made in connection with a money-laundering transaction.

102. By the autumn of 1996, payments totalling £144 million (£88 million net after the recovery of funds from the liquidation or administration) had been made to depositors by the Deposit Protection Board of a total of 29 institutions (Bank of England/SIB, 1996b).

103. A special levy, of 0.025516 per cent of an institution's average sterling deposit base, was imposed in December 1992 on UK-authorized institutions to finance payments made by the Deposit Protection Board to depositors of BCCI. The levy was designed to raise £80 million, £58 million having already been paid out by the Bank in connection with the collapse of BCCI by mid December 1992.

104. That is, the application of (capital) requirements on a consolidated basis.

105. Securities regulators have traditionally concentrated on the financial condition of regulated securities firms on a solo basis, taking account of the risks which a wider group poses for those firms in a qualitative fashion, if at all. Accordingly, securities regulators do not typically set capital requirements at levels which are guaranteed to prevent the failure of securities firms, but rather to ensure that, if they fail, they can be wound up in a controlled manner, with all creditors receiving the amounts due to them. Some, however, under pressure from IOSCO and other bodies, are beginning to develop group-based risk assessment in a manner which adopts a more quantitative approach to group-based supervision, not least because of a growing recognition of the extent of the systemic risks posed by the operation of large securities firms, and of the importance of receiving early warnings of underlying problems.

106. International efforts to secure convergence in the approaches adopted by different regulators towards the assessment of capital adequacy have so far focused on banks and securities firms. The EU has already made significant moves on this front (*see* the text) but has agreed to review its position in the light of market developments and any agreement reached between the IOSCO and the Basle Committee. Convergence with insurance regulation remains further in the distance.

107. The US Securities and Exchange Commission, for example, is far from convinced of the merits of prudential consolidation, arguing that financial groups should be supervised along functional lines (i.e. the banking supervisor supervising the banking operations, the securities supervisor the securities operations, etc.), with the focus of attention being on the regulated firms and their capital adequacy.

108. Perhaps in the form of a subordinated loan or guarantee.

109. This is also suggested for consideration by bank supervisors when such subsidiaries are not included in the prudential consolidation.

110. The experience of BCMB (*see* Chapter 10) is a testament to this.

111. Banks are subject to the solvency requirements of the Own Funds and Solvency Ratio Directives and, in respect of their trading book activities, to the capital requirements laid down in the CAD in respect of market and other miscellaneous risks, as well as to the Large Exposures Directive.

Investment firms, in turn, are subject to the capital requirements of the CAD (*see* Chapter 9).

112. That is, groups which are composed either exclusively or mainly of banks or other financial institutions.

113. That is, where there is a non-financial holding company and at least one of the subsidiaries is a bank. (The group may include insurance companies.)

114. In certain circumstances, however, consolidation can be waived.

115. For a critique of the Bank's approach, *see* Hall, 1993, pp. 204–6, and Hall, 1996a.

116. This amending notice set out certain restricted circumstances in which the Bank was willing to extend the range of intra-group exposures not weighted in the calculation of a bank's unconsolidated RAR (to avoid double counting). In such circumstances (i.e. when the group has a UK bank at its head and is managed as an integrated banking business by that bank; the other group company is consolidated for the purposes of calculating the group's consolidated capital ratios; and capital resources are freely transferable between the other group company and the bank at the head of the group), the Bank was prepared to agree the same target and trigger RARs (*see* Chapter 17) for all banks in the group.

117. Under this notice, the Bank revised its approach to consolidation of subsidiaries in the computation of solo capital ratios by stating that it is now prepared to allow such consolidation in cases where *all* of the following applied:

    1. The subsidiary is at least 75 per cent owned.
    2. Either the subsidiary is wholly funded by its parent bank or all of its exposure to risk is wholly in respect of its parent bank.
    3. The management is under the effective direction of the parent bank.
    4. It is clear that there are no potential obstacles to the payment of surplus capital up to the parent bank, in particular taking account of overseas exchange controls, potential legal and regulatory problems, and taxation.
    5. There is sufficient capital in the bank's own balance sheet to fund its investment in those subsidiaries which are to be solo consolidated.

118. Although the CSD (92/30/EEC) was adopted in April 1992 and implemented on 1 January 1993 (*see* Chapter 9), it did not involve any substantive changes to existing Bank policy (*see* Bank of England, 1993a).

    Under the new Directive, consolidated supervision covers both capital adequacy and large exposures to a single counterparty, and extends beyond banks' financial subsidiaries to banks' parents and the financial subsidiaries (excluding insurance subsidiaries) of parents where the majority (i.e. over 50 per cent) of the group's activities are of a financial nature. Where banks belong to a group in which the majority of activities are not of a financial nature, consolidation is not required, although supervisors have the power to require banks to supply information about the group to which they belong.

The main issue for the Bank concerned the position of regulated securities subsidiaries of the banks, whose capital adequacy positions were supervised under the Financial Services Act regime and were not included in consolidated supervision by the Bank. A decision was taken to put in place an interim arrangement pending implementation of the CAD, required by end-December 1995 (*see* Chapter 9), which governed the treatment of the capital adequacy of such subsidiaries for the purposes of consolidated supervision. Under this arrangement, the then existing supervisory regimes were employed as a close approximation to the CAD. In the event that a financial company had a capital deficiency, this would be deducted from group capital in addition to the investment in the group company. Where the financial company had 'adequate' capital, only the value of the investment in it would be deducted from the group's consolidated capital.

119. In assessing the adequacy of the group capital, for example, the Bank will *not* usually make an independent quantitative assessment of the adequacy of capital in those non-bank group companies which are subject to supervision by other UK supervisory authorities. Accordingly, such companies undertaking an investment or insurance business which is supervised by another UK supervisory body (such as the SFA and DTI respectively) are not, generally, included with banks' consolidated statistical returns, except in relation to the consolidated country exposures return and the large exposures return. They will, however, be included in the Bank's consolidated supervision of the group, and close liaison will be maintained with the relevant supervisory bodies.

120. Consolidated supervision also takes into account a bank's management policies on liquidity, foreign exchange exposure, interest rate exposure and sectoral exposures, although consolidated data on these subjects are not collected on a regular basis.

121. With effect from February 1993, the date of implementation of BSD/1993/1, consolidation extended to all 'financial' companies in the group, including the parent company itself, subsidiaries of the parent company and companies in which the parent company or its subsidiaries have a 'participation' of 20 per cent or more of the voting rights or capital of a company.

122. Special arrangements apply to *single* institutions subject to multiple authorization under the Financial Services Act 1986. To minimize the problems of supervisory overlap, Memoranda of Understanding were agreed between the Bank on the one hand and the SROs on the other (see Chapter 15), under which the Bank is recognized as the lead regulator for all banks in the assessment of their financial position, and the financial services supervisor is responsible for monitoring an institution's compliance with its 'conduct of business' rules.

123. A study published by the Bank in October 1997 suggested that, as far as *options* were concerned, too many London-based investment banks still had insufficient understanding of how to evaluate and assess the risks involved. The report, which came in the wake of a number of options-mispricing scandals – notably that which resulted in NatWest Markets incurring a loss of £77 million – claimed that some banks rely too heavily on computer models to evaluate the options they own, blindly accepting the results of their in-house models 'without any intuitive feel for its reasonableness'. Similarly, some managers were criticized for failing to grasp the workings of options, leaving it to computers to provide the answers. The answer was perceived to lie in additional training of back office staff, particularly to help them understand the more 'exotic' products gaining ground in the market place.

124. A particularly thorny issue which arose was the question of whether or not disclosure requirements should be imposed on fund managers which buy money-market instruments on behalf of pension funds and hedge funds. The banks are obviously keen, for sound risk management reasons, to identify the ultimate counterparties to their over-the-counter sale of derivatives, yet the ultimate purchasers do not want their investment strategies revealed and tend to shun publicity. Unilateral action by the Bank to enhance transparency simply risked moving the business elsewhere.

125. The Bank was also concerned with the accounting treatment of derivatives – *see* Bank of England, 1995a, p. 31, and Bank of England, 1996a, p. 31.

Bibliography: Part II

APB (1992), *Future Development of Auditing* (McFarlane Report), November.

APB (1994), *The Audit Agenda*, December.

Baestaens, D. (1987), 'The UK–US Joint Proposals on Bank Capital Requirements: A Critical Overview', *Journal of International Securities Markets*, Vol.1, Autumn, pp. 47–58.

Bank of England (1980), 'The Measurement of Capital', *BEQB*, London, September.

Bank of England (1981), 'Foreign Currency Exposure', *BEQB*, London, June.

Bank of England (1982), 'The Measurement of Liquidity', *BEQB*, London, September.

Bank of England (1984a), 'Foreign Currency Options', London, April.

Bank of England (1984b), 'Supervisory Aspects of Country Risk', *BEQB*, London, June.

Bank of England (1984c), *Bank of England, Report and Accounts*, London, June.

Bank of England (1986a), *Measurement of Capital* (BSD/1986/4), London, June.

Bank of England (1986b), *Subordinated Loan Capital Issued by Recognised Banks and Licensed Deposit-Takers* (BSD/1986/2), London, March.

Bank of England (1986c), *Off-Balance-Sheet Business of Banks*, consultative paper, London, March.

Bank of England (1986d), *Consolidated Supervision of Institutions Authorised Under the Banking Act 1979* (BSD/1986/3), London, March.

Bank of England (1987a), 'Supervision and Central Banking', *BEQB*, London, August.

Bank of England (1987b), *Guidance Note on Accounting and Other Records and Internal Control Systems and Reporting Accountants' Reports Thereon* (BSD/1987/2), London, September.

Bank of England (1987c), *Potential Credit Exposure on Interest Rate and Foreign Exchange Rate Related Instruments*, London, March.

Bank of England (1987d), *Large Exposures Undertaken by Institutions Authorised Under the Banking Act 1987* (BSD/1987/1), London, September.

Bank of England (1987e), 'Ownership and Control of UK Banks', *BEQB*, London, November.

Bank of England (1987f), *The Regulation of the Wholesale Markets in Sterling, Foreign Exchange and Bullion*, consultative paper, London, July.

Bank of England (1988a), *Implementation of the Basle Convergence Agreement in the United Kingdom* (BSD/1988/3), London, October.

Bank of England (1988b), *Proposals for a Stock of High Quality Liquidity*, consultative paper, London, March.

Bank of England (1988c), *Large Underwriting Exposures* (BSD/1987/1.1), London, February.

Bank of England (1988d), *Banking Act 1987, Section 16: Statement of Principles*, London, May.

Bank of England (1989a), *Banking Act Report for 1988/89*, London, June.

Bank of England (1989b), *Amendment to BSD/1986/3* (BSD/1989/2), London, March.

Bank of England (1989c), *Loan Transfers and Securitisation* (BSD/1989/1), London, February.

Bank of England (1990a), *Implementation in the UK of the Directive on Own Funds of Credit Institutions* (BSD/1990/2), London, December.

Bank of England (1990b), *Implementation in the UK of the Solvency Ratio Directive* (BSD/1990/3), London, December.

Bank of England (1990c), *Amendment to BSD/1987/1* (BSD/1990/1), London, February.

Bank of England (1990d), *Amendment to BSD/1986/3* (BSD/1990/4), London, December.

Bank of England (1992a), *Banking Act Report for 1991/92*, London, June.

Bank of England (1992b), *Implementation in the UK of the Directive on Own Funds of Credit Institutions*, Amendment to the 1990 Notice (BSD/1992/1), London, January.

Bank of England (1992c), *Verification of Interim Profits in the Context of the Own Funds Directive* (BSD/1992/5), London, August.

Bank of England (1992d), *Implementation in the United Kingdom of the Solvency Ratio Directive (amendment to the 1990 paper)* (BSD/1992/6), London, November.

Bank of England (1992e), *Further Amendments to BSD/1987/1* (BSD/1992/2), London, February.

Bank of England (1992f), *Loan Transfers and Securitisation (amendments to the 1989 paper)* (BSD/1992/3), London, April.

Bank of England (1992g), *The London Code of Conduct*, London, May.

Bank of England (1993a), *Implementation in the United Kingdom of the Directive on the Consolidated Supervision of Credit Institutions* (BSD/1993/1), London, March.

Bank of England (1993b), *On-Balance-Sheet Netting and Cash Collateral* (BSD/1993/3), London, December.

Bank of England (1993c), *Implementation in the United Kingdom of the Directive on the Monitoring and Control of Large Exposures of Credit Institutions* (BSD/1993/2), London, October.

Bank of England (1993d), *Letter to Authorised Institutions Concerning Debt Provisioning (the new matrix)*, London, February.

Bank of England (1993e), 'The London Approach', *Bank of England Quarterly Bulletin*, London, February, pp. 110–15.

Bank of England (1994a), 'The Pursuit of Financial Stability', *BEQB*, London, February, pp. 60–66.

Bank of England (1994b), *Guidance Note on Reporting Accountants' Reports on Accounting and Other Records and Internal Control Systems* (BSD/1994/2) London, March.

Bank of England (1994c), *Subordinated Loan Capital Issued by UK-Incorporated Authorised Institutions* (BSD/1994/3), London, May.

Bank of England (1994d), *Treatment of Repurchase Agreements and Stock Lending and Borrowing for Capital Adequacy and Large Exposures Purposes* (BSD/1994/4), London, November.

Bank of England (1994e), *Implementation of the Capital Adequacy Directive for UK-Incorporated Institutions Authorised under the Banking Act 1987*, consultative paper, S&S Division, London, December.

Bank of England (1995a), *Banking Act Report for 1994/95*, London.

Bank of England (1995b), *Implementation in the United Kingdom of the Capital Adequacy Directive* (S&S/1995/2), London, April.

Bank of England (1995c), *Implementation in the United Kingdom of the Capital Adequacy Directive (amendments to S&S/1995/2)* (S&S/1995/4), London, December.

Bank of England (1995d), *Amendments to the Bank's Notices on: (i) The Verification of Interim Profits in the Context of the Own Funds Directive; and (ii) The Implementation in the United Kingdom of the Solvency Ratio Directive (BSD/1990/3)* (S&S/1995/5), London, December.

Bank of England (1995e), *Netting of Counterparty Credit Risk Associated with Sale and Repurchase Agreements and OTC Derivatives* (S&S/1995/3), London, December.

Bank of England (1995f), *Implementation in the United Kingdom of the Solvency Ratio Directive (further amendment to the 1990 paper)* (S&S/1995/1), London, March.

Bank of England (1996a), *Banking Act Report 1995/96*, London.

Bank of England (1996b), *The Bank of England's Relationship with Auditors and Reporting Accountants* (S&S/1996/5), London, April.

Bank of England (1996c), *Guidance Note on Reporting Accountants' Reports on Accounting and Other Records and Internal Control Systems* (S&S/1996/6), London, April.

Bank of England (1996d), *Guidance Note on Reporting Accountants' Reports on Bank of England's Returns used for Prudential Purposes* (S&S/1996/7), London, April.

Bank of England (1996e), *Netting of Counterparty Credit Risk Associated with Sale and Repurchase Agreements and OTC Derivatives* (S&S/1996/3), London, March.

Bank of England (1996f), *Implementation in the United Kingdom of the Solvency Ratio Directive (further amendment to the 1990 paper)* (S&S/1996/2), London, March.

Bank of England (1996g), *Treatment of Potential Future Exposure for Off-Balance-Sheet Contracts; Implementation in the United Kingdom of the Solvency Ratio Directive (further amendments to the 1990 paper)* (S&S/1996/4), London, March.

Bank of England (1996h), *Further Amendment to the Implementation in the United Kingdom of the Solvency Ratio Directive (BSD/1990/3)* (S&S/1996/10), London, December.

Bank of England (1996i), *Definition of Marketable Assets for Liquidity Purposes (amendment to July 1982 policy notice: 'Management of Liquidity')* (S&S/1996/1), London, January.

Bank of England (1996j), 'Risk Reduction in Payment and Settlement Systems', *Bank of England Quarterly Bulletin*, London, November, pp. 481–6.

Bank of England (1996k), *Developing a Supervisory Approach to Credit Derivatives*, London, November.

Bank of England (1996l), *Securitisation of Revolving Credits (amended annex to BSD/1989/1, replacing Part C of BSD/1992/3)* (S&S/1996/8), London, April.

Bank of England (1997a), *A Risk-Based Approach to Supervision (the RATE framework)*, consultative paper, London, March.

Bank of England (1997b), *A Risk-Based Approach to the Supervision of Non-EEA Banks (the SCALE framework)*, consultative paper, London, July.

Bank of England (1997c), *Objectives, Standards, and Processes of Supervision*, London, February.

Bank of England (1997d), *Banking Act Report 1996/97*, London.

Bank of England (1997e), *Banks' Internal Controls and the Section 39 Process*, consultative paper, London, February.

Bank of England (1997f), *A Revised Method for Measuring Liquidity Mismatches*, consultative paper, London, June.

Bank of England (1997g), *A Risk-Based Approach to Supervising Foreign Exchange and Other Market Risks*, London, July.

Bank of England (1998a), *Banking Act Report 1997/98*, London.

Bank of England (1998b), *Letter to UK Incorporated Authorised Institutions Clarifying Treatment of Perpetual Non-Cumulative Preference Shares*, London, January.

Bank of England/HM Treasury (1986), *The Future Regulation of the Wholesale Markets in Sterling, Foreign Exchange and Bullion*, consultative paper, London, December.

Bank of England/SIB (1996a), 'Rating Sovereign Risk', *Financial Stability Review*, No. 1, London, Autumn, pp. 31–7.

Bank of England/SIB (1996b), 'Deposit Protection and Bank Failures in the United Kingdom', *Financial Stability Review*, No. 1, London, Autumn, pp. 38–43.

Bank of England/SIB (1996c), 'Bancassurance: European Approaches to Capital Adequacy', *Financial Stability Review*, No. 1, London, pp. 58–63.

Bank of England/SIB (1996d), 'Crest: Its Recognition and Approval', *Financial Stability Review*, No. 1, London, pp. 51–7.

Basle Committee/IOSCO (Technical Committee) (1995), *The Prudential Reporting of Derivatives*, Basle, May.

Baumol, W.K. (1982), 'Contestable Markets: An Uprising in the Theory of Industry Structure', *American Economic Review*, Vol. 72, pp. 1–15.

BIS (1983), *Principles for the Supervision of Banks' Foreign Establishments* (revised *Basle Concordat*), Basle, May.

BIS (1987), *Proposals for the International Convergence of Capital Measurement and Capital Standards*, consultative paper, Basle, December.

BIS (1991), *Proposals for the Inclusion of General Provisions/General Loan Loss Reserves in Capital*, consultative paper issued by the Basle Committee, Basle, February.

BIS (1992), *Recent Developments in International Interbank Relations* (Promisel Report), Basle, November.

BIS (1994), *A Discussion Paper on Public Disclosure of Market and Credit Risks by Financial Intermediaries* (Fisher Report), Basle, September.

BIS (1996), *Settlement Risk in Foreign Exchange Transactions* (Allsop Report), Committee on Payment and Settlement Systems, Basle, March.

Board, J. *et al.* (1995), 'Derivatives Regulation', *LSE Financial Markets Group*, Special Paper No. 70, March.

Clarotti, P. (1997), 'EU Directives and their Impact on Netting', *Journal of Financial Regulation and Compliance*, Vol. 5, No. 2, pp. 154–62.

Committee on Corporate Governance (1998), *Final Report* (Hampel Report), London, January.

Cooke, W. (1982), 'The Communities and the Banks in the 1980s: Supervisory Aspects – A Central Banker's View', speech given at a British Bankers' Association Seminar, London, January.

Davies, D. (1997), 'Remuneration and Risk', *Financial Stability Review*, Issue No. 2, pp. 18–22.

EC (1983), *First Consolidated Supervision Directive* (83/350/EEC), Brussels, June.

EC (1986), *Bank Accounts Directive* (86/635/EEC), Brussels, December.

EC (1989a), *Own Funds Directive* (89/299/EEC), Brussels, April.

EC (1989b), *Solvency Ratio Directive* (89/647/EEC), Brussels, December.

EC (1989c), *Second Banking Coordination Directive* (89/646/EEC), Brussels, December.

EC (1991), *Money Laundering Directive* (91/308/EEC), Brussels, June.

EC (1992a), *Large Exposures Directive* (91/121/EC), Brussels, December.

EC (1992b), *Second Consolidated Supervision Directive* (92/30/EEC), Brussels, April.

EC (1993), *Capital Adequacy Directive* (93/6/EEC), Brussels, March.

EC (1994), *Deposit Guarantee Schemes Directive* (94/19/EEC), Brussels, May.

EC (1995), *Post-BCCI Directive* (95/26/EC), Brussels, June.

Federal Home Loan Bank Board (1983), *Agenda for Reform: A Report on Deposit Insurance to the Congress from the Federal Home Loan Bank Board*, Washington DC.

Fédération des Experts Comptables Européens (1993), *Survey on the Involvement of the Auditor in the Prudential Control of Banks by the Supervisory Authorities*, Brussels, October.

FSAu (1998), Plan and Budget 1998/99, London, February.

FSAu (1998), *Guide to Banking Supervisory Policy*, London, July.

Fitchew, G. (1992), 'The Regulation of International Financial Conglomerates', paper presented at the XVIIth Annual IOSCO Conference, London, 29 October.

Group of Thirty (1993), 'Derivatives: Practices and Principles', Appendix 1 of the Working Paper of the Accounting and Reporting Subcommittee, Washington, July.

Group of Thirty (1994), *Derivatives: Practices and Principles: Follow-up Survey of Industry Practice*, Washington, December.

Hadjiemmanuil, C. (1996), 'Financial Reporting and Auditing in the Regulated Sector: The Case of Banking', *Journal of International Banking Law*, Vol. 3, pp. 104–14.

Hall, M.J.B. (1987a), *The City Revolution: Causes and Consequences*, London: Macmillan.

Hall, M.J.B. (1987b), *Financial Deregulation: A Comparative Study of Australia and the United Kingdom*, London: Macmillan.

Hall, M.J.B. (1988), 'Managing Liquidity', Chapter 3 in J.S.G. Wilson (ed.), *Managing Bank Assets and Liabilities*, London: Euromoney Publications.

Hall, M.J.B. (1989), 'The BIS Capital Adequacy "Rules": A Critique', *Banca Nazionale del Lavoro Quarterly Review* June, pp. 207–27.

Hall, M.J.B. (1990), 'Fit and Proper?: Harrods Bank and the Fayed Brothers', *Banking World*, May, pp. 20–1.

Hall, M.J.B. (1993), *Handbook of Banking Regulation and Supervision*, 2nd edition, Aldershot: Woodhead-Faulkner.

Hall, M.J.B. (1995), 'The Capital Adequacy Directive: An Assessment', *Journal of International Banking Law*, Vol.10, No. 3, pp. 78–87.

Hall, M.J.B. (1996a), 'The Collapse of Barings: The Lessons to be Learnt', *Journal of Financial Regulation and Compliance*, Vol.4, No. 3, pp. 255–77.

Hall, M.J.B. (1996b), 'Barings: The Bank of England's First Report to the Board of Banking Supervision', *Butterworths Journal of International Banking and Financial Law*, Vol. 11, No. 3, March, pp. 128–30.

Hall, M.J.B. (1997), 'The Capital Adequacy Directive: Implications for UK-Incorporated Banks', *The Service Industries Journal*, Vol.17, No. 2, April, pp. 320–53.

HMSO (1982), *Hong Kong and Shanghai Banking Corporation, Standard Chartered Bank Ltd. and The Royal Bank of Scotland Group Ltd., Monopolies and Mergers Commission Report on the Proposed Mergers*, Cmnd 8472, London, January.

HMSO (1991), *Banking Supervision and BCCI: The Role of Local Authorities and Money Brokers*, Treasury and Civil Service Committee, London, December.

HMSO (1995), *Board of Banking Supervision: The Report on the Collapse of Barings*, Minutes of Evidence, Treasury and Civil Service Committee, House of Commons Paper 746-i, London, July.

House of Commons (1996), *First Report of the Treasury Committee for the Session 1996–97*, House of Commons Paper 65-i, London, December.

IIF (1994), *A Preliminary Framework for Public Disclosure of Derivatives Activities and Related Credit Exposures*, New York, August.

IOSCO (1992), *Principles for the Supervision of Financial Conglomerates*, New York, October.

Jamison, N. (1998), 'Developments in Voluntary Self-Regulation', *Journal of Financial Regulation and Compliance*, Vol.6, No. 1, pp. 31–8.

Lewis, M.K. (1988), 'Off-Balance-Sheet Activity and its Regulation', Chapter 9 in J.S.G. Wilson (ed.), *Managing Bank Assets and Liabilities*, London: Euromoney Publications.

Llewellyn, D.T. (1988), 'The Policy Framework: Capital Adequacy', Chapter 2 in J.S.G. Wilson (ed.), *Managing Bank Assets and Liabilities*, London: Euromoney Publications.

Price Waterhouse (1993), *The Regulation of Market Risk: The Impact of the European Community's Capital Adequacy Directive and the Basle Proposals*, London, December.

Salt, M. and Southern, D. (1997), 'Black–Gold–Blue: Banking Regulation's New Banner', *Butterworths Journal of International Banking and Financial Law*, July–August, pp. 303–8.

Walker, G. (1996a), 'Consolidated Supervision – Part 1', *Butterworths Journal of International Banking and Financial Law*, February, pp. 74–83.

Walker, G. (1996b), 'Consolidated Supervision – Part 2', *Butterworths Journal of International Banking and Financial Law*, March, pp. 131–9.

Index